Heritage Tourism

Heritage tourism has become an increasingly significant component of the global tourism industry, particularly in countries striving to diversify away from sea, sand and sun. This growth has had profound influences on the presentation and representation of both tangible and intangible heritage within tourism. The concept of heritage continues to evolve with its fast-changing political, economic and socio-cultural surroundings. Therefore it is essential that heritage tourism engages with the new form of globalised communities and societies, which have become more assimilated to each other but yet strive to sustain their own distinctive locality.

This book aims to offer a thorough critical examination and systematic evaluation of the unique dynamics of heritage and tourism development from both social sciences and management perspectives. It incorporates both global and local perspectives in theorising and managing heritage tourism. While focusing on reviewing and analysing key academic concepts and debates including commodification, globalisation and heritage interpretation, this book also discusses and evaluates topical issues such as sustainable development, marketing strategies and digital technologies including social media. It theoretically locates heritage discourses in the analysis of heritage tourism development and management drawing on various perspectives, from tourism, heritage studies, sociology, anthropology, politics and geography to management and marketing studies. Including case studies of topical concerns, controversies and challenges it will encourage readers to develop a new and insightful understanding of the dialectical relationship between heritage and tourism development.

This book is essential reading for students studying tourism, heritage studies and cultural studies, as well as related disciplines.

Hyung yu Park is Senior Lecturer of Tourism Studies at Middlesex University, UK. Her main area of research and teaching is cultural heritage tourism, particularly its dialectic role in the reconstruction of identity and memory. Other research interests include: heritage interpretation and consumption; heritage management and sustainable development; the politics of heritage tourism; anthropology of tourism and qualitative (ethnographic) research in methods in tourism studies.

Heritage Tourism

Hyung yu Park

Routledge
Taylor & Francis Group

LONDON AND NEW YORK

First published 2014
by Routledge
2 Park Square, Milton Park, Abingdon, Oxon OX14 4RN

and by Routledge
711 Third Avenue, New York, NY 10017

Routledge is an imprint of the Taylor & Francis Group, an informa business

© 2014 Hyung yu Park

British Library Cataloguing in Publication Data
A catalogue record for this book is available from the British Library

Library of Congress Cataloging in Publication Data
Pak, Hyong-yu.
Heritage tourism / Hyung yu Park.
pages cm
Includes bibliographical references and index.
1. Heritage tourism. I. Title.
G156.5.H47P35 2013
338.4'791--dc23
2013017454

ISBN: 978-0-415-59582-7 (hbk)
ISBN: 978-0-415-59583-4 (pbk)
ISBN: 978-1-315-88209-3 (ebk)

Typeset in Times New Roman
by GreenGate Publishing Services, Tonbridge, Kent

For my mum
who inspired my journey in all its dimensions

Contents

Figures

Tables

Case studies

Acknowledgements

I would like to begin by acknowledging Routledge for supporting this book from the very start. Special thanks must go to the editorial team – Emma Travis, Carol Barber, Philippa Mullins for their efficiency and professionalism. I am also grateful for Karen Wallace, Production Editor at GreenGate Publishing who has kindly guided me through the whole process of producing this book. This book would not have been possible without inspiration, encouragement and critical insights from Aram Eisenschitz and Maureen Ayikoru. During my academic journey of exploring heritage and tourism, teaching has provided me with a great wealth of ideas and motivations, which served as a platform upon which this book is founded. Particularly, I am indebted to the students whom I have taught in classes at Middlesex University for interesting and thought-provoking debates and discussions. A deepest gratitude goes to my parents, both in Korea and England, who never cease to believe in me. Without emotional support from my family and friends despite the distances in time and space I would have never managed to complete this book. Thanks, too, to my friends in London who have accompanied me through all its ups and downs. I hope that both my academic and personal journey searching for the meanings in the bygone days will continue to inspire and challenge me.

 # Introduction

Heritage tourism is predominantly concerned with exploring both material (tangible) and immaterial (intangible) remnants of the past. Importantly, heritage is not a fixed or static outcome of the past, particularly when it is presented and represented in the context of tourism. Heritage is constantly reconstructed and reinterpreted in an attempt to meet the specific demands of tourists and reflect the socio-cultural changes of the contemporary world. Therefore, the relationship between heritage and tourism is complex, intricate and symbiotic. This book aims to critically examine and evaluate the complex and unique dynamics of heritage and tourism development from both social sciences and management perspectives. It incorporates both social-science-based and management-driven discourses on heritage and tourism, illustrating the professional practices of heritage tourism in both developed and developing countries. Critical focus is placed on employing multidisciplinary and interdisciplinary perspectives, drawing key theoretical concepts and debates from heritage studies, sociology, anthropology, political economy, archaeology, management and marketing studies. This interdisciplinary and multidisciplinary approach has been dichotomous in theorising heritage in tourism contexts. It has substantially expanded the theoretical foundations of heritage tourism studies. However, too many academic orientations and interests in heritage tourism have also acted as an impediment to consolidating key theoretical frameworks (Garrod and Fyall, 2000; Jamal and Kim, 2005). Therefore, this book hopes to contribute to diversifying and enriching the critical understanding of dialectic and discursive relationships between people and places within the context of heritage tourism. While focusing on analysing key academic concepts and debates including authenticity, commodification, globalisation and heritage interpretation, this book discusses such topical and current issues as sustainable development, marketing strategies and digital technologies and their implications in heritage tourism development. A range of case studies of topical concerns, controversies and challenges are provided to develop a new and insightful understanding of contemporary heritage tourism development. Integrating case studies with relevant theories and issues will help to enhance formative, inclusive and comprehensive approaches to conceptualising and contextualising heritage tourism.

Heritage: an interface between past and present

Heritage is both a complex and multifaceted concept. Heritage is not a fixed and unchanging entity but a culturally ascribed and socially constructed process (see Smith, 2006). Heritage needs thus to be understood as a flexible and malleable concept, open to multiple interpretations and negotiations. The present-centred nature of heritage is deeply associated with an increasing contemporary use of the past, as manifested in the popularity of a 'heritage industry' (Hewison, 1987). Heritage is criticised for creating shallow pastiches of the past that thrive on 'historicism' (Jameson, 1984), an elegiac sense of the past. This is consistent with Hewison's (1987: 144) fierce criticism that views heritage as a 'bogus history' commercially contrived for entertainment. Walsh (1992) argues that increasing commodification of heritage distances people from their own heritage and dilutes a sense of place. The past is thus turned into a 'reservoir of shallow surfaces which can be exploited in the heritage centre or on the biscuit tin' (Walsh, 1992: 3). The heritage industry is denounced not only for the emergence of quasi-heritage (pseudo) products, but also for the distortion of intrinsic meanings. The commodified portrayal of pastness is described as 'romanticised fiction' (Merriman, 2000: 3) and 'shallow titillation' (Walsh, 1992: 1), as well as 'retrochic' (Samuel, 1994: 83). However, growth of the heritage industry has undoubtedly contributed to expanding the scope and appeal of heritage (see Samuel, 1994). The process of commodification in heritage has led to creating and fabricating a new environment in which different possibilities and potentials of heritage can coexist for different audiences. Too much focus on the monumental, aesthetic and authoritative approach to heritage has increasingly been replaced by a more inclusive approach, incorporating ordinary, popular and intangible heritage. Here, heritage can be contextualised as an 'alternative way of mediating the past to popular audiences' (Johnson, 1999: 187), thus leading to the 'proliferation of alternative histories' (Urry, 1990: 121). Furthermore, it is important to recognise that heritage is firmly grounded in historical knowledge and performance, not just created through the socio-economic changes of the late twentieth century. Heritage illustrates and signifies the change of society rather than being a by-product of the change. Heritage should thus be seen as 'living history incorporating social processes of both continuity and change' (Barthel-Bouchier, 2013: 9). Heritage as a complex and multifaceted concept is deeply embedded in both past and present, tradition and modernity, and time and space.

Story-telling heritage through tourism

There often exist 'multiple constructions of the past' that are 'endlessly revised from our present positions' (Crang, 1994: 341). Likewise, the concept of authenticity, particularly in relation to developing heritage attractions for tourists' consumption, is neither static nor fixed. It is of paramount significance that increasing attention is paid to creating, recreating and promoting reliable stories and images of the past rather than just attempting to deliver the real stories of the past associated with the actual sites of historical significance. The notion of story-telling in heritage presentations and representations is thus fundamental in enhancing their appeal. It is not necessarily the physical manifestations of heritage resources but the images, meanings and symbols attached to them that are of greater significance in making heritage resources more attractive and appealing. Heritage often depends entirely on the stories being created, recreated, told and retold. Importantly, story-telling heritage through tourism is often conditioned by a 'complex and often discordant array of identifications and potential conflicts' (Ashworth et al., 2007: 36). The issues of heritage as dissonant and conflicting uses and purposes of the past are clearly implicated in the way heritage is created, marketed and consumed in tourism contexts. In official heritage discourses and displays local, ordinary and informal representations of heritage remain largely unrecognised or under-represented. As a conspicuous change and challenge to the dominant stories of heritage, increasing focus is now placed on articulating the different perceptions and multiple interpretations of heritage. Individual narratives and subjective experiences of heritage play a substantial role in broadening the scope and range of story-telling heritage within tourism contexts (see Park, 2010a). There has been a gradual shift in understanding heritage tourism from descriptive approaches to experiential approaches. The descriptive approach is mainly concerned with conceptualising and contextualising heritage tourism on the basis of the supply side of heritage tourism focusing on heritage sites, attractions and settings. To the contrary, the experiential approach challenges the excessive focus on tourists' appreciation of historic places and sites in the descriptive approach (Poria *et al.*, 2003; Kim and Jamal, 2007). Instead, heritage tourism is a phenomenon related to tourists' motivations and perceptions of the site itself rather than simply site attributes and specific artefacts presented. It is therefore important to critically acknowledge tourists' socio-psychological needs and interests of the heritage setting in an endeavour to advance a dialectic relationship between tourists and heritage as tourism settings. This book thus hopes to contribute to diversifying and enriching an understanding of the complex and discursive relationships between people and places within the context of heritage tourism.

Heritage tourism: a play between the global and the local

Heritage is increasingly seen as part of the wider debates surrounding ways in which the relationship between heritage and power is reconfigured and repositioned in the global–local nexus. Heritage tourism is becoming an increasingly significant component of the global tourism industry. The growth in popularity of a recreated and reinterpreted past has had profound influences on the presentation and representation of both tangible and intangible heritage within the tourism context. It continues to evolve with fast-changing political, economic and socio-cultural surroundings. Heritage tourism contributes to community economic development (Chhabra *et al.*, 2003), security and stability (Halewood and Hannam, 2001) and 'ideological framing of history and identity' (Johnson, 1999: 187). Heritage tourism serves as both economic incentives and political principles. According to Salazar (2010: 130):

> On the domestic level, cultural heritage is commonly used to stimulate pride in the (imagined) national history or to highlight the virtues of particular ideologies. In the supranational sphere, heritage sites are marketed and sold as iconic markers of a local area, country, region or even continent, and the journey abroad as an opportunity to learn about the 'Other' – some go as far as promising a contribution to worldwide peace and understanding.

Heritage resources are generally non-renewable and irreplaceable resources requiring management and conservation (Shackley, 1998; du Cros, 2001; Timothy, 2011). Tourism has widely been regarded as both an opportunity and a threat to heritage. Too much emphasis on heritage as economic assets for tourism development can devalue and demoralise the social and cultural values of heritage. However, Ashworth (2012) contradicts a popular assumption that heritage is in fixed supply, characteristic of being limited, non-renewable or non-replicable. Heritage, within tourism contexts, offers a wide array of possibilities and potentials that are often created and positioned by tourists' demand. According to Ashworth (2012: 283):

> As heritage is a demand-derived set of contemporary uses constructed as required then the resources of which it is composed have no limits other than the limits of the human creative imagination. There can be no question of resource shortage or depletion: the resource is ubiquitous and can be created according to the demand for it.

Heritage and tourism cannot be, as Bushell and Staiff (2012) maintain, regarded as homogeneous or essentialised entities. Heritage and tourism need to be considered as a process and performance, which are constantly negotiated and renegotiated in both global and local contexts. Therefore, it is essential that heritage tourism engages with the new forms of globalised communities and societies, which have become more assimilated to each other but yet strive to sustain their own distinctive locality. There is an urgent need to incorporate both global and local perspectives and approaches in theorising and managing heritage tourism. In this book critical focus is thus placed on the discursive role of heritage tourism in enhancing the nuanced and intricate dynamics between the global and the local, the universal and the particular, and ultimately the past and the present.

Layout of the book

This book seeks to draw out certain connections and divergences between various debates surrounding heritage and tourism, thereby opening up further discussions. A variety of topical international case studies are presented and linked with relevant concepts and theories in order to facilitate a broader understanding of both theoretical frameworks and contemporary practices of heritage tourism development. Further learning material including useful weblinks, mainly video links, is provided as an option to further examine some key themes and issues raised and developed in each chapter.

The main aim of Chapter 1 is to conceptualise and contextualise heritage by expanding the conceptions and meanings of the present-day use of the past. It discusses the critical literature that comments on ways in which heritage has evolved as a symbolic medium in reappropriating and recreating the past in contemporary societies. New social and cultural dimensions of heritage experiences emerging from postmodern changes are explored and systematically analysed, particularly in relation to the advent of the 'heritage industry'.

Chapter 2 is mainly concerned with identifying and examining both the supply and demand sides of heritage tourism. Increasing popularity of purposefully artificial heritage tourism environments harnessed by the heritage industry and their contributions to heritage production and consumption is also discussed and illustrated. The latter part of this chapter focuses on enhancing the critical understanding of heritage tourists' motivations and their changing expectations and experiences regarding heritage tourism.

Chapter 3 explores and examines ways in which effective heritage management is crucial in both enhancing heritage conservation and facilitating tourism development. Such areas as visitor facilities, retailing and interpretive media will be reviewed as essential elements of heritage tourism management. A wide range of new management strategies employed in various heritage settings including World Heritage Sites (WHSs) are illustrated with appropriate examples.

Chapter 4 addresses and examines the complex polemics over authenticity issues in the context of heritage tourism. Authenticity is an important factor to consider in enhancing heritage tourism experiences. The debates over authenticity are unmistakably bound up with the issues of commodifying heritage for touristic consumption. This chapter thus seeks to examine and encapsulate how the process of commodification has influenced the recreation and reappropriation of the past in contemporary tourism contexts, thereby repositioning authenticity as a flexible and context-specific concept. A more nuanced and intricate understanding of the dynamics between authenticity and commodification is essential in broadening their meanings and implications in heritage tourism experiences.

Chapter 5 offers a detailed analysis of the politics of heritage. Central to this chapter is a consideration and (re)contextualisation of power relations in heritage production and consumption, particularly in relation to tourism development. The focus is placed on examining the political dimensions of heritage by drawing attention to its contested and dissonant nature. Heritage production and consumption is often closely related to power relations. In many heritage attractions, official and state-based discourses and interpretations of heritage can exclude certain elements of the past or people that are also an essential part of history. The latter part of this chapter further elaborates upon some critical issues surrounding the development and promotion of sensitive pasts, including slavery heritage.

Chapter 6 is mainly concerned with exploring ways in which heritage tourism contributes to maintaining and enhancing a sense of national belonging and national solidarity. The discussions demonstrate that heritage tourism experience acts as a symbolic mechanism through which national belonging can be reconstructed and communicated. The symbolic and spiritual dimensions of heritage are highlighted in recognising heritage tourism as an effective tool in facilitating a sense of national belonging and continuity in everyday contexts. Finally, attention is drawn to discussing how visits to homeland can encourage diasporas to realise their hybrid and fluid identities, while reaffirming their cultural connections with the homeland.

Chapter 7 looks specifically at globalisation and its influences on heritage tourism development. It aims to examine ways in which heritage is incorporated in a wider framework of the economic, political and cultural ramifications of globalisation. A critique of WHSs as global heritage products is established. Neoliberal forces in privatising heritage, as one conspicuous illustration of global heritage, are discussed and illustrated with relevant examples. Although increasing global assimilation and interdependence has unmistakably led to certain degrees of homogenisation in heritage tourism development worldwide, it is crucial to note that globalising forces may not necessarily overpower the essential dynamics of local cultures and identities. Here, focus is placed on exploring ways in which heritage tourism development can play an important role in reasserting distinctive local cultures and identities, while sustaining its global approaches.

Chapter 8 aims to explore the role of marketing in developing and promoting heritage to both actual and potential heritage tourists. The ways in which such key marketing concepts as branding and market segmentation are incorporated in heritage marketing are critically assessed. New marketing strategies including experiential marketing and emotional branding are introduced and illustrated with examples and case studies on an international scale. Despite the efficacy and relevance of employing marketing in heritage, however, careful focus needs to be placed on recognising the political implications of heritage marketing.

The main theme of Chapter 9 is sustainable development and community participation in heritage tourism development. Key principles of sustainable development are examined and applied to tourism contexts. It then highlights the significance of incorporating sustainable development strategies and methods in the context of heritage tourism. Further considerations are also made to the possibility of further developing sustainable heritage tourism in both developed and developing countries. Different stakeholders in developing and managing heritage tourism define sustainability in a way that reflects their particular interests. Stakeholder management and collaboration is thus essential in achieving the long-term sustainability of destinations. Finally, this chapter emphasises the importance of community participation as an essential element in enhancing the long-term sustainability of heritage tourism destinations.

Chapter 10 provides an in-depth analysis of the implications of heritage tourism development within the context of cities. It is mainly concerned with examining ways in which cities have become major consuming places and the role heritage has played in the process of reinventing and reconfiguring urban landscapes. Substantial emphasis is placed on discussing and evaluating ways in which urban regeneration can lead to homogeneous commercial development and the process of gentrification. The relationships between festivals and urban tourism are briefly discussed given a recent upsurge of heritage festivals as an effective tool for urban regeneration and cultural revival.

Chapter 11 aims to conceptualise and contextualise museums as important sources of national and local heritage. This chapter also seeks to critically evaluate the changing socio-cultural roles of museums facilitated by their repositioning as major leisure and tourism spaces. New opportunities and challenges that contemporary museums currently face in order to enhance their appeal are discussed and illustrated with some relevant examples. Museums need to be continually redefined and repositioned within the context of new technological changes and new social demands in contemporary societies.

Finally, Chapter 12 mainly discusses new opportunities, choices and challenges generated by contemporary heritage tourism development including intangible heritage, digital technologies, social media and climate changes. It also aims to critically evaluate the complex dynamics and situations inherent in current and new heritage tourism trends and activities.

1 Heritage: from history to commodity

Heritage as contemporary use of the past

The past has become a world force that 'inhabits a complex matrix of economic, political and global processes' (Weiss, 2007: 416). Appadurai (2001: 48) perceives the past as a 'boundless resource, endlessly open to variety, elaboration, reinvention and social empowerment'. Heritage encompasses a wider scope of meanings ranging from cultural and historical significances, political implications, spiritual and intellectual connotations to communications. Increasingly, heritage becomes an ephemeral and vague concept, which is in a state of constant flux. The complexities and intricacies in conceptualising and contextualising heritage are clearly pointed out by Di Giovine (2009: 91), highlighting that:

> Heritage is a powerful word in its own right, for it is at once extraordinarily suggestive and ideologically charged, but simultaneously vague enough to be applied to nearly everything across any space and time. It is a word whose significance changes with its myriad invocations, designations or legislations. Depending on its usage, heritage can determine personal property, explicate unknown qualities, foster patriotism among disparate peoples, become a tourist destination, exacerbate geopolitical tensions, or call for help in the form of preservation, among other usages.

Heritage needs thus to be understood as a 'socially produced, negotiated entity', whose meanings vary depending on the context and over time (Williams, 2009: 237) rather than a fixed and unchanging entity. Understanding of heritage as a flexible and malleable concept is particularly applicable in relating heritage to tourism contexts. Heritage becomes a raw material that authenticates and fabricates the past and the present for touristic consumption. In this light, Samuel's explication further stretches the remit of heritage: '"heritage" is a nomadic term, which travels easily... a term capricious enough to accommodate widely discrepant meanings' (Samuel, 1994: 205).

As Hewison (1987: 32) succinctly argues, heritage means 'anything you want' in this new era of insatiable obsession with the past. The desire for the past has superseded the desire for the future in Western societies since the 1980s (Huyssen, 2000). This obsession with the past is inextricably bound up with post-industrial social changes in which individuals are often dislocated from families, neighbourhood and nations and even one's former selves. It is stated: 'Dismay at massive change stokes demands for heritage... Beleaguered by loss and change, we keep our bearings only by clinging to remnants of stability... Mourning past neglect, we cherish *islands of security* in seas of change' (Lowenthal, 1998: 6, emphasis added).

In the context of Britain, the relative economic decline since the late nineteenth century has been attributed to its anti-industrial and anti-business culture, which has propelled

British society to generally become 'rooted in the past, pre-modern and anti-modern in most respects, and ill-equipped to deal with the modern world' (Rubinstein, 1993: 3). Collective longing for the past emerged from the 1970s as a reaction to the onset of economic recession, the demise of manufacturing industry and the subsequent mass unemployment and social instability. In the 1980s, heritage was important in the urban restructuring of British cities. Wright (1985) claims that newly developed capitalist and industrial society is future-oriented and evolves around progress, whereas pre-capitalist society was past-oriented and cherished a sense of stability. Present-day concerns over the disconnection with the past affect people's sense of security and identity. Therefore, it is inevitable for people to develop a collective longing for the past in the midst of turmoil and change, as a means to consolidate a sense of security and belonging. As a consequence, heritage serves as 'islands of security' that people can cling to amidst the economic crisis of contemporary society. In a similar vein, Horne (1984) claims that the growing obsession with the past reflects the crisis of contemporary reality. The incessant search by tourists for 'discarded dreamlands' (1984: 1) is one rather conspicuous illustration of a process of harking back to the past in order to evade the reality of the present. He maintains:

> Why should tourists be seeking the past? Why should the past have any particular resonance?... Throughout the age of industrialism there has been a nervousness in finding valid expressions of modernity. The tourist experience, with its seeking for an authentic (and well-researched) past, has been part of the same crisis in reality that has produced so much scholarship, so much sociology and so many experiments in art forms... Uneasiness with the present was so great that... the past was nostalgically plundered to provide a modern sense of dignity and meaning.
>
> (1984: 21–2)

Here, a sense of nostalgia plays an important role in enhancing the appeal of heritage as a secure and stable platform. Nostalgia implies a sense of homesickness and sentimental yearning for the past. In growing dissatisfactions of everyday life, nostalgic past becomes appealing and ever present. Accordingly, Shackel (2003: 3) highlights: 'Heritage creates a useable past, and it generates a precedent that serves our present needs... and we live in a society that has an unquenchable thirst for nostalgia.'

Nostalgia exerts a strong influence on how certain elements of the past are symbolically constructed and reconstructed in present contexts. Increasingly, heritage becomes the nostalgic expressions of a recent and lived past. Knudsen (2010: 150) explicates:

> Nostalgia is a storing feeling of longing triggered by a sensation, a material thing, a place, an encounter or an experience. Nostalgia is a feeling arising due to sensuous stimuli. For the memory to become nostalgic longing, a qualitative change has to happen. The memory transforms into an idyllic image of the past, a utopia of the past... Nostalgia does not have to be conservative and something that only reactionary people experience.

The recognition of the reactionary nature of nostalgia in people's experiences is significant in understanding how the appeal of heritage is steadily sustained in present contexts. It can be argued that heritage tourism encourages people to react to and experience nostalgia. Hewison (1987) attributes the burgeoning of the heritage industry to individual and collective fears over severance from the past. He emphasises that the rapid transformation of the urban environment, resulting from industrial and technological change, poses a threat to traditional ways of life that are nostalgically perceived to be authentic, stable and secure. It is claimed: 'In the face of apparent decline and disintegration, it is not surprising that the past seems a better place. Yet it is irrecoverable, for we are condemned to live perpetually in the present' (Hewison, 1987: 43).

The idealised and beautified perceptions of the past underpin the growing popularity of heritage in tourism development (e.g., the heritage industry). Heritage is an essential re-enactment of the past, which is largely conditioned by the concerns and needs of the present and future. Recent literature increasingly focuses on elements of the present and future in enhancing the understanding of heritage. Heritage is thus conceptualised as the 'contemporary use of the past' (Graham, 2002: 1004). The past is constantly adapted and modified by present demands, in which the creative side of culture, history and tradition plays a crucial role in facilitating and maintaining the process of symbolic construction. Therefore, the study of heritage should carefully consider the present-centred nature of heritage which is created and shaped by, and in response to, the demands of the present in which tourism is an essential part. Heritage can be viewed as a symbolic embodiment of the past, reconstructed and reinterpreted in the collective memories and traditions of contemporary societies rather than being perceived as a mere apotheosis of bygone times (Park, 2010a). Inevitably, heritage is open to constant change and revision, thereby leading to multiple interpretations, usages and purposes.

Democratisation of heritage?

As a socially constructed and negotiated concept, heritage evolves through time and across space. Heritage has significantly expanded its base and market appeal over the recent decades. Heritage was once exclusive to the elitist group as part of high culture. In this regard, heritage was a symbolic embodiment of power and hegemony and geography of heritage was confined to the sites of power, including palaces, stately homes and governmental buildings. The era of the 'Grand Tour', for instance, was a testimony of the rights of social elites to travel to places for the purpose of acquiring cultural knowledge and intellectual advancement (Towner, 1985; Black, 1992; Timothy and Boyd, 2003); see Case study 1.1. Until the 1960s there existed clear demarcations between two realms of culture, reinforced by stringent class divisions: high culture and low culture. Germane to this demarcation between high and low culture is the understanding of culture as properties that belong to specific individual groups. However, these divisions became less clear as a result of rapid socio-economic changes in the 1960s (see Williams, 2009). Throughout this period, the appeal of heritage spread to a wider section of society. A growing popularity of encountering and experiencing the realms of the past among the general public is perceived as one clear manifestation of democratising heritage. Lowenthal (1998: 11) explains the pervasive appeal of a nostalgic past:

> In times past, only a small minority sought forebears, amassed antiquities… Such pursuits now lure the multitude. No longer are only aristocrats ancestry-obsessed, only the super-rich antique collectors, only academics antiquarians, only the gentry museum visitors; millions now hunt their roots, protect beloved scenes, cherish mementos, and generally dote on times past.

However, this idea of democratising heritage can be contentious since it is difficult to demonstrate that heritage has been democratised in a real sense. Obviously, heritage

Case study 1.1: Grand Tour

Most of the people on the Grand Tour were aristocrats for whom a trip to continental Europe such as Italy, France and Germany was a part of their classical education. The trip involved visiting sites connected with classical culture, in particular the cities of Italy. The Grand Tour was originally initiated under the reign of Queen Elizabeth I as a form of refined education for young men who sought positions at court. They were encouraged to travel to mainland Europe to study classical culture and antiquity of arts. At that time Italy saw the culmination of Renaissance and it was admired for its vast cultural assets and refined arts tradition. Unlike the medieval period, the main focus was placed on human creativity and inspiration, leading to the culmination of such areas as arts and literature. The tradition of travelling to Europe soon became a trend that was followed by young aristocrats and clergymen who aimed to acquire cultural knowledge and intellectual advancement. This new breed of grand tourists undertook the Grand Tour from several months to several years, travelling through France, Italy, Germany, Switzerland, Austria and Holland. The Grand Tour reached its peak in the seventeenth and eighteenth centuries and its tradition was firmly established as a form of travelling with educational and cultural purposes. In the latter decades of the eighteenth century the focus of the Grand Tour shifted to nature with more people travelling but taking shorter trips. Nature and scenic landscapes became a major force of attraction, largely stimulated by the growth of the Romantic Movement which highlights the force of nature as an artistic imagination. Visits to countryside destinations became extremely popular, including the Alps, the Lake District and the Scottish Highlands. By the mid-nineteenth century, the Grand Tour as an opportunity to explore European antiquity and culture became popular among early American tourists. The most popular cities such as Florence, Venice and Rome on the Grand Tour still remain popular for contemporary cultural and heritage tourists.

Sources: Towner (1985); Black (1992).

in contemporary contexts has become part of mass culture which produces different products to serve different audiences. Forms of high culture have been changed and transformed to meet the newly developed interests and demands of the mass market. But the products consumed by the mass market are often new and different inventions and modifications of heritage. It would thus not be wrong to assert that the manifestation of cultural differences is still palpable in certain heritage sites and practices. Heritage as connoisseurship or scholarship is predominantly linked with the elitist groups, which is not necessarily emphasised in the way heritage is consumed on a mass scale. However, this view of heritage may not be the value of heritage other groups look for in their heritage experiences. Therefore, democratising heritage is deeply associated with challenging the dominant values and discourses of heritage by way of popularising the notion of heritage, rather than arguing over the diffusion of cultural hegemony. Democratisation of heritage thus testifies to the expansion of heritage beyond its traditional boundary as the property of high culture. The scope and appeal of heritage has substantially been broadened, particularly in relation to actively recognising and incorporating the heritage of the general public. Furthermore, heritage not only broadens its appeal but also incorporates alternative approaches and positions to understanding heritage in contemporary contexts.

Within a British context, Hall (2005: 27–8) explicates the wider processes of democratising heritage:

> Increasingly, the lives, artefacts, houses, work-places, tools, customs and oral memories of ordinary everyday British folk have slowly taken their subordinate place alongside the hegemonic presence of the great and the good. The inclusion of domestic vernacular architecture and the agrarian and industrial revolutions, together with the explosion of interest in 'history from below', the spread of local and family history, of personal memorabilia and the collection of oral histories… have shifted and democratised our conception of value: of what is and is not worth preserving.

Heritage has become symptomatic of the choices being made, driven by public enthusiasm and involvement of their own past. Accordingly, heritage is no longer defined solely by antiquities or historical and aesthetic values and qualities. Humble creations and mundane endeavours of ordinary people have been recognised as something worthy of remembrance, protection and preservation. Increasing emphasis on heritage of the working classes, minority ethnic groups and communities has challenged dominant and traditional understanding of heritage and heritage making (see Smith et al., 2011). Moreover, geography of heritage has been realigned and repositioned with new heritage attractions and locations, as evidenced in the examples in Case study 1.2.

Theorising heritage has been characterised by a focus on the monumentality and aesthetics of material heritage, particularly in Western contexts. In this traditional Western understanding of heritage, heritage is perceived as an intrinsic value of objects, places or practices (Smith, 2006). The value becomes immutable, consensual and unquestioned over time, which becomes supposedly regarded as a quality inherent in heritage. Here, the process of assessing heritage is simply concerned with uncovering the heritage values that already exist in an object, place and practice, without recognising heritage as social relation or process. However, Smith contends that heritage is not something that is self-defining:

> At one level, heritage is about the promotion of a consensus version of history by state-sanctioned cultural institutions and elites to regulate cultural and social tensions in the present. On the other hand, heritage may also be a source that is used to challenge and redefine received values and identities by a range of subaltern groups. Heritage is not necessarily about the stasis of cultural values and meanings, but may equally be about cultural change.
>
> (2006: 4)

Heritage is thus not static, open to ongoing negotiations and contestations in different temporal contexts. Here, the present-centred nature of heritage acts as a creative force in diversifying and democratising heritage. Heritage is, in essence, culturally ascribed and socially conditioned rather than being intrinsic to objects and places. This point is of crucial significance in realising and recognising the relative, reflective and relational nature of heritage which is essential in understanding heritage as a social and cultural practice (see Smith, 2006). Accordingly, heritage needs to be constantly re-evaluated and repositioned by social needs, desires and practices. It is also important to recognise and incorporate a more holistic, wide-ranging and all-inclusive understanding of heritage in heritage management and conservation practices.

Case study 1.2: Heritage of the working classes

Humberstone and Santa Laura saltpeter works, Chile

Humberstone and Santa Laura works contain over 200 former saltpeter works where workers from Chile, Peru and Bolivia lived in company towns and forged a distinctive communal Pampinos culture. That culture is manifest in their rich language, creativity and solidarity, and, above all, in their pioneering struggle for social justice, which had a profound impact on social history. Situated in the remote Pampas, one of the driest deserts on Earth, thousands of Pampinos lived and worked in this hostile environment for over 60 years, from 1880, to process the largest deposit of saltpeter in the world, producing the fertilizer sodium nitrate that was to transform agricultural lands in North and South America, and in Europe, and produce great wealth for Chile. The Humberstone and Santa Laura saltpeter works are two that have managed in part to survive the asset stripping that followed the decline of the nitrate industry. None of the buildings are now in use apart from some bathrooms that have been restored for the use of visitors and a reception building. The Pampinos, those who live in the Pampa, are now seen as pioneers in the social struggle for better working conditions, and their distinctive and creative culture is celebrated in print and film.

Berlin modernism housing estates, Germany

The property consists of six housing estates that testify to innovative housing policies from 1910 to 1933, especially during the Weimar Republic, when the city of Berlin was particularly progressive socially, politically and culturally. The property is an outstanding example of the building reform movement that contributed to improving housing and living conditions for people with low incomes through novel approaches to town planning, architecture and garden design. The estates also provide exceptional examples of new urban and architectural typologies, featuring fresh design solutions, as well as technical and aesthetic innovations. Bruno Taut, Martin Wagner and Walter Gropius were among the leading architects of these projects, which exercised considerable influence on the development of housing around the world.

The Workhouse, Southwell in Nottinghamshire, UK

Built in 1824 by the Reverend John Becher, the Workhouse in Southwell was a prototype of the nintheenth-century workhouse. It introduced a revolutionary system of welfare that was later adopted nationwide after the passing of the Poor Law Amendment Act 1834 in the UK. The Workhouse provided housing for the poor, but only in return for submission to a harsh regime that was intended to achieve moral improvement. Even after the abolishment of the New Poor Law system in 1929, workhouses including this one continued to provide housing for the poor into the 1970s and 1980s. The National Trust purchased this workhouse in 1997 and one room in the Workhouse has been recreated to show how it looked in the 1980s when the Workhouse was used for temporary housing. It is also a Grade II listed building and restoration work is ongoing.

Sources: http://whc.unesco.org/en/list; The Open University (2009).

According to Fairclough (2008: 298):

> The spatial dimension of heritage has grown from 'monument' to the slightly larger concept of 'site', thence to 'setting', areas and 'landscapes' and cities and, finally to the landscape. The chronological spread of heritage has been expanded until there are no significant temporal boundaries at all. Growing interest in 'contemporary archaeology', and the concepts of future heritage, suggests that heritage does not even need to be of the past.

Furthermore, the increased recognition of cultural diversity and the proliferation of multiculturalism in Western societies have brought a new and challenging dimension in discourses of heritage. The recognition of representativeness in assessing and appropriating heritage is critical in emphasising different and diverse exemplars of ethnic and multicultural heritage as key constituents of heritage in increasingly multiracial and multicultural societies. Cultural difference and heterogeneity needs to be clearly reflected in the process of heritage selection, interpretation and management. (Please see Chapter 12 for further discussions on heritage as citizenship.)

Changing society, changing heritage

Transition from Fordism to post-Fordism in the late twentieth century has substantially impacted economic structures and relations. This transition has led to the advent of a 'post-industrial' or a 'service' economy in which large-scale and supply-driven production is replaced by a focus on small-scale and demand-driven production. Contrary to the Fordist mode of mass consumption, as well as the mass production of standardised goods and styles, post-Fordist mode is characteristic of flexible production, individualistic consumption and multiple preferences (Henry, 1993). The 'post-industrial' and 'post-Fordist' transition has unmistakably influenced the tourism industry, particularly with respect to the new consumption styles of tourists, the changing perceptions of tourist experiences and the subsequent changes in tourism products (see Table 1.1).

There are contentions and disputes surrounding a clear transformation from 'Fordist' to 'post-Fordist' modes of production and consumption in societies (see Kumar, 1995; Ioannides and Debbage, 1998; Shaw and Williams, 2004). It is argued that both Fordist and post-Fordist patterns coexist in the production systems including tourism. The transition to post-Fordism needs thus to be understood as one way of understanding contemporary socioeconomic changes rather than a fait accompli. Undeniably, this transition has impacted on the ways in which heritage is produced and consumed, particularly within the context of tourism. Post-Fordist orientations make both tourism production and consumption flexible. More specialised niche markets are created to accommodate post-Fordist tourist consumption, compared to the collective consumption of such undifferentiated products as package tourism (Shaw and Williams, 2004). The development of niche markets including special-interest tourism, of which heritage tourism is part, is expected to cater for the varied and specialised tastes of contemporary tourists, i.e., 'post-tourists' (Feifer, 1985: 259). Different motivations and demands of contemporary heritage tourists lead to facilitating the (re)construction of varied heritage experiences and settings. Ioannides and Debbage (1997) claim that the post-Fordist focus on flexible consumption and specialisation can be understood as part of a broader framework of the postmodern phenomenon.

Postmodernism refers to a wide-ranging movement that describes the development of new socio-cultural, political and economic spheres, thereby representing a shift towards distinctive experiences that are somewhat split from the organised, structured and rational

Table 1.1 *Fordism versus post-Fordism*

Fordist production in manufacturing (1920s–1970s)	Post-Fordist production in manufacturing (post-1970s)
Mass production of homogeneous goods Uniformity and standardisation Resource driven and supply oriented Dedicated and inflexible production line Mass consumption Inexperienced customers, motivated by price	Small-scale production of a variety of customised product Niche market Information technologies and robotics Demand-driven production Individualised and differentiated consumption Experienced consumers Increasing preference for non-mass forms of production and consumption
Fordist production in tourism (1950s–1990s)	Post-Fordist production in tourism (post-1990s)
Mass, standardised and all-inclusive holidays Narrow range of standardised travel products Tour industry determines quality and type of product Mostly unskilled labour force Mass tourists Inexperienced and predictable tourists, motivated by price	Emergence of specialised operators, tailor-made holidays Development of niche (alternative) tourism System of information technologies (SIT) Flexible and custom-designed holidays Experienced, independent and sophisticated tourists

Source: adapted from Ioannides and Debbage (1997).

contexts of modern society. Postmodernism has substantially transformed the cultural and social formations of contemporary societies. Postmodernist perspectives attempt to counteract modernistic ways of understanding the nature and function of social and cultural spheres, especially the emphasis on perceiving cultures and societies in an overly essentialist manner. It is generally believed that there exists neither absolute truth nor objective reality under conditions of postmodernism. In this light, postmodernism encompasses 'an appreciation of the plasticity and constant change of reality and knowledge, a stress on the priority of concrete experience over fixed abstract principles, and a conviction that no single a priori thought system should govern belief or investigation' (Tarnas, 1991: 395). Modernism is undeniably associated with 'structural differentiation' (Urry, 1990: 84), which develops normative and institutional distinctions within various cultural and social spheres, including heritage. The process of differentiation in cultural spheres implies that each domain of culture is selected and interpreted by different class-oriented audiences. In sharp contrast to modernism, the main gist of postmodernism is to recognise the 'complexity and nuances of interests, cultures, places, and the like' (Harvey, 1989: 113). Lash (1990: 11) focuses on the process of 'de-differentiation' in the cultural realm. He believes that the boundaries between high culture and low culture have become less strong and clear. A monolithic discourse of culture has increasingly been replaced by a plurality of competing ideas and styles. The distinctive boundaries between such cultural spheres as high and popular culture, history and heritage, past and present, and entertainment and education have been less visible under the influences of postmodernism. According to Urry (1990: 82): 'Postmodernism involves a dissolving of the boundaries, not only between high and low cultures, but also between different cultural forms, such as tourism, art, education, photography, television, music, sport, shopping and architecture.'

Uriely (2005: 203) further highlights the processes of blurring the distinctions among 'normative, aesthetic and institutional spheres of social activity'. Under the increasing influences of postmodernism, relatively uniform and modernist historical discourses have given way to discourses and representations that are more varied, postmodernist, vernacular and regional (Lash and Urry, 1987). Harvey (1989: 156) claims: 'The relatively stable aesthetic of Fordist modernism has given way to all the ferment, instability, and fleeting qualities of a postmodernist aesthetic that celebrate difference, ephemerality, spectacle, fashion, and the commodification of cultural forms.'

Overarching meta-narratives concerning the differentiations of socio-cultural spheres have thus come to be replaced by accounts of popular mass culture. Featherstone (2007: 94) specifically explains the essence of postmodern change in direct relation to changing perceptions of cultural consumption, commenting:

> Here one can point to the increasing salience of forms of leisure consumption in which the emphasis is placed upon the consumption of experiences and pleasure (such as theme parks, tourist and recreational centres) and the ways in which more traditional forms of high cultural consumption (museums and art galleries) become revamped to cater for wider audiences through trading in the canonical, auratic art and educative–formative presentations for an emphasis upon the spectacular, the popular, the pleasurable and immediately accessible.

What is also pertinent about the postmodern perspective is that the past, especially the way it is articulated, perceived and negotiated, is merged into the postmodern present. Thus the past and the present have become no longer perceived as separate and discontinuous realms. Nonetheless, Harvey (1989: 54) cynically notes: 'Postmodernism abandons all sense of historical continuity and memory, while simultaneously developing an incredible ability to plunder history and absorb whatever it finds there as some aspect of the present.'

Harvey's observation thus implies a critical awareness that postmodernism is fundamentally concerned with using elements of the past for present purposes. Postmodernism is then accused of commodifying and domesticating modernism following 'anything goes' market eclecticism (Harvey, 1989: 42). Despite the controversial nature of postmodernism, however, it is important to recognise its key roles as a condition in manifesting the changing nature of heritage. Heritage can be seen as an important signifier of change in the nature of society. Heritage illustrates postmodernism in the way its use and purpose reflects the manifestation of postmodernism such as focus on experience and multiple narratives. Traditionally, sites of cultural and historical significance tend to be more frequented by those individuals who had sufficiently high forms of economic and cultural capital. Likewise, an initial form of cultural appreciation through tourism was ultimately preoccupied by those who represented high culture, as highlighted in Case study 1.1 about the 'Grand Tour'. However, since heritage places such as visitor attractions appeal to a wider section of society, the social significance of heritage sites has dramatically changed in recent years. Development in communication and travel networks, and the increase in disposable income and leisure time, pave the way for diversifying and enriching tourist experiences (Urry, 1990). More recently, the dissolution of class culture has provided individuals with increased opportunities to participate in activities considered to be a social right for elite groups. For Urry (1994), the expansion of heritage tourism is closely associated with the rise of postmodern forms of consumption. A variety of heritage products are produced and marketed as commodities for this new group of tourists, who distinguish themselves by highly diversified patterns of consumption. Although questions remain as to how significant or large this group is, which will need further exploration, increasing growth in heritage production and consumption is explicable in terms of fascination with the past in contemporary societies.

History versus heritage

History and heritage are often interrelated and interchangeable in certain contexts. Nonetheless, history and heritage have generally been understood as being dichotomous, contrasting and contradictory. History is perceived to be objective and veritable, while heritage is often accused of being subjective and unscrupulous.

> [H]istory and heritage are typically placed in opposite camps. The first is assigned to the realm of critical inquiry, the second to a merely antiquarian pre-occupation, the classification and hoarding of things. The first, so the argument runs, is dynamic and concerned with development and change; the second is static. The first is concerned with explanation, bringing a sceptical intelligence to bear on the complexities and contradictoriness of the record; the second sentimentalizes, and is content merely to celebrate.
>
> (Samuel, 1994: 270)

Within the context of tourism development, heritage often becomes a commercially driven entity that is carefully selected, packaged and promoted. Heritage is therefore accused of packaging and commodifying the past and turning it into tourist kitsch (Samuel, 1994). Subsequently, heritage is clearly differentiated from history in that

> history is the remembered record of the past; heritage is a contemporary commodity purposefully created to satisfy contemporary consumption... the raw materials... are a wide and varied mixture of historical events, personalities, folk memories, mythologies, literary associations and surviving relics, together with the places, whether sites or towns, with which they are symbolically associated. The past is thus best viewed as a quarry of possibilities, only a very small proportion of which will ever be utilized as heritage.
>
> (Ashworth, 1994: 16)

Unsurprisingly, historians' leitmotiv of heritage criticism is unmistakably bound up with the assumption that heritage is a commercial, vulgar and denigrating exploitation of the past, which is the main tenet of the 'heritage industry'. Heritage is, at best, a commercial and political misuse of history, presenting a 'history that stifles, but above all, a history that is *over*' (Hewison, 1987: 141, original emphasis). Similarly, Lowenthal emphasises:

> It [heritage] is not a testable or even a reasonably plausible account of some past, but *a declaration of faith* in that past. Critics castigate heritage as a travesty of history. But heritage is not history, even when it mimics history. It uses historical traces and tells historical tales, but these tales and traces are stitched into fables that are open neither to critical analysis nor to comparative scrutiny.
>
> (1998: 121, original emphasis)

English country houses (stately homes) are widely regarded as the 'quintessence of Englishness' and the 'culmination of English aristocratic history'. Exploring the historical evolution and the changing roles of English country houses can be a good illustration of understanding the conflictual and dialectic relationship between history and heritage (see Case study 1.3).

Case study 1.3: Country houses (stately homes) in England: history or heritage?

Integral to the country house are grand architectural styles, the rural landscapes or parks and the collections of art and antiquities. Country houses are about power; their architectural design is not about ensuring a sense of 'home', but is an explicit statement about the status and power of the family within.

Figure 1.1 Blickling Hall, Norfolk, UK

It was with the Tudor period that castles tended to be replaced by non-fortified halls and other elite dwellings. From the seventeenth century, much of the political power in England was largely in the hands of the owners of the country houses. Although highly symbolic of elite privilege, these houses are also deeply emblematic of a sense of England's national heritage. During the nineteenth century, the country house became caught up in a European drive to develop a sense of national history and, by the mid-nineteenth century, the country house was viewed as 'common property', belonging to all 'England' and the first wave of mass country house visiting occurred. After the Second World War, country houses went into a rapid decline. However, country houses became revalued as a national heritage icon by the work of the National Trust and organisations such as SAVE Britain's Heritage throughout the 1970s and early 1980s. A significant event in the preservation history of the country house was the 1974 exhibition at the Victoria and Albert Museum: The Destruction of the Country House, 1875–1975. Organised by members of SAVE, this exhibition, and the SAVE campaign itself, raised pubic interest over the fate of the country houses when a plan for a Wealth Tax was introduced. A new tax aimed to replace death duties with a Capital Transfer Tax (CTT), which would tax the transfer of capital assets made during the owner's lifetime or after death. The exhibition proved very successful in order to raise the interests of the public in the country houses in crisis. Over the last several decades, country houses have regained their fame and popularity, particularly in relation to their broadened appeal to the general public. As popular heritage tourism attractions ranging from living museums to heritage hotels, country houses still play an important role in maintaining national identity in modern Britain. The ownerships of country houses are varied: public, private and voluntary. In order to meet the changing needs and interests of contemporary heritage tourists, country houses have eagerly tried to incorporate new interpretational methods and visitor management strategies. For all the critique of 'Disneyfication' of the past as theme parks, country houses are keen on enhancing their appeal in the tourism industry. Some notable examples of country houses as popular heritage tourism attractions are Longleat in Wiltshire (with the safari park), Harewood in Yorkshire, Harewood House in Leeds, Tatton Park in Cheshire and Highclere Castle in West Berkshire, which has recently been used as a film set of *Downton Abbey*.

Source: an excerpt from Smith (2006).

It can be argued that clear and rigid demarcation between history and heritage is somewhat elitist based and outmoded. It seems to be rather unjust to claim that heritage only distorts, fabricates and exaggerates historical facts and events, thereby leading to falsification and trivialisation of the past. Samuel (1994) argues against the 'heritage-baiting' of critics such as Wright and Hewison, on the grounds that heritage is progressive. He perceives heritage as a more inclusive vision of collective memories rather than rigid ramifications of the past supported by the conservatives. Cassia (1999) also draws attention to a need to refine Lowenthal's clear distinction between history and heritage. He further argues that Lowenthal fails to fully explore the similar and overlapping social bases of history and heritage and their dialectical relationship. According to Cassia (1999: 260):

> History as scholarly activity can be seen as the means of production of knowledge about the past, and heritage as celebratory activity can be seen as the means of consumption of that historical knowledge. This consumption is realized through the signification of preservation. 'History' and 'heritage-tradition' are thus intimately related. This enables us to move beyond the debate on 'truth' versus 'relativism' in history and view history and heritage-as-tradition as joint productions and celebrations of the past.

The critical understanding of heritage should thus be grounded in the theoretical premise that heritage, like history, is an essential creation and consumption of historical knowledge. The interrelated and interdependent nature of history and heritage needs to be recognised rather than perceiving them as conflicting and discrepant. It is history that provides the foundation upon which heritage is conceived and developed. History is thus an essential element to establish heritage's own version of legacy and tradition, be it personal, local or national, particularly within the context of tourism. History becomes constantly deconstructed and reconstructed as heritage with different uses and purposes, as evidenced and illustrated in the advent of the heritage industry.

The heritage industry: commodification and sanitisation of the past?

The transition from a manufacturing to a service-based economy has facilitated the consumption of culture and heritage in contemporary societies (McCrone *et al.*, 1995). As indicated earlier, another conspicuous phenomenon of the tourism industry that is influenced by postmodern change is the growing popularity and consumption of the representations of the past. Many theorists have discussed ways in which the increasing demand for past representations is closely related to the needs of contemporary societies to encourage and enhance a clear continuity with the past (Wright, 1985; Hewison, 1987; Walsh, 1992; Ashworth, 1994; Graham *et al.*, 2000; Ashworth *et al.*, 2007). This concern leads to the advent of a commercialised 'heritage industry' institutionally linked to the leisure and tourism industries (Hewison, 1991: 166–7). Collective and personal nostalgia for the past serves as a main motivation for tourism and other leisurely activities. Robert Hewison coined the term 'heritage industry' describing the commodification and sanitisation of the past as heritage in the UK in the late 1980s. He cogently argues that heritage is mainly created to capture middle-class nostalgia for the past as an ideal retreat amidst a climate of decline. Both remote and recent past has been made alive and influential in the present. In an era of the 'heritage industry' the past has become an essential commodity both materially and symbolically. Furthermore, the heritage industry promotes entertainment and commercial values by presenting a past that is a hollow pastiche of history rather than accurately portraying its truth. Commodified heritage is often criticised as a denigrated version of history, which fails to capture the essence of the nation's cultural and social identities. Hewison (1987) emphasises that the commercial need for exploiting historical tales has consequently led to the advent of the heritage industry. He (1987: 138) states:

> Yet we have no real use for this spurious past, any more than nostalgia has any use as a creative emotion. At best we turn it into a commodity, and following the changed language of the arts, justify its exploitation as a touristic resource. The result is a devaluation of significance, an impoverishment of meaning.

The tourism industry is often blamed for being responsible for the excessive commodification of heritage, which is often systematically packaged and sold for tourist consumption. The range of heritage attractions, which is nostalgically motivated and commercially contrived, has become more appealing and palatable to tourists (Hewison, 1987; Urry, 1990; Halewood and Hannam, 2001; Vesey and Dimanche, 2003). Hewison (1987: 32) argues that heritage 'means everything, and it means nothing, and yet it has developed into a whole industry'. Interestingly, Richards (1996: 13) indicates that the heritage industry has been founded upon a 'whole new breed of attractions and intermediaries who supply culture specifically for tourist consumption'. According to Hannabuss (1999: 297):

Everything appears to be 'heritage' these days. A mine that closes yesterday becomes industrial heritage today. Breweries and aqueducts, fishing ports and jute factories, tenement flats and car factories go the same way… Obsolete industries like fishing and agriculture are generated heritage centres to celebrate bygone ways and crafts, national parks and forestry areas are promoting themselves as never before.

The aegis of the heritage industry is inextricably bound up with such key tenets of postmodernism as 'simulation' (Baudrillard, 1983), 'historicism' (Jameson, 1984) and 'hyper-reality' (Eco, 1986). Baudrillard (1983) claims that meaning has been replaced with spectacle in postmodern society. According to Eco (1986: 43), a copy of the original, a 'total fake', reproduces reality, namely 'hyper-reality' in postmodern tourism environments. Hewison (1987: 135) appropriately contends:

Post-modernism and the heritage industry are linked, in that they both conspire to create a shallow screen that intervenes between our present lives, and our history. We have no understanding of history in depth, but instead are offered a contemporary creation, more costume drama and re-enactment than critical discourse.

Commercial heritage attractions display and promote a constructed and false history playing on nostalgia. The spurious past includes popular culture which allows for nostalgia to be commodified. Themes such as Vikings, Romans and Tudors reproduce popular preconceptions and stereotypes in the commercially contrived heritage settings as well as popular culture. The Tudors are, for example, popular themes for heritage centres in the UK in which banquets and jousting mainly symbolise and represent this historical period. Hampton Court Palace in London is, for example, renowned for its connection with the Tudor period, particularly as the favourite palace of Henry VIII (see Figure 1.2). One of the main palace highlights is a programme entitled 'A living Tudor world', through which visitors can experience various aspects of the Tudor life, including a Tudor kitchen.

However, Raphael Samuel argues, in '*Theatres of Memory*', that heritage needs to be understood as a possibility for promoting social change as well as a democratic phenomenon. He states that heritage criticism is often grounded in aristocratic snobbery which attacks the commodification of the past. Samuel (1994: 266) summarises the prevalent criticism of heritage:

Aesthetes condemn it [heritage] for being bogus: a travesty of the past, rather than a true likeness, let alone – the preservationist's dream – an original. In other words, in spite of the charge that heritage is imprisoning the country in a time-warp, and the accusation that it is sentimentalizing the past, heritage is being attacked not because it is too historical but because it is not historical enough. It lacks authenticity. It is a simulation pretending to be the real thing. It is not because heritage is too reverent about the past that it provokes outrage, but on the contrary the fact that, in the eyes of the critics at least, it seems quite untroubled when it is dealing with replicas and pastiche.

The development of the heritage industry has blurred boundaries between history and heritage. As Samuel (1994) argues, heritage makes the past more democratic by emphasising the lives of ordinary people. He therefore supports the 'museumification' of society, observing that this process enables heritage settings to appeal to wider sections of society.

Figure 1.2 Hampton Court Palace, UK

The process of commodification could create and fabricate a new environment in which different possibilities and potentials of heritage are created and recreated. Recognising the transformative nature of heritage has redefined and repositioned the values of heritage as socially constructed, thereby broadening the appeal of heritage to a wider section of society. In a similar vein, Urry (1990) challenges the prevalent criticism of the heritage industry, particularly in relation to the use of heritage as tourism resources. He puts a great emphasis on the role of the consumers in selecting what is and what is not heritage through developing a gaze on history. It therefore follows that heritage is to a large extent co-created by its consumers, particularly as an object for visual consumption within tourism contexts. Read (1999) also notes that a heritage industry that makes the past popular in the present plays an essential role in making historical resources more accessible. Likewise, intellectual opposition to the growing popularity of the commercialised nature of the heritage industry has become more moderate during the past decade, especially as significant attention has focused on the positive aspects of utilising the past through commercially led approaches. Some heritage attractions including heritage theme parks and heritage centres never intend to become an accurate historical reconstruction. Their main intention is to establish a true replica for which there is no original. Here, searching for objective authenticity becomes rather meaningless. It is also important to recognise that contemporary heritage tourists are generally aware that some heritage attractions are simulated and replicated, thus providing an inauthentic tourism environment (Hall and Bombardella, 2005). Heritage, particularly in relation to the process of commodification, has challenged high culture and its aesthetics, thereby forming a middle-ground culture. Commodified heritage makes high culture more accessible by opening new markets for the middle class such as the dramatisation of books and retailing business. Heritage can be seen as a form of 'cultural production' expressing new social identities, packaged and promoted within tourism development contexts (Robb, 1998). Such observations thus draw caution to theorists such as Hewison (1987) and Lowenthal (1998), who denounce heritage as a commercial and political misuse of history.

Conclusion

Heritage is identified as both a tangible and intangible outcome of the past inherited from one generation to the next. Heritage is not a fixed and unchanging entity, instead, it is a socially produced, conditioned and negotiated process. Heritage often maintains a strong correlation with political power and cultural hegemony. This tendency can still be palpable in some heritage practices such as national heritage representations. The scope and range of heritage has substantially expanded, thereby creating and managing different heritage products to attract a wider section of society, particularly in relation to the emergence of the 'heritage industry'. Academic critiques of the commercialisation of the heritage industry have been prevalent in studies of heritage and tourism. Economic commodification of the past could lead to trivialising and distorting history for touristic consumption. In addition, the popularity of the nostalgic pastiche of a bucolic and idealised past, a popular theme of a commercial heritage industry, often involve dispiriting and suppressing the present. Nonetheless, more recently there is an increasing realisation that the process of utilising the past can be socially and culturally constructive, even though commercial orientations are purposefully pursued. Thus discussions concerning the role of the heritage industry in the context of postmodern change imply that as historical resources are becoming more available, access has become more democratised and consumption has become less socially differentiated.

Research questions

1   Try to conceptualise heritage in your own words and explain what heritage means to you.
2   Explain and critically assess the socially constructed nature of heritage. Why is the notion of nostalgia important in the appeal of heritage?
3   Discuss the increasing focus on the present-centred nature of heritage and heritage making.
4   What does 'democratisation of heritage' mean? Illustrate your answer with relevant examples.
5   Discuss and evaluate the ways in which postmodernism has influenced heritage tourism development.
6   Develop a critique of the dichotomy between history and heritage.
7   Using relevant examples, explain some positive aspects of the burgeoning of the 'heritage industry'.

Learning material

Ashworth, G.J. (1994) From history to heritage – from heritage to identity: in search of concepts and models, in G.J. Ashworth and P.J. Larkham (eds) *Building a New Heritage: Tourism, Culture and Identity in the New Europe*, London: Routledge, pp. 13–30.

Ashworth, G.J., Graham, B. and Tunbridge, E. (2007) *Pluralising Pasts: Heritage, Identity and Place in Multicultural Societies*, London: Pluto Press (Chapter 3).

Cassia, P. (1999) Tradition, tourism and memory in Malta, *Journal of the Royal Anthropological Institute* (N.S.), 5(2): 247–63.

Eco, U. (1986) *Faith in Fakes*, London: Secker & Warburg.

Fairclough, G. (2008) New heritage, an introductory essay: people, landscape and change, in G. Fairclough, R. Harrison, J.H. Jameson and J. Schofield (eds) *The Heritage Reader*, London: Routledge, pp. 297–312.

Graham, B. (2002) Heritage as knowledge: capital or culture? *Urban Studies*, 39(5–6): 1003–17.

Graham, B., Ashworth, G.J. and Tunbridge, J.E. (2000) *A Geography of Heritage: Power, Culture and Economy*, London: Arnold (Chapters 1 and 4).

Harvey, D. (1989) *The Condition of Postmodernity: An Enquiry into the Origins of Cultural Change*, Oxford: Blackwell (Chapters 3, 9 and 10).

Hewison, R. (1987) *The Heritage Industry*, London: Methuen (Chapters 2 and 4).

Jameson, F. (1984) Postmodernism, or the cultural logic of late Capitalism, *New Left Review*, 146(July–August): 53–92.

Lowenthal, D. (1998) *The Heritage Crusade and the Spoils of History*, Cambridge: Cambridge University Press (Chapters 1, 6 and 7).

McCrone, D., Morris, A. and Kiely. R. (1995) *Scotland – the Brand: The Making of Scottish Heritage*, Edinburgh: Edinburgh University Press (Chapters 1 and 2).

Poria, Y. and Ashworth, G.J. (2009) Heritage tourism: current resource for conflict, *Annals of Tourism Research*, 36(3): 522–5.

Poria, Y., Butler, R.W. and Airey, D. (2003) The core of heritage tourism, *Annals of Tourism Research*, 30(1): 238–54.

Samuel, R. (1994) *Theatres of Memory Vol. 1: Past and Present in Contemporary Culture*, London: Verso (the section on heritage-baiting).

Smith, L. (2006) *Uses of Heritage*, London and New York: Routledge (Chapter 1).

Smith, L., Shackel, P.A. and Campbell, G. (2011) *Heritage, Labour and the Working Classes*, London: Routledge.

Towner, J. (1985) The grand tour: a key phase in the history of tourism, *Annals of Tourism Research*, 12(3): 297–333.

Urry, J. (1990) *The Tourist Gaze: Leisure and Travel in Contemporary Societies*, London: Sage (Chapter 6).

Weiss, L.M. (2007) Heritage-making and political identity, *Journal of Social Archaeology*, 7(3): 413–31.

Wright, P. (1985) *On Living in an Old Country: The National Past in Contemporary Britain*, London: Verso (Chapter 2).

Weblinks

What is heritage? OpenLearn (The Open University, UK)
http://www.open.edu/openlearn/history-the-arts/history/heritage/what-heritage/content-section-0

Photo journal: rise and fall of mass production
http://news.bbc.co.uk/1/shared/spl/hi/picture_gallery/07/business_rise_and_fall_of_mass_production/html/1.stm

Excess baggage: England
http://downloads.bbc.co.uk/podcasts/radio4/excessbag/excessbag_20111231-1032a.mp3

American icons
http://www.studio360.org/series/american-icons

Visit to Thomas Jefferson's Monticello, USA
http://www.youtube.com/watch?feature=player_embedded&v=dqqKYyT5kS8#

Their homes: our heritage 1950
http://www.britishpathe.com/video/their-homes-our-heritage/query/heritage

Stately homes of old England (1921): Hampton Court
http://www.britishpathe.com/video/stately-homes-of-old-england

Behind the Tudors: Hampton Court
http://www.youtube.com/watch?v=mX7ABmAlcAE

Henry VIII's kitchens, Hampton Court
http://www.hrp.org.uk/MediaPlayer/ViewPlaylist.aspx?PlaylistId=24

Life for the servants of Erdigg Hall in Wales, UK
http://www.bbc.co.uk/programmes/p00k9c1m

Geopolitics of archaeology: archaeological tourism's effect on people and heritage (an interview with Lynn Meskell)
http://www.wbez.org/episode-segments/geopolitics-archaeology-archaeological-tour-isms-effect-people-and-heritage-0

UK targets heritage tourism
http://news.bbc.co.uk/1/hi/programmes/fast_track/8989610.stm

Heritage tourism in York, UK
http://learnenglish.britishcouncil.org/ar/word-street/heritage-tourism

What is your heritage?
http://www.youtube.com/watch?v=bYPNKoDm0e4

Museum of Jewish heritage in New York, USA
http://watch.thirteen.org/video/2364994111

Tweed Run 2010, London
https://www.youtube.com/watch?v=qMdGMiX1KHQ&feature=player_embedded

2 Heritage tourism supply and demand

Heritage tourism supply

Heritage tourism supply includes both tangible and intangible elements of the past that form and constitute tourism products and services. This section aims to briefly summarise the key characteristics of the existing typologies and elaborate the ways in which contemporary changes in society have influenced the spectrum of heritage supply, rather than developing an exhaustive list of heritage attractions. Within the context of tourism development, Nuryanti (1996) groups heritage into three main categories: built heritage that can be described as historic and artistic heritage such as relics, forts and modern towns (see Figure 2.1); scientific heritage encompasses elements such as plants, birds, animals, rocks and natural habitats; and cultural heritage comprises folk and fine arts, customs and languages. The 1972 United Nations Educational, Scientific and Cultural Organization (UNESCO) World Heritage Convention provides a useful definitional framework for deciding both cultural and natural sites that can be considered for inscription on the World Heritage (WH) List. 'Cultural heritage' is composed of:

- Monuments: architectural works, works of monumental sculpture and painting, elements or structures of an archaeological nature, inscriptions, cave dwellings and combinations of features, which are of outstanding universal value from the point of view of history, art or science.

Figure 2.1 Carthage, Tunisia

- Groups of buildings: groups of separate or connected buildings that, because of their architecture, their homogeneity or their place in the landscape, are of outstanding universal value from the point of view of history, art or science.
- Sites: works of man or the combined works of nature and man, and areas including archaeological sites that are of outstanding universal value from the historical, aesthetic, ethnological or anthropological point of view.

The following is considered as 'natural heritage':

- Natural features consisting of physical and biological formations or groups of such formations, which are of outstanding universal value from an aesthetic or scientific point of view (see Case study 2.1).
- Geological and physiographical formations and precisely delineated areas that constitute the habitat of threatened species of animals and plants of outstanding universal value from the point of view of science or conservation.
- Natural sites or precisely delineated natural areas of outstanding universal value from the point of view of science, conservation or natural beauty.

(UNESCO, 1972)

It is important to recognise the interrelated relationship between natural heritage and cultural heritage. Many natural heritage sites, such as national parks, have cultural components that humans ascribe to them. Cultural heritage sites, such as architectural remains, archeological sites, artefacts or monuments, despite being mainly classified as tangible heritage, encompass intangible values and meanings construed from aesthetic and historical values, architectural styles or stories to people associated with the sites. Various types and scopes of heritage attractions within the context of tourism have been identified and illustrated in great detail by authors, including Prentice (1993), Leask and Yeoman (1999), Timothy and Boyd (2003) and Timothy (2011). Prentice (1993) makes a distinction between heritage and heritage attractions, particularly drawing on the heterogeneity of heritage attractions for tourism consumption. Here, the role of intermediary agencies in developing heritage into heritage attractions is discussed as the main producers of heritage products. Harnessed by the emergence of the heritage industry and subsequent competitiveness in tourism, the supply of heritage attractions often exceeds the demand of heritage. There has been an over-supply of heritage sites in contemporary tourism scenes (Jenkins, 1992). The heritage market has reached saturation due to an increasing influx of newly established and commodified heritage attractions.

Within the context of heritage tourism, heritage is not just confined to ancient monuments and historic sites. Heritage as a tourism resource is, as emphasised, present-centred as much as past-oriented. The past is created and recreated for contemporary purposes of tourism development. Tunbridge and Ashworth (1996: 9) claim: 'The recycling, renewal and recuperation of resources, increasingly important in the management of natural resources, can be paralleled in historic resources where objects including buildings can be moved, restored and even replicated.'

Heritage tourism is both a spatial and temporal phenomenon (Jamal and Kim, 2005). Situating the past in a wider context of political, socio-cultural and economic changes is essential in understanding the intricate dynamics between heritage and tourism. Spatial context can be categorised as individual, local, national and international, while temporal context can be divided by the stratum of past, present and future. Here, it is fundamental to understand that heritage is not just material remnants of the past that are of aesthetic and historical value. The increasing present-centred nature of heritage has led to facilitating the

Case study 2.1: 'Natural' WHSs

The Dorset and East Devon Coast, UK

The Dorset and East Devon Coast, also known as The Jurassic Coast, was the first ever site in the UK to be inscribed as a 'natural' WHS in 2001. WH status was achieved because of the site's unique insight into the earth sciences as it clearly depicts a geological 'walk through time' spanning the Triassic, Jurassic and Cretaceous periods. The Jurassic Coast covers 95 miles of truly stunning coastline from East Devon to Dorset, with rocks recording 185 million years of the Earth's history. The area's important fossil sites and classic coastal geomor-phologic features have contributed to the study of earth sciences for over 300 years. All along the coast there are picturesque 'Gateway' towns and villages, including Charmouth, Sidmouth, Lyme Regis, Exmouth and Wareham.

Source: www.jurassiccoast.com.

Purnululu National Park, Australia

Purnululu National Park is located in the East Kimberley Region of Western Australia located 300km by road south of Kununurra in Western Australia's Ord Region; the listed area is almost 240,000ha. The park comprises four major ecosys-tems: the Bungle Bungle Mountain Range, a deeply dissected plateau that dominates the centre of the park; wide sand plains surrounding the Bungle Bungles; the Ord River valley to the east and south of the park; and limestone ridges and ranges to the west and north of the park. Purnululu also has a rich Aboriginal cultural herit-age spanning over some 20,000 years. The park provides exceptional testimony to this hunter–gatherer cultural tradition, which has survived to the present day despite the impact of colonisation.

The Sundarbans, Bangladesh

The Sundarbans, the only natural heritage designation in Bangladesh, was inscribed as a UNESCO WHS in 1997. The Sundarbans mangrove forest, one of the largest such forests in the world (140,000ha), lies on the delta of the Ganges, Brahmaputra and Meghna rivers in the Bay of Bengal. It is adjacent to the border of India's Sundarbans WHS inscribed in 1987. The site is inter-sected by a complex network of tidal waterways, mudflats and small islands of salt-tolerant mangrove forests, and presents an excellent example of ongoing ecological processes. The area is known for its wide range of fauna, includ-ing 260 bird species, the Bengal tiger and other threatened species such as the estuarine crocodile, flying foxes, spotted deer and the Indian python.

Source: http://whc.unesco.org/en/list.

development of a plethora of recent heritage attractions. Amid the influx of not-so-old, rec-reated and replicated heritage attractions, however, Weaver (2011) insightfully observes that scant attention has been placed on identifying tourism heritage as part of heritage supply for touristic consumption. The remnants of contemporary, consumer-driven mass tourism and hospitality, such as mature seaside resorts, are hardly recognised as being legitimate and worthy of heritage designation. He pinpoints that recent commodification of industrial heritage as popular heritage attractions tends to be clearly incorporated and illustrated in the practices of heritage supply. It is further argued that tourism heritage needs to be recognised and valued as authentic industrial and cultural heritage. Given the significance of tourism development as a global recreational activity, a call for recognition and legitimacy of contemporary tourism is a timely contribution to broadening the understanding of the changing dynamics of heritage supply (see Case study 2.2).

The increasingly competitive and saturated supply side of heritage tourism development has undoubtedly led to a call for understanding and systematically analysing the needs and expectations of heritage tourists.

Experience economy and heritage tourism

Contemporary consumers are not satisfied with merely consuming products and services, however varied and diverse they are. There has been an upsurge of new demand for unique and memorable experiences as a distinctive consumption pattern (Pine and Gilmore, 1998, 1999; Oh *et al.*, 2007). Pine and Gilmore (1999) conceptualise experience as a distinct economic offering that pervades a wide range of industries. In the industrial economy, tangible and standardised products were the main economic offering, which gradually gave way to customised services as the main focus of the service economy in the 1970s and 1980s. Eventually, these services have become recreated and presented as experiences that are 'events that engage individuals in a personal way' (Pine and Gilmore, 1999: 12). These

---

Case study 2.2: Benidorm as a WHS?

As the first high-rise resort in Europe, Benidorm is the most popular beach tourism destination in the Costa Blanca, Spain. It has been the mecca of sun-seeking beach tourists, particularly British tourists, since its transformation from a peaceful fishing village to a bustling tourist resort for package tourists in the 1950s and 1960s. High skyscrapers densely built along the coast are the epitome of the town, which is often criticised as a main factor in deteriorating its architectural values. But interestingly, there is an opposing perspective in viewing this recent tourism heritage. Professor Philippe Duhamel, a geographer at the University of Angers, adds immense cultural importance to Benidorm's 'unique collection of skyscrapers'. He even terms it as 'the Dubai of Europe' and emphasises its remarkable and unique contribution to mass tourism development. It is added: 'For many years, everybody spoke badly of Benidorm, but with time it has gained value, as has happened in other examples of architectural world heritage.' While trying to remake its image as a luxury destination, authorities in Benidorm have been trying to apply for WHS status.

Source: Walsh (2008).

experiences are expected to create a closer link between the providers (heritage supply) and the customers (heritage demand) (Hayes and MacLeod, 2007). Here, the customers, redefined as heritage tourists in this context, are recognised both as main recipients of memorable experiences and main actors of enriching the experiences. The emergence of an experience economy is also closely related to the transition from Fordist to post-Fordist operations. The shift of focus from production-driven to consumer-driven in the tourism industry creates a need for a unique experience (Apostolakis, 2003). Pine and Gilmore (1998) propose four different realms of experience: education, entertainment, aesthetics and escapism. The four experience dimensions have been incorporated into a conceptual framework in various tourism studies: tourists' experiences of lodging, the bed-and-breakfast industry (Oh *et al.*, 2007); designing heritage trails and visitors' engagement (Hayes and MacLeod, 2007); and examining the effects of theatrical elements of theme parks on tourists' experiential quality and satisfaction (Kao *et al.*, 2008). Regardless of mainly relating to the changes in economic offerings underpinning contemporary business arenas, the concept of an experience economy bears significant implications in heritage tourism development, particularly in relation to its contemporary trends and characteristics in both heritage supply and demand. Increasingly, heritage attractions pay greater emphasis in enhancing tourist experiences. This change is clearly manifest in heritage attractions and settings where elements of the past are recreated and re-enacted in staged experiences. There has also been a shift of focus on active participation on the part of heritage tourists. Heritage tourists play key roles in creating the event or the performance that yields the experience.

Furthermore, it is strongly recommended to theme the experience in order to be able to design and facilitate memorable experiences. Pine and Gilmore (1998: 103) emphasise:

> Consider the Forum Shops in Las Vegas, a mall that displays its distinctive theme – an ancient Roman marketplace – in every detail… These include marble floors, stark white pillars, 'outdoor' cafes, living tress, flowing fountains – and even a painted blue sky with fluffy white clouds that yield regularly to simulated storms, complete with lightning and thunder. Every mall entrance and every storefront is an elaborate Roman re-creation. Every hour inside the main entrance, statues of Caesar and other Roman luminaries come to life and speak. 'Hail, Caesar!' is a frequent cry, and Roman centurions periodically march through on their way to the adjacent Caesar's Palace casino.

Increasing focus on tourist experiences is also evident in more traditional types of heritage attractions, including palaces, stately homes and museums. Eltham Palace, a medieval royal palace and childhood home of Henry VIII, is run by English Heritage. It is usually closed during the winter months (November–March) for maintenance and upkeep. But the palace still occasionally runs special events in which tourists' active participation is a critical element. It organised, for example, the Great Hall Sleepover on the 17 February 2013. Families were invited to spend an exclusive evening including a supper, a late night tour of the palace and a story-telling session.

The annual event of 'Museums at Night' is another interesting example of encouraging tourists' active participation, thereby creating memorable personal experiences in museums. It is the annual after-hour celebration in which museums, galleries, libraries and heritage sites remain open for special evening events and exhibitions during one weekend in May in the UK. It is funded by the Arts Council England, the Heritage Lottery Fund and the Norfolk Museums and Archaeology Service. Museums at Night 2013 took place in various museums and heritage sites across the UK during the evenings of 16–18 May. 'Calke by Candlelight' in Calke Abbey, Ticknall, 'Evening Walk around

Historic Dunbar' in East Lothian, Scotland and 'Museum at Night Dinner at Bateman's' in East Sussex were some notable examples in 2013.

Likewise, the application of effective and compelling themes has been clearly adopted in heritage attractions that focus on enhancing tourist experiences by employing differing and diverse presentational and representational methods. Open air museums and heritage trails, for example, are good examples of heritage with a focus on unique and innovative presentational methods including living history presentations and heritage tourists' active participation in facilitating memorable experiences (see Case study 2.3).

Case study 2.3: Open air museums

Sirogojno Zlatibor, Serbia

Sirogojno is a village located on Mt. Zlatibor in West Serbia. In Sirogojno an open air museum, or 'ethno-village' known as the Old Village Museum (Serbian: Muzej 'Staro selo'), represents the village dwelling culture covering nearly 15ha with authentic elements of ordinary life collected from all over the Zlatibor region from the nineteenth century. The ethno-village displays a set of traditional wooden build-ings, including a bakery, a dairy and an inn, some of which have been transferred to the present site of the museum and conserved for further research and display for the public. It is also known all over the world for its hand-made wool jumpers that have been designed by Dobrila Vasiljevic-Smiljanic for 30 years and knitted by Zlatibor peasant women. This traditional art and craft of knitting has been recognised all over the world as a timeless fashion. The museum has a particularly elaborate programme to revive old local arts and crafts. Copies of objects of fine workmanship are produced in the workshop of the museum: pottery, hand printed textiles, utensils of wood and iron. It also runs summer schools for learning traditional arts and crafts such as pottery, knitting and mosaic-making and graphic skills. It is possible to book accommodation in the cottages that have kept the traditional appearance and feel, but that have been adapted to accommodate the needs of modern tourists.

Source: http://www.uzice.net/sirogojno.

Beamish Open Air Museum, UK

The North of England Open Air Museum at Beamish was first opened in 1970. Its main purpose was to display the remnants of the industrial and agricultural north-east-ern England. As the main hub of the Industrial Revolution, the region experienced the dramatic economic and social changes. Using 'living history' presentational and rep-resentational methods, the Beamish Open Air Museum encourages visitors to have a feel of their past. The museum's collections were built around what was already on the site, and donated property through a successful policy of unselective collect-ing – 'you offer, we collect' – employing communicators or interpretive media. Its founder, Frank Atkinson, was an entrepreneurial museum curator who had a vision for providing an authentic site portraying everyday life of the ordinary people in the Georgian, Victorian and Edwardian periods. Despite a barrage of criticism that relates Beamish to a Disneyfied past, its living history presentations incorporating interpretive media and costumed impersonators are key to attracting heritage tourists both locally and internationally.

Source: Cross and Walton (2005); www.beamish.org.uk.

Figure 2.2 Beamish Open Air Museum, UK (courtesy of Beamish Open Air Museum)

Nazareth Village, Israel

As an open air museum in Nazareth, Israel, Nazareth Village reconstructs and re-enacts village life in Galilee in the time of Jesus. The main aim of the site is to create a first-century village based on biblical, historical and archeological research. Its website unmistakably emphasises memorable experiences its visitors will soon discover:

> Come meet the people and experience first-century hospitality. Step through a stone doorway into the dim interior, and smell the smoke from the oil lamps. You will begin to imagine life in another time, when Jesus lived here in Nazareth. In the courtyard peer into the cistern, a vital part of any household. Hand-hewn caves store wheat and other supplies.

A range of guided group tours are available and biblical meals served by villagers dressed in first-century costumes are available upon request. The village also runs a volunteer programme that can last from one week to one year. As visitor facilities it offers both a gift shop and an online shop as well as a visitor centre that is designed to enrich visitors' understanding of the history of the Nazareth Village and the life and times of Jesus. The following comments are from its webpage of visitors' comments:

> By reading the Bible we can make a picture of the first century. By visiting Nazareth Village we can feel life really walking inside the Bible.

> I thank God for the wonderful opportunity of visiting the Nazareth Village. It was like stepping into the ancient world of Jesus and the Nazarite community! It was an unforgettable, most memorable and life changing experience!

Source: www.nazarethvillage.com.

Heritage tourism demand

Critical focus is increasingly placed on the significance of heritage in global tourism development. The fascination with experiencing and consuming the past continues to grow all across the globe. On an international scale heritage tourism experiences encourage people to encounter and appreciate diverse historic environments and cultural assets, thereby enhancing the understanding of different people and cultures. At a time of fast socio-cultural changes, heritage visits are expected to contribute to enhancing personal and collective memories, a sense of cultural and national identity and community cohesion and belonging on a domestic scale. As highlighted, heritage means different things to different people. It is thus obvious that tourists visit heritage sites with different motivations and demands. It is essential to recognise the significance of understanding the different motivations of heritage tourists, which subsequently influence heritage interpretations and representations. In general, there is substantial lack of detailed information as regards global patterns and trends in the area of heritage tourism (Timothy, 2011). However, it is evident that heritage tourism is a fast-growing sector in both developed and developing countries. For countries including the UK and the USA where heritage sites and events are the main stimulant for both domestic and international tourists, understanding motivations for heritage consumption is critical in developing and enhancing the management and promotional strategies of heritage attractions and events. The size of the heritage tourism sector in the UK is in excess of £12.4 billion a year and supports an estimated 195,000 full-time jobs (Heritage Lottery Fund, 2010). Similarly, many developing countries have recently seen a surge of interest in heritage sites, settings and events as the main pull factors of both inbound and outbound tourism development. As evident in the case study below, China has recently experienced a sharp increase in domestic heritage tourism development (see Case study 2.4).

In the existing literature on heritage tourists' motivations, substantial focus has been placed on identifying heritage tourist demographics: age, gender, education, income, social status and lifestyle (Prentice, 1993; Herbert, 2001; Chhabra et al., 2003). It is believed that understanding demographic variables are of use for heritage managers in identifying specific markets and developing relevant management and marketing strategies catered to specific desires and needs of tourists. Education is, in general, regarded as a prominent characteristic of heritage tourists. Serious heritage tourists tend to be often well educated, with qualifications in higher education. Heritage tourists are likely to be more affluent than other types of tourists, mostly from higher socio-economic backgrounds. Heritage tourists also tend to stay longer and spend more in an area than other types of tourists (Taylor et al., 1993). Moreover, heritage tourists show more willingness to explore places in greater depth, with the intention to 'usually seek an informed visitor experience rather than merely gazing' (Prentice et al., 1998: 7). They thus expect outcomes that include learning about their destination and gaining an insight into its past. While enjoyment is still crucial, heritage tourists often expect a greater degree of involvement with, or immersion into, heritage sites and settings. In terms of gender, women tend to visit heritage sites more than men (Timothy, 2011). Timothy (2011) further observes that heritage tourists are younger and middle aged; however, the majority of heritage tourists in the USA tend to be older and retired, which is increasingly a visible trend in other countries. Here, Bourdieu's (2010) [1984] concept – 'habitus' – has a clear bearing on the main characteristics of heritage tourist demographics, with specific reference to social classes and lifestyles. 'Habitus' refers to the ways in which social classes strive to maintain differentiation from other classes. It is not economic and financial assets but cultural and symbolic capital that embodies and sustains certain attributes of different social

Case study 2.4: Domestic heritage tourism development in China

The Chinese are increasingly in search of their history, their spiritual traditions, their temples and their places of natural beauty. The Chinese are now travelling through their own country as tourists in a way they have never done before. This new phenomenon is undoubtedly encouraged by the advent of a new Chinese middle class, who are increasingly affluent and less prohibited in the way they choose their travelling preferences. In October's Golden Week in 2011 (one of the country's semi-annual, seven-day national holidays), 302 million tourist trips were recorded. At the heart of this new domestic tourism development lies heritage attractions and settings, either genuinely old or partly constructed. The traditional communities, such as the Wuzhen water village on the Changjiang river near Hangzhou in Zhejiang province, are very popular destinations, often leading to excessive commodification of their heritage. Some traditional villages actually thrive on constructed and contrived heritage settings. For example, the hotel complex of Nanping in Anhui is, in fact, based on a film set used by the director Zhang Yimou for his 1989 film *Ju-Dou*. More traditional types of heritage attractions are also popular among the Chinese tourists, such as the Confucius' temple in the old city of Qufu, Shandong province. Following Confucius' death in 478 BC, Lu Aigong, King of Zhou, changed the three rooms of his residence into a temple, which has since been sustained as a historic site. Natural heritage attractions are big draws to domestic heritage tourists. Huangshan, literally known as 'Yellow Mountain' in China, is a mountain range in southern Anhui Province in eastern China that is renowned for its breathtaking scenery including peculiarly shaped granite peaks. It has been a frequent subject of traditional Chinese mountain and water paintings, as well as modern photography. Including Huangshan, which was designated a WHS in 1990, China currently ranks third in the world with 43 enlisted WHSs, only superseded by Italy (47) and Spain (44).

Source: Woollacott (2012).

classes. Unlike economic capital, cultural capital cannot be easily acquired or replicated. According to Bourdieu (2010: 59):

> The competence of the 'connoisseur', an unconscious mastery of the instruments of appropriation which derives from slow familiarization and is the basis of familiarity with works, is an 'art', a practical mastery which, like an art of thinking or an art of living, cannot be transmitted solely by precept or prescription.

In this light, heritage tourism can be, in a traditional sense, one form of symbolic and cultural consumption to maintain the 'habitus' of certain social groups, thereby maintaining social class differentiations. However, the increasing democratisation of heritage, facilitated by the advent of the heritage industry, has to some extent challenged the stringent notion of heritage as the specific cultural capital of certain social classes and groups, as discussed in greater detail in Chapter 1.

Another variable for classifying heritage tourists is psychographic segmentation, focusing on tourists' attitudes and behaviour. Following Plog's (1990, 1991) model, heritage tourists can be categorised into two different groups: allocentric and psychocentric. Plog (1990: 43) defines the allocentric type of tourists as being 'self-confident, not suffering from unfocused anxiety, and liking to travel, especially to exotic or very unique destination areas'. Allocentric heritage tourists are thus very eager to gather information and search for new and challenging heritage experiences and places whereas psychocentric heritage tourists rather choose to visit historic sites or heritage attractions close to home (Timothy, 2011). However, these variables are predominantly hypothetical and quantitative based. Moreover, they are generally predetermined by academic or professional researchers, without systematically examining visitors' own interpretations and explanations of their motivations and attitudes towards heritage. Concurrently, Masberg and Silverman (1996) contend that very little research has been adequately designed to explore visitors' perspectives at heritage sites. They bring attention to the significance of employing qualitative approaches, particularly phenomenology based, in uncovering and understanding heritage tourists' conceptions and experiences. Heritage tourists describe their experiences as more personal, emotional or experiential than just being educational and factual based. Central to this assumption is a recognition that heritage tourists are not necessarily drawn to historical and educational elements of heritage. Rather, they place substantial significance on personal and emotional encounters with heritage through which their perspectives and experiences become differentiated and specialised. In sharp contrast to Prentice's (1993) argument that heritage tourists display general and similar behaviour, Kerstetter *et al.* (1998) examine if travel behaviour characteristics of heritage tourists are related to visitations at industrial heritage attractions. They argue that the travel behaviour of individuals in certain types of industrial heritage attractions such as historic railways and trains is unique and individualised. Since the 1970s, there has been an increasing growth of heritage railways that cater to tourists, particularly those with special interest in railroads and trains (Timothy, 2011). A growing number of people are keen on seeing and travelling on a preserved mode of transport, thus experiencing the images, emotions and past memories they stimulate (Halsall, 2001) (see Case study 2.5). It is thus important to recognise that the demographic and psychographic variables need not be understood as an ultimate factor in understanding the motivations of heritage tourists. Instead, they should be understood as an auxiliary factor in enriching the understanding of heritage tourism demand. There is a critical need to acknowledge the multidimensional and multifaceted nature of tourists' experiences at heritage attractions and events.

For heritage professionals, it is important to realise and identify latent demand of heritage, not to mention of its current demand. A clear understanding of latent demand for heritage can help heritage professionals, particularly heritage site managers and event organisers, develop new management and marketing strategies to attract new and prospective tourists (Timothy and Boyd, 2003) (see Table 2.1). Given an increasing business-oriented and commercial nature of heritage attractions, heritage tourists are increasingly seen as customers seeking 'value for money' in their tourism experiences. Contemporary heritage tourists are keen on experiencing heritage in emotional, intuitive and interactive ways. They are in constant search of individually tailored and differentiated experiences reflecting their personality and interest in their encounters with heritage. The heritage tourist may be also described as a 'thoughtful consumer', one who is culturally competent and wary of the process of commodification in heritage arenas (Voase, 2002).

Case study 2.5: The North Norfolk Railway, UK

The North Norfolk Railway (NNR), also known as the 'Poppy Line' by its locals, started its service as a commercial railway in 1887 across north Norfolk in the UK. Due to the rapid development of the railways in the UK in the early twentieth century, the line became deflected and used as a secondary route, which gradually led to decreased passenger numbers. The service was finally ceased in 1924. Since reconstituted as a heritage railway in 1973, the NNR has offered a 10.5 mile round trip by steam or vintage diesel trains between the coastal town of Sheringham and Holt. Currently, the NNR is a private limited company with active status that owns all the land, structures and tracks. NNR PLC has 50 shareholders including the Midland and Great Northern Joint Railway Society (M&GN), which is a supporting charity and a key player in the preservation, conservation and survival of the NNR. The NNR is now one of Britain's most scenic heritage railways. The heritage railway currently offers additional services and private hire for events such as weddings, birthdays, filming and other seasonal occasions. It also runs various events including a Steam Gala, a 1940s weekend, a Santa Special and Murder Mysteries throughout the year. The trains can also be hired for individual driving experiences. In addition, there is a museum, restaurant and educational workshops available for the use of both tourists and the community.

Sources: http://www.nnrailway.co.uk; http://www.mandgn.co.uk/page.php?pid=12.

Figure 2.3 The North Norfolk Railway, UK (taken by Aneta Kaczmarek)

Some examples of popular heritage railways

UK
The Heritage Railway Association: www.heritagerailways.com
Vintage Trains: www.vintagetrains.co.uk

Chiltern Railways: www.chilternrailways.co.uk
North Yorkshire Moors Railway: www.nymr.co.uk
Northern Belle: http://www.orient-express.com/web/uktr/uk_day_trains.jsp

USA
The Texas State Railroad: www.texasstaterr.com
Grand Canyon Railway: www.thetrain.com

India
The Darjeeling Himalayan line in northern India (WHS): www.dhrs.org

Australia
The Association of Tourist and Heritage Railways Australia: www.athra.asn.au
Australian Steam: www.australiansteam.com
Great Rail Experiences Tasmania: www.greatrailexperiencestasmania.com.au

Table 2.1 *Key constraints underlying latent demand/non-use of heritage*

Inaccessibility	Physical inaccessibility: harsh weather, topographic barriers, lack of infrastructure and transportation and a lack of handicap access Market inaccessibility: work and domestic responsibilities, lack of time and money (admission fees and transportation)
Lack of educational preparation	A perceived lack of educational preparation/a lack of visitation during childhood and informal education
Disabilities	Physical, psychological or cognitive disabilities/ environmental barriers/communications barriers
Psychological constraints	A lack of interest or desire
Other constraints	Widely-held perceptions of high-quality customer service/'museum fatigue'

Source: Timothy and Boyd (2003: 75–8).

Motivations and experiences of heritage tourists

Tourism motivations are directly linked to the demand of tourism. It is thus important to understand and analyse tourists' motivations of visiting heritage sites in order to better understand the demand side of heritage tourism. Tourist motivation is defined as 'a state of need, a condition that exerts a push on the individual towards certain types of action that are seen as likely to bring satisfaction' (Moutinho, 1987: 16). Here, clear emphasis is placed on human behaviour, be it an intrinsic or extrinsic motive. Intrinsic motives include escape from personal/social pressures, social recognition/prestige, socialisation/bonding, self-esteem, novelty and learning/discovery, whereas extrinsic motives are usually viewed from the supply side, mainly actual tourist attractions (Kim and Lee, 2002). Intrinsic motives are 'push' factors that refer to the intangible, intrinsic desires of the individual traveller, mainly origin related. 'Pull' factors are, as extrinsic motives, mainly related to the appeal of each attraction or destination, which entails both tangible resources including heritage attractions and intangible resources including tourists' perceptions and expectations (Uysal and Juroski, 1994). As emphasised previously, some of the key motivations for visiting heritage sites have not yet been fully explored (Poria *et al.*, 2006a, b). Here, the main difficulties lie in the multidimensional and multifarious nature of heritage tourists' motivations. Light and Prentice (1994: 27) acknowledge that the demand for heritage is heterogeneous and divergent, further claiming that 'demand will vary at different types of site, and among different groups of visitors. Identification of these variations is essential to enable individual sites to design their development and promotion policies in accordance with the requirements of their consumers.'

Importantly, tourism motivation is not a fixed and static variable. It can change over time and in different spatial and temporal contexts. Therefore, Pearce (1993) brings attention to the flexible design of motivation lists that 'incorporate individual changes across the life-span and consider the effects of broad cultural force on tourist motivation'. It is important to note that visits to heritage sites are not just recreational or leisure purposes despite a common assumption inherent in motivation studies. Poria *et al.* (2003) challenge the existing perceptions of heritage tourism, especially those mainly linked to tourists' appreciation of historic places and sites. Instead, they contend that heritage tourism is a phenomenon related largely to tourists' motivations and perceptions of the site itself rather than simply site attributes and specific artefacts presented. However, attempts to investigate the significance of the demand side of heritage, particularly people's subjective perceptions and aspirations, are overshadowed by an over-concentration on the supply aspects of heritage, together with a significant emphasis on heritage management as a tool for economic development (see Wiendu Nuryanti, 1997; Rowan and Baram, 2004; Hausmann, 2007). Accordingly, it is important to critically acknowledge tourists' socio-psychological needs and perceptions of the heritage setting in an endeavour to advance an alternative approach to understanding the role of heritage tourists and tourists at heritage places. This can be explained by considering the motivations of the visit and the relationships between tourist perceptions and tourist behaviour patterns. A deep understanding of heritage tourism based on tourists' motivations and perceptions can be further effective and relevant in such contexts as domestic heritage settings, religious sites and places of ancestral connection.

Apostolakis (2003) believes that the categorisation of 'heritage tourists' depends on the consumption patterns of heritage attractions. From the existing literature concerning heritage tourists, he classifies two contrasting groups: the descriptive group and the experiential group. The first definitional group places an emphasis on the 'material components of culture and heritage such as attractions, objects of art, artifacts, relics, as well as more intangible forms of culture and heritage such as traditions, languages, and folklore' (2003: 799). The second definitional group focuses on the individual's experiences and her/his perceptions of the destination site, and when choices need to be made to consume heritage attractions. Apostolakis (2003: 799) further claims: 'The experiential definition of heritage tourism thus embodies an interpersonal element. The linkages between the site, the potential tourists' motives and their perceptions can be conceived as an interactive process.'

The experiential definition of heritage tourism seems to be of particular relevance in understanding possible influences derived from the motivations and perceptions of tourists visiting heritage sites. In relation to this, the embodied interpersonal element plays a pivotal role in exploring the meanings and perceptions of visiting specific heritage settings, particularly where the meanings attached to the sites are closely related to issues of cultural and national identity. In their study on investigating the association between the perception of the site in relation to tourists' own heritage and behaviour, Poria *et al.* (2006a) attempt to examine tourists' motivations before the visit takes places compared to previous studies in which motivations were explored after the actual visit. With regard to specific motivations for a visit to the Anne Frank House in Amsterdam, the Netherlands, the following three categories were identified: willingness to feel connected to the history presented; willingness to learn; and motivations not linked with the historic attributes of the destination, particularly the willingness to feel emotionally linked to the heritage tourists perceive as their own (Poria *et al.*, 2006a: 172). It is emphasised that the emotional link between the tourist and the heritage setting visited should be explored in order to enhance the understanding and management of historic settings (see also McCain and Ray, 2003; Caton and Santos, 2007; Park, 2010a).

There have also been few studies examining and evaluating the actual experiences of heritage tourists. Using a framework of heuristic inquiry, Caton and Santos (2007) aim to unravel the different and varied travel experiences along Route 66 in the United States. Established in 1926, Route 66 is one of America's first transcontinental highways (from Chicago to Los Angeles), attaining the status of an American cultural icon. The study challenges the prevailing assumption in heritage tourism literature that heritage tourists are mainly driven by nostalgia, a collective longing for a forgotten past. Nostalgic yearning has been identified as one of the main motivations of heritage tourists (Davis, 1979; Chhabra *et al.*, 2003; Vesey and Dimanche, 2003). Nostalgia is conceptualised as a 'positively toned evocation of a lived past in the context of some negative feeling toward present or impending circumstance' (Davis, 1979: 18). However, Caton and Santos (2007) criticise that nostalgia theory perceives history as something that exists independent of tourists' perceptions and interpretations. Furthermore, it is argued that the implication of nostalgia theory subscribes to the view that tourists are not capable of assessing individual features of the past and present, thereby leading to an uncritical and undifferentiated consumption of heritage. Therefore, tourists' insatiable obsession with the past as something that is purported to be better than the present can be a 'product of irrational emotional attachments, rather than logical reasoning' (Caton and Santos, 2007: 372).

Subsequently, it is critical to note that heritage tourists' motivations are somewhat complex, divergent and multifaceted (Moscardo, 1996; Park, 2010b). Park (2010b) emphasises the significance of individual experiences and multiple interpretations in heritage tourism experiences. Therefore, tourists need to be aware of their reflexive role in actively constructing and reconstructing the past in present contexts. They are not just passive recipients but active creators of heritage. They can play a significant role as key actors in building stronger links with the present as well as the past. It is highlighted '[b]y demonstrating that visitors' experiences were multifaceted, rather than solely focused on learning about or connecting with history, and that visitors frequently left sites with an appreciation for the present, rather than a longing for the past' (Caton and Santos, 2007: 373). It is also clear that travelling Route 66 challenges tourists to move beyond their ordinary life experiences and to reflect various intrapersonal, interpersonal and societal issues. A sense of personal growth is accompanied with embracing challenges. Here, heritage tourism is reconceptualised and recontextualised as an embodied and emotive experience:

> Participants did not merely gaze at historic sites and gain information from interpretive displays; rather, they interact with history through vivid visceral experiences that directly engaged their bodies and senses (e.g., driving/riding,

consuming food). They also experienced profound social interactions through their travels. In turn, these experiences became the raw material from which individual participants forged personal narratives of the journey… Thus, the experience was about connecting with history, not by romanticizing the past as a lost golden era, but by choosing to participate in an ongoing, dynamic cultural legacy, which is rooted in the past but continues to spur new encounters that become part of the participants' biographies in the present. In this case, heritage tourism, often portrayed as a past-oriented endeavour, provided the raw material for active self-making, a future-oriented pursuit.

(Caton and Santos, 2007: 384)

This focus on active and dynamic experiences of heritage tourists can also be related to the concept of 'existential authenticity' (Wang, 1999) in which focus is placed on individual perceptions, feelings and articulations (see Chapter 4 for discussions on authenticity). Despite recognising that the significance of individual perceptions of visits to heritage sites contributes to broadening the spectrum of heritage tourism formations, too much emphasis on the demand side could then lead to neglecting the supply side of heritage tourism, including the attributes of sites and objects on display (and their relationship to patterns of tourism consumption). Accordingly, conceptual and empirical studies associated with elements of the heritage industry ought not to lose sight of the interconnections and interrelationships between the demand and supply components of heritage tourism. Hence, concentration on one component should duly acknowledge the ontological relevance of the other component.

Conclusion

Heritage tourism is directly related to experiencing both tangible and intangible heritage, be this at a local, national or international level. A variety of heritage attractions and events, including recent creations of heritage driven by the process of commodification, are an essential part of heritage supply. Given the increasing influx of newly established and commodified heritage, heritage supply often surpasses heritage demand in contemporary heritage tourism development. Certain socio-economic changes, including the transition to an experience economy, have also contributed to broadening the scope and range of heritage, particularly focusing on developing and facilitating memorable experiences, as is clearly evidenced in heritage sites such as open air museums. Here, there has been a shift of focus on active participation on the part of heritage tourists as both creators and recipients of heritage. Understanding tourists' motivations to visit heritage sites, the demand side of heritage, is of paramount significance in enhancing heritage interpretations, representations and overall management strategies. It is clear that tourists visit heritage sites with different motivations and demands. There have been increasing academic interests in recognising and appreciating personal values and emotional connections with heritage sites, rather than merely focusing on the historic and factual attributes of sites. Understanding individual perceptions and articulations underpinning heritage tourism experiences contributes to unraveling the intricate, multifaceted and complex nature of heritage tourists' motivations. There must be a balanced approach to understanding heritage supply and demand, focusing on the interconnections and interrelationships between the demand and supply components of heritage tourism.

Research questions

1 Try to devise your own typologies of heritage as tourism attractions.
2 Discuss how a focus on an experience economy has influenced the supply side of heritage.
3 How can an experience economy model be further developed and implemented in order to produce effective strategies for managing and marketing heritage?
4 Why is it important to understand the underlying motivations of heritage tourists?
5 Explain the ways in which the concept of cultural capital is associated with understanding the motivations of heritage tourists.
6 Discuss the ways in which emotional or experiential focus of heritage tourists' experiences influence the operation of the heritage supply side.
7 Explain the main changes in heritage tourism demand in recent years.

Learning material

Apostolakis, A. (2003) The convergence process in heritage tourism, *Annals of Tourism Research*, 30(4): 795–812.
Bourdieu, P. (2010) *Distinction*, London: Routledge (Chapter 3).
Caton, K. and Santos, C.A. (2007) Heritage tourism on Route 66: deconstructing nostalgia, *Journal of Travel Research*, 45(4): 371–86.
Ioannides, D. and Debbage, K. (1997) Post-Fordism and flexibility: the travel industry polyglot, *Tourism Management*, 18(4): 229–41.
McCain, G. and Ray, N. (2003) Legacy tourism: the search for personal meaning in heritage travel, *Tourism Management*, 24(6): 713–17.
Pine, B.J. and Gilmore, J.H. (1998) Welcome to the experience economy, *Harvard Business Review*, July–August, 97–105.
Poria, Y., Butler, R.W. and Airey, D. (2004) Links between tourists, heritage, and reasons for visiting heritage sites, *Journal of Travel Research*, 43(1): 19–28.
Poria, Y., Reichel, A. and Biran, A. (2006) Heritage site perceptions and motivations to visit, *Journal of Travel Research*, 44(3): 318–26.
Shaw, G. and Williams, A.M. (2004) *Tourism and Tourism Spaces*, London: Sage (Chapter 10).
Timothy, D.J. (2011) *Cultural heritage and tourism: an introduction*, Bristol: Channel View Publications (Chapters 2 and 3).
Vesey, C. and Dimanche, F. (2003) From storyville to Bourbon Street: vice, nostalgia and tourism, *Journal of Tourism and Cultural Change*, 1(1): 54–70.
Weaver, D.B. (2011) Contemporary tourism heritage as heritage tourism: evidence from Las Vegas and Gold Coast, *Annals of Tourism Research*, 38(1): 249–67.

Weblinks

Carthage, Tunisia
http://whc.unesco.org/en/list/37/video
http://www.youtube.com/watch?v=EdYhshaAZDY

Mount Huangshan, China
http://whc.unesco.org/en/list/547/video

Bompas & Parr at the SS Great Britain (Museums at Night 2012)
http://www.youtube.com/watch?v=lUjSnUsCa4k

Old Village of Sirogojno in Zlatibor, Serbia
http://www.youtube.com/watch?v=59kJNG9kO0k

The Man Who Made Beamish (1986)
http://www.youtube.com/watch?v=YwuDCIo4hUU#t=32

Beamish Museum: pit village
http://www.youtube.com/watch?v=2o0tL8OFFWA

Beamish Museum: 1980s television adverts
http://www.youtube.com/watch?v=avTZEfjGuuk

Beamish Museum: the living museum
http://www.flickr.com/photos/beamishmuseum/sets/72157624163461491

Nazareth Village Promotion 2012
http://www.youtube.com/watch?v=-CCs6Xm5FC8

1940s Weekend: the North Norfolk Railway
http://www.youtube.com/watch?v=4oU5Hibxxfc

3 Managing heritage tourism

Heritage: conservation or development?

The values of heritage in the past were mainly associated with preservation and conservation. Preservation and conservation, as terms, are often used interchangeably. However, conservation entails a broader and more holistic understanding of the uses and purposes of heritage, considering its present and future needs as well as past integrity. Conservation is thus conceptualised as:

> the process of understanding, safeguarding and, where necessary, maintaining, repairing, restoring, and adapting historic property to preserve its cultural significance. Conservation is the sustainable management of change, not simply an architectural deliberation but also an economic and social concern.
>
> (Orbaşli and Woodward, 2012: 316)

Heritage implies a sense of stability and continuity whereas tourism is by nature a form of modern development and consumption (Li, 2003). However, heritage has become more popular and prevalent in contemporary tourism development. This new change has led to increasing and ongoing conflicts among the ideas of heritage conservation and tourism development. Despite increasing tourism development in heritage sites and events, there is a fundamental desire to preserve and protect the realms of the past as a means to maintain historical integrity and cultural continuity. There thus exists a dichotomy between preservation of the past for its intrinsic values and development of the past in response to fast-changing society in heritage planning and management (Nasser, 2003). The relationship between tourism and conservation can be classified into:

1   conflict, where tourism is detrimental to the local environment;
2   coexistence, where tourism has no impact on the area in which it operates; and
3   symbiosis, where conservation values are enhanced by tourism.
         (Budowski, 1976, cited in Lindsay *et al.*, 2008: 730)

Too much focus on preserving heritage would undermine its economic potential, particularly in relation to tourism development. On the contrary, excessive tourism development could lead to damaging and destroying heritage in the long term. Tourism development without proper consideration for conservation would result in excessive commodification of heritage sites, which will increase the risk of permanent physical damage, as well as the loss of cultural values and authenticity (du Cros, 2001). Therefore, heritage professionals and managers need to strive to keep a symbiotic relationship between conservation and tourism development (see Case study 3.1).

Case study 3.1: The second fall of Pompeii

As one of the most visited heritage sites in Italy, Pompeii receives approximately 2.5 million visitors annually. Since its excavation Pompeii has been subject to both natural and man-made forces including erosion, light exposure, pollution, poor methods of excavation and reconstruction, tourism, vandalism and theft. The signs of deterioration have been evident for years. Pompeii was included on the World Monuments Watch List of 100 Most Endangered Sites in 1996, 1998 and 2000. There ensued a critical concern to desperately repair the site and a 'conservation master plan' was drafted. Despite this, Pompeii's House of the Gladiators, which had survived the cataclysmic volcanic eruption in AD79 and heavy Allied bombing in 1943, collapsed in November 2010. The Italian newspaper *La Repubblica* dubbed this catastrophe as a 'world scandal' and UNESCO claimed that it had had 'a devastating effect internationally'. Though it may be possible to rebuild it from the ground, the richly decorated frescoes of gladiators that gave the building its name may be lost forever. The political system of Berlusconi's government has been blamed for making significant cuts to heritage spending, thereby reducing maintenance budgets in 2010 from €30 million to €19 million. *Il Sole 24 Ore*, Italy's leading business newspaper, claims that the collapse of the House of the Gladiators was proof that responsibility for Pompeii should be removed from the state and given to private sponsors. Excessive tourism development could be another main culprit. Sandro Bondi, the then culture minister, announced in the following week after the disaster the establishment of a new foundation responsible for assessing the state of decay and devising necessary action plans. But critics point out that his insistence that work would resume on five key Pompeii houses ignored the need for a more modest programme of continual and small-scale maintenance across the city. Rather than a few prestige renovation projects, it is critical to focus on infrastructural stabilisation and maintenance across the entire site in the long term.

Source: an excerpt from Addley (2010).

Compared to widely held distrust in tourism development as a hindrance to sustain the historical integrity of heritage, it is critical to note that tourism can serve as a vehicle for conservation, particularly in financial terms (Orbaşli and Woodward, 2012). Concomitantly, tourism is increasingly recognised as an opportunity for conservation. Heritage needs a popular base and public support for its conservation, which is often attained from tourism development. In his comparative analysis on heritage tourism development in Singapore and Hong Kong, Li (2003) argues that inherent contradictions between conservation and tourism development serve more as resources than threats for developing heritage tourism. It is emphasised that both Singapore and Hong Kong began to make a concerted effort to conserve their heritage, as late as the 1980s and 1990s respectively, when each government realised the economic potential of utilising heritage for tourism development. Tourism development in heritage sites inevitably influences what should be conserved and how it should be conserved. Regular and permanent maintenance measures need to be employed in heritage sites in order to ensure the preservation of heritage. Furthermore, raising tourists' awareness of the significance of conservation is critical in the effective management of heritage sites. There is a critical need for the tourism industry to develop effective long-term planning and understanding regarding the importance of heritage (Millar, 1989). It is also vital to have efficient heritage management strategies that redress a balance between the requirements of heritage sites and the requirements of tourists. Importantly, relevant management strategies need to be employed before any visible signs of degradation and destruction of heritage resources.

The tradition of conservation within the European context is rooted in the development of the Grand Tour through which a need to preserve important works of art and historic monuments was recognised and stressed. Collective concerns over linking with the past in the twentieth century were, as previously explicated, unmistakably bound up with notions of conservation and national and cultural pride at a time of uncertainty and ongoing changes. It is quite surprising that the principal measures to systematically protect historic sites and buildings were not clearly identified and legislated until as late as the 1880s, even in European countries. It was not until 1882 in the UK when the Ancient Monuments Protection Act, the prototype of legislative protect, was introduced by Sir John Lubbock. It recognised the need for a government administration on protecting ancient monuments. However, it only covered mainly historical sites and monuments (e.g., archaeological ruins) and earthworks. It was not until 1944 and 1947 that Town and Country Planning Acts enlisted historic buildings for preservation. In America, the conservation movement of the nineteenth and early twentieth centuries contributed to public interest in protecting historic and archaeological sites, for example, the Antiquities Act signed by President Roosevelt in 1906 and the National Trust for Historic Preservation in 1949. The passage of the National Historic Preservation Act (NHPA) of 1966 paved the way for systematically preserving historical sites in America. This act established several institutions: the Advisory Council on Historic Preservation, the State Historic Preservation Office and the National Register of Historic Places. Importantly, the NHPA has led to major changes in the field of cultural resource management (CRM) which developed as a 'system for site and resource protection' in America (Jameson, 2008: 42). CRM is an umbrella term that encompasses archaeology, historic preservation and other disciplines when employed for the purposes of compliance with NHPA and other federal and state-mandated historic preservation laws (see Table 3.1). The major international organisations involved in the management of heritage in the Western world currently include the Council of Europe, the International Council of Museums (ICOM), ICOMOS, the International Committee on Archaeological Heritage Management (ICAHM, a committee of ICOMOS), the International Federation of Library Associations and Institutions (IFLA), the Organisation of World Heritage Cities (OWHC), UNESCO and the World Monuments Fund (WMF).

Despite concerted attempts to conserve heritage on an international scale, as illustrated above, heritage conservation and management remains as a big challenge in many developing countries. There exists a lack of the governance in dealing with a huge rise in global tourism and encouraging long-term local engagement, with specific reference to conserving and managing WHSs. Here, the active involvement of such independent conservation organisations as the Global Heritage Fund (GHF) is crucial in protecting and preserving heritage. The GHF is an international conservancy whose mission is to protect, preserve and sustain the most significant and endangered cultural heritage sites in the developing world. Since 2002, the GHF has invested over $25 million and secured $20 million in co-funding for 18 global heritage sites to ensure their sustainable preservation and responsible development (see Case study 3.2).

Too much reliance on governments in protecting heritage can be problematic in some countries where governments do not operate properly or function only in the interest of the elite. It is therefore important to note that a certain level of non-state stakeholder involvement including the private sector is often necessary in monitoring and facilitating

Table 3.1 *Cultural heritage charters regarding heritage conservation and management*

The Athens Conference (1931)	The Athens Conference, organised by the International Museums Office, established basic principles for an international code of practice for conservation. Some key principles include the legislation of preserving historic sites at the national level and the inclusion of areas surrounding historic sites for protection.
Hague Convention (1954)	UNESCO adopted the Convention for the Protection of Cultural Property in the Event of Armed Conflict after the Second World War. As the first international treaty, the Hague Convention aimed to protect cultural heritage in the context of war and highlighted the concept of common heritage.
The Venice Charter (1964)	The Venice Charter, an important cornerstone for the modern conservation movement, was published by the International Council on Monuments and Sites (ICOMOS). The Venice Charter for the Conservation and Restoration of Monuments and Sites (CATHM) is a treaty that gives an international framework for the preservation and restoration of ancient buildings. The Venice Charter particularly stresses the importance of the traditional setting, respect for original fabric, careful evaluation with scientific standards and precise documentation in the form of analytical and critical reports.
The Declaration of Amsterdam (1975)	As part of the European Architectural Heritage, The Declaration of Amsterdam emphasises the role of planning, education, legal and administrative measures in protecting the region's architectural heritage. The concept of integrated conservation and broad identification of heritage was introduced and the justification for conserving the architectural heritage is clearly manifest in the document. Critical focus was placed on recognising the significance of integrating conservation of the architectural heritage into urban and regional planning.
The Burra Charter (The Australian ICOMOS Charter) (1981)	The Burra Charter for the Conservation of Places of Cultural Significance defines the basic principles and procedures that are essential in the conservation of Australian heritage settings. Foreground in the Venice Charter, it introduces the concept of cultural significance, the 'aesthetic, historic, scientific or social value for past, present and future generations', which needs to be (re)defined and (re)contextualised for each heritage setting. It also identifies three different levels of conservation, such as preservation, restoration and reconstruction.
The Washington Charter on the Conservation of Historic Towns and Areas (1987)	The Washington Charter mainly concerns historic urban areas, including cities, towns and historic centres and quarters, together with their natural and man-made environments. Critical focus is placed on encouraging the participation and involvement of the residents as essential for the success of the conservation programme.
The Nara document on Authenticity (1984)	The Nara document on Authenticity by Japan and UNESCO expanded the Venice Charter in the context of cultural and heritage diversity. The understanding of authenticity plays a fundamental role in all scientific studies of cultural heritage and its conservation and restoration planning. It also emphasises the integration of the preservation of the intangible cultural heritage together with the safeguarding of sites and monuments.
The ICOMOS Charter for interpretation and preservation of cultural heritage sites (2008)	The ICOMOS Charter for interpretation and preservation of cultural heritage sites aims to contribute to the sustainable conservation of cultural heritage sites, through promoting public understanding of, and participation in, ongoing conservation efforts, ensuring long-term maintenance of the interpretive infrastructure and regular review of its interpretive contents.

Case study 3.2: Mirador Archaeological and Wildlife Area in Guatemala

Mirador Archaeological and Wildlife Area, located in the heart of the Maya Biosphere in northern Guatemala, is home to the earliest and largest Preclassic Maya archeological sites in Mesoamerica and includes the largest pyramid in the world – La Danta. Therefore, the Mirador Basin is regarded as the Cradle of Maya Civilization, but according to the World Wildlife Fund, the Maya Biosphere has lost 70 per cent of its forests in the past ten years. Establishing sustainable tourism in this area with active local community participation will provide economic alternatives to the currently ongoing destructive activities such as illegal logging, archeological looting, and human, wildlife and drug trafficking. The GHF is working with the Guatemalan government, community leaders, the Foundation for Anthropological Research and Environmental Studies (FARES) and the US Department of the Interior (which includes the US National Park Service) to create an economically sustainable cultural and natural sanctuary. Many factors threaten the archaeology and the ecology of the Mirador Basin. Drug trafficking profits are fueling a massive ranching industry which requires large areas of jungle to be cleared and has virtually destroyed the Maya Biosphere within the past five years in northern Guatemala. Forest is also cleared for agricultural purposes, generally in a slash-and-burn practice that employs fire to clear the land. This practice has been so extensive, though, that the intensity of the fires and the resulting smoke has closed down schools as far north as Houston, Texas, in 2003 and 2004. Logging has also had a devastating effect on the Mirador Basin as clearcutting destroys the forest, and the roads needed to remove the cut trees allow access for poachers and looters. The looters, in fact, have targeted virtually every site in the Mirador Basin, with most sites damaged or destroyed by scores of looters' trenches. The project has taken an active role in combating looting, deforestation, poaching and depredation of Maya cultural heritage and the natural environment through placement of numerous guards, implementing education programmes and vocational training, as well as providing major employment opportunities for communities and towns in northern Guatemala. Public films, publications and scientific documentaries have contributed to awakening international interest in the Mirador Basin, and the unusual cultural and natural heritage contained therein. The GHF has equipped and trained 60 guides in the community association and funded Mirador's 30 park rangers who have been instrumental to stop the burning, looting, poaching and illegal logging within the Mirador area. The project provided employment for 318 workers, 40 specialists and 22 Guatemalan and American students, while continuing with programmes of tourism infrastructure, health, potable water systems, computer systems for schools in communities, schools for tourism guides including the first graduating class of 28 students from the first school of community guides, and literacy and education programmes for workers.

Source: http://globalheritagefund.org/what_we_do/overview/current_projects/mirador_guatemala.

government's role, thereby achieving more positive links between heritage conservation and economic development.

In various discourses surrounding conservation, the concept of authenticity remains a central and grave concern. Ashworth and Tunbridge (2000) argue, in their co-authored book *The Tourist–Historic City*, that authenticity needs to be understood as a flexible concept and a range of factors including building types, materials and socio-economic changes through time should be taken into consideration in evaluating authenticity of conservation. Ashworth (1992) perceives heritage as the product of a 'commodification' process in which selection is inevitable. In this regard, heritage conservation entails a new creation rather than just preserving what already exists. Detailed discussions on authenticity and commodification are developed in the Chapter 4. This perspective challenges prevalent perceptions of heritage conservation as an accurate and precise record of the past. It is further elaborated:

> Heritage changes over time in the way it is presented and also in the ways in which the public reacts to its presentation. Hence, there is a tendency to change the past to suit changing requirements; relics can be adapted, added to, copied, and interpreted, all of which idealise the past. Since heritage cannot logically exist without a consumer, then, in effect, the consumer defines heritage. Then, the perceived problem of authenticity is largely irrelevant in heritage planning, because the consumer authenticates the resource.
>
> (Nasser, 2003: 471)

In this light, the main focus lies in managing changes, not just preventing changes. It is rather impossible to avoid changes in peoples' perceptions and attitudes towards heritage over time. This change needs to be unmistakably reflected and incorporated in the conservation and management strategies of heritage. Furthermore, new approaches in heritage management employ broader holistic and comprehensive definitions of the historic environment (Fairclough, 2008). The scope and range of the historic environment has significantly widened over recent years. Fairclough (2008: 298) cogently claims:

> From originally being a qualitative measure or a badge of significance, the word 'historic' has become an adjective applied to the whole environment, irrespective initially of significance. The term 'historic environment' carries a dual implication: the environment is not purely natural but has a strong (and culturally predominant) humanly-created aspect, and, conversely and in consequence, the historic environment is not free-standing but part of a wider interconnected environmental whole.

The spatial dimension of heritage management is now stretched to incorporate the landscape-based understanding of heritage, which is more complex, inclusive and discursive than merely focusing on a monument-based and rather fragmented understanding of heritage. There has been increasing recognition that issues of conservation need to be carefully realised and considered within the remit of intangible heritage or intangible values of tangible heritage. In particular, the value of cultural heritage in the Asian context is unmistakably related to its intangible aspects and dimensions (Taylor, 2004; Ahmad, 2006; Park, 2011). Heritage conservation is not just driven by sheer intention of protecting and sustaining the historic environment. Heritage is increasingly regarded as a value-added entity that improves the images of the places or destinations concerned. In this regard, heritage conservation is also fairly capital-driven economic activity (see

Herzfeld, 2010). For future development of heritage management and conservation, it is of paramount significance to integrate new changes and perspectives in understanding heritage and to facilitate its varied contextualisations, either locally or nationally, in different heritage practices.

Managing heritage for tourism

Heritage is mainly associated with fulfilling such social functions as conservation and protection of historic settings and assets, whereas tourism is characterised by its business-driven approaches and economic focuses. However, it is crucial to recognise the interrelated and interdependent nature of heritage and tourism. The ideological and institutional context of heritage tourism is fundamentally different from that of general tourism (Garrod and Fyall, 2000, quoted in Aas *et al.*, 2005). Aas *et al.* (2005) identify and summarise several challenges encountered in the relationship between tourism and heritage. First, it is suggested, following Peters (1999), that there is a clear need to establish channels of communication between the concerned stakeholders. The lack of communication often leads to a detrimental and destructive development of heritage. Second, there is a need to find the balance between heritage conservation and use of heritage for touristic consumption. The excessive focus on tourism could lead to the deterioration of heritage harnessed by the process of commodification, as is often evident in WHSs, while conservation focus may not fully exert the appeal of heritage for the wider section of society. Finally, it is highlighted that tourism generates income for heritage conservation. This point is of paramount significance in that tourism serves as a major economic resource for conserving the past. In this regard, tourism development should not be conceived as an antithesis to heritage conservation. Careful consideration in both sustaining a sense of place and maximising economic potential is critical to the successful management of heritage tourism. Heritage managers have incorporated business-oriented dimensions in their traditional 'curatorial approach', which mainly focuses on collection and academic research. Increasing and enhancing public access and providing quality experiences have become a main focus of heritage sites.

The growing popularity of heritage tourism can be, however, attributed as a destructive force to the long-term sustainability of heritage sites and places if it is not properly managed. The failure to manage the flux of tourists often leads to putting heritage sites in danger. The ancient city of Thebes and its Necropolis was declared a WHS in 1979. Since its inscription excessive tourism development has posed a threat to the safety of the tomb and paintings in the Valley of the Kings and Queens. Particularly, such popular tombs as Pharaoh Tutankhamum are under serious threat from the high volumes of tourists. Increased vibrations and humidity caused by tourists' breathing have even led to fungus growing on the walls. The Supreme Council of Antiquities (SCA) in Egypt has created management plans to give added protection to the tombs, such as installing cool lighting systems to allow visits in the evening and to spread visits over the whole day (El-Aref, 2009). Furthermore, a 'replica valley' of the tombs at the Valley of the Kings is being created near to the original valley, using hi-tech equipment to create exact replicas of the artefact within the tombs.

Since Garrod and Fyall's (2000) attempt, increasing academic attention has been paid to examining the relationship between heritage tourism and sustainability (see Chapter 9 for detailed discussions on sustainable development of heritage tourism). The term 'sustainability' has come to mean an enormous array of different things, as has often been the case with the term 'heritage'. Both terms need to be redefined and (re)contextualised, reflecting differing contexts, changing perceptions and multiple interpretations. A successful management of heritage sites and places is of pivotal significance in enhancing and enriching tourists' experience and appreciation. The fundamental aim of the heritage sector lies in ensuring an appropriate balance between the contemporary use of heritage assets and their conservation for future uses (Garrod and Fyall, 2000). In order to comply with the requirements posed by heritage sites and tourists, site management and visitor management must work mutually to moderate the needs of both. The ultimate goal of effective visitor management at heritage sites should lie in enhancing visitors' experience, encouraging both deeper appreciation of the unique values of the sites and visitors' higher spending (Cooper *et al.*, 2005). Furthermore, effective visitor management can reduce the possible negative socio-cultural and environmental impacts on the local communities and foster a sense of local cultural identity (Shackley, 2001) (see Figure 3.1).

According to Shackley (1998), cultural heritage sites can be separated into two different categories: monuments, groups of buildings and individual sites and, second, groups of urban buildings. Both these groups require proper visitor management but present different management issues of their own. In an urban heritage context, Orbaşli (2007: 183–4) states:

> Visitor management is not only a matter of traffic or pedestrian flow management, but also involves imaginative solutions to enhance the visitor experience, maintain a favourable reputation for the destination, while at the same time ensuring a high-quality environment for residents to live and work in, and visitors to enjoy. Chosen visitor strategies have to respond to specific needs and remain appropriate to the local culture.

Figure 3.1 Tourists in Tokapi Palace, Istanbul in Turkey

There should also be different management strategies, for example, employed for site-specific heritage attractions or historic cities and towns. With respect to managing tourism for historic cities and towns, there emerge conflicts between local use of living environment and tourist expectations, as encapsulated in the concept of 'tourist–historic' city (Ashworth and Tunbridge, 2000). Mordue (2005: 179) argues that the 'historic core' of old cities and towns has entered a new phase of tourism development over the past two decades, which is 'characterized by a typically postmodern coupling of enterprise and heritage'. Drawing on the case study of York in the UK, Mordue (2005) observes the conflicts between maintaining the local integrity and cultural authenticity of the city and enhancing its market status as a popular tourist attraction. Here, the preservation of heritage is regarded as something necessarily antithetical to the development of tourism. Urban conservation, however, needs to be understood not just as a means to protect the historic environment but as an effective tool for city development and regeneration (Sirisrisak, 2009). Conservation and development complement each other, without necessarily causing conflicts. Orbaşli (2000) clarifies three interrelated objectives in urban conservation: physical, spatial and social. The social dimension of conservation is, as argued, the most important factor, although it is often neglected and underestimated compared to the other two objectives. The social attitudes and aspirations of local communities need to be incorporated in planning and managing heritage conservation and development.

It is important to note that management strategies differ and vary depending on the types and ownership of heritage. Different ownership implies different management orientations and strategies. In general, there are public ownership, private ownership and voluntary ownership of heritage. Public ownership means that a site is owned and possibly operated by government agencies and bodies. This can exist on national and sub-national (regional) levels. The examples include archaeological ruins, ancient monuments, historic buildings and parks. The primary motivation for public ownership is to conserve and preserve heritage sites, to enable and widen public access, education and tourism development. The best example of public ownership is English Heritage in the UK. English Heritage is the government's statutory adviser on the historic environment. Officially known as the Historic Buildings and Monuments Commission for England, English Heritage is an executive non-departmental public body sponsored by the Department for Culture, Media and Sport (DCMS). Its powers and responsibilities are set out in the National Heritage Act (1983) and it is funded in part by the government and in part from revenue earned from historic properties and other services. In 2010/2011, its public funding was worth £129 million, and income from other sources amounted to £41.9 million (English Heritage, 2011). Apart from managing the historic sites that are open to the public, substantial focus is placed on looking after the historic environment as a whole, including historic buildings, monuments and areas, and archaeological remains. In comparison with public ownership, private ownership refers to the types of heritage attraction privately owned and managed. They are mainly historic theme parks, industrial heritage centres, including mines, factories and distilleries, art galleries, private museums and cultural centres. Their primary motivation is to make a profit. In tandem with this, emphasis is placed on enhancing entertainment values and public images, thereby achieving commercial success and quality branding. Merlin Entertainments Group, which acquired Legoland parks in 2005, Gardaland in 2006 and the Tussauds Group in 2007, is now the clear market leader in the UK and Europe and second only to Disney worldwide. It now manages over 70 attractions in 17 countries, including the Madame Tussauds waxworks, Legoland parks, Sealife Centres, Gardaland in Italy, The London Dungeons and the London Eye, Alton Towers, Thorpe Park and Chessington World of Adventures in the UK. Finally, voluntary ownership encompasses non-profit organisations including charities. Given that there is no direct grant or subsidy available from the government, the primary motivation of voluntary ownership is conservation by self-sufficiency and it mainly relies on volunteer guides to staff its properties. Most of the money raised on entrance fees is spent on site maintenance and conservation. The National Trust in the UK is a private charity governed by an executive committee. Originally, the desire to preserve and recreate the traditional landscape of rural England was strongly implicated in the creation of the National Trust. The National Trust was established to halt further enclosure of common land and to provide open spaces for urban workers (Short, 1991). Davison (2008) emphasises that the British heritage movement is firmly grounded in the process of idealising 'unspoilt' and 'peaceful' rural England and its country houses. The National Trust was at the forefront of saving the country houses during the inter-war years. High taxation, reduced income and changing fashion led many country houses around the UK to come up for sale. Under the auspice of a special Act of Parliament in 1937, the National Trust managed to keep land and invest in maintaining and upkeeping the country houses. Finance comes from a variety of sources and in 2010/2011 these amounted to legacies (£46.2 million) and grants and contributions (£30.1 million), membership subscriptions (£124.3 million), enterprises (£53.5 million), admission fees (£18.9 million) and catering (£39.3 million). Membership of the trust currently stands at 3.8 million and there is also support for the National Trust from overseas, especially the Royal Oak Foundation which is the United States membership-affiliate of the British National Trust.

Heritage interpretation

Interpretation is conceptualised as an 'educational activity which aims to reveal meanings and relationships through the use of original objects, by firsthand experience, and by illustrative media, rather than simply to communicate factual information' (Tilden, 1977: 7–8). It is defined within the heritage tourism context as a 'particular set of professional practices designed to engage heritage visitors with the meanings of their encounter' (West, 2010: 4). Light and Prentice (1994) view heritage interpretation as an increasingly common and popular form of product development at heritage sites, including ancient monuments, due to the small impact on the perceived authenticity of such sites. The main roles of heritage interpretation include constructing and enhancing visitor experiences (Moscardo and Ballantyne, 2008), encouraging preservation through education (Timothy and Boyd, 2003) and ensuring the sustainability of tourism (Moscardo, 1996). Heritage interpretation refers to

> the full range of potential activities intended to heighten public awareness and enhance understanding of cultural heritage site. These can include print and electronic publications, public lectures, on-site and directly related off-site installations, educational programmes, community activities, and ongoing research, training, and evaluation of the interpretation process itself.
>
> (ICOMOS, 2008: 2)

There has been a prevalent assumption that the main motivation for visiting heritage sites is related to gaining and broadening knowledge. Therefore, the traditional methods of interpretation were mainly related to effectively delivering the factual information and knowledge in order to educate tourists. However, it is argued that developing interpretational methods to communicate information to tourists in both educational and entertaining ways is of paramount significance in enhancing heritage tourism experiences (Holloway and Taylor, 2006). Increasingly, interpretation in heritage settings needs to be understood as 'an informational and inspirational process designed to enhance understanding, appreciation, and protection of our cultural and natural legacy' (Beck and Cable, 2002: 1).

Concurrently, the introduction of entertainment in heritage interpretation is rather inevitable in contemporary heritage scenes. The role of entertainment as a means of enhancing the educational purposes of heritage has been widely recognised. Introducing entertainment in heritage interpretation should not be understood as a threat to sustaining authentic and educational credibility of heritage sites. Here, enjoyment and education are not mutually exclusive, rather complementing each other. 'Living history' presentations are good examples of incorporating education and entertainment to increase the appeal of heritage sites. 'Living history' is defined as 'first-person applications of costumed characters presenting or recreating events and activities from the past' (Saxe, 2009: 34). It is generally considered to have strong educational values (Robertshaw, 1997; Tivers, 2002; Saxe, 2009), while adding the commercial and entertaining dimensions to ways in which heritage is presented and represented, particularly within the context of tourism (see Case study 3.3).

Case study 3.3: Llancaiach Fawr in Wales, UK

Built in 1530 for Dafydd ap Richard, Llancaiach Fawr was designed to be easily defended during the turbulent reigns of the Tudor kings and queens and is one of the finest examples of a semi-fortified manor in Wales today. The Manor House has been restored and furnished as it would have been in 1645 during the Civil War. All the furnishings in the rooms are accurate reproductions of items from the time of the Prichards and many of the originals can be found in the Museum of Welsh Life at St. Fagans. Llancaiach Fawr presents the social world of a seventeenth-century gentry household from a multiplicity of perspectives, mainly servants including needlewoman, bodyservant, groom, under dairy maid and man of all work. Its website gives, for example, a detailed description of historical characters revived in living history presentation. The introduction for the needlewoman is as follows:

> You may well meet Elisabeth Proude… A rather prim sort of person – until she lets down her guard! She is the wife of a cattle drover, Iestyn Proude. Because he is so often away from home trying to find markets for the Colonel's cattle, she is frequently to be found in the Manor carrying out all sorts of work, usually sewing… She is a skilled needlewoman so of great value to Mistress Prichard. She is also from the county of Surrey and so Mrs. P. likes to hear tales about the nobility Elisabeth has seen when she was a girl, as they 'progressed' from one palace to another during the summer months. How did she come to be living in South Wales? Well, you'll have to ask her!

Llancaiach Fawr is a good living history exemplary and is an attempt to portray and present the authentic lives of servants of the seventeenth century as accurately as possible. The living history presentation of the site aims to provide an entertaining learning experience for all ages.

Source: http://your.caerphilly.gov.uk/llancaiachfawr/content/welcome-llancaiach-fawr.

However, first-person interpretation could hinder the authentic portrayal of the past, lead-ing often to historical inaccuracy or distortion. In this light, 'living history' presentations are accused of turning history into saleable heritage products. It is claimed that '"living history" stands in some respects to one side of the general commodification of history which creates heritage, although it may well be used to commercial advantage by tourism managers' (Tivers, 2002: 198).

In examining the phenomenon of 'living history' presentations of heritage, however, Tivers (2002) states that most of the performers regard their participation as a leisure activity rather than a performance. The major concern of the performers relates to the degree of authenticity of the performance. The performers are encouraged to experience heritage that is meaningful to them, thereby enhancing their sense of identity and under-standing of society, both past and present. Irrespective of the different dimensions to heritage interpretation, a search for authenticity remains a significant drive for visiting a heritage setting. Reisinger and Steiner (2006) emphasise that the on-site information presented and interpreted is often neither truthful nor authentic. It is claimed that there are two main factors that facilitate the differences between the 'real thing' and its presenta-tion. First, the display of heritage justifies and validates the version of history supported by the elitist groups. This issue is closely associated with the political nature of heritage, which is examined in greater detail in Chapter 5. The second factor that is not often fully recognised is the managerial orientation of heritage sites. As a main source of income, heritage sites strive to attract tourists and this growing significance of tourism develop-ment in heritage sites can influence the way heritage is presented and interpreted. This is an interesting claim in that it clearly recognises ways in which the commercial orienta-tions of contemporary heritage sites influence their presentational and interpretational methods. In examining visitors' understanding and evaluation of authenticity in the con-text of heritage tourism, Goulding (2000) claims that most of the visitors interviewed, regardless of their age, class and education, mention the significance of authenticity in their heritage experiences. For them, however, methods of display or interpretation are not overtly important. Unlike fierce criticism surrounding the postmodern pastiche of the past as a commercial and spurious version of history, simulacrum and hyper-reality are major features of the visitor experiences in the reconstructed heritage settings of Blists Hill Living Museum in Shropshire. It is interesting to note that a reconstructed reality of the past does not act as an impediment to visitors' appreciations and experiences. This finding has significant implications in enhancing heritage representations and interpreta-tions employed in heritage settings. It is further emphasised that a careful balance needs to be achieved between obvious spectacle and scholarly presentation:

> This juxtaposition where 'genuineness' clocks the absence of historical social processes means that attention to object detail becomes the criteria against which credibility and authenticity are evaluated. The challenge therefore is to strike a balance between providing accurate information whilst at the same time engaging the interest of the visitor in as stimulating a manner as possible. The individual must feel that what is on offer is genuine.
>
> (Goulding, 2000: 849)

Heritage interpretation is often unmistakably influenced by power relations (Hall, 1994; Poria, 2007; Poria and Ashworth, 2009). Heritage interpretation is thus utilised as a means to sustain the power of the dominant and hegemonic groups in society (see Tunbridge and Ashworth, 1996; Graham et al., 2000). Hall (1994) argues that heritage settings provide a single, monolithic interpretation supporting a particular ideological framework. Here, heritage is employed as a symbolic signifier of power and hegemony, with a particular emphasis on state-centred and official interpretations of heritage. However, critical focus is increasingly placed on multiple interpretations and diversified experiences of heritage, especially the subjective nature of heritage interpretations and experiences (Bruner, 1996; Austin, 2002; Park, 2010a). It is argued that the study of heritage settings needs to shift from the uses of heritage to the users themselves, thereby focusing more on the consumers than the producers of heritage (Tunbridge and Ashworth, 1996; Voase, 2002; McCain and Ray, 2003). The shift from monolithic and rigid to multiple and varied interpretations of heritage is clearly encapsulated in the way heritage is presented and represented for contemporary tourism consumption. The recent emphasis in heritage interpretation is thus grounded in the fact that individuals are interested in multiple and diverse interpretations (Wight and Lennon, 2007). Heritage interpretation should aim to enhance the 'various means of communicating heritage to people' (Howard, 2003: 244). Copeland (2006a) draws attention to the distinctions between positivist and constructivist approaches to interpreting heritage. Within the constructivist approaches meanings are always variable and individual, highly complex and contingent. Here, greater emphasis is put on the roles of visitors as an active agent in heritage interpretation by way of bringing ideas, preconceptions and images to heritage sites. It is also emphasised that visitors are increasingly keen on interpretation as a means of generating emotional involvement and strengthing the link with the site (Poria *et al.*, 2009). In a similar vein, Nuryanti (1996: 253) states:

> Interpretation is not only a description of physical facts and tangible elements: it moves into the realms of spiritual truth, emotional response, deeper meaning and understanding. Meaning lies in the observer or participant (i.e. the tourist) rather than as some objective quality inherent in the object itself.

Poria *et al.* (2009) reveal that heritage visitors show interest in having the interpretation generate emotional involvement, thereby strengthening the link between the site and visitors themselves. Obviously, some visitors are keen on regarding heritage interpretation as a source of education. But interestingly, their findings indicate that visitors view interpretation as an effective tool to enhance their emotional experiences as well as gain knowledge. It is further emphasised that heritage tourism is not just a search for nostalgia or a romantic version of the past but a complex phenomenon. In this light, heritage site experiences cannot be monolithic as is the case with heritage interpretation. Therefore, heritage sites need to provide varied interpretational strategies given the fact that tourists are interested in different experiences. This can be further expanded to planning and promoting marketing strategies specific to the different segments of heritage tourists.

There has been scant attention paid to examining the role of the tour guide in enhancing the experience in heritage settings (Poria *et al.*, 2006b). Tour guides play a significant role in both transmitting information and facilitating its interpretation in heritage settings. Given their perceived mediating roles between tourists and heritage settings, it is critical to examine ways in which tour guides' performances could influence tourists' interpretations of the site, thus enhancing the individual experiences of heritage. Tour guides can serve as major actors in facilitating and communicating the symbolic relevance of heritage to tourists, particularly in terms of staging and inscribing the socio-cultural implications of national heritage within tourism performances (see Edensor, 1998; Macdonald, 2006). In heritage settings, tour guides are not merely pathfinders. Their mediating roles are critical in constructing a discursive understanding between tourists and the site itself. Tour guides, viewed as 'upkeepers' of national heritage, are keen on providing tourists with an enlightened insight into the spiritual meanings of heritage settings, particularly within the remit of domestic heritage tourism (Park, 2007). Heritage interpretation and education programmes are crucial in any visitor management plan. The quality of promotional material, such as brochures, guidebooks, site maps and audio guides, and the availability of guides needs to be closely monitored as a main educational tool. A variety of media for site interpretation and education should be chosen with the intention of making the visit as enjoyable and informative as possible. The concept of 'edutainment', incorporating educational elements with entertainment, has been increasingly employed in various heritage sites. Due consideration should also be given to the needs of different categories of tourists (e.g., scholars, school children and the general public), as well as providing information in different languages, according to the provenance of the major visitor markets. Signage should be complementary to interpretation and the effective use of a visitor centre that focuses on interactivity between visitors and site or display is essential in improving visitors' experiences.

New management strategies for heritage tourism

Given the unprecedented popularity of heritage tourism across the globe, with specific reference to WHSs, new effective management strategies are essential in reducing possible damage caused by an influx of tourists to heritage sites (see Bennett, 2005). Timed tickets are increasingly popular to limit and control visitor numbers. The Alhambra, for example, attempts to limit visitor numbers by offering timed visits. Entry to the areas accessible to visitors within the palace is strictly limited to the relevant time of day shown on the purchased ticket (morning, afternoon or evening visit). A limited number of tourists is only allowed for different time scales: 3,300 in the morning, 2,100 (1 November – 28 February), or 3,300 (1 March – 31 October) in the afternoon and 400 at night. Admission pricing can serve as an important potential source of funds for managing tourist impacts and for undertaking repair and conservation programmes (Garrod and Fyall, 2000). There are also two-tier pricing policies, as is the case with the Taj Mahal in India, Angkor Wat in Cambodia and Petra in Jordan. As the single most visited monument in India, the Taj Mahal attracts between 2–4 million tourists annually. In order to tackle such issues as congestion and pollution, it introduced a two-tier pricing system in 2001 in which the admission fees for foreign visitors increased by approximately 6,000 per cent. Along with the benefit of limiting unnecessary visits on a mass scale, two-tier pricing policies encourage local access and participation, thereby enhancing their connections with heritage settings. There is a growing interest, on the part of heritage managers, in developing and promoting other heritage sites and settings located within the proximity of iconic sites. In this regard, developing and promoting heritage trails can be employed as an effective and useful management strategy in controlling the congestion issues of popular heritage sites and enhancing the tourism appeal of less popular heritage sites and events in the areas and regions concerned (see Case study 3.4).

Du Cros's (2007) study investigates congestion issues at the two most popular heritage attractions in Macao, the St. Paul's Ruins and the A-Ma Temple. While the St. Paul's ruins suffer from permanent congestion, the A-Ma Temple needs to deal with fluctuating congestion issues, particularly during various festivals and rituals. Fluctuating congestion is often more difficult to deal with, such as the difficulties of resources allocation. At the A-Ma Temple, the government created a formal entry route from the official bus parking area, however, illegal parking around the site has also been observed during peak hours. Senior officials in the government

Case study 3.4: Heritage trails

Although the enjoyment of guided or 'informed' walking has a long history, dating back to ancient pilgrim and trade routes, the specific development and promotion of self-guided trails by conservation bodies in 1970s was a fairly new phenomenon. A range of stakeholders, such as local authorities, tourism organisations, local development agencies and civic societies, are all interested in developing trails as they see heritage trails as flexible and multifaceted products with wide-ranging benefits. For trails, developing a coherent story is essential in enhancing visitor experiences. It is suggested that the developer needs to aim to incorporate both rational and evocative appeals using a variety of linguistic approaches. The use of experiential and action-based language, graphical devices and sensory triggers can create an evocative mood and multiple stories which provide tourists with a range of options to reflect their preferences and interests. Dedicated websites in which tourists can share experiences and memories can contribute to maximising the potential of media and involving the community at large. Developing opportunities for enrolment, engagement and personalisation is essential in further enhancing tourist experiences in heritage trails. Enrolment provides a valuable opportunity to acquire data that can be utilised to enhance planning and management. More imaginative engagement opportunities are provided, such as activities particularly designed for children and special interest groups. Finally, opportunities for personalisation are much needed. The use of web technology encourages interaction and facilitates personalisation and service enhancements such as individualised route planning based on specific interests, a choice of engagement devices and links to further information. This approach could avoid a bland offering of heritage trails for a homogeneous market as tourists could access contested stories and differing perspectives of place.

Source: an excerpt from Hayes and MacLeod (2007).

Figure 3.2 The plaque used in a heritage trail, Lublin in Poland

departments do not seem to realise the significance of political and horizontal coordination for the effective management of these heritage sites. It is argued that congestion studies of heritage sites should be carried out prior to WH inscriptions. In order to enhance effective heritage management, it is also essential to recognise a wider array of stakeholders involved in both heritage and tourism sectors, ranging from curators and conservators, planners, policy-makers, operations managers, marketing and management professionals. Top-down approaches often employed in the conservation plan can cause conflicts between stakeholders (Sirisrisak, 2009). It is thus important to make a concerted effort to make bottom-up approaches, facilitating local involvement and active participation (see Chapter 9). Importantly, it is the political support that often determines the success of conservation and management. Ensuring governments' support and enhancing collaboration with various bodies involved are essential in successful heritage management practices. Both heritage and tourism professionals need to take a careful consideration in maintaining an optimum balance between conservation and management, thereby improving the long-term sustainability of heritage sites.

Conclusion

Heritage conservation and tourism development are often regarded as being contradictory and conflicting. The relationship between heritage and tourism is complicated since the main aim of heritage organisations is to preserve and protect the historical environments, whereas tourism strives to maximise the economic uses of heritage. However, heritage and tourism are interrelated and interdependent. As emphasised, heritage has become an invaluable tourism product that is marketed to meet the demands of the tourists. Tourism plays a significant role in increasing public support and awareness for heritage conservation. To ensure the long-term sustainability of heritage sites, there is a critical need to make an optimal balance between tourism development and conservation. It is also essential to note that heritage does not simply exist in the domain of tourism, but is closely intertwined with notions of cultural identity and ethnicity and is very much part of everyday experiences. Therefore, a need for heritage conservation is as critical as a drive for tourism development. Poor and ineffective visitor management in heritage sites can lead to increasing the risk of degradation and destruction. The excessive influx of tourists to the major heritage tourism attractions including WHSs can also pose a serious threat to members of the local community, potentially leading to a growing hostility towards visitors. Heritage interpretation is critical in enhancing visitors' experiences and appreciations of heritage sites. Increasingly, integrating education with entertainment gains recognition in heritage interpretation. Furthermore, the shift from monolithic to multiple interpretations of heritage is embedded in the way heritage is presented and represented for contemporary tourism consumption. Heritage professionals need to be aware that heritage means different things to different people. Therefore, heritage interpretation needs to be diversified and varied to meet the different interests and needs of heritage tourists. The use of new and innovative management strategies is of pivotal significance in minimising any deterioration or damage caused by an increasing flux of tourists to heritage sites. Effective heritage management facilitating local participation is essential in ensuring the long-term sustainability of heritage sites, as well as maintaining an optimal balance between conservation and tourism development.

Research questions

1   Explain and discuss the interrelated and interdependent nature of heritage and tourism.
2   Discuss and evaluate the ways in which heritage conservation and tourism development can be complementary to each other.
3   Why is effective visitor management important in managing heritage?
4   Explain and discuss the ways in which entertainment is increasingly incorporated in heritage interpretation. Use relevant examples to substantiate your points.
5   Explain how different ownership of heritage influences the ways in which heritage sites are managed and conserved.
6   What are the accepted and acceptable goals for heritage interpretation?
7   Using relevant examples, develop a critique of 'living history' presentations, which are increasingly popular in heritage tourism development.
8   Try to devise and develop a heritage trail in your chosen town or region.
9   Develop new and innovative management strategies in effectively dealing with excessive tourism development in heritage sites.

Learning material

Ashworth, G.J. and Tunbridge, J.E. (2000) *The Tourist–Historic City: Retrospect and Prospect of Managing the Heritage City*, Oxford: Pergamon/Elsevier (Chapters 3 and 6).

Copeland, T. (2006a) Constructing pasts: interpreting the historic environment, in A. Hems and M. Blockley (eds) *Heritage Interpretation*, London: Routledge, pp. 83–95.

Fairclough, G. (2008) New heritage, an introductory essay: people, landscape and change, in G. Fairclough, R. Harrison, J.H. Jameson and J. Schofield (eds) *The Heritage Reader*, London: Routledge, pp. 297–312.

Garrod, B. and Fyall, A. (2000) Managing heritage tourism, *Annals of Tourism Research*, 27(3): 682–708.

Li, Y. (2003) Heritage tourism: the contradictions between conservation and change, *Tourism and Hospitality Research*, 4(3): 247–61.

Moscardo, G. (1996) Mindful visitors: heritage and tourism, *Annals of Tourism Research*, 23(2): 376–97.

Nasser, N. (2003) Planning for urban heritage places: reconciling conservation, tourism and sustainable development, *Journal of Planning Literature*, 17(4): 467–79.

Orbaşli, A. (2000) *Tourists in Historic Towns: Urban Conservation and Heritage Management*, London: Spon Press.

Poria, Y., Biran, A. and Reichel, A. (2009) Visitors' preferences for interpretation at heritage sites, *Journal of Travel Research*, 48(1): 92–105.

Reisinger, Y. and Steiner, C. (2006) Reconceptualising interpretation: the role of tour guides in authentic tourism, *Current Issues in Tourism*, 9(6): 481–98.

Robertshaw, A. (1997) 'A dry shell of the past': living history and the interpretation of historic houses, *Interpretation*, 2: 1–7.

Timothy, D.J. (2011) *Cultural heritage and tourism: an introduction*, Bristol: Channel View Publications (Chapters 9 and 10).

Tivers, J. (2002) Performing heritage: the use of live 'actors' in heritage presentations, *Leisure Studies*, 21(3–4): 187–200.

Weblinks

1954 Hague Convention and protocols
http://portal.unesco.org/en/ev.php-URL_ID=13637&URL_DO=DO_TOPIC&URL_SECTION=201.html

Geopolitics of archaeology: archaeological tourism's effect on people and heritage
http://www.wbez.org/episode-segments/geopolitics-archaeology-archaeological-tour-isms-effect-people-and-heritage-0

The heritage curse
http://www.aljazeera.com/programmes/101east/2012/07/20127295539315179.html

China's heritage under threat
http://edition.cnn.com/2012/08/14/world/asia/china-heritage-tourism

Beyond Angkor
http://www.youtube.com/watch?v=neP7K9F9hSA

Saving Asia's ancient heritage sites
http://edition.cnn.com/video/#/video/world/2012/05/03/intv-asia-historic-sites-morgan.cnn

Profit through preservation (Stone Town, Zanzibar)
http://edition.cnn.com/video/#/video/international/2010/12/27/ia.mbweni.profit.preser-vation.cnn?iref=videosearch

UNESCO determined to help Mali
http://m.youtube.com/watch?v=cehUJPm2NCI

Mirador, Guatemala
http://globalheritagefund.org/video/mirador_update2012

Heritage trail in the UK
http://www.theheritagetrail.co.uk

Tamworth (Staffordshire, UK) heritage trail app
https://itunes.apple.com/gb/app/tamworth-heritage-trail/id446206465?mt=8

Auld Reekie Trail: explore the old and new towns in Edinburgh around the year 1780
http://www.ewht.org.uk/uploads/downloads/EWH%20Auld%20Reekie%20Trail%20FINAL.pdf

4 Authenticity and commodification in heritage tourism

Authenticity in tourism studies

Both conceptual and empirical applications of understanding authenticity have been a major focus and concern in tourism studies (MacCannell, 1976; Cohen, 1988; Hughes, 1995; Selwyn, 1996; Wang, 1999; Steiner and Reisinger, 2006; Chhabra, 2010; Lau, 2010; Zhu, 2012; Brown, 2013). There has been a growing upsurge of academic interest in reconstructing, reinterpreting and renegotiating the concept of authenticity over the past decades. In particular, the issues of authenticity are constantly discussed and evaluated in the context of heritage tourism in which the past is recreated and reappropriated for touristic consumption. Boorstin (1964) is one of the earliest theorists who developed the social critique of American mass tourists. His main premise is that contemporary tourism development has led to the burgeoning of superficial activities and inauthentic experiences. He draws a sharp distinction between travel and tourism, claiming that certain key aspects of travel including adventure and authenticity have been replaced by those of tourism, which is fundamentally neither 'real' nor 'authentic'. Contemporary tourists are either unable or unwilling to directly experience the travel reality, thus merely thriving on contrived experiences, inauthentic attractions and 'pseudo-events'. In contrast to Boorstin's elitist approach, MacCannell (1973, 1976) views contemporary tourists as modern pilgrims who are eager to search for authenticity in other places and cultures. He argues that tourism is fundamentally a search for authenticity which is rarely found and experienced in our modern world. Accordingly, tourist attractions and experiences are created through a search for authentic meanings for tourists. For MacCannell, the search for authenticity often becomes meaningless due to the strategically contrived and constructed nature of tourism settings and experiences. What tourists experience as authentic often turns out to be 'staged authenticity' which is carefully manufactured and promoted by the local and the tourism industry.

MacCannell (1976) applies Goffman's (1959) differentiation of the 'front region' from the 'back region' to tourism settings. The back stages are often regarded as a realm of 'truth', 'reality' and 'intimacy' in which the personal space of local is kept intact, whereas staged encounters between tourists and locals, often 'false' and 'contrived', take place in the front stages of tourism settings. What tourists experience as authentic in the front stages can be, however, a deliberately contrived staging of local culture and heritage, which is conceptualised as 'staged authenticity'. MacCannell notes that tourists are thwarted in experiencing reality and the authentic truth due to the commercial role of the tourism industry. Subsequently, 'staged authenticity' in tourism settings seems to discourage modern tourists to search for authentic experiences. Authenticity in a back region, furthermore, has also been transformed and staged for touristic consumption when the tourists seek something more authentic and real, as evident in contemporary heritage attractions. In this light, the distinction between front and back regions in these attractions in terms of authenticity seems to be meaningless. Despite its widely acknowledged contribution to systematically examining authenticity in tourism contexts, MacCannell's analysis predominantly relates authenticity to an object-related and essentialist notion emphasising that the touristic search for authentic experiences is thus no more than an epistemological experience of toured objects that are found to be authentic (Wang, 1999). Certainly, his focus on authenticity is mainly supply-oriented, without fully recognising the demand side of authenticity, including tourist motivations and experiences. It also fails to recognise the differing levels and perceptions of authenticity. Given the nature of authenticity as a variant specific to each time and place, the tendency in which the authentic is closely correlated to absolute and objective criteria such as old, primitive and traditional contexts needs to be reconsidered and re-evaluated. As discussed in greater detail in the sections below, the expectations and experiences of tourists play a significant role in conceptualising and contextualising authenticity. The changing roles and expectations of modern tourists in their consumption of heritage need thus to be carefully considered given that they are no longer passive in their experiences of authenticity.

Authenticity is a cultural and textual phenomenon that relies on the ability to 'utilise', 'recreate' and 'project' (Graham, 2001). According to Graham (2001), it is the loyalty of one's self that needs to be created and moulded depending upon the specific resources of the self's own cultural and historical background rather than a universal and worldwide context. Individuals tend to select varying authentic manifestations from different realms of the past and heritage, often influenced by their personal choices and experiences. Individual tourists' perceptions, preferences and interpretations of authenticity are increasingly recognised as crucial agents in broadening and enriching the understanding of the complex notion and practice of authenticity. Cohen (1979) criticises both Boorstin and MacCannell in that both theories fail to recognise the different and varied motivations of tourists. Cohen's typology of tourists contributes to understanding the varying degrees of authenticity as a travelling motivation in different types of tourists. Authenticity is, in this light, perceived as a socially constructed phenomenon, rather than an absolute attribute of objects or places – 'emergent authenticity' (Cohen, 1988: 379). Consequently, authenticity emerges over time and becomes an ever-changing system of representation rather than a fixed setting of objects or ideas. Cohen (1988) further argues that authenticity needs to be understood as a negotiable concept. Here, tourist motivations and meaning-making processes play a significant role in encouraging a constructivist approach to authenticity (Bruner, 1994). This constructivist perspective is clearly encapsulated in Bruner's position to see all cultures continually invented and reinvented. Bruner (1994: 407) claims:

> socialization is at best an imperfect mechanism for cultural transmission, and that each new performance or expression of cultural heritage is a copy in that it always looks back to a prior performance, but each is also an original in that it adapts to new circumstances and conditions.

Wang (1999, 2000) classifies the nature of authenticity in tourist experiences into two separate issues: one is tourist (authentic) *experiences* and the other is *toured objects*. Based on this division, Wang (1999) identifies three dominant and different approaches to understanding authenticity: 'objective', 'constructed' and 'existential'. Both objective and constructive authenticity are understood as being object-related, whereas existential authenticity is activity-related. Constructive authenticity is differentiated from objective authenticity in that the role of tourists or tourism producers in terms of their beliefs or expectations is recognised as a key variable with less focus on the authenticity of originals. Wang (1999: 352) conceptualises existential authenticity as:

> a potential existential state of Being that is to be activated by tourist activities. Correspondingly, authentic experiences in tourism are to achieve this activated existential state of Being within the liminal process of tourism. Existential authenticity can have nothing to do with the authenticity of toured objects.

Importantly, Wang emphasises 'existential authenticity' that encompasses 'personal or intersubjective feelings that are activated by the liminal process of tourist behaviors' (Wang, 2000: 49). 'Intrapersonal authenticity' refers to the bodily feelings of pleasure, spontaneity and self-making construed from tourists' engagement in non-ordinary activities outside their constrained everyday life. On the contrary, 'interpersonal authenticity' is achieved when tourists make cultural and emotional interactions with the 'other'. Recognising both 'intrapersonal' and 'interpersonal' authenticity is crucial in recognising the significance of tourists' self-realisation in the actualisation of authentic experiences during their encounters with new cultures and places. In sharp contrast to objective authenticity focusing primarily on the genuineness or the originality of objects and sites, existential authenticity in tourism contexts focuses on tourists' experiences. Steiner and Reisinger (2006) claim that existential authenticity is a state of being that can be produced or pursued through tourism. Interestingly, it is argued:

> Because existential authenticity is experience-oriented, the existential self is transient, not enduring, and not conforming to a type. It changes from moment to moment. As a result, a person is not authentic or inauthentic all the time. There is no authentic self. One can only momentarily be authentic in different situations... At the most extreme, some tourists might prefer to be authentic most of the time while some prefer being inauthentic most of the time.
>
> (Steiner and Reisinger, 2006: 303)

Existential authenticity in this regard relates to the subjective manifestation of individual perceptions, personal feelings and unique situations, which can be changing and contingent. However, as Wang (1999) pinpoints, existential authenticity also includes essentialist connotations in that it suggests a state in which a person is true to his or her real self. It is widely recognised that tourists experience symbolic and spiritual inversions, thus discovering an 'existential self' during tourism experiences alienated from inauthentic everyday life (see Bruner, 1991; Graburn, 2001; Brown, 2013). Insightfully, Brown (2013) emphasises the role of tourism as a catalyst for existential authenticity, rather than a substitute, further arguing that tourism can encourage the adoption of an authentic life beyond the trip. The main premise is that existential authenticity during tourism experiences can be sustained as a transformative force of knowledge, values or attitudes in everyday life. Given this study is conceptually based and philosophically oriented, it will be informative and interesting to examine the ways in which certain aspects of tourists' experiences may or may not contribute to catalysing existential authenticity in future studies.

Authenticity issues in heritage tourism

Authenticity is regarded as the most important criterion for the development of heritage tourism (Xie and Wall, 2003). The use of the term is popularised in both areas of supply (heritage promoters) and demand (heritage tourists). Heritage promoters are keen on promoting authentic settings and experiences while heritage tourists are constantly in search of authenticity in their encounters with heritage. Within heritage tourism contexts authenticity is often a social construct, which is elaborately created by heritage managers and subjectively perceived by tourists' own knowledge and frame of reference. Authenticity has been, as elaborated in the previous section, increasingly recognised as a 'struggle, a social process, in which competing interests argue for their own interpretation of history' (Bruner, 1994: 408). Authenticity can form different meanings and encompass countervailing claims, contextualised from varied interpretations of individuals, societies and nations. It is not a fixed and permanent but a fluid and mutable concept depending on the present circumstances in which it is marked and represented. Critical focus is here placed on varied and differentiated assertions and interpretations of authenticity. Accordingly, Martin (2010: 550) claims:

> The 'original' that is present is always of course itself a product of the present; carefully constructed through the selective remembrance and forgetting of elements of the past. The selections made naturally reflect a diversity of different perspectives and the same person or set of persons might make radically different selections in different contexts or conversations.

Recognising the 'original' as a product of the present and different perspectives and contexts in which the 'original' is located is of fundamental significance in broadening the understanding of authenticity. Similarly, Golomb (1995: 9) argues that authenticity does not need any particular contents or consequences, to the contrary, it focuses on 'the origins and the intensity of one's emotional-existential commitments'. In this regard, the notions of authenticity are more associated with tourists' individualised and personal processes of emotionally and existentially appropriating and reappropriating the past rather than merely encountering the very outcomes of the past during their heritage tourism experiences. Steiner and Reisinger (2006) identify heritage tourism as an area that manifests existential authenticity. They argue that the way people look to the past to identify and understand themselves during visits to heritage is closely linked to finding what Heidegger conceptualises as one's existential identity and meaning. Jamal and Hill (2002) differentiate between 'objective authenticity', which usually refers to traditional or historical sites or artefacts, and 'constructed authenticity', which may be associated with staged events, moderated art objects or artificially created cultural attractions. The category of 'personal authenticity' may refer to the emotional and psychological experience of travel, subjective responses to, and interpretations of, sites and events experienced, or deeper existential aspects relating to personal meaning and identity. It is emphasised:

> 'Authenticity' is neither a unified static construct nor an essential property of objects and events. It is better to approach it more holistically as a concept whose objective, constructed and/or experiential dimensions are in dialectical engagement with each other and with both the home and world of tourists. Tourism becomes a metaphor for a changing, bio-political world in which (post)modernity, capitalism and globalization furnish complex meanings to authenticity and the authentic in everyday life.
>
> (Jamal and Hill, 2002: 103)

It is thus crucial to recognise the competing and varied claims on the authenticity of local heritage practices, thereby leading to the understanding of the wider social contexts within which tourism is practised. Authenticity can be more broadly sought for, within heritage tourism contexts, as 'a projection of tourists' own beliefs, expectations, preferences, stereotyped images, and consciousness onto toured objects, particularly onto toured Others' (Wang, 1999: 355). Authenticity attached to heritage seems to be not so much original facts as emotive and existential perceptions depending on tourists' feelings, perceptions and values in a given time and place. It is thus correct to assert that the issues of originality need to be less emphasised in judging authentic/inauthentic contexts. In a sense, the question of originality in itself seems quite problematic because the standards of originality are difficult to define and characterise. Furthermore, it is rather impossible to seek an absolute and definite point of origin (Wang, 1999). There are a lot of examples showing that things regarded as original and old are somewhat contrived and created depending on the circumstances. Hobsbawm (1983) asserts that the modern 'nation' comprises various artificial constructs and 'invented traditions'. These traditions are conceptualised as: 'A set of practices, normally governed by overtly or tacitly accepted rules and of a ritual or symbolic nature, which seek to inculcate certain values and norms of behavior by repetition, which automatically implies continuity with the past' (Hobsbawm, 1983: 1). As one conspicuous example of 'invented traditions', the choice of Gothic style architecture for the nineteenth-century reconstruction of the Houses of Parliament in London was aimed at instilling a sense of continuity through shared beliefs relating to long-cherished traditions in architecture and design – see Chapter 6 for more detailed discussions on 'invented traditions'.

Martin (2010) argues that the debates over authenticity within tourism contexts are grounded in the clear demarcation between 'Western tourists' and 'exotic others' of the Western imagination. The Western gaze voraciously seeks the exotic, pristine and unspoilt images of others, which are, in many cases, the by-products of Western fantasies and preconceptions. Boorstin's (1964) elitist approach to differentiate travellers from tourists is somewhat in line with this Western-focused understanding of authenticity. This approach is useful in understanding ways in which authenticity issues and concerns are particularly prevalent in the touristic display of local culture and heritage in non-Western contexts. Here, 'exotic others' are rather constructed and posited as a 'unified and temporalised object' (Martin, 2010: 545) which resonates with objective authenticity. Objective authenticity refers to a 'property of a tourist object', including life processes, activities and artefacts (Lau, 2010: 480). However, objective authenticity is no longer perceived, as discussed previously, as a main determinant in evaluating authenticity in contemporary heritage tourism discourses and practices. Differing and varied conceptualisations of authenticity need to be employed in order to enhance the critical understanding of tourists' authentic heritage tourism experiences in specific spatial and temporal contexts. Both toured objects as attributes of heritage sites and heritage tourists' motivations and preferences have been recognised as essential agents of authenticity. Scant attention has been, however, placed on conceptualising the authenticity of actors in heritage performances. Knudsen and Waade (2010: 5) encapsulate the notion of performative authenticity as a 'feeling you can experience in relation to place'. Performative authenticity emphasises the transitional and transformative qualities inherent in the processes of authentication. Concurrently, performative authenticity brings, as Zhu (2012) argues, attention to the roles of actors in 'becoming' authentic through embodied practice. In examining how the dongba as the ritual practitioner perceives his authenticity during the marriage ceremony in the Naxi Wedding Courtyard in Lijiang, China, Zhu (2012) observes that the ritual performance of the dongba, influenced by his life story and the external world, gives rise to the performative experience of authenticity. This study adds an interesting yet different dimension to an in-depth understanding of complex dynamics inherent in authenticity discourses. The authenticity of performance-based intangible heritage can, even when commodified for touristic consumption, be facilitated and actualised by the performer's powerful act of meaning-making.

Handler and Saxton (1988: 243) state that an authentic experience is 'one in which individuals feel themselves to be in touch both with a "real" world and with their "real" selves'. Selwyn (1996) classifies the concept of authenticity into two distinctive experiences: the experience of a 'real' world as 'authenticity as knowledge' – 'cool' authenticity, and the experience of the 'real' self as 'authenticity as feeling' – 'hot' authenticity. The 'hot' authenticity as the quest for the self and the Other can exert a substantial influence on understanding the spiritual characteristics of places visited, particularly in the context of heritage tourism. It is suggested that the quest for the 'authentic Other' in contemporary tourism involves understanding 'the Other' as the 'authentically social' (Sewlyn, 1996: 21). The benign and pre-commoditised character of 'the Other' looks authentically social to the tourists, thereby playing a crucial role in creating the authentic visions in contemporary contexts. This point is pertinent in developing and enhancing authentic experiences in heritage tourism attractions by way of facilitating and promoting 'hot' authenticity as well as 'cool' authenticity through a variety of interpretational methods and strategies focusing on education and identity. The symbols of national weakness and vulnerability – 'cool' authenticity – can be, for example, transformed into those of national reconstruction with emotionally powerful coherence – 'hot' authenticity – as is the case of the Jewish museum in Israel or Hiroshima Peace Park in Japan (Sewlyn, 1996: 23). The whole process is closely associated with recreating heritage of inglorious and shameful pasts as a tourist attraction providing more 'authentically social' experiences in a given socio-spatial context (see Figure 4.1).

Figure 4.1 Hiroshima Peace Memorial (Genbaku Dome), Japan

Kierkegaard illustrates authenticity as 'namely, the return to the genuine origins of our-selves, our feelings and our beliefs' (Golomb, 1995: 39). The return to genuineness seems to be of initial importance in the quest for authenticity. But the notion of genuineness does not necessarily mean a faithful reinstatement of what was felt and believed in the past. The self needs to be understood as 'something that should be created and formed, not something possessing an intrinsic essence to be further developed' (Golomb, 1995: 54). McIntosh and Prentice (1999) draw attention to the difficulty of assessing how 'authentic' a destination can be and the authenticity of a destination is dependent on the interpretation of how the destination portrays its heritage to the public in various meth-ods. Heritage presentations and representations for tourism purposes could be idealised, distorted and over(under)-represented, depending on the intentions and purposes of the tourism developers and promoters – see Chapter 5 for further discussions on the politics of representing heritage.

Under the influences of postmodern perspectives, issues of authenticity within the context of heritage tourism have become more diverse and divergent. The concept of 'hyper-reality' represents a typical postmodern approach to the issues of authenticity in the contemporary world (Eco, 1986). It is argued that the boundaries between the copy and the original, or between sign and reality have been blurred and deconstructed. Within the context of Disneyland, fantasy and imagination are identified as the main conceptual signifiers of the place, since there is no original to refer to. In this con-text, 'emergent authenticity' (Cohen, 1988), which is not primitively given but emerged from the newly constructed contexts, becomes authentic with the passage of time. The authentic is regarded as evidence of the loss of, or change in, the real. It is suggested that authenticity becomes the reproduction and simulation of origins where they may not be influential any more. Wang (1999: 357) claims that the approach of postmodernism lies in the 'justification of the contrived, the copy, and imitation'. Furthermore, he empha-sises that 'a postmodernist deconstruction of the authenticity of the original implicitly paves the way to define existential authenticity as an alternative experience in tourism' (Wang, 1999: 358).

Baudrillard (1983) closely relates the issues of authenticity to the process of postmod-ernism in which a sense of nostalgia, a sentimental yearning for the past, plays a significant role in reconstructing and simulating the past in contemporary contexts – e.g., the advent of the 'heritage industry'. He explains three historical 'orders of simulacra' (1983: 83) concerning the different relationships between simulacra and the real. First, the dominant simulacrum in the period of Renaissance is 'counterfeit', which indicates the emergence of representation. Second, newly developed technologies in industrial changes enable the exact reproduction of 'production'. Simulation is, finally, prevalent in the contemporary condition that has no connection with originals or realities:

> When the real is no longer what it used to be, nostalgia assumes its full meaning. There is a proliferation of myths of origin and signs of reality; of second-hand truth, objectivity and authenticity… there is a panic-stricken production of the real and the referential, above and parallel to the panic of material production.
> (Baudrillard, 1983: 12–13)

Interestingly, Ritzer and Liska (1997) comment that many tourists today are, in stark contrast to MacCannell (1976), in search of inauthenticity. The contrived and imitated attractions have increasingly broadened their appeal to postmodern tourists. Even in completely contrived heritage tourism settings, tourists' quests for an alternative exis-tential authenticity can be understood as an attempt to facilitate authentic experiences.

Mitrašinovic (2006) accuses contemporary heritage tourists of seeking entertainment and pleasure in inauthentic attractions, events and performances without questioning what they see and experience (see Case study 4.1). Similarly, McCrone *et al.* (1995: 46) emphasise:

> Authenticity and originality are, above all, matters of technique... What is interesting to postmodernists about heritage is that reality depends on how convincing the presentation is, how well the 'staged authenticity' works... the more 'authentic' the representation, the more 'real' it is.

Chhabra *et al.* (2003) argue that the focus should now be placed on tourists' perceptions and experiences regarding the authenticity and quality of heritage attractions and practices. Within heritage tourism contexts, authenticity becomes fairly subjective, increasingly conditioned and reconditioned by its demand side. The recent shift in emphasising interactivity and tourist experiences in various heritage attractions is closely associated with increasingly recognising and valuing 'perceived authenticity', which is, to a greater or lesser extent, place- and context-specific. Despite an increasing significance on 'perceived authenticity', however, there exists an ongoing request for maintaining certain degrees of essentialist and object authenticity in heritage tourism experiences. Accordingly, Chhabra (2010) argues that the demand for objective authenticity remains within the conventional boundaries of heritage tourism. It is interesting to realise that younger generations, particularly Generation Y in Chhabra's research context, are very keen on experiencing essentialist authenticity in heritage settings. Belhassen and Canton (2006) also recognise the continued relevance of object authenticity to tourists and tourism settings. It seems to be of crucial importance to argue that the quest for authenticity has to be achieved through a negotiated compromise between tradition and modernity and object and experience.

In this postmodern-based society, the search for authenticity is too simple a foundation for explaining contemporary tourism (Urry, 1991). Authenticity is often regarded as an outdated and redundant concept in tourism contexts. However, Mkono (2012) asserts that tourists are still concerned with authenticity in their travelling experiences. In particular, the quest for authenticity remains, as discussed before, of fundamental importance to both attractions and motivations of heritage tourism closely associated with the representation of the past and identity. It follows, therefore, that authenticity within heritage tourism contexts needs to be understood as a constant search for and a struggle with realising and repositioning the individual selves and their individuality during encounters with heritage. The convergent and heterogeneous nature of authenticity needs to be clearly recognised and utilised as a drive, rather than an impediment, to diversify and enrich the academic debates and enquiries surrounding authenticity. Subsequently, authenticity should not be perceived as a static and fixed concept, but a flexible, negotiable and malleable concept reflecting both the attributes of heritage and individual tourists' perceptions and interpretations. Clearly, both theoretical and empirical analysis of authenticity will be sustained as an ongoing research subject in future heritage tourism studies.

Commodification of heritage for tourism

Commodification is a process by which 'things (and activities) come to be evaluated primarily in terms of their exchange value, in a context of trade, hereby becoming goods and services' (Cohen, 1988: 380). Tourism activities and experiences generally encompass the

Case study 4.1: Postmodern heritage attractions

The Texas Renaissance Festival

The Texas Renaissance Festival is a recreated theme park of historical European villages, located in Plantersville, Texas. It is the most acclaimed and popular Renaissance theme park in the US. It is open to the public, every weekend and Thanksgiving Friday in October and November. Each weekend has been variously themed, ranging from Oktoberfest, 1001 Dreams and Roman Bacchanal to Highland Fling. All the employed staff wear period costumes and they attempt to reincarnate the characters they perform. The re-enactment of history is achieved through living history presentations and representations. Visitors are also encouraged to come in period or fantasy costumes. There are also demonstrating artists and costumed performers (e.g., armourer, broom maker, coin minting, pole lathing and wax chandler) showcased in over 200 daily performances. The 36th Annual Texas Renaissance Festival received 450,000 tourists in 2010, including more than 76,500 people for closing weekend alone. A range of history lessons are run in the School Days programme, which is a two-day event when the Texas Renaissance Festival opens its gates exclusively to school groups grades K–12 (tickets are priced at US$8 per person). The festival also organises wedding services under the slogan of 'create the royal wedding of your dreams in 16th-century-style within the walls of our charming English village'. Kim and Jamal's (2007) study has revealed that repeat participants who are highly committed to engage in costumed and ritualistic practices at the festival were likely to gain multiple personal benefits, ranging from self-enrichment, renewal of self to more evident hedonistic enjoyment, including fun and fantasy. Participants were also able to experience some interpersonal benefits, including the development of unique subcultures, authentic social interaction and a strong sense of belonging. Here, the notion of existential authenticity is fundamental in understanding repeat participants' commitment to the festival. The hyper-real experiences of constructed heritage settings encourage tourists to perceive their visit as authentic. General Manager, Terre Albert, highlights that

> the success of the festival relies on exciting, authentic and diverse programming and we had tremendous feedback regarding the new performers, activities and games. We know people come to see their favorite acts year after year, but we continue to seek out themes and performers that will appeal to a wide-array of people in order to keep them coming back for more each year.

The festival features on Facebook, Twitter, YouTube, Vimeo and Pinterest to enhance interactivity with tourists. A new mobile app was also introduced recently as part of their promotional and marketing activities.

Sources: www.texrenfest.com; Kim and Jamal (2007).

Global Village, Dubai

The Global Village is located in Dubailand, which is a massive-scale entertainment complex being built in Dubai, United Arab Emirates. The Global Village was first launched in 1996 on the Deira side of Dubai Creek as a small cultural event. It began as an annual pseudo festival during the Dubai Shopping Festival but has now moved to Dubailand. The project construction began in 2003, and is now one of the main tourist attractions in Dubai. It aims to be the world's largest tourism, leisure and entertainment project. It incorporates cultural, entertainment and shopping, with diverse cultures, theatre, art, commerce and cuisine from across the world in order to create surreal tourism experiences. For example, the World Culture Stage hosts a wide array of shows featuring Irish, Sri Lankan, Cuban, Japanese, Indian and African performers. New kiosks from Austria, Brazil, Greece, Hong Kong and South Africa, restaurants, entertainment venues and an open air theatre are now being added in order to meet increasing commercial demand. The Global Village, following Las Vegas and Macau, is a good example of inauthentic and surreal experiences of cultural heritage, mainly contrived and promoted for touristic consumption.

Source: www.globalvillage.ae.

The Holy Land Experience, Orlando

The Holy Land Experience (HLE) is a living biblical museum and theme park located in southwest Orlando. It was opened on 5 February 2001 by Marvin Rosenthal, the president and CEO of Zion's Hope, a non-profit evangelical Christian ministry. The period that the park attempts to recreate and re-enact is the time of Moses (1450BC) and the Exodus to Jesus' teachings and eventual crucifixion (AD70). In its mission statements, it is clearly specified that the HLE aims to recreate historically significant biblical points of interest in Jerusalem and Israel, from an accurate depiction of Herod's Temple to the Upper Room, thereby bringing the visitor into a place of understanding of Christianity's historical roots. The main exhibits include the Church of All Nations, the Scriptorium, Jerusalem Street Market, Oasis Palms Café, Jerusalem Model AD66 and the Theatre of Life. On its website, the Church of All Nations is promoted as follows:

> The 2,000 seat Church of All Nations auditorium is a must-see highlight for guests visiting the Holy Land Experience. This beautiful, state of the art facility features spectacular dramatic productions such as live presentations of 'Behold the Lamb', the powerful re-enactment of the passion and crucifixion of Jesus, and 'We Shall Behold Him', the glorious depiction of His resurrection and ascension to heaven. There are wonderful, live Praise the Lord programs, with the best of today's ministry and music guests, plus praise and worship concerts, church and baptismal services… and more!

Multimedia presentations, costumed employees, reconstruction of buildings and towns and replications of historical events are the main presentational and representational methods employed at the HLE. The online store sells a range of products including anointing oils, DVDs, clothing, jewellery as well as Holy Land Experience themed souvenirs. The price for a one-day ticket is adult (13+) $40; youth (6–12) $25; and pre-school (3–5) $10.

Sources: Rowan (2004); http://www.holylandexperience.com.

consumption of commodities, either objects or practices. Hannam and Knox (2010: 38) further explicate that:

> The major difference between a commodity and an object is that a commodity has an exchange value in addition to its use value. A commodity is thus purchasable and is subject to market forces. The economic laws of supply and demand will determine the economic price attached to a commodity... Once an object or space is commodified then only those that have the means to pay the purchase price or entrance fee are able to experience that commodity or service. Commodification is thus a political issue as it shifts objects and spaces that were formerly thought of as free and communal into the economic domain of scarcity.

MacCannell (1976: 25) discusses 'cultural productions', a term that refers not only to the process of culture, but also to the products that result from that process. He identifies tourism as an ideal arena in which to investigate the nature of such cultural production, which in essence expresses the concept of commodification applied to tourism. The appropriation and utilisation of the past for tourist experiences have unmistakably led to commodifying culture and heritage. Due to the growing popularity, heritage sites and attractions are being modified and transformed as a consumable product to enhance tourist experiences, which is often criticised as resulting in the loss of meaning and authenticity. Intangible heritage as events and performances has also become increasingly commodified for touristic consumption. Once heritage gets transformed into a tourism product, its 'cultural value' is often replaced by 'commercial value', leading to exploiting the past for economic purposes (Lanfant, 1995: 37). Commodification occurs due to tourist demand, facilitating the alterations of heritage as a commodity (Lominé and Edmunds, 2007), as illustrated in Chapter 1. Samuel (1994) explicates that the advent of heritage, like the popularity of retrochic, has undeniably brought the issues of commodification to the fore. It is claimed that retrochic, like heritage, is

> dazzled by surface appearances; that it is more interested in style than in substance, and that it is obsessed with the language of looks. It is also charged with fraud – creating copies, as Baudrillard puts it in *Simulations*, for which there are no originals, using hyperreality to camouflage the absence of the real. Then – in a residue of 1960s jeremiads against consumerism – retrochic is charged, like heritage, with 'commodifying' the past, instrumentalizing it for the purposes of commercial gain, exploiting the sacred in the interests of the profane.
>
> (Samuel, 1994: 113)

Heritage has thus been criticised as exploiting the past for commercial purposes. Heritage is accused of turning the past into a spectacle that is divorced from its original context. Walsh (1992: 103) contends that the heritage site is often a spurious simulacrum:

> Unlike real places these heritage environments are not historic environments which have developed 'naturally' over time as the town, village or city has developed. Heritage sites are constructed as 'time capsules' severed from history, islands of mediated image, sites of out-of-town heritage shopping... In many ways they represent a form of historical bricolage, a melting pot for historical memories.

Critical concerns over commodification of heritage do not just rest in the area of tangible heritage as above. Greenwood's (1989) research on the Alarde celebrations in Fuenterrabia, Spain, has been the most quoted and debated study in discussing the commercial exploitation of culture and heritage in tourism contexts. The Alarde was an important commemoration of local history, celebrating a distinctive sense of locality. However, when its potential to attract tourists was recognised, the municipal government ordered the Alarde celebrations to be formed twice in one day to attract more visitor attention. In only two years, the celebration had lost its appeal for the local population and had ceased being a celebration for the villagers and had become a tourist spectacle, and community leaders found it difficult to incite enthusiasm among residents to participate. It is argued that the packaging, staging and promoting of local culture for touristic consumption renders it meaningless and inauthentic. Therefore, local cultural celebrations are easily turned into a mere tourist spectacle by the process of commodification within tourism contexts. It is stated:

> The ritual has become a performance for money. The meaning is gone... this decision directly violated the meaning of the ritual, definitively destroying its authenticity and its power for the people... Making their culture a public performance took the municipal government a few minutes; with that act, a 350-year-old ritual died.
>
> (Greenwood, 1989: 178–80)

Greenwood's premise is based on understanding traditions as being distinct from market forces. His argument is firmly grounded in an essentialist understanding of tradition which focuses on cultural integrity and continuity. Essentialist perspectives often impose strict and fixed criteria in evaluating the authenticity of traditions in present contexts. The search for an authentic heritage experience is often identified as the search for 'the unspoiled, pristine, genuine, untouched and traditional' (Handler, 1986: 2), which is rather one-dimensional and restrained. Commodification of heritage in essentialist perspectives is thus perceived as a destructive force in sustaining its authenticity. But there emerges one critical question here: which authenticity does this concern? As discussed in greater detail in the previous sections, authenticity is a relative, subjective and malleable concept. Commodifying the past can thus lead to creating, recreating and negotiating authenticity in certain contexts. The process of commodification has revived an old cultural event, the Alarde, thereby turning it into a source of both community cohesion and tourism development (Wilson, 1993). Cohen (1988) supports the process of commodification as a means for the survival of culture and heritage. Furthermore, MacDonald (1997) perceives commodification as a means of intensifying the traditional for local communities, rather than diluting it. Drawing on Viking heritage tourism markets, Halewood and Hannam (2001: 578) claim that commodifiation can also be seen as a 'process which is both resisted and embraced in order to develop local cultural values'. Here, there emerges a need to recontextualise Appadurai's (1986) claim in appropriating heritage for touristic consumption that commodification is not a singular or irrevocable process. It is argued that objects have social lives and their commodity status can only be certain stages of their wider social lives. Therefore, an object that is once regarded as a commodity may not necessarily be regarded as a commodity at other stages of its social life. This is in line with Samuel's (1994) perspective on commodifying heritage as a social process. This point is pertinent in a 'constructivist' understanding of culture and heritage, particularly in relation to tourism-led commodification processes. In examining how the commodification of culture for tourism affects traditional practices in a Mayan village in Belize, Medina (2003: 356) distinguishes a 'constructivist' understanding of tradition from an 'essentialist' one, by claiming that:

> While essentialists have focused on the persistence of a cosmological core that has shaped Maya culture across time, 'constructivists' have argued that the culture of contemporary communities is not an artefact of pre-Columbian times; rather, it is the product of their interactions with powerful non-Maya forces.

This focus on interactions with different cultural forces and influences lies at the core of a 'constructivist' understanding of tradition. Here, authenticity is socially constructed and positioned through the 'collaborative production of culture in negotiations between tourists and tourees' (Medina, 2003: 365). The process of commodification is not necessarily negative. It can facilitate constructivist-based recreation and reappropriation of culture and heritage in relation to tourism development. In commodifying heritage and tradition for tourism development, it is thus important to differentiate 'touristic authenticity' from 'historical authenticity'. Both 'essentialist' and 'constructivist' understandings of heritage and tradition are of specific relevance in evaluating the issues of both authenticity and commodification in heritage tourism contexts. In the recent academic studies on traditional (heritage) festivals and tourism development, critical focus has been placed on examining their discursive and symbiotic relationships. In his study on the Trinidad Carnival, Sampath (1997) states that the host population adopts the tourists' culture, mainly Euro-Americans. Despite the worries over the process of Westernisation in the re-enactment of vernacular living heritage, he ensures that the touristification of this carnival reflects and contributes to a constant reconstruction and repositioning of local identity with the appropriation of global and local nexus. Tourism development has made a positive contribution to increasing both formal and informal participation of locals and tourists, thereby incorporating global influences with local characters, where a greater emphasis is placed on localising and, at the same time, globalising the different aspects of their identity. It is elaborated:

> it is possible that 'authenticity' can be safely sacrificed to tourism, if that authenticity is never strongly claimed to have existed in the first place. By having allowed a constant stream of 'foreign' influences to affect it during its segmented cultural construction, carnival has ameliorated negative effects on the society from which it sprang. In fact, carnival provides a celebratory forum for a society to express its fears of global influence *by displaying them*.
>
> (Sampath, 1997: 167–8, original emphasis)

In their ethnographic study examining the complex social spaces and political structures underpinned in an annual festival in Sardinia, Italy, Azara and Crouch (2006) emphasise that newly invented and modified elements of festivals still function as an efficient medium in encouraging community participation and cohesion, fulfilling different social roles and identity performances. La Cavalcata Sarda is primarily regarded as an annual celebration of local identity and culture regardless of invented romantic imagery portrayed and promoted to further tourism development. The successful transformation and restructuring of La Cavalcata Sarda as a popular tourism destination has made a positive impact on local reappreciation of their intangible cultural practices. This festival has made Sardinia recreate its image from a mass beach tourism destination back in the 1960s and 1970s to a specialised cultural and heritage destination which attracts new segments of tourists. During this process, the government has encouraged the active involvement of different communities, thereby reviving varying elements of local cultures from possible extinction or degradation. Here, both real and potential effects of tourism development have led to rediscovering local cultural traditions and recognising the importance of preserving them for future generations (see Case study 4.2).

It appears that historical accuracy or objective authenticity become less significant in creating tourists' meaningful and embodied experiences of culture and heritage. Appropriately, Carnegie and McCabe (2008: 353) emphasise that:

> in the field of tourism, the issues of authenticity and post-modern experience has been advanced to the point where such experiences can be seen as authentic and meaningful to participants and spectators even within the context of a largely commoditised and 'staged' experiential setting.

Despite increasing attention to a flexible and fluid understanding of authenticity, however, the adaptation of heritage for tourism demand should carefully be considered in order not to fully distort or negate original meanings and values inherent in heritage. Moreover, it should be noted that touristic representations of national (sacred) sites or places can be significantly different from local appreciation and understanding. For local people, places and sites can have cultural and symbolic value, and personal and localised meaning, especially as such spaces are inhabited and contextualised as part of everyday life. Newly manufactured meanings of heritage for tourism purposes can tarnish traditionally upheld values of heritage. But these newly acquired meanings of heritage through commodification can enrich and enhance the values of heritage. Therefore, the interaction of heritage and tourism should possibly entail a reinterpretation of both sectors, only then can an informed approach and critical engagement be made to achieve a harmonised balance between tradition and modernity. Heritage tourism has a role to play in meeting the changing demands of cultural consumption, and enhancing the overall quality of touristic experiences and maximising the potential of historical resources by way of enhancing the discursive and organic relationship between authenticity and commodification.

Case study 4.2: Commodification and authenticity of souvenirs

Souvenirs are regarded as one of the most significant material and tangible markers and mementos of travelling experiences and memories. They play a significant role in mediating cultural interaction between tourists and host people. But it is often said that the meanings of souvenirs as unique cultural markers have become tainted with the mass production and replication of souvenirs, particularly traditional local arts and crafts. Local arts and crafts, which used to be traditionally produced on a small scale, have become commercially manufactured on a mass scale to meet the increasing demands of tourists.

Unique cultural and heritage products have thus been modified and transformed 'in response to the impositions or temptations from large-scale and sometimes far-away consumers' (Appadurai, 1986: 47). Hence, the debates over the commodification of souvenirs and its subsequent impact on the authenticity of local cultural products have consistently attracted scholastic attention (see Graburn, 1967; McKean, 1976; Cohen, 1988; Hume, 2009). 'Airport art' (Graburn, 1967) refers to local arts and crafts that have been produced and marketed to look authentic to mislead tourists. Souvenirs have even been demeaned as 'tourist kitsch' or 'tourist tat', tasteless and tawdry products transformed through excessive commodification. The uncontrolled proliferation of tasteless souvenirs has had a negative impact on promoting and sustaining the unique cultural traditions of destinations. Even in 2011, a summit was held in Tuscany, Italy, with the aim of regulating the souvenir trade in renowned cultural heritage tourism destinations in the region. However, the process of commodification in turning local arts and crafts into souvenirs has also led to some positive changes in a variety of contexts. Using the example of the commodified figurative embroideries of Hmong (Meo) refugees from Laos, Cohen (1988) brings attention to the possibility of conferring different authentic messages to cultural products targeted for external audiences, including tourists. Here, souvenirs can act as new cultural expressions manifesting emergent authenticity. It is thus possible that certain cultural and heritage products developed for tourists have become authentic over time, facilitating new interpretations and purposes. Hitchcock (2000) also pinpoints the difficulty of distinguishing between a 'touristic' and 'traditional' artefact in some places where there is a long experience of international trade. The process of commodification has unmistakably impacted on the production, promotion and distribution of cultural products as souvenirs. Instead of destroying the meaning of cultural products, it may create new cultural meanings of souvenirs. In explicating the increasing recognition and inclusion of tourist art in museums and art galleries, Hume (2009) argues that the repetitive production in the making of souvenirs does not always result in reducing the aesthetic standards of local cultural products. He also emphasises tourists' roles as consumers in the generation of the collective memory. However, Briassoulis and der Stroaten (2000) warn that emergent authenticity dislocates local culture and heritage, encouraging the transformation of cultural heritage as an idealised product for touristic consumption. According to Ooi (2002), the concept of emergent authenticity ignores the resistance and concerns of the host societies. Academic debates over the commodification and authenticity of souvenirs will continue to grow. Issues such as empowerment and cultural property rights in the commodification of local arts and crafts need to be more rigorously investigated in future studies. Furthermore, examining and evaluating the authenticity of souvenirs needs to take into account such variables as originality, workmanship, aesthetics, function, cultural and historic integrity and shopping experience (see Littrell *et al.*, 1993).

Figure 4.2 Mass production of traditional Vietnamese potteries in Bát Tràng

Conclusion

Despite the increasing popularity and prevalence of simulated and replicated tourist sites in a contemporary tourism environment, searching for authenticity is still a major concern for tourists, tourism developers and promoters. There is an ongoing contestation and negotiation of cultural meanings and social relations in the way the past is reconstructed, represented and consumed in heritage tourism contexts. The debates on authenticity and commodification are regarded as one of the most significant controversies in heritage tourism contexts, particularly in relation to staging and promoting heritage for touristic consumption. The processes of commodifying heritage for touristic consumption are now quite common all around the globe. Both heritage products and experiences have been increasingly turned into commodities, which are then promoted for attracting heritage tourists. It follows, therefore, that newly contrived and purely commercial heritage attractions have also gained their own momentum as popular tourism attractions. Authenticity is an important factor to consider in enhancing heritage tourism experiences, however it cannot be completely relied upon as a medium of assessing the quality of heritage tourism experiences. Furthermore, recognising authenticity as a relative, subjective and malleable concept focusing on tourists' existential state in which they consume cultural objects rather than constructing and reconstructing objective authenticity is of crucial relevance in further facilitating the context-specific understanding of authenticity in tourism contexts. It is pertinent to note that academic debates now acknowledge the crucial importance of accounting for tourists' own perceptions and experiences in evaluating authenticity. A balanced and flexible approach needs to be made in incorporating both 'essentialist' and 'constructivist' understandings of tradition and heritage in order to broaden and enhance ways in which issues of authenticity and commodification influence heritage tourism products, services and experiences. A more nuanced and intricate understanding of authenticity and commodification and their dynamics is essential in broadening its meanings and implications in heritage tourism experiences.

Research questions

1. Can you explain what major differences there are in conceptualising 'staged authenticity', 'emergent authenticity', 'existential authenticity' and 'perceived authenticity'?
2. What does 'commodification of heritage' mean? Using relevant examples, critically evaluate both positive and negative aspects of commodifying heritage for touristic consumption.
3. How significant or insignificant are the issues of authenticity for contemporary heritage tourists?
4. Discuss ways in which postmodern tourists seek inauthenticity in their heritage tourism experiences.
5. How different is the 'constructivist' understanding of tradition from the 'essentialist' perspective?
6. How important do you think 'objective authenticity' is in experiencing historical sites, including WHSs?
7. Discuss ways in which commodification of heritage can be reconciled with other aims of heritage such as preservation.
8. What are the main effects of turning heritage into commodities on local communities and their practices?
9. Is heritage turning merely into a spectacle or entertainment through the process of commodification?
10. Based on this chapter, try to conceptualise and contextualise authenticity and commodification in the context of heritage tourism in your own words.

Learning material

Belhassen, Y. and Caton, K. (2006) Authenticity matters, *Annals of Tourism Research*, 33(3): 853–6.

Bruner, E.M. (1994) Abraham Lincoln as authentic reproduction: a critique of postmodernism, *American Anthropologist*, 96(2): 397–415.

Chhabra, D., Healy, R. and Sills, E. (2003) Staged authenticity and heritage tourism, *Annals of Tourism Research*, 30(3): 702–19.

Cohen, E. (1988) Authenticity and commoditization in tourism, *Annals of Tourism Research*, 15(3): 371–86.

Eco, U. (1986) *Faith in Fakes*, London: Secker & Warburg.

Greenwood, D.J. (1989) Culture by the pound: an anthropological perspective on tourism as cultural commoditization, in V.L. Smith (ed.) *Hosts and Guests: The Anthropology of Tourism*, 2nd edn,

Philadelphia: University of Pennsylvania Press, pp. 171–85.

Halewood, C. and Hannam, K. (2001) Viking heritage tourism: authenticity and commodification, *Annals of Tourism Research*, 28(3): 565–80.

Handler, R. and Saxton, W. (1988) Dissimulation: reflexivity, narrative, and the quest for authenticity in 'living history', *Cultural Anthropology*, 3(3): 242–60.

Jamal, T.B. and Hill, S. (2002) The home and the world: (post)touristic spaces of (in)authenticity, in G.M.S. Dann (ed.) *The Tourist as a Metaphor of the Social World*, Wallingford: CAB International, pp. 77–108.

MacCannell, D. (1976) *The Tourist: A New Theory of the Leisure Class*, London: Macmillan.

McIntosh, A.J. and Prentice, R.C. (1999) Affirming authenticity: consuming cultural heritage, *Annals of Tourism Research*, 26(3): 589–612.

Meethan, K. (2001) *Tourism in Global Society: Place, Culture, Consumption*, Hampshire: Palgrave (Chapter 4).

Mkono, M. (2012) Authenticity does matter, *Annals of Tourism Research*, 39(1): 480–3.

Rowan, Y. (2004) Repackaging the pilgrimage: visiting the Holy Land in Orlando, in Y. Rowan and U. Baram (eds) *Marketing Heritage: Archaeology and the Consumption of the Past*, Oxford: Altamira Press, pp. 249–66.

Steiner, C.J. and Reisinger, Y. (2006) Understanding existential authenticity, *Annals of Tourism Research*, 33(2): 299–318.

Wang, N. (1999) Rethinking authenticity in tourism experience, *Annals of Tourism Research*, 26(2): 349–70.

Weblinks

Titanic memorial cruise sets sail
http://www.guardian.co.uk/uk/video/2012/apr/09/titanic-memorial-cruise-sets-sail-video

Titanic II plan unveiled
http://www.guardian.co.uk/world/video/2013/feb/27/titanic-australian-billionaire-video

Texas Renaissance Festival
http://vimeo.com/21820651

Weddings at Texas Renaissance Festival
http://vimeo.com/21821501

The Holy Land Experience
http://www.youtube.com/watch?v=odY8IaW-LhM
http://www.holylandexperience.com/resources/video_gallery.html

Celebrating carnival in Trinidad
http://www.youtube.com/watch?v=zMyI4GKHcZE

La Cavalcata Sarda, Sardinia
http://vimeo.com/channels/lacavalcatasarda/808737

5 **Politics of heritage tourism**

Power and politics in heritage

Heritage is inherently embedded in an 'often-bewildering array of identifications and potential conflicts, not least when heritage places and objects are involved in issues of legitimisation of power structures' (Ashworth *et al.*, 2007: 41). Heritage attests to the dissonant and conflicting uses and purposes of the past. The past can be purposefully selected, modified and reappropriated to meet the political agendas and ideological frameworks that underpin heritage in the present. It is often the case that heritage reflects the governing assumptions, beliefs and values of its time and context (Hall, 2005). Hall (2005: 26) emphasises:

> It [heritage] is always inflected by the power and authority of those who have colonized the past, whose versions of history matter. These assumptions and co-ordinates of power are inhabited as natural – given, timeless, true and inevitable. But it takes only the passage of time, the shift of circumstances, or the reversals of history to reveal those assumptions as time – and context – bound, historically specific, and thus open to contestation, re-negotiation, and revision.

Heritage can segregate social and ethnic groups as a means of aestheticising and reinforcing differences rather than unity. Heritage is often utilised as a clear barometer to discern and differentiate the social class and stratum. Such concepts as 'dissonant heritage' (Tunbridge and Ashworth, 1996), 'undesirable heritage' (Macdonald, 2006), 'ambivalent heritage' (Chadha, 2006) and 'negative heritage' (Meskell, 2002) are deeply associated with the political dimensions of heritage, with specific reference to denial of or struggle with certain elements of past. The official and hegemonic understanding of heritage is predicated upon the assumption that heritage encompasses fixed and unchanging values and standards (see Weiss, 2007). However, perceiving heritage as a monolithic establishment with a fixed identity often leads to the suppression of differing perceptions and the exclusion of varying interpretations of heritage. Graham *et al.* (2000: 93) draw attention to the dissonant nature of heritage, commenting that

> heritage cannot exist as a universal absolute. Ultimately, because it is what and where we say it is (the pivotal variable being 'we') then one person's heritage is the disinheritance of another... Heritage dissonance can be defined as the mismatch between heritage and people, in space and time. It is caused by movements or other changes in heritage and by migration or other changes in people, transformations which characteristically involve how heritage is perceived and what value systems are filtering those perceptions.

Importantly, tourism can serve as an effective means in reinforcing the legitimacy of state-based and hegemonic representations and interpretations of the past. Both heritage and tourism can play an active role in politically reconstructing and reappropriating national memories. It is thus essential to note that heritage tourism strategically promotes or suppresses certain elements of shared memories inherent in specific heritage settings (Park, 2011). The political uses of heritage tourism are often evident in ex-communist regimes including some East European and Indochine countries, where communist heritage is actively employed as an effective tourism resource with which to legitimate their political ideologies and emphasise their nationalist sentiments (see Light, 2000, 2001; Henderson, 2007). Various sites and events originating from communism have been recreated and promoted as popular tourism attractions – Memento Park (Budapest, Hungary); Survival Drama in a Soviet Bunker (Lithuania); The House of the People (Bucharest, Romania) and Killing Fields (Cambodia). It is apparent that heritage tourism often distorts and manipulates the past by way of selecting what should be remembered and forgotten. It is also critical to recognise that utilisation of the past for forging and maintaining national cohesion and solidarity within tourism contexts is often closely associated with facilitating the acts of intentional forgetting (social amnesia) as well as collective remembering (Tunbridge and Ashworth, 1996; Walsh, 2001; Buzinde and Santos, 2008). In this regard, the reconstruction of communist heritage can be understood as a collective struggle of post-communism that attempts to forget its undesirable pasts. A collection of the communist statues and monuments was relocated in Memento Park outside Hungary after having been removed immediately after the fall of the communist regime in 1989. The relocation of the communist heritage thus reflects an attempt to sanitise the memory of the Soviet era (see Case study 5.1).

Case study 5.1: '1984. Survival Drama' in a Soviet Bunker, Lithuania

'1984. Survival Drama' in a Soviet Bunker was a part of the official programme of events during Vilnius' year as European Capital of Culture in 2009. It was aimed at enabling visitors to experience first-hand the ideology and brutality of the communist regime during the Soviet era. Survival Drama in a Soviet Bunker represents past conflicts, which resulted in human atrocities. Survival drama is a good illustration of the heritage attractions that have gradually evolved from passive to interactive and from the authenticity of the object to the authenticity of the visitor's experience. Since its opening in 2008, the museum has been visited by more than 7,000 people. The creation of 1984: Survival Drama in a Soviet Bunker was deemed to be appropriate for various reasons: preserving the memory of Nazi and communist terror for younger Lithuanian generations and providing unique opportunities for international visitors to glimpse the country's turbulent past. Lithuania is one of the Eastern European countries that has decided to capitalise on their Socialist past in the form of tourism development, including Grutas Park. Under the regime of the USSR, the bunker was originally used as a base by Soviet troops for an attack on the TV tower in Vilnius in which 14 people were killed. Its website promotes unique visitor experiences:

You'll be taken to the maze, watch TV shows and shops of 1984, be interrogated in a KGB office, learn the anthem of the USSR and get used to wearing a gas mask. You'll dance to the music of those times and will eat a Soviet dinner yourself. Before leaving the bunker you will receive a special certificate and an authentic present from the Soviet times.

Visitors need to sign a disclaimer that informs them that they risk verbal abuse and will have to perform physical exercise. To make it more stressful all the instructions are provided in Russian. There is a deliberate intent not to run the tours in English, in order to recreate more authentic settings and experiences. All of the actors involved were originally in the Soviet army and some were authentic interrogators. The performances for the school children are specifically tailored. It is the aspect of participation that is the major premise behind the Survival Drama. Tourists' active involvement makes the presented heritage more compelling as it provokes emotion. Furthermore, actors' interactions with tourists are the mainstay of the whole experience which intensifies edutainment elements. The interpretation of Survival Drama caused intense debates as Russia never admitted to occupying Lithuania. The conflicts and subsequent human atrocities presented by Survival Drama led to political tension between the two countries.

Source: www.sovietbunker.com.

Figure 5.1 '1984. Survival Drama', Lithuania (courtesy of the Soviet Bunker)

With regard to ownership, heritage can create serious conflicts and tensions between different ethnic or religious groups, regions and nations. The Preah Vihear temple, designated a WHS in 2008, has become a cause of serious border conflicts between Thai and Cambodian soldiers. This ancient Hindu sanctuary, partially in ruins, is located on the cliffs of the Dang Raek mountains which constitute the boundary between Cambodia and Thailand. The International Court of Justice (ICJ) declared the temple to be part of Cambodia in 1962. But both Thailand and Cambodia make different yet conflicting claims over the site's sovereignty and history. However, the ICJ in The Hague awarded the temple to Cambodia. During two outbreaks of hostilities in 2011 heavy shelling resulted in 17 fatalities and more than 50,000 people were evacuated on both sides of the militarised border. Its WH designation, celebrated by Cambodia, led to a series of nationalistic and xenophobic protests in Thailand (Fawthrop, 2011). Tourism is often employed as a strategic political tool to reinforce a nation's ideological agendas and political stances. Rivera (2008) examines ways in which the Croatian government has represented the country to international audiences, with particular reference to tourism promotion and marketing. The state has successfully managed to cover and reframe the country's recent difficult past in order to enhance the nation's images as a tourism destination. The recent war, a crucial part of Croatian history, has been strategically omitted in tourism promotional materials. Excessive focus on promoting Croatia as being similar to Western Europe can lead to losing its distinctive socio-cultural and geo-political characteristics, thereby being merely incorporated into a homogenising global culture. Implicit in this study is a claim to consider that official representations of heritage often fail to incorporate different versions of history and individual identifications of nationhood. Another interesting example is the role of the state in Dracula tourism development in Romania. Light (2007) argues that the state plays an important role in the cultural politics of tourism as well as planning and policy-making. The state in Romania has been reluctant to promote the supernatural associations of Dracula in the Western imagination as the country's main tourism attraction. Compared to the stereotypical images of Romania as Dracula's country, the state wants to promote the country's images as a modern, developed European country. However, the state needs to compromise to meet the popular demand from international tourism, particularly from the West. Light (2007) concludes that this example illustrates wider issues of power, representations and inequality within international tourism development by way of highlighting the tensions between the power to represent and those who are represented.

The changing dynamics and relations immanent in heritage settings should be carefully considered to enhance the reflexive understanding of the various episodes in the past. The heritagisation process has been defined as a 'social process whose final outcome is the presentation and interpretation (rather than archiving or sustaining) of heritage' (Poria and Ashworth, 2009: 523). The main goal of heritagisation is to articulate and consolidate the identities and solidarities of various groups and individuals and their different interpretations in the tourism context. It is further argued:

> Heritagization is at times intentionally based on an invented, hidden, as well as purposely chosen past. Additionally, heritagization centres on ideas and ideological frameworks in contrast to preservation and conservation which focus on objects... In heritagization, history is captured as completed, something that belongs to the inhabitants of the present who can choose how to interpret and use it to their advantage... Heritagization, for which heritage tourism is often the means, aims at legitimizing a certain social-political order and ideological framework.
>
> (Poria and Ashworth, 2009: 523)

Following Smith's (2006) premise that heritage is often seen as privileged and exclusive cultural symbols of the white elite groups, Waterton (2009) aims to challenge the ways in which image and imagery have been represented and consumed in heritage studies. The idea of heritage visually embedded within a range of promotional brochures and policy documents is rather implicated in a dominant and exclusive understanding of heritage and its associated identity categories are mainly linked with the white, middle and upper classes. He further argues that the consciously designed objectives (New Labour policy in the UK) have also opened up a conceptual space within which images of heritage are drawn upon to undertake a course of ideological work that affectively reaffirms and legitimises the cultural symbols of an elite social group as a consensual representation of national heritage. Being fundamentally political by its nature, heritage becomes 'something that is beyond the familiar, and beyond the banal, carrying a perceived significance that clothes it in a "see, but do not touch" reverence' (Waterton, 2009: 50) for certain social and ethnic groups or communities, which are often excluded and discriminated in the presentations and representations of national heritage. The varying perceptions and perspectives of different ethnic, religious and cultural groups are not necessarily integrated in the official and hegemonic discourses of heritage. In his study of Beamish, the open air museum depicting the everyday life of North East England during the Georgian, Victorian and Edwardian periods, Bennett (1995) reveals that certain political issues such as labour and trade union movements have not been represented and the site largely ignores the activities of the women of the North East in suffrage and feminist campaigns. According to Bennett (1995: 112):

> Many of the artefacts displayed might well have been exhibited in such a way as to suggest their associations with popular political movements. However, the tendency is for them to be severed of such associations and to serve, instead, as vehicles for the nostalgic remembrance of sentimentalized pasts.

Consequently, the display of the site mainly focuses on the role of men as a dominant power base of the era, largely under-representing such groups as women, children, disabled people and ethnic minorities. The utilisation of heritage in the tourism context could be selective, as is often the case with education and media.

Conflicts and contests over the meaning of the past often result from conflicts and contests inherent in the present. The conflicting and contradictory discourses of heritage in post-colonial contexts are clearly illustrated in the existing literature in both tourism and heritage studies. In unravelling the ways in which Fort Jesus is represented in post-colonial Kenya, Sarmento (2010) claims that heritage sites in post-colonial contexts are eager to discard colonial histories as undesirable national pasts while striving to promote their colonial connections as tourism resources. Memories of a colonial past embedded in certain heritage settings are recontextualised, repositioned and renegotiated in the context of tourism development. There exist ongoing contestations between the promotion of heritage as tourism resources and the obliteration of colonial heritage as an undesirable past. The cultural and architectural heritage of a colonial power is suppressed or even discarded in favour of the cultural legacy of a pre-colonial period that is appropriated for the creation of 'new' national identities (Harrison, 2005). In examining the significance of colonial cemeteries in contemporary India, Chadha (2006) claims that it is the ambivalent meaning of a heritage site that leads to the neglect and abandonment of colonial cemeteries in the post-colonial landscape. Colonial experiences are often regarded as 'national shame' in which national pride is inevitably damaged by foreign and non-indigenous forces. However, it is argued that the public recognition of the difficult pasts of a nation can be beneficial for societies (Henderson, 2001). They often play an impetus in encouraging nationals to redefine and redetermine their national identity and cultural integrity throughout generations (see Smith, 1991a). Henderson's (2001) study draws attention to ways in which heritage presentations in Hong Kong contribute to the construction and negotiation of meanings associated with national identity formations. Hong Kong's heritage, representing a mixture of Chinese and colonial cultural elements, is perceived as an important signifier in defining a distinctive identity at a time of social transition and cultural uncertainty, influenced by the process of de-colonisation. In a similar vein, Basu (2008) considers the roles of cultural heritage in Sierra Leone in post-conflict recovery. Sierra Leone is one of the poorest countries in the world, whose recent history has been tainted with a violent civil conflict. Critical focus has been placed on recognising heritage as a main remedy for post-conflict recovery, with specific reference to tourism development. However, the official list of protected ancient and historical monuments and sites in Sierra Leone mainly reflect mid-twentieth-century colonialist values. Here, European influences are rather emphasised while undervaluing local indigenous heritage. History and heritage of local communities and indigenous people have been marginalised and under-represented in recreating and representing national heritage in international tourism contexts. The country's recent civil war conflict is largely excluded in the official discourses of national heritage. It is suggested that it is better to confront and accept the historical narratives of conflict than to neglect this difficult heritage as a pretext of rewriting its history.

Dark heritage sites, media and tourism development

Dark, difficult and dissonant heritage sites and attractions are essential components of dark tourism development (see Lennon and Foley, 2000). This form of tourism has also been labeled as 'thanatourism' (Seaton, 1996), 'black spot tourism' (Rojek, 1999) and 'morbid tourism' (Blom, 2000). Dark tourism is regarded as a complex phenomenon as it combines features from educational, cultural, heritage and special interest tourism (Tarlow, 2005). As a phenomenon, dark tourism development is closely associated with individuals' increasing fascination concerning visiting places of death, disaster and atrocity. On a supply side, dark tourism development also refers to the growing expansion of death- and disaster-related attractions and experiences in the tourism environment. The concept of postmodernism, which is discussed in greater detail in Chapter 1, is critical in understanding the unprecedented growth of dark tourism in contemporary contexts. A range and scope of dark tourism attractions have increasingly become vast and diverse due to the increasing exploitative and commodified nature of tourism development. However, heritage sites construed from difficult and contested pasts are only considered in this section. A wide array of dark heritage sites is as follows: touristic appeal of war (Henderson, 2000), Holocaust (Lennon and Foley, 1999), cemeteries (Seaton, 2002), slavery (Dann and Seaton, 2001) and prisons (Strange and Kempa, 2003). In old days pilgrimage was a common form of travel involving a journey to places relating to the death of an individual of special religious and mystical significance (Fladmark, 1998). The consumption of the disturbing past is driven and shaped by tourists' needs as well as changes in political and socio-cultural settings (Ashworth and Larkham, 1994; Lennon and Foley, 2000; Rátz, 2006). Rátz (2006: 245) maintains 'the selection of culturally significant themes and the interpretation of sensitive political issues depend on the socio-economic framework that heritage and cultural tourism exist in'.

The development of global media has contributed to constantly reproducing dark heritage sites and events (Foley and Lennon, 1997; Lennon and Foley, 1999). Through the process of remaking films and television programmes, death and disaster becomes a saleable and promotable commodity in a global communication market (Palmer, 1993). Not only television and films, but also books, travel blogs, websites and computer games may contribute to triggering the growth of dark heritage tourism by stimulating the perceived reality of dark heritage sites and events. Media and commercial businesses see opportunities in promoting death and disaster as a lucrative heritage attraction, as clearly evidenced in the recent upsurge of commercial interest in the Titanic disaster (see Case study 5.2).

Case study 5.2: The *Titanic* memorial cruise in 2012

In commemoration of the centenary of the *Titanic* disaster, *MS Balmoral* retraced the ship's voyage in the Atlantic in April 2012. This reconstructed, 12-night memorial cruise attracted 1,309 passengers from 28 different countries worldwide. It began its epic journey from Southampton on 8 April despite an uproar of criticism and ethical concerns surrounding the commodification of the tragedy since its conception. Dr. Philip Stone, a professor at the University of Central Lancashire who is an executive director of the Institute for Dark Tourism Research, suggests ways in which people can learn from this memorial cruise without feeling guilty of exploiting a tragedy. He claims that this dark tourism event opens up the discussion of much broader issues of morality, ethics and politics. There existed a strict division of class among the passengers and when the disaster struck, the rich were best positioned to escape, while the rest struggled to escape from the sunken ship. He further argues that the process of burial of the dead was even hierarchical by social class. The first-class passengers were the first to be embalmed and taken for burial, while those in lower classes or steerage were buried at sea. He also emphasises the role of the media in the process of touristification of the tragedy. It is often the media that selects and promotes the stories. He notes that the real *Titanic* was largely forgotten in the decades after the disaster. It was only with the 1953 hit movie *Titanic* that it began to attract public attention. The worldwide success of the 1997 James Cameron version of the film – *Titanic* – propelled the increase of *Titanic* enthusiasts. The memorial cruise's operators, Miles Morgan Travel, endeavoured to recreate and revive the original *Titanic* characters and tastes as much as possible. Dancing classes were prepared to teach passengers how to dance 1912-style and each meal featured at least one '*Titanic* dish of the day'. This fascination with experiencing historical authenticity was also well received on the part of the passengers. Many passengers were dressed up in period costumes of the Edwardian era including a woman wearing a splendid replica of the 'boarding dress' worn by Kate Winslet in the film *Titanic*. Both tour operators and passengers claim that this is not a commodified re-enactment of the tragedy. Rather it aims to remember and commemorate the tragic event. However, there seem to be crucial differences between the memorial voyage and the original. In 1912, 700 third-class passengers had to share two bath tubs, however, all cabins this time around were en suite. Furthermore, Miles Morgan assured everyone that *MS Balmoral* has 'more than sufficient' lifeboats for everyone on board. There exists a thin line here between the tragedy and the commerce.

Sources: Pidd (2012) and Stone (2012).

Crouch *et al.* (2005: 6) draw attention to ways in which the media influences people's imagination, focusing on 'overarching interdependence between tourism and the media'. Seaton and Lennon (2004) distinguish the media as a central driver to the growth of tourism to sites, attractions and exhibitions of death and atrocity, harnessed by the help of global communication technology. The media representations of dark heritage sites have affected the way they are perceived and experienced by tourists. Certainly, the media plays a critical role in shaping and promoting contemporary modes and patterns of dark heritage tourism consumption.

Issues of interpreting and promoting dissonant and sensitive pasts

The central challenge in heritage tourism is to reconstruct the past in the present through interpretation (Dewar, 1989; Timothy and Boyd, 2003; Hems and Blockey, 2006). Interpretation does not only describe historic facts, but creates an understanding or emotional response, thereby increasing appreciation and awareness (see Richards, 1996; Hems and Blockey, 2006). Interpreting and promoting dissonant and sensitive heritage sites can be problematic and controversial, particularly when hegemonic power affects ways in which they are represented and promoted. Heritage interpretation can be a resource used as a political instrument in shaping national identities or legitimising dominant ideologies and hegemonies (Harrison and Hitchcock, 2005; Hems and Blockley, 2006; Rivera, 2008). Therefore, heritage of atrocity may be a powerful political tool, as controversial events are often effective in creating a sense of division between victims and oppressors (see Graham *et al.*, 2000; Smith, 2003; Timothy and Boyd, 2003). In her study examining the motivations of different stakeholders in the commodification of conflict heritage in Northern Ireland, McDowell (2008) reveals that official agencies put an emphasis on the economic potential of this form of heritage while community-based groups often perceive the sites as a symbolic medium through which to propagate their political perspectives. Tourism development of conflict heritage in this context, often dubbed as 'political tourism', is expected to contribute to a 'broader process of external legitimization for localized sectarian politics and geographies' (McDowell, 2008: 418). However, the transformation and commodifiaction of conflict heritage and landscape for tourist consumption encompasses serious political, social and economic ramifications (see Case study 5.3).

Strange and Kempa (2003) observe the marketing and interpretation of Alcatraz and Robben Island as a dark tourism attraction. These sites were formerly prisons that were subsequently converted into museums and heritage sites. Critical focus is placed on examining the ways in which the history of a site has been used to educate and inform visitors. They state that tourism has played a significant role in providing the financial security for heritage sites that could otherwise have been unstable. Although the tourism development may jeopardise the authenticity of these sites, the economic pressures have led to commercialising the representations of the heritage sites, thereby gaining appeal in the mass market. It is also maintained that the state is responsible for the ways in which these sites are presented and represented, along with the information provided to visitors. In this regard, certain parts of history or history of some groups can be under-interpreted or over-interpreted, as previously explicated. Lennon and Foley (1999) analyse how the involvement of the US government has affected the nature of the education offered to visitors. Governmental involvement in dark heritage sites has led to negatively influencing the integrity of the site, mainly focusing on portraying the positive images of American values. This conveys a restriction on authenticity that is

Case study 5.3: Conflicting heritage in Northern Ireland

Coiste Belfast Political Tours

Belfast is the capital of Northern Ireland. It has been the centre of various sectarian conflicts between its Roman Catholic and Protestant populations. The civil conflicts stretching over three decades (1969–98), widely known as the Troubles, badly affected Belfast. The opposing groups in this conflict are now often termed republican (Roman Catholic) and loyalist (Protestant) respectively. They are also widely referred to as 'nationalist' and 'unionist'. Belfast now sees an increasing development of political tourism through which local conflicts can be understood and shared by tourists. The political-themed tours aim to provide tourists with experiences of the republican and loyalist viewpoints in the form of authentic tours delivered by former political prisoners who have first-hand experience of the civil conflict. The guides weave their own personal stories into the tour as they visit many different sites that explain both the local and wider history of Northern Ireland. For these guides this project is a living history. These guides are a primary source and an invaluable link into the most recent phase of struggle. Below are the guided tours offered:

• Falls Road Wall Mural Tour
• Milltown Cemetery Tour
• The Ballymurphy Story – from Guerilla War to Government
• United Irishmen Tour.

Source: www.coiste.ie.

Duchas Oral History Archive

In response to the experiences of the nationalist community of West Belfast, the Duchas Oral Archive project was established in 2000. It aims to document life in West Belfast during the Troubles, thereby enhancing the role of public history-making surrounding conflict. Since its inception, the project has created an oral history sound and personal photographic archive containing 100 interviews, which reflect a range of individual experiences. The interviews cover a wide range of experience from many different perspectives, including campaigners, combatants and activists. Each comment on their own experiences of the conflict provides interesting contextual background information about themselves and local events. Interviews can be read or listened to through an interactive computer database which can be searched by defined criteria or by keyword. Interviews can also be accessed through tape cassette or CD recordings. The collection is situated at The Falls Community Council Offices where it can be simultaneously read and listened to.

Sources: http://duchasoralhistoryarchivebelfast.blogspot.co.uk; http://www.rascal.ac.uk/index.php?CollectionID=205&navOp=locID&navVar=39.

controlled by politics. Similarly, Wight (2005) suggests that the government is mainly responsible for the inaccurate presentation of dark tourism sites, often leading to a loss of authenticity. Butler (2001) conducts a textual analysis of promotional materials from 102 plantation brochures to examine the extent to which slavery is actually depicted and narrated. It is revealed that slavery is hardly mentioned in comparison with other features of the plantations, including crops. The promotional materials that are used to advertise the plantations to tourists attempt to hide the real history of slavery. The owners of the plantations want to hide the way slaves were treated in the plantations so that their reputations would not be affected. It is also observed that tourists seek pleasurable experiences when on holiday and are not really keen on confronting the dark reality of the actual historical events. More rigorous empirical research looking into various motivations of dark heritage tourists would thus be desirable.

Despite controversies, many destinations are eager to develop and promote dark heritage tourism sites due to their economic benefits. However, using the reputation of the victims as a means of marketing these sites not only damages the highly sensitive nature of these sites but also conflicts with ethical and moral issues. Lennon and Foley (2000) note that commercialisation and promotion of death and atrocity as tourism products may raise a number of ethical issues. Similarly, developing heritage attractions connected with historical events that are sensitive to tourists can be highly contentious (Austin, 2002). In examining the nature of visitation at sensitive historical sites, focusing on the Cape Coast Castle in Ghana, Austin (2002) observes that tourists exhibit different emotional states in relation to the site. For heritage managers, marketing challenges thus lie in recognising the link between visitor emotional states and visitor satisfaction and incorporating the differing emotional states of prospective tourists in the interpretational and promotional activities and services. Use of new technologies is regarded as a strategic and effective management and marketing activity in enhancing tourist experiences. However, the overuse of entertainment factors in interpreting and promoting dark heritage sites may trivialise or distort their historical integrity (Hewison, 1987; Dewar, 1989; Boniface and Fowler, 1993). Marketing activities in sensitive sites need to prioritise the opportunities of learning as the primary and dominant motivation for visitation (Austin, 2002). As emphasised, heritage interpretation is often endowed with political messages. A selective use of the past for current purposes and its transformation through interpretation is a widely experienced phenomenon in heritage tourism (Garrod and Fyall, 2000). The interpretation and promotion of dark heritage can be a particularly sensitive and complex issue. But enhancing public awareness by employing relevant interpretational methods and strategies in sensitive heritage may contribute to the healing process of sensitive pasts through remembering.

Slavery heritage and tourism development

As 'one of the worst crimes perpetrated against humanity' (Dann and Seaton, 2001: 19), the slave trade is regarded as the 'African Holocaust' (Adi *et al.*, 2005). The loss and exploitation of over 12 million Africans led to ravaging and displacing local African communities and corrupting local culture and social structures (Bressey and Wareham, 2011). The dispersal of Africans by the Transatlantic Slavery Trade (TST) has resulted in a large diaspora of African people scattered all over the world. African-Americans now comprise a significant proportion of roots tourism, hugely influenced by Alex Haley's popular novel, *Roots*, and a later adaptation for television in the late 1970s. For diasporic Africans these visits could be a sacred pilgrimage to the homeland, provoking emotional connections with their roots. This recent upsurge of interest in slavery heritage has been closely associated with place promotion and tourism development (Dann and Seaton, 2001; Austin, 2002; Catalani and Ackroyd, 2013). There is now a number of slavery heritage sites open to the public in Africa and the Caribbean: the village of Juffure (Home Coming Festival), Gambia; Goree Island, Senegal; Cape Coast Castle and Elmina Castle, Ghana; the former slave market in Stone Town, Zanzibar (see Figure 5.2); the Clifton National Heritage Park in the Bahamas; and the slave route heritage trail in Barbados.

In this section, the main focus is placed on briefly reviewing Britain's involvement in the TST and examining the ways in which Britain has recently attempted to confront this difficult heritage and incorporate it as part of national heritage. Britain's involvement in the TST has long been denied by the British state, as is often the case with former colonial governments. It is explicated that 'Britain's involvement in slavery has not been a subject for heritage development since it may have been seen to have more potentially socially and politically divisive results' (Seaton, 2001: 121).

Interpreting slavery heritage and the TST had virtually been non-existent until 1999 when a local British terrestrial television channel produced a serial documentary on British slavery heritage (Beech, 2001). Britain's role in the management and control of the trade during the era of slavery and the profits earned from the TST had never been emphasised in standard historical texts. However, the growing multicultural society of post-war Britain has become increasingly aware of their past and their ancestors' involvement in slavery and the TST. The teaching of slavery heritage has become part of the curriculum in British schools since 2000 (USI, 2011), thereby creating more public awareness of the

Figure 5.2 Church of Christ, the former slave market, Stone Town in Zanzibar (taken by Sarah Razzaq)

contribution and role of slavery in Britain's heritage. Cities like Liverpool and Bristol began to present slavery heritage as an essential part of their maritime heritage. However, it is argued that London has noticeably unrecognised its link with slavery heritage (Beech, 2001). It is the discords or contestations about slavery heritage that have been the bane of slavery heritage development in the UK. Lennon and Foley (2000: 34) insightfully suggest 'to retain only the positive aspects of one's past and to obliterate all trace of evil is to present a cultural and historical landscape that is, to say the least, incomplete'.

The British government commemorated in 2007 the bicentenary of the abolition of slavery, resulting in issues regarding British involvement in slavery and the TST coming to the fore. Just before the bicentenary of the abolition of slavery, English Heritage launched a research project aiming to reinvestigate the connections of Britain's stately homes to the slave trade. All of English Heritage's properties dating from between 1600 and 1840 were re-examined with the purpose of revealing the hidden and untold stories of their pasts. It is believed that a major proportion of stately homes, architectural representations of British aristocratic culture and heritage, were built on the profits of the TST and plantation wealth (Weaver, 2006). This new progressive approach led to representing and reinterpreting long-suppressed memories of the past. In 2007, the world's first International Slavery Museum opened in Liverpool, which once controlled 80 per cent of the British slave trade (Beech, 2001). As an inaugural exhibition of a new permanent gallery at the Docklands museum in London in 2007, the portraits of both slave merchant George Hibbert and slave abolitionist Robert Wedderburn, whose images were recreated by the contemporary artist Paul Howard, went on display together (Kennedy, 2007). Robert Wedderburn, a radical preacher and campaigner against the slave trade, was born to an enslaved mother and a plantation-owning father, James Wedderburn. As explicated above, the revelation and acceptance of slavery links to British heritage sites including stately homes have also become prevalent, with specific reference to launching various projects such as Re:interpretation by the National Trust and UNESCO's Slave Route Project. Kenwood House in Hampstead, London, has revealed its close link with slavery and its abolition movement. Kenwood House is the former home of Lord Mansfield, who won a series of legal victories for the abolitionist movement in the eighteenth century. Interestingly, Dido Elizabeth Belle (1761–1804), an illegitimate daughter of the nephew of Lord Mansfield and an enslaved African woman known as Belle, was brought up under the care of Lord Mansfield and his wife at Kenwood House. It can be assumed that Lord Mansfield's close relationship with Dido influenced him in supporting many important court cases concerning the freedom and lives of the enslaved people, including the Somerset case. The portrait of Dido with her cousin was finally put on public display at Kenwood House in 2007.

Harewood, located near Leeds in West Yorkshire, is another example of a stately home that commemorated the bicentenary of the abolition of the slave trade with a range of exhibitions, performances and displays as part of 'Harewood 1807'. By 1787, the Lascelles family had interests in 47 plantations and owned thousands of slaves in Barbados and across the West Indies. 'Harewood 1807' paved the way for Harewood to search for its roots, particularly where the money came from to build this stately home. In conjunction with the University of York, Harewood has strived to discover the exact nature of the Lascelles family's involvement with the sugar trade and the slave trade and to investigate the Yorkshire election in 1807 contested by William Wilberforce, Henry Lascelles and Lord Milton (Harewood, 2007). Along with concerted attempts to reveal the connections with the slave trade, increasing attention has also been placed on unravelling and critically analysing the motivations and experiences of the visitors in relevant heritage sites, as evidenced at the permanent exhibition London, Sugar & Slavery at the Museum of London Docklands in Case study 5.4.

Case study 5.4: London, Sugar & Slavery, the Museum of London Docklands, UK

London, Sugar & Slavery gallery at the Museum of London Docklands was established in 2003 to commemorate the bicentenary (abolished 1807, commemorated 2007) of Britain's involvement in slavery; and its role in the abolition of the TST which lasted for about 400 years. The museum is located on the Isle of Dogs which is where the West India Dock trading company of 1802 was originally built. At that time, it housed enormous warehouses that stored up to 80,000 hogsheads of sugar and 20,000 'puncheons' or small caskets of rum (Bressey & Wareham, 2011) that were brought back from America and the Caribbean.

Responses by specific groups

- Specific responses from those of African descent tended to be positive in that they were pleased the museum was giving 'space' to the subject rather than hiding it, although some did express bitterness and sadness for both what happened to their ancestors and the legacy of racism that the slave trade has left behind.
- Conversely, there were many responses from white Britons expressing guilt, regret and sadness at both their ancestors' role in the slave trade and how again the legacy pervaded in terms of lingering racism.
- Although a small number, US visitors were also engaged as the issue of slavery and its aftermath is so critical to US social history.
- It was appreciated that the exhibition tackles the issue of the legacy of slavery in attitudes in modern Britain, the continuing difficulties faced by those of African descent and the gains that Britain and London made as a result of the trade.

Critical feedback

- The criticisms of the exhibition focused on a perceived lack of coverage of the role of Africans in running the slave trade, the enslavement of white Europeans and a sense that the story has in some way been sanitised to tell it from one perspective only.
- Other critical feedback suggested more content on African history in general, the role of the abolitionists and more context on the conditions and treatment of the poor in general at the time.

Some believed the museum was breaking new ground in covering a history not often made public: 'Finally, a museum exhibition in London that deals with British colonialism! Fantastic balance in displaying historical artefacts and dealing with the legacy of slavery in twenty-first-century Britain' (general visitor).

Learning from past mistakes was another theme that was often raised, so that the horrors of the past would not be repeated: 'Thank you for this exhibition. The only way we can learn from and not repeat our mistakes is by talking about them, however uncomfortable it may be. Thank you for making this so accessible by keeping the price low!' (general visitor).

Source: Museum of London Docklands (2012).

It is now important to openly embrace the slavery heritage, albeit undesirable and painful, thereby reconfiguring and repositioning its significance in contemporary multicultural Britain. The complicated cultural and historical dynamics of Britain need thus to be acknowledged and integrated in relevant heritage attractions by way of utilising them as informative educational sources, which can also be practised in slavery heritage attractions worldwide. However, careful consideration needs to be made in order not to overly exploit the slavery heritage for economic purposes such as place branding and promotion in tourism. Tourism development can only be meaningful when its main purpose is seen as providing people with new opportunities to reinterpret and reappreciate the complexities and subtleties of sensitive pasts.

Conclusion

The dissonant and contested nature of heritage is implicated in the way the past is shaped, managed and promoted for present uses and purposes, including tourism development. Heritage tourism is undeniably influenced by power structures and relations, marked by whose (and which) heritage is preserved, discarded and represented for touristic consumption. As emphasised, heritage tourism is often employed as a strategic political tool to legitimise certain socio-political and ideological frameworks (see Tunbridge and Ashworth, 1996; Poria and Ashworth, 2009). In this light, the past can be purposefully selected and transformed to meet the political agendas and ideological frameworks of a nation, thereby supporting and reinforcing an official version of national history and heritage. This selective use of the past is strongly implicated in facilitating collective remembering and forgetting. Difficult and undesirable pasts including slavery heritage are often suppressed or discarded in the official interpretations and representations of national heritage. It is also evident in many cases that local indigenous history and heritage have been rather unrecognised or under-represented in the mainstream heritage discourses and displays. However, critical focus is increasingly placed on the differing perceptions, varying interpretations and multiple perspectives of heritage. Furthermore, dark heritage sites representing the conflicting discourses of heritage have been actively utilised and promoted as popular tourism attractions. The media plays a significant role in increasing the visitation of dark heritage sites, often turning heritage sites into a marketable and promotable commodity. Despite the potential economic benefits, it should be noted that promoting dissonant and sensitive pasts can be a complicated and difficult issue. Heritage tourism developers and marketers need to be sensitive in what they select to develop as tourism resources. Tourists also need to be aware that what they consume and experience is not necessarily an accurate portrayal of the past and the people concerned.

Research questions

1   Explain the ways in which heritage is closely related to politics.
2   What does 'dissonant heritage' mean? Try to illustrate three examples of 'dissonant heritage'.
3   Why is it important to incorporate the varying perceptions and different perspectives in the official and hegemonic discourses of heritage?
4   Why are tourists drawn towards sites or experiences associated with death and suffering?

5   Examine and critically assess the role of the media in dark heritage tourism development.
6   What ethical issues surround the exploitation of tragic history?
7   What would be the justification of commodifying dark heritage, particularly 'heritage that hurts'?
8   What role does ethics and morality play in (re)presenting and interpreting slavery heritage development in tourism contexts?

Learning material

Ashworth, G.J., Graham, B. and Tunbridge, E. (2007) *Pluralising Pasts: Heritage, Identity and Place in Multicultural Societies*, London: Pluto Press.

Austin, N.K. (2002) Managing heritage attractions: marketing challenges at sensitive historical sites, *International Journal of Tourism Research*, 4(6): 447–57.

Basu, P. (2008) Confronting the past? Negotiating a heritage of conflict in Sierra Leone, *Journal of Material Culture*, 13(2): 233–47.

Buzinde, C.N. and Santos, C.A. (2008) Representations of slavery, *Annals of Tourism Research*, 35(2): 469–88.

Catalani, A. and Ackroyd, T. (2013, in press) Inheriting slavery: making sense of a difficult heritage, *Journal of Heritage Tourism*.

Foley, M. and Lennon, J. (1997) Dark tourism: an ethical dilemma, in M. Foley, J. Lennon and G. Maxwell (eds) *Strategic Issues for the Hospitality, Tourism and Leisure Industries*, London: Cassell, pp. 153–64.

Golden, J. (2004) Targeting heritage: the abuse of symbolic sites in modern conflicts, in Y. Rowan and U. Baram (eds) *Marketing Heritage: Archaeology and the Consumption of the Past*, California: Altamira Press, pp. 183–202.

Graham, B., Ashworth, G.J. and Tunbridge, J.E. (2000) *A Geography of Heritage: Power, Culture and Economy*, London: Arnold (Chapters 2 and Chapter 3).

Hall, S. (2005) Whose heritage? Un-settling 'the heritage', re-imagining the post-nation, in J. Littler and R. Naidoo (eds) *The Politics of Heritage: The Legacies of 'Race'*, London: Routledge, pp. 23–35.

Henderson, J.C. (2007) Communism, heritage and tourism in East Asia, *International Journal of Heritage Studies*, 13(3): 240–54.

Lennon, J.J. and Foley, M. (2000) *Dark Tourism: The Attraction of Death and Disaster*, New York: Continuum.

Light, D. (2000) An unwanted past: contemporary tourism and the heritage of communism in Romania, *International Journal of Heritage Studies*, 6(2): 145–60.

Light, D. (2007) Dracula tourism in Romania: cultural identity and the state, *Annals of Tourism Research*, 34(3): 746–65.

Macdonald, S. (2006) Undesirable heritage: fascist material culture and historical consciousness in Nuremberg, *International Journal of Heritage Studies*, 12(1): 9–28.

McDowell, S. (2008) Selling conflict heritage through tourism in peacetime Northern Ireland: transforming conflict or exacerbating difference? *International Journal of Heritage Studies*, 14(5): 405–21.

Meskell, L. (2002) Negative heritage and past mastering in Archaeology, *Anthropological Quarterly*, 75(3): 557–74.

Poria, Y. and Ashworth, G. (2009) Heritage tourism: current resource for conflict, *Annals of Tourism Research*, 36(3): 522–5.

Rivera, L.A. (2008) Managing 'spoiled' national identity: war, tourism, and memory in Croatia, *American Sociological Review*, 73(4): 613–34.

Sarmento, J. (2010) Fort Jesus: guiding the past and contesting the present in Kenya, *Tourism Geographies*, 12(2): 246–63.

Strange, C. and Kempa, M. (2003) Shades of dark tourism: Alcatraz and Robben Island, *Annals of Tourism Research*, 30(2): 386–405.

Tunbridge, J.E. and Ashworth, G.J. (1996) *Dissonant Heritage: The Management of the Past as a Resource in Conflict*, Chichester: Wiley (Chapters 1, 2 and 3).

Waterton, E. (2009) Sights of sites: picturing heritage, power and exclusion, *Journal of Heritage Tourism*, 4(1): 37–56.

Weiss, L.M. (2007) Heritage-making and political identity, *Journal of Social Archaeology*, 7(3): 413–31.

Weblinks

Preah Vihear Temple, Cambodia
http://www.youtube.com/watch?v=7lQiAwE9ylA

What is the plan for Hampi (India)?
http://www.youtube.com/watch?v=N9docvUG0mM

Iraq war 10 years on: the museum's story
http://www.guardian.co.uk/world/video/2013/mar/19/iraq-10-years-museum-video

Syria's cultural heritage under attack during bloody civil war
http://www.foxnews.com/world/2013/03/29/syria-cultural-heritage-at-risk-amid-bloody-two-year-battle

The destruction of ancient Aleppo, Syria
http://watch.thirteen.org/video/2364994111

What compels us to visit sites of mass death?
http://news.bbc.co.uk/1/hi/programmes/fast_track/9724775.stm

Titanic in Nova Scotia
http://titanic.gov.ns.ca

History: Titanic centenary 1912–2012
http://pinterest.com/jenniferlstone/history-titanic-centenary-1912-2012

Titanic 2
http://www.bbc.co.uk/news/uk-21597371

Holocaust Memorial Day
http://www.guardian.co.uk/world/video/2013/jan/27/holocaust-memorial-day-commemorated-across-world-video

Interactive Map of the Falls Road (Coiste political tours)
www.coiste.ie/map

Image and video gallery (Coiste political tours)
http://www.coiste.ie/gallery

Re:interpretation (the project examining the connections between the TST and National Trust properties)
www.reinterpretation.co.uk

Remembering slavery: evaluation report
http://www.twmuseums.org.uk/slavery/_files/research-zone/REMEMBERING
SLAVERYEVALUATIONREPORT.pdf

International Slavery Museum, Liverpool
http://www.liverpoolmuseums.org.uk/ism/index.aspx

BBC history: Abolition
www.bbc.co.uk/history/british/abolition

6 Heritage tourism, nation and identity

Heritage, memory and identity formation

Material culture in a given society is viewed as a visual expression of identity (Hitchcock, 1996). The use of material culture is thus understood as one of the most obvious manifestations of identity communication. As an essential element of material culture, heritage serves as a symbolic medium through which identity is created, recreated and maintained. Heritage is deeply associated with constructing and legitimising collective constructs of identity, ranging from class, gender, ethnicity to nationalism (Graham et al., 2000). Macdonald (2006: 11) identifies heritage as a 'material testimony of identity', which is primarily interpreted as a 'discourse and set of practices concerned with the continuity, persistence and substantiality of collective identity'. However, Park (2011) places an emphasis on immaterial elements of heritage as an active agent in the process of identity communication. The meanings, values and emotions, embodied as immaterial elements of heritage, are essential in the intricate dynamics of heritage and identity. Heritage is not just a tangible asset of the past represented as artefacts and sites, as elaborated in Chapter 1, but an intangible phenomenon manifesting diverse symbolic meanings and national embodiments. Therefore, heritage can be better understood as both a material and symbolic testimony of identity. Here, heritage serves as a 'unifying sign' (Bessière, 1998), which helps to preserve and reconstruct the collective memory of a social group, thereby enhancing the group's social and cultural identities. Bessière (1998: 26) emphasises:

> Heritage, whether it be an object, monument, inherited skill or symbolic representation, must be considered as an identity marker and distinguishing feature of a social group. Heritage is often a subjective element because it is directly related to a collective social memory... social memory as a common legacy preserves the cultural and social identity of a given community, through more or less ritualized circumstances.

Heritage tourism could play a pivotal role in providing certain 'ritualised circumstances' through which shared social memory can be collectively reminded and effectively communicated within specific heritage settings. Heritage tourism experiences encourage nationals to realise the essential elements of their own unique culture and history, thereby symbolically constructing and reconstructing cultural and national identities (Palmer, 1999). Heritage tourism is inextricably bound up with experiencing both physical and psychological remnants of the nation's past. Heritage tourism experiences can thus greatly contribute to the processes of identity formation, maintenance and communication, particularly within the context of domestic tourism. According to Park (2010b: 29): 'The popularity of heritage tourism, particularly within domestic settings, relates to the fact that its images and symbols encountered and experienced during visits reveal a past that is "ours", which appears to be both socially familiar and communally enduring.'

Recollecting, materialising and commemorating shared memory is essential in the construction and reconstruction of national identity. Shared memories of the past are essential in maintaining and fortifying a sense of national belonging and solidarity (Bell, 2003). Nation is continuously revived, reimagined and reconstituted through shared memories among its nationals. It is maintained that:

> This memory acts as a powerful cohesive force, binding the disparate members of a nation together… Such binding memories can be passed from generation to generation, transmigrating across multiple historical contexts. They can (allegedly) be invented, acquired, and embellished, although more often than not they assume a lifeforce of their own, escaping the clutches of any individual or group and becoming embedded in the very fabric, material and psychological, of the nation.
>
> (Bell, 2003: 70)

The existence of shared collective memory as representing a nation's unique legacy, whether glorious or disgraceful, is thus crucial in encouraging nationals to experience a heightened sense of national belonging. Shared collective memory of a nation is partly based on individually selected recollections of past events and reminiscences and serves as a substantive base for the construction of cultural and national identities. According to Park (2010b: 66):

> Collective memory is not just an accumulation of mainstream public opinion and major past events. It entails a sense of nostalgia concerning those opinions and events, a shared psychological empathy constantly reproduced and communicated throughout generations. However, it is also important to note that collective memory comprises of differing meanings and varying interpretations that people bestow in present contexts. It is a dynamic concept reflecting present needs, circumstances and changes.

Memories induce different interpretations and represent various interpretive contexts. Graham et al. (2000) argue that the distinction and variation between official and unofficial renditions of memory become a recurring theme in framing and interpreting the past for contemporary uses. In a similar vein, Shackel (2003: 3) emphasises the roles of various individuals and institutions in influencing certain versions of the past that become part of the collective memory. This point is of crucial significance in recognising the individual and different uses of collective memory for the construction and maintenance of national identity.

In essentialist approaches, heritage and identity are perceived as a given form and structure based on the physical remains of the past. However, historical and social discourses of identity represented in heritage contexts, as with memory, need to be carefully handled, particularly since representations of the past are open to falsification or exaggeration via the construction of partial truths (Read, 1999). Hall (1993: 362) views identity as an 'open, complex, unfinished game – always under construction'. Identity is neither fixed nor static, open to constant modifications, reappropriations and reinterpretations. Particularly in an age of rapid global changes, identity has increasingly become mobile, hybrid and flexible. As Hall (1996: 212–13) further claims:

> Cultural identities come from somewhere, have histories. But, like everything which is historical, they undergo constant transformation. Far from being eternally fixed in some essentialised past, they are subject to the continuous 'play' of history, culture, and power. Far from being grounded in a mere 'recovery' of

the past, which is waiting to be found… identities are the names we give to the different ways we are positioned by, and position ourselves within, the narratives of the past.

It is thus important to understand that national identities are reconstructive and reflexive representations, which change with varying contexts and situations. The notion of national identity is inextricably multifaceted, complex and plural (Hall, 1992). The situational approach places an emphasis on the significance of differing contexts and varied situations in identifying ethnicity and identity, thereby challenging the existing concept of culture as a fixed and unchanging entity. Critical focus has been placed on discursively examining how people's ethnic identities are articulated within a range of social contexts and situations, and how people's self and collective identities serve to represent cultural differences and similarities with other individuals, groups and societies (see Barth, 1969; Eriksen, 1991). Given that heritage institutions and settings are operated by and composed of a range of social actors, they have a crucial role in projecting notions of ethnicity and identity. As Barth (1969) considers how such social organisations as kinship and community networks enable people to express the 'cultural features' of their ethnic unit (1969: 14), heritage institutions may be another important (contemporary) illustration of how cultural features of one's ethnicity are socially communicated through (inter)personal encounters and (inter)subjective relationships. As with collective memory, the systematic analysis of national identity and its core attributes thus need to clearly reflect fast-changing norms and values of contemporary society and culture.

National heritage, national identity and tourism development

The past is an indispensable element of defining and understanding nations. Nation is a political entity that also produces meanings, 'a system of cultural representation' in which the idea of nation is represented (Hall, 1992: 292). This system of cultural representation shapes and maintains a nation's own distinctive identity. As an essential part of cultural representation, national heritage is perceived as manifesting the fundamental attributes of people's ethnicities and identities. It becomes a primary instrument in forging, maintaining and strengthening nationalism and national identity. Newly established nation-states, for example in Europe in the nineteenth century, were in a desperate need of strengthening national cohesion and solidarity. Establishing national heritage was thus quintessential for newly established nation-states in that

> [i]t supported the consolidation of this national identification, while absorbing or neutralizing potentially competing heritages of social-cultural groups or regions. Again, a national heritage helped combat the claims of other nations upon the nation's territory or people, while furthering claims upon nationals in territories elsewhere.
>
> (Graham *et al*., 2000: 12)

As a fundamental element of cultural distinction and national representation, heritage is bestowed with the potential to perpetually remind nationals of the foundations upon which the idea of a nation and 'felt history' (Connor, 1993: 382) is reminded and productively communicated. Nora (1989) stresses the significance of 'milieu de mémoire', sites of memory, in an endeavour to retain and enhance the vitality and continuity of memory. National heritage acts as 'milieu de mémoire' in which 'memory crystallizes and secretes itself' (Nora, 1989: 7). In this sense, national heritage acts as a symbolic medium through which a nation's shared memory can be commemorated and communicated throughout generations. But maintaining and promoting national heritage in tourism contexts often involves value-added representations and interpretations. National heritage representations for touristic consumption are often invented, manipulated and strategically promoted.

Invented traditions and imaginary national narratives are essential, as discussed in Chapter 1, in constructing and reconstructing national heritage and identity. Hobsbawm (1983: 1) refers invented tradition to 'a set of practices, normally governed by overtly or tacitly accepted rules and of a ritual or symbolic nature, which seek to inculcate certain values and norms of behaviour by repetition, which automatically implies continuity with the past'. The modern 'nation' comprises of various artificial constructs and 'invented traditions', which include 'fairly recent symbols or suitably tailored discourses (such as "national" history)' (Hobsbawm, 1983: 14). The adaptation of old traditions to fit into new situations and the deliberate invention of new traditions for novel purposes facilitates the process of 'social engineering' in a modern nation through which group cohesion is facilitated and the consequences of rapid socio-cultural change are controlled. Furthermore, invented traditions encourage people to believe that contemporary customs are deeply rooted in an unchangeable and stable past (Tomlinson, 1991). Hobsbawm (1983: 9) outlines three main modes of social inclusion and control: (1) creation of such institutions as festivals, sports and unions; (2) invention of such new systems and modes of socialisation as hierarchical educational systems and royal ceremonies; and (3) formation of such 'communities' as nations, clans and associations that establish or symbolise 'social cohesion or the membership of groups, real or artificial communities'. Invented traditions can thus be perceived as a lucid manifestation for reinterpreting and reappropriating deep-seated cultural traditions and values of a nation in modern contexts (see Case study 6.1). Despite its contribution to enriching the modernistic accounts of nation and nationalism, the notion of 'invented traditions' is not exempt from criticism. Smith (1991b: 357) contends that 'invented traditions' are more akin to 'rediscovery' or 'reconstruction' of certain elements of ethnic pasts, affirming the socio-cultural continuity of a nation throughout history. In a similar vein, Edensor (2002) criticises an overemphasis on the novelty of national cultures without fully taking account of earlier cultural continuities in the practices of 'invented traditions'.

National heritage settings are generally perceived as symbolising 'national badges of high culture' (Edensor, 2002: 15) representing an authoritative and official version of history. National heritage including national museums, monuments and royal palaces thus portrays and disseminates the essence of high culture and national hegemony. In exploring interrelationships between nationalism and tourism, Pretes (2003) examines three tourist sites in the American state of South Dakota: Mount Rushmore National Memorial, Wall Drug Store and Rapid City Dinosaur Park. It is argued that visiting these places helps to 'create' and 'strengthen' national identity through identifying and recognising hegemonic-based discourses of the nation. Mount Rushmore signifies the USA's presidential power and elements of nationhood, as well as such national values as independence, freedom and liberation by way of presenting the images of four 'great American presidents'. However, the range and scope of these 'sacred centres', which stand as a nation's unique 'moral geography' (Smith, 1991a: 16), should not necessarily be restricted to the presentation of heritage settings driven or imposed by an official ideology of high culture. Furthermore, it should be pinpointed that an excessive focus on disseminating the state-led official discourses embodying nationalistic elements could neglect attention to the crucial significance of individual narratives and unofficial discourses, which are also

Case study 6.1: The making of Scotland: Tartanry and Scottish heritage

Tartan was 'made' for the modern world in the relatively short time between the late eighteenth and mid-nineteenth century. During this period, a sequence of events occurred that gave tartan its modern meanings. In the first place, the Proscription Act, which had forbidden the wearing of 'highland garb' after the defeat of the Jacobites in 1746 at Culloden, was repealed in 1782 under political pressure from a group of rich and influential 'chieftains' living in London who were becoming conscious of the interest in the Gael, as were Scotland's elite generally. This interest had been generated by the Romantic movement, the search for a suitable 'noble savage', primitive people closer to nature, without the encumbrance of modern living and manners. The kilt and tartan came to signify the mystery of primitive society and consequently what had been lost since 1746 or had never been known was simply invented. By the 1820s, the commercial production of tartan was in full swing under the auspices of William Wilson of Bannockburn, who developed a list of tartans in a fairly opportunistic way by reclassifying designs to fit clan names. There was little evidence of systematic association between family names/clans and specific designs as appear in the sales catalogues of tartan manufacturers of today. After 1746, the only possible public use of tartan was as army colours, and both kilt and tartan were appropriated by the British state to kit out its erstwhile enemies while in its military employ. New muted tones of tartan were invented to make it more seemly as a uniform, and its haphazard excesses were reduced through regimentation and standardization. This proved to be a master-stroke by the British state in literally stealing its enemy's clothes, and helped to incorporate tartanry into an elite rather than a rebel form of dress. By the late nineteenth century, the myth of tartan had been made. Using the term 'myth' might seem to imply a value judgement, as if the whole thing was a fraud, but myths provide guides to the interpretation of social reality and if we want to know what tartan means today, that is where we have to begin. On the one hand, it is a common dress for males at ceremonial occasions, like weddings and graduations. It also has its wilder manifestations. Football fans, for example, bedeck themselves in shades of tartan like the colours of the rainbow.

Source: an excerpt from McCrone *et al.* (1995).

Figure 6.1 Scottish tartans (taken by Brian Anderson)

essential in maintaining national sentiments. Winter (2004) brings attention to the ways in which domestic tourism at Angkor (Cambodia) contributes to ongoing formations of collective identity. He challenges the popular and normalised notion of heritage landscape as 'abstract, objective and value neutral' (2004: 330), where the notion of objective and official history is deemed to be deeply grounded in unbiased truths and dispassionate commentaries. Instead, emphasis is placed on the concept of memory as a fundamental agent in actively constituting and reconstituting times and places in multiple and varied ways in a given heritage landscape. Shared memory, evoked through personal and subjective experiences of the heritage setting thus plays a more significant role in the upkeep of cultural and national identities as opposed to such physical manifestations as buildings and objects of historical significance.

In examining the conceptual and symbolic interrelationship between heritage tourism and national identity in Changdeok Palace, Seoul, South Korea, Park (2010a) reveals that the communication of national memories and shared recollections during the heritage tourism experience does not necessarily mean there is a governing consensus on the nature of heritage interpretations and national identifications. Instead, it is argued that the heritage setting facilitates different and subaltern viewpoints concerning the relevance of national memories to individual's perceptions and experiences (see Case study 6.2).

Case study 6.2: Heritage tourism as emotional journeys into nationhood, Changdeok Palace, Seoul, South Korea

Changdeok Palace, interpreted as the 'Palace of Prospering Virtue', was originally built in 1405 under the reign of King Taejong. It was the eastern detached palace of Gyeongbok Palace, which was the main palace of the Joseon Dynasty. Changdeok Palace was designated a WHS in 1997 on the grounds of an outstanding example of 'Far Eastern palace architecture and garden design'.

Figure 6.2 Changdeok Palace, South Korea

This ethnographic study aims to examine the role of unofficial and informal mechanisms of national identity formation via heritage tourism experiences. It is revealed that the socio-psychological dimensions of heritage are of paramount importance in understanding how personal perceptions, individualised meanings and subjective sentiments concerning collective social memories contribute to the long-standing tourism appeal of heritage institutions. National consciousness is facilitated by the process of individually appropriating and reinterpreting national memories provoked within Changdeok Palace:

> People say that Changdeok is our precious heritage which conveys the nation's legacy. This is an indispensable fact but the ways in which people perceive it are different. We all have individual preferences and personal viewpoints on our nation's past (woman in her 30s).

Importantly, feelings of comfort and familiarity facilitated by personal memories are pertinent in fortifying people's emotional attachment to the nation. By engaging with their own personal memories, individuals may be more at ease in establishing an intimate sense of national belonging. Tourist narratives imply the importance of feelings of comfort and familiarity as integral to the Changdeok experience: 'It makes my stomach churn to feel I am naturally connected with this place. I am part of it and it is part of me' (man in his late 40s).

Tourists tend to initiate the process of conceptualising an essence of national belonging through oral narratives focusing on personal memories and subjective experiences. Here, personal memories should not necessarily be perceived as self-indulgent recollections of lived experiences as they are instrumental in serving the purpose of imagining the nation's past and shaping it into a coherent and meaningful entity, which lies at the core of a collective sense of national belonging. Their function in familiarising the nation's past is profound in making the abstract and conceptual elements of national belonging more concrete and directly related to people's life experiences. Importantly, individual and subjective perceptions of heritage are closely related to experiential ways of articulating and enacting national consciousness.

Source: an excerpt from Park (2010a).

Smith (1991a) claims that national identity entails dual functions: 'external' and 'internal'. External functions of national identity are mainly associated with the territorial, economic and political components of a nation. On the contrary, the internal functions of national identity are closely related to intangible and subjective accounts of the nation, which mainly focus on psychological bonds and collective memories of the past. The internal functions are of pivotal significance in enhancing and strengthening a sense of national belonging through the provision of shared values, symbols and traditions, thereby relocating our 'individual selves' at a time of intense, socio-cultural change (Smith, 1991a: 16). National heritage as a main signifier of shared values, symbols and traditions plays a significant role in facilitating and enhancing the internal functions of national identity. The relationship between national heritage and national identity is thus closely interrelated and intercontextualised. Heritage presentations and representations are systematically developed and promoted in order to enhance a distinctive culture and exalt a sense of national belonging (Pitchford, 1995; McLean, 1998; Henderson, 2001). The craving for heritage in relation to exalting a sense of history, real or fabricated, is regarded as a conspicuous effort to solidify a sense of belonging to a nation at a time of significant cultural and social change. National heritage is expected to be 'appealing in one covertly projective way or another to the historical and sacrosanct identity of the nation' (Wright, 1985: 2). In this light, heritage has a symbolic as well as a physical function. As emphasised, the relationship between heritage and national identity has been more complicated by the expansion of the heritage industry and heritage tourism development (Light and Dumbraveanu-Andone, 1997; McIntosh and Prentice, 1999; Kohl, 2004). Tourism and nationalist policies are often complementary in the way they promote a sense of historical past and revive cultural heritage (Leong, 1997), particularly in contexts where tourism is strategically deployed as an effective tool in supporting the officially sanctioned past and heritage. Red tourism development in China clearly illustrates this close interrelationship between the officially sanctioned past and tourism development (see Case study 6.3).

The discursive and interrelated relationship between heritage and identity seems only to be reflected and emphasised in heritage sites with no commercial orientations. There exists a consensus that commercially oriented heritage sites or attractions do not fully fulfill their role in supporting identity formation and maintenance. Their main focus on economic viability and commercial orientations is believed to counteract the identity formation and maintenance of heritage. Nonetheless, it should be noted that a heritage industry with commercial orientations can play an essential and unique role in maintaining and reinforcing notions of national identity (Johnson, 1999). In a similar vein, McIntosh and Prentice (1999: 590) claim that

> [a]t a deeper level, commodification of pastness can be interpreted as marking needs for identity, and the finding of the true self through the appropriation of pastness... Identities are thereby created through amassing insights into what is associated with the emergence of a culture, and appropriating these insights is pertinent to the consumer's own understanding of his or her place in time and space.

Insight is gained from the ways in which the creation and reaffirmation of identity is encouraged through visitation of places with associations of pastness. The findings emphasise that heritage appreciation is enhanced for the personal, familiar or affective responses generated during visits to heritage sites, whether contrived or real. This perspective is closely associated with the discussions of existential authenticity in Chapter 4. Heritage becomes constantly reconstructed and reinterpreted, as discussed in Chapter 1, in an attempt to meet the specific demands of tourists and reflect the socio-cultural changes of the contemporary world. Heritage constantly changes in relation to space and time. Appropriately, Ashworth and Tunbridge (1996: 105) emphasise contemporary usages of the past:

> The interpretation of the past in history, the surviving relict buildings and artifacts and collective and individual memories are all harnessed in response

Case study 6.3: Red tourism in China

Since 2004, the Chinese government has promoted 'red tourism' in an attempt to reinvigorate the national ethos of domestic tourists and the economies of mostly deprived and less-developed areas such as Shaanxi in Yan'an, Shaoshan, Mao Zedong's Hunan hometown and Xibaipo in Hebei, another communist base. The strategic development of red tourism was understood as an effective means to bring vitality to cultural traditions and political ideologies that are believed to rapidly disappear at a time of fast economic and socio-cultural changes in contemporary China. The political heritage of the Chinese Communist Party (CCP) ranging from past revolutionary events and monuments to birthplaces and residences of former communist leaders was actively utilised and promoted as the main appeal of red tourism. The main gist of communist ideological values including collectivism and revolutionary spirit is explicitly promoted in this state-driven and officially sanctioned heritage tourism development. Tourists flocking to the sites relating to the communist past are, however, not just the Communist Party members. Red tourism experiences also appeal to younger generations who have never experienced the country's turbulent political history. Red tourism is an interesting example of active, nation-state involvement in provoking collective nostalgia, thereby reviving the nation's communist heritage for touristic consumption.

The most popular red tourism destinations are as follows:

- Yan'an: the birthplace of the revolution, which was used as Chairman Mao's wartime base. Mao Tse-tung's Red Army (the Communist Party) came here in 1935 and planned its takeover of China. On-site performances include the re-enactment of the communist victory over the Nationalist Party in China's civil war. The admission charge is 150 yuan (approximately £14.50).
- Shaoshan: the birthplace of Mao Tse-tung in Hunan province, which includes Mao's old renovated home, a memorial museum and a dedicated park. Local restaurants even serve the chairman's favourite dish, red-braised fatty pork.
- Jinggang Mountain: the place where Mao Tse-tung and his comrades founded the Red Army in 1927. Today, the mountain has more than 100 revolutionary attractions, including on-site performances.
- Dalian: the former residence and memorial of Guan Xiangying in Jinzhou district and war remains and some military buildings from the former Soviet Union in Lvshun district.

Interestingly, the scope and range of red culture have constantly evolved and expanded beyond the remit of the country's communist past, further incorporating industrial and technological development of modern China.

Sources: Branigan (2009); www.telegraph.co.uk/news/worldnews/asia/china/8489488/Chinas-Top-Five-Red-Tourism-destinations.html#.

to current needs which include the identification of individuals with social, ethnic and territorial entities and the provision of economic resources for commodification within heritage industries.

Appadurai (1990: 9) argues that the past cannot merely be engaged in representing a 'golden glow of nostalgia ruled by the politics of the good old days', but should actually symbolise a 'synchronic warehouse of cultural scenarios' that serve to develop and facilitate various ways of reaffirming and reinterpreting connections with the past in ever-changing cultural and social contexts. But there still remains a critical need for national heritage, despite increasing focus on its creative and economic potential, to serve its intrinsic purpose in maintaining and enhancing national solidarity.

Heritage tourism and banal nationalism

There has been a surge of interest in developing a critical understanding of nationalism with respect to its modes and patterns of reproduction inherent in ordinary and normal circumstances (Billig, 1995; Edensor, 2002; Jones and Merriman, 2009). It is argued that an idea of nation is constantly re-enacted and re-embodied as a 'vernacular and informal sense of history' in everyday contexts (Wright, 1985: 5). As a main contributor in systematically analysing the mundane elements of nationalism, thus advocating the concept of 'banal nationalism', Billig (1995) elaborates the ways in which nationalism is constantly reproduced on a daily basis, mainly within the context of the 'West'. Billig (1995: 8) criticises existing analyses of nationalism and national identity for comprehending the manifestations of nationalism and national identity in 'passionate and exotic exemplars'. He points out that academic enquiries generally disregard the routine and mundane reproduction of nationalism and national identity. The concept of 'flagging the homeland daily' (Billig, 1995: 93) is thus inextricably bound up with ways in which nationhood is constantly reminded and reproduced in everyday life. It is claimed:

> The latency of nationalistic consciousness does not depend on the vagaries of individual memory... Nor does national identity disappear into individuals' heads in between salient situations... The 'salient situation' does not suddenly occur, as if out of nothing, for it is a part of a wider rhythm of banal life in the world of nations. What this means is that national identity is more than an inner psychological state, or an individual self-determination: it is a form of life, which is daily lived in a world of 'nation-states'.
>
> (Billig, 1995: 69)

His advocacy of 'banal nationalism' challenges the widely held assumption that nationalism is a hot and political ideology mainly inherent in 'salient situations' such as wars or national events. Particular focus is placed on unravelling the unconscious, nuanced and rather implicit manifestations of nationalism embedded in daily life. In everyday contexts, most people maintain a notion of the nation and familiarise its existence in more mundane and routined ways. Similarly, Brubaker (1996: 10) reconceptualises nationalism as a 'heterogeneous set of "nation"-oriented idioms, practices, and possibilities that are continuously available or "endemic" in modern cultural and political life' rather than a 'force to be measured as resurgent or receding'. Edensor (2002: 17) concurs with Billig's notion of banal nationalism, claiming that 'national identity is grounded in the everyday, in the mundane details of social interaction, habits, routines and practical knowledge' rather than the 'spectacular, the traditional and the official'. For example, the influence of the media (e.g., newspapers and television programmes) is of profound significance as an effective tool to disseminate nationalist ideologies and sentiments in everyday contexts (Edensor, 2002).

The issues of national identity, heritage and shared memory have become at the forefront of contemporary societies where a strong sense of local nationalism has been revived and re-emphasised in the midst of neoliberal globalisation, which will be discussed in greater detail in Chapter 7. According to Hall (1993: 353–4, original emphasis):

> this latest phase of capitalist globalization, with its brutal compressions and reordering across time and space, has not necessarily resulted in the destruction of those specific structures and particularistic attachments and identifications which go with the more localized communities which a homogenizing modernity was supposed to replace... Paradoxically, globalization seems also to have led to a strengthening of 'local' allegiances and identities *within* nation-states; though this may be deceptive, since the strengthening of 'the local' is probably less the revival of the stable identities of 'locally settled communities' of the past, and more that tricky version of 'the local' which operates within, and has been thoroughly reshaped by 'the global' and operates largely within its logic.

The mundane nature of national identity is deeply embedded in everyday contexts of cultural formations which play a role in 'all these forgotten reminders' (Billig, 1995: 8), thus enabling people to be constantly aware of the social and cultural significance of their homelands amidst changing perceptions of national boundaries and global interdependence. Heritage settings, along with other mediums such as the print technology as advocated by Anderson (1983), can be one important distinctive cultural product that enables the essence of nationhood to be reproduced in everyday experiences, especially in contributing to the development of innate and latent manifestations of national awareness and belonging. In line with this observation, people's experience of heritage tourism could be considered as another important medium in enabling people to conceive, imagine and confirm their belonging to the community (Palmer, 1999). Visits to heritage settings in everyday contexts could encourage nationals to feel part of and connected to the nation's past in their national imagination. Heritage tourism experiences in domestic contexts can generally be conceived as a conspicuous effort to solidify a sense of national belonging at a time of rapid socio-cultural change. The identification of national belonging needs to be regarded as a dynamic process in which individuals are required to reproduce the contexts of existing material and symbolic resources in the changing circumstances of everyday life. Consequently, it is essential to recognise that the discursive construction of national identity in banal and mundane contexts, developed through individual constructions of shared national memory, is of particular relevance to analytical approaches concerning the study of national identity, nationalism and heritage construction.

Heritage tourism and the identity of the diaspora

Regardless of the ambivalent nature of using diaspora in tourism (see Hannam, 2004), research into diaspora and tourism has proliferated over the last decades. Diasporas are conceived as 'nations or ethnic groups living outside their traditional homelands but which are being bound together either literally or figuratively by spatial concentration, culture, religion, ethnicity or national identity' (Timothy, 2011: 407). Diasporas travel in search of their roots, making connections with their personal heritage. Research on tourism perceptions amongst diasporic communities draws critical attention to ways in which the nation can be imagined through cultural ties and social meanings, as well as being embodied in the homeland (tourism) experience (see Stephenson, 2002; Duval, 2003; Coles and Timothy, 2004). Safran (1991) suggests a 'myth of return' as being inherent to the cultural framework of diasporas, a paradigm within which displaced people, what Hollinshead (1998) terms as 'halfway populations' following Bhabha, retain their emotional ties and identification with the homeland in a longing for an eventual return there. Diasporas thus remain emotionally 'stuck' to their homeland even if they have become physically 'unstuck' from it (Falzon, 2004: 89). Homeland, as a place of symbolic significance, provides diasporans with a sense of identity, thereby strengthening their cultural connections and continuity. Therefore, visits to their homeland can play a pivotal role in forging and maintaining a sense of belonging and continuity in the memory and imagination of diasporic communities. According to Kelner (2010: 3):

> it [tourism] provides a means for diasporans to encounter their ethnic homelands, regardless of whether or not they have direct social and material ties there… nation-states commodified as diasporic 'homelands' have been made available for mass consumption by diaspora tourists who use them as sites of memory and imagination, spaces to reflect on the perennial questions of diasporic existence and the individual's relationship to place.

Park (2010a) argues that the overall experience of heritage settings enables diasporas to feel connected to a country representing their ancestral roots. Here, the socio-psychological dimension of heritage acts as a powerful agent for perpetuating emotional association and cultural affinity with their homeland. Heritage tourism experiences encourage diaspora tourists to experience primordial attributes of a nation's culture and history, which leads to strengthening their cultural and ethnic ties to their ancestral homeland. Increasing interest and desire in experiencing tourists' own personal and familial past is clearly reflected in the widespread and ongoing popularity of this travelling pattern of diasporas, also referred to as roots tourism, genealogy tourism and personal heritage tourism. The development and promotion of diaspora tourism make substantial contribution to enhancing the destination branding and marketing. The main appeal of diaspora tourism is the local heritage and tradition of homeland, which act as a symbolic medium through which a sense of belonging and cohesion can be encountered and communicated. The connection between the local and the global is important in developing diasporic heritage practices. For diasporans, heritage serves as a 'powerful language of place and community around which individuals and groups can mobilize a series of technologies for producing "the local" at a global level' (Harrison, 2010: 245).

There are some popular destinations for diaspora tourism: Scotland, Ireland, Israel, Ghana and China to name a few. Scotland's Homecoming 2009 is a good example of promoting the destination utilising the benefits of diaspora tourism. In Scotland, 2009 was promoted as the year of homecoming and subsequently a number of events including a clan gathering were organised. The main aim of promotion was to attract Scots from around the world, while increasing local tourism both directly, by attracting an influx of foreigners (with an average ten-day stay per participant), and indirectly, by educating Scots to be 'better ambassadors' of a cosmopolitan, modern Scotland, one that has gone beyond kilts, swords and smokestacks (Newland and Taylor, 2010). The popular 'I Am a Scot' campaign videotaped those with Scottish roots saying what made them a Scot. Scotland is now organising the Year of

Homecoming Scotland 2014 with specific emphasis on celebrating Scottish food and drink. There will also be a number of exciting events commemorating the 700th anniversary of the Battle of Bannockburn during the Year of Homecoming 2014, including an exciting battle re-enactment event. The re-enactment will be the largest ever hosted at the memorial battlefield, featuring costumed characters throughout the site, weaponry displays, a medieval village and traditional food and drink (VisitScotland, 2013) (see also Case study 6.4).

Tourism can often be employed as a power to legitimise or authenticate ethnic identity and culture (Adams, 1997; Hitchcock, 1999; Xie, 2010). Utilising diasporic identity and culture as the main markers of ethnic tourism development in various destinations is another interesting theme in the lines of research enquiry on tourism and diaspora. Xie (2010) examines the relationship between tourism and the diaspora community – the Chinese Indonesians on Hainan Island, China – particularly focusing on the tensions between the tourism businesses and the community in terms of manipulating and commodifying diasporic resources. It is argued that tourism can help to 'fulfill the nostalgia of the homeland while connecting with the reality of the hostland' (Xie, 2010: 368). Here, the diasporic identity and culture of the Chinese-Indonesians are utilised and commercially exploited as the main markers of ethnic

Case study 6.4: Taglit-Birthright Israel

Launched in December 1999, 'Taglit-Birthright Israel' is a $0.5 billion joint initiative of individual philanthropists, the State of Israel and diaspora Jewish organisations. The programme provides free ten-day pilgrimage tours of Israel to college-age diaspora Jews, primarily from North America but with significant representation from Western Europe, the former Soviet Union, South America and Oceania. Since its inception, more than 300,000 participants have visited Israel. 'Taglit' means discovery in Hebrew and tours aim to encourage young diaspora Jews to discover Israel and its people, and their own personal connection to Jewish values and tradition, thereby feeling a part of the larger Jewish communities. Taglit-Birthright Israel does not itself operate tours but functions as an umbrella organisation financing, supporting and licensing the operation of trips. As an organised peer group educational programme, tours are run semi-annually in winter and summer sessions. Young Jewish adults aged 18–26 who have never been on a peer educational Israel experience can join the tours. Each pre-assigned group comprises of about 40 participants, accompanied by Israeli guides ('the *Mifgash*'), two or three counselors from the tourists' country of origin and eight Israeli soldiers or students in the mifgashim programme. Tours include travels, lectures, group discussions and informal activities which together reflect their educational goals. Tours are structured around three core themes: the narratives of the Jewish People, contemporary Israel and the ideas and values of the Jewish people. Fulfillment of the core theme – the narratives of the Jewish People – encompasses all five types of heritage sites: a Jewish heritage site, a Zionist heritage site, a national heritage site, a 'natural' heritage site and a Shoah heritage site. Utilising heritage and shared social memory of the Jewish people, Birthright Israel attempts to achieve a balance between emotional attachment and intellectual contextualisation in the maintenance of Jewish identities. Birthright Israel is thus regarded as an effective model for utilising tourism in fostering and enhancing state–diaspora relations.

Sources: Kelner (2010); www.birthrightisrael.com.

tourism development. It is pointed out that the Indonesian village, albeit presented as authentic Chinese-Indonesian cultural representations, does not really represent the Chinese-Indonesian community on Hainan Island. Instead, it is like a theme park where commodified ethnic culture for touristic consumption has no bearing on the community. This is attributed to a poor level of community involvement and an excessive focus on economic development. It is important to note that diasporic identity becomes reconstructed, re-evaluated and reinterpreted by various stakeholders, including the tourism industry. It is suggested that a complex interplay of identity, commodification and authenticity needs to be carefully considered and understood in order to successfully develop the ethnic identity and culture for touristic consumption.

Interestingly, Cohen (1997) argues that Safran's (1991) concept of a 'myth of return' places too much emphasis on the relationship between the diaspora and its homeland. Instead, a reorientation of conceptualising diaspora beyond the homeland is proposed. The positive virtues of retaining a diasporic identity in the host countries and the power of collective identity, are expressed not just with the homeland, but also in the host countries and with co-ethnic members in other countries. Several authors interpret diasporic identities as being hybridised, a process in which they adapt to the host culture, then rework, reform and reconfigure their own identity to produce new hybrid cultures and identities (Lowe, 1991; Featherstone, 1996; Iorio and Corsale, 2013). Homeland visits could thus lead to 'troubling, disconcerting and ambiguous experiences as well as newfound ambivalences' (Coles and Timothy, 2004: 13). Ambivalent connection to homeland becomes established during visits to homeland. Frequently, homeland is not any more a 'myth' but a 'reality' which delimits and demarcates diaspora identity as sources of complexity and diversity. As Xie (2010) argues, diasporic identity is more malleable than other identities given the fact that diasporic identity oscillates between homeland and hostland. The recognition of increasing hybridity in both homeland and diasporic identities suggests a new dimension in studying diaspora tourism, thereby generating new practices of identity formation and communication between homeland and diaspora, particularly in the age of globalisation and transnationalism. Inherent in diaspora tourism is a potential to facilitate the process of reflexively constructing hybrid and competing identities, and incorporating new social contexts, multiple agents and discursive relationships between homeland and diasporic communities.

Conclusion

Both material and immaterial remnants of historical significance are embodied as symbols and icons of national legitimacy and solidarity. As an essential element of national culture, heritage plays a fundamental role in enhancing the identity of a nation or region, and is a major vehicle for expressing national and regional cohesion and unity. The view of heritage as a cultural production seems to play a fundamental role in imagining an essence of national identity. It is important to note that it is not necessarily the physical manifestations of heritage resources but the meanings and symbols attached to them that are of greater significance in shaping an essence of identity and history. Heritage tourism acts as a symbolic mechanism through which shared social memories and experiences can be evoked, conceptualised and reconceptualised. Representations of national heritage are often predominantly attributed to state-centred, official and hegemonic discourses without significant attention to the importance of subjective narratives and individual interpretations pertaining to social memories and national sentiment, evoked and shared within heritage settings. However, informal, subjective and individual significations and interpretations of heritage are closely associated with maintaining and enhancing emotional connections to a nation. Furthermore, a systematic analysis of national identity and heritage and its interrelated dynamics requires a wider application of differing theoretical underpinnings and contextualisation of varying situational contexts. Encountering and experiencing national heritage, viewed as an essential constituent of a nation's history, plays a significant role in inculcating a sense of national stability and cultural continuity in the social spheres of everyday life. Homeland visits can help diasporas to reaffirm their cultural and emotional connections with their homeland, while at the same time making them feel more grounded in their everyday life in their country of residence by way of recognising their hybrid and fluid identities. Both identity and heritage are discursive and dynamic entities that change with time and space. In particular, it is important to emphasise the potential of diasporic identity in facilitating new and hybrid identities, incorporating multiple agents, differing social contexts and discursive relationships between homeland and diasporic communities.

Research questions

1   Explain ways in which heritage serves as a symbolic medium of identity formation and communication.
2   Discuss the significance of national heritage in maintaining and enhancing a sense of national belonging.
3   Based on your own experiences discuss the emotional and emotive dimension of domestic heritage tourism.
4   Why are personal perceptions and individualised experiences of heritage significant in contextualising national identity during heritage tourism experiences?
5   Using relevant examples illustrate how 'invented traditions' are incorporated within heritage tourism contexts.
6   Discuss and evaluate ways in which the concept of 'banal nationalism' contributes to understanding the significance of heritage tourism in everyday contexts.
7   Discuss how heritage tourism experiences in homeland contribute to the hybrid and heterogeneous identities of the diaspora.

Learning material

Anderson, B. (1983) *Imagined Communities*, London: Verso (Chapters 1 and 2).
Ashworth, G.J. and Tunbridge, J.E. (1996) *Dissonant Heritage: The Management of the Past as a Resource in Conflict*, Chichester: Wiley.
Billig, M. (1995) *Banal Nationalism*, New York: Sage (Chapters 3 and 5).
Coles, T.E. and Timothy, D.J. (eds) (2004) *Tourism, Diasporas and Space*, London: Routledge.
Duval, D.T. (2003) When hosts become guests: return visits and diasporic identities in a Commonwealth Eastern Caribbean, *Current Issues in Tourism*, 6(4): 267–308.
Graham, B., Ashworth, G.J. and Tunbridge, J.E. (2000) *A Geography of Heritage: Power, Culture and Economy*, London: Arnold (Chapters 3 and 5).
Hall, S. (1992) The question of cultural identity, in S. Hall, D. Held and T. McGrew (eds) *Modernity and its Futures*, London: Polity Press, pp. 273–326.
Hobsbawm, E. (1983) Introduction: inventing traditions, in E. Hobsbawm and T. Ranger (eds) *The Invention of Tradition*, Cambridge: Cambridge University Press, pp. 1–14.
Johnson, N.C. (1999) Framing the past: time, space and the politics of heritage tourism in Ireland, *Political Geography*, 18(2): 187–207.
Kelner, S. (2010) *Tours that Bind: Diaspora, Pilgrimage, and Israeli Birthright Tourism*, New York: New York University Press.
Light, D. (2007) Dracula tourism in Romania: cultural identity and the state, *Annals of Tourism Research*, 34(3): 746–65.

Macdonald, S. (2006) Undesirable heritage: fascist material culture and historical consciousness in Nuremberg, *International Journal of Heritage Studies*, 12(1): 9–28.

Palmer, C.A. (1998) From theory to practice: experiencing the nation in everyday life, *Journal of Material Culture*, 3(2): 175–99.

Park, H.Y. (2010a) Heritage tourism: a journey into nationhood, *Annals of Tourism Research*, 37(1), 116–35.

Park, H.Y. (2011) Shared national memory as intangible heritage: re-imaging two Koreas as one nation, *Annals of Tourism Research*, 38(2): 520–39.

Safran, W. (1991) Diaspora in modern societies: myths of homeland and return, *Diaspora: A Journal of Transnational Studies*, 1(1): 83–99.

Smith, A.D. (1991a) *National Identity*, London: Penguin.

Stephenson, M.L. (2002) Travelling to the ancestral homelands: the aspirations and experiences of a UK Caribbean community, *Current Issues in Tourism*, 5(5): 378–425.

Winter, T. (2004) Landscape, memory and heritage: new year celebrations at Angkor, Cambodia, *Current Issues in Tourism*, 7(4&5): 330–45.

Xie, P.F. (2010) Developing ethnic tourism in a diaspora community: the Indonesian village on Hainan Island, China, *Asia Pacific Journal of Tourism Research*, 15(3): 367–82.

Weblinks

The mystery of the Basques
http://www.guardian.co.uk/travel/video/2010/jun/24/travel-basque-culture

Changdeok Palace in Seoul, South Korea: 3D CG animation
http://vimeo.com/53053369

Red tourism in China
http://www.guardian.co.uk/world/video/2009/sep/28/china-communism?intcmp=239

Taglit-Birthright Israel
http://www.birthrightisrael.com/Pages/Default.aspx#

The Year of Homecoming Scotland 2014
www.homecomingscotland.com

African Diaspora Tourism
http://www.africandiasporatourism.com

7 Heritage tourism and globalisation

Globalisation, tourism and heritage

It is difficult to develop a singular or unequivocal definition of globalisation due to its complex and multifarious nature both as an ideology and a phenomenon (see Mak *et al.*, 2012). Globalisation refers 'both to the compression of the world and the intensification of consciousness of the world as a whole' (Robertson, 1992: 8). According to Held and McGrew (2003: 3), globalisation refers to the 'entrenched and enduring patterns of worldwide interconnectedness'. The phenomenon of globalisation has made a substantial impact on the social structures of everyday life by enabling individuals to live in a more homogeneous world facilitated by the process of global interdependence. The process of globalisation is often regarded as a fairly recent economic and social–cultural phenomenon. Different forms and varying patterns of intercontinental contacts and interactions have, however, existed throughout history. The European imperialism in the eighteenth and nineteenth centuries is one conspicuous example of intercontinental expansion as an early form of global assimilation. But there also exist much earlier examples of the movement of populations and trades such as the Silk Road, Genghis Khan's invasion of Europe and the Muslim incursions into Spain and other parts of Europe (Long and Labadi, 2010). It would thus be wrong to assume that globalisation is a really recent phenomenon that only began in the 1980s, although the most recent form of globalization – free market capitalist 'neoliberal' globalization – has become the most predominant and influential force, which draws both positive and negative attention. The sheer scale, intensity and speed of global cultural communications in contemporary society have reached alarming and unprecedented levels. This new age of global communication has been harnessed by technological innovations in communication and transportation (Held and McGrew, 2003; Reiser, 2003; Hopper, 2007). Under conditions of globalisation, geographical boundaries have become rather meaningless in an increasingly interconnected world. Waters (2001) believes that globalisation makes geography less relevant for social and cultural arrangements. Furthermore, imposing and enforcing regulatory mechanisms and standards developed at a global level in local contexts have become pervasive.

Increased and unimpeded flow of movement of people through tourism development is another crucial agent in facilitating globalising processes in our contemporary world. Hannam (2002) maintains that tourism development is integral to the processes of globalisation, which leads to restructuring and reconfiguring economic, political and cultural power relations. Globalisation and tourism development are reciprocal in terms of the ways in which each makes a significant impact on the other (Keller, 2000). Globalisation has enabled both capital commodities and tourists to be easily transported and transferred across the world (Mowforth and Munt, 2009). To a certain extent, global tourism development leads to homogenising and standardising tourism products, services and facilities.

It is generally acclaimed that tourist destinations are increasingly managed and marketed in a way that is placeless, lacking in a unique sense of place and identity (see Judd, 1999). Moreover, increasing global interdependence and cultural assimilation seriously question the sovereignty of nationalism and singular notions of nationhood. Appropriately, McGrew (1992: 63) claims:

> In a 'shrinking' world, where transnational relations, networks, activities and interconnections of all kinds transcend national boundaries, it is increasingly difficult to 'understand local or national destinies', without reference to global forces... the enormous flow of peoples across national boundaries; and the emerging authority of institutions and communities above the nation-state: all these factors provide a powerful case for reassessing the traditional conception of society... as a bounded, ordered, and unified social space – a coherent totality.

The development and expansion of high technological forms of communication and internationalised business transactions have made national borders appear fluid and flexible in an era of transnationalism (Ong, 1999). The increasing dominance of economic globalisation contributes to the denationalisation of national territory, thereby repositioning the roles of individual nation states (Sassen, 1996). The process of denationalisation and deterritorialisation has unmistakably impacted cultural and social spheres across the world. In particular, the process of deterritorialisation in culture and heritage is further accelerated by increased movement of people through travelling and migration, including diasporic communities. It is emphasised:

> under conditions of increased mobility, culture becomes increasingly detached from territory... Arguably, it can lead to culture and cultural forms evolving largely free from association with a particular place... The new cultural forms that emerge from such hybrid encounters are therefore frequently not tied to or associated with any specific territory.
>
> (Hopper, 2007: 50)

The process of deterritorialisation and homogenisation driven by global tourism development poses a big challenge in managing heritage. Globalising forces in heritage conservation and management have brought to the fore many challenging issues and concerns in both academic and practical applications of such themes as authenticity, interpretation, social inclusion and heritage preservation. They have also influenced ways in which stakeholders including local communities interact with heritage. The increasing influx of globalisation undermines, as emphasised above, the power of nations to determine their own identities and notions of nationhood, thereby diminishing the symbolic significance of national and local heritage. The values of traditional culture and national heritage are being dominated by new meanings associated with the ascendancy of international and transnational cultures, practices and events (Urry, 1990). There emerges an urgent need, therefore, for heritage to adapt itself to the rapid homogenising trends of global tourism, while striving to commodify its local distinctiveness in order to enhance its competitiveness in global tourism markets (Salazar, 2010). Globalisation plays a significant role in transforming heritage in both global and local contexts. The reorganisation of time and space within the framework of globalisation inevitably leads to a situation where heritage necessitates reappraisal and reconfiguration. Heritage in global contexts becomes deconstructed, deterritorialised and commodified, thereby turning itself into cultural products for global consumption. Here, rapid tourism development has further accelerated the process of recreating and repositioning heritage as a global commodity. Due to tourists' incessant search for 'new' and 'different' experiences, their increased mobility on a global scale to more and more 'exotic' and 'far-flung' destinations has become developed and promoted (Azarya, 2004). Both natural and cultural heritage of these 'exotic' and 'far-flung' destinations are commodified as main tourist attractions. It is elaborated that:

> Western notions of property – both 'real' and 'intellectual' – have established a system whereby anything can be isolated, decontextualized, packaged for consumption, marketed, and traded – in short, commodified. This has become even more prevalent in a global era where individuals are increasingly seeking to distinguish themselves from the increasingly similar crowd. Culture, perceived as a resource for supplying consumers with innovative, different, and 'authentic' (and 'unique') objects and experiences, has thus become the ultimate commodity.
>
> (Bauer, 2007: 697)

Despite the prevailing criticism of commodifying local culture and heritage in global tourism development, however, it should also be noted that globalisation has allowed different aspects of cultural and natural heritage resources to become recognised and valued beyond their local contexts, which will be discussed in greater detail later in the section on 'glocalisation'. Furthermore, increased competition under the conditions of globalisation has pushed heritage tourism development to take a new direction, with particular regard to the new production of heritage tourism and its subsequent marketing strategies. Heritage, as a commercial and commodified entity, is recognised as a lucrative tourism resource that can provide new and different attractions and experiences. Heritage is increasingly attuned to global market interests and demands. But it should also be noted that heritage is simultaneously confronted with a challenge to sustain its locality and heterogeneity. Local heritage assets become transformed into global heritage, with a new need to serve a global community, while striving to maintain its cultural integrity and locality as a resistance to globalisation.

WHSs: globalising heritage

In tandem with global tourism development, the popularity of WHSs as heritage tourism destinations has been unprecedented. WHSs are, in general, perceived as the centrepieces of global heritage tourism (Shackley, 1998). The designation of WHS, by nature, is the process of creating and maintaining global heritage products (see Salazar, 2010). According to Frey and Steiner (2011), the list can be beneficial where heritage sites are undetected and disregarded by national decision-makers, not commercially exploited and where national financial resources are insufficient and inadequate, or there is lack of political control and technological support for conservation. Based in Paris, UNESCO's World Heritage Centre is, as an intergovernmental organisation, in charge of defining, protecting and promoting both cultural and natural heritage sites. The idea of protecting cultural heritage on a global scale was first initiated by the League of Nations at the Conference of Athens in 1931 between the two world wars, in which an international code of practice for the preservation and restoration of ancient buildings was established. Founded in 1945, UNESCO focused on promoting peace and harmony between nations by way of rescuing, preserving and promoting historic sites. At its 1946 Constitution, the main obligation of UNESCO lay in 'the conservation and protection of the world's inheritance of books, works of arts and monuments of history and science'. Critical focus in The Hague Convention in 1954 was placed on the Protection of Cultural Property in the Event of Armed Conflict, in particular relation to post-war European reconstruction of cities damaged by war. When a decision was made to build the Aswan High Dam in Egypt in 1954, which would have flooded the valley containing the Abu Simbel and other temples of Ancient Egyptian civilisation, an international campaign to save the local heritage was soon launched. With the help of funding partly donated by some 50 countries (US$80 million), the Abu Simbel and Philae temples were disassembled, moved to dry ground and reassembled and the temple of Dendur was moved to New York, where it is now exhibited in the Metropolitan Museum of Art. The success of the campaign resulted in subsequent international campaigns to safeguard Venice, Borobudur and Angkor (UNESCO Brief History, http://whc.unesco.org/en/convention/#Brief-History).

'The UNESCO Convention on the Protection of the World' in 1972 is regarded as the first systematic effort to select and protect a variety of sites of historical and archeological significance. The convention has since been ratified by 187 countries. By signing the convention, each nation is committed to conserve the sites situated within its borders, some of which may be designated as WHSs. WH status is the highest accolade a site can receive and UNESCO has been acclaimed for emphasising the importance of conserving physical and cultural heritage (Nasser, 2003). The WH List designates unique cultural sites of outstanding universal value, values measurable in both cultural and economic terms (Shackley, 1998: 1). Responsibility is shared by the international community as a whole for the preservation of these sites for future generations, particularly where an array of non-governmental organisations (NGOs) are actively involved (see Table 7.1).

The early operation of the convention distinguished between natural and cultural sites overlooked the long-standing human presence in outstanding landscapes designated for their natural value (West and Ansell, 2010). Both the White House conference in Washington DC in 1965 and the IUCN in 1968 developed proposals that called for an international recognition of protecting natural and scenic areas. The World Heritage Committee gradually recognised a concept of cultural landscape, which encompasses human and cultural elements of landscape. Countries such as the USA and Australia include a range of natural sites as an essential part of their WH inscriptions. Furthermore, UNESCO's original definition of cultural heritage failed to recognise the scope for intangible elements of heritage, representing cultural diversity and sensitivity. In 2001, the Proclamation of the Masterpieces of Oral and Intangible Heritage of Humanity was initiated, which paved the way for a new list for intangible heritage. Finally, the UNESCO Convention for the Safeguarding of the Intangible Cultural Heritage of 2003 was agreed. Detailed discussions on intangible heritage are developed in Chapter 12. There emerge several critical issues and concerns in the way WHSs are inscribed, managed and promoted. WHSs are, as emphasised, global heritage products (Kirshenblatt-Gimblett, 2006; Di Giovine, 2009; Salazar, 2010). Local heritage is transformed into global assets through the process of selecting and designating WHSs. Local heritage is, in this way, aestheticised and sanitised for global mediatic and touristic consumption. The inscription on the WH List often leads to creating iconic and global attraction, thereby increasing visitations on a global scale (M.K. Smith, 2002; Boyd, 2008; Peter, 2009; Roders and van Oers, 2011; Frey and Steiner, 2011). Newly designated WHSs often receive an unprecedented and extensive level of publicity in global media coverage, including tourism promotional and marketing material. Despite its primary focus on protecting sites, ironically, the designation of WHSs often leads to excessive tourism development, which can lead to substantial

Table 7.1 *WH List Nominations*

Tentative List	A country must make an 'inventory' of its important natural and cultural heritage sites located within its boundaries, known as the Tentative List. It is an important first step since the World Heritage Committee cannot consider a nomination for inscription on the WH List unless the property has already been included on the state party's Tentative List.
The nomination file	By preparing a Tentative List and selecting sites from it, a state party can plan when to present a nomination file. The World Heritage Centre offers advice and assistance to the state party in preparing the nomination file, which needs to be as exhaustive as possible, including the necessary documentation and maps. The nomination is submitted to the World Heritage Centre for review. Once a nomination file is complete, the World Heritage Centre sends it to the appropriate Advisory Bodies for evaluation.
The Advisory Bodies	A nominated property is independently evaluated by two Advisory Bodies mandated by the World Heritage Convention: ICOMOS and the International Union for Conservation of Nature (IUCN). Both bodies respectively provide the World Heritage Committee with evaluations of the cultural and natural sites nominated. The third Advisory Body is the International Centre for the Study of the Preservation and Restoration of Cultural Property (ICCROM), an intergovernmental organization that provides the committee with expert advice on conservation of cultural sites, as well as on training activities.
The World Heritage Committee	Once a site has been nominated and evaluated, the intergovernmental World Heritage Committee makes the final decision on its inscription. Once a year, the committee meets to decide which sites will be inscribed on the WH List. It can also defer its decision and request further information on sites from the States' Parties.
The Criteria for Selection	To be included on the WH List, sites must be of outstanding universal value and meet at least one out of ten selection criteria. These criteria are explained in the *Operational Guidelines for the Implementation of the World Heritage Convention* which, besides the text of the convention, is the main working tool on WH. The criteria are regularly revised by the committee to reflect the evolution of the WH concept itself. Until the end of 2004, WHSs were selected on the basis of six cultural and four natural criteria. With the adoption of the revised *Operational Guidelines*, only one set of ten criteria exists.

Source: UNESCO WH List Nomination.

threats to heritage conservation. Here, some important questions can be raised: what can be considered worthy of inclusion on the WH List? How is inclusion determined and who decides what is included and what is not included? What political, social and economic implications would WHSs have in their communities? What impact do WH inscriptions and related development including tourism have on the local communities and people? How are the benefits of development distributed? What is the relationship between tourism and WH?

Hoi An in central Vietnam is renowned for its well-preserved historic centre, which represents its glorious past as one of the main South-East Asian trading ports dating from the fifteenth century (see Figure 7.1). Hoi An maintains the traditional architecture of the

Figure 7.1 Hoi An old town, Vietnam

nineteenth and twentieth centuries, mainly wooden buildings. The architecture is a by-product of cultural exchange occurring during this period in which traditional Vietnamese architectural designs and building techniques were mixed with foreign architectural elements coming from China, France and Japan. Hoi An and its heritage values remained largely undiscovered until the 1980s. With exposure in the global media, the Lonely Planet guide in the early 1990s subsequently attracted individual travellers, mainly backpackers to Hoi An. Its designation as a WHS in 1999 has further accelerated an increase of tourists from all over the globe, receiving 1.5 million tourists, including 750,000 international tourists in 2011. There is no doubt that WH designation has enhanced the international appeal of Hoi An as a main heritage tourism attraction in Vietnam, thereby vitalising and enhancing the local economy. However, excessive tourism development has brought about some negative consequences. Almost all of the historic houses in the centre have turned into shops, hotels, cafes and restaurants serving tourists. There are no traces of living community in the centre, which has been aestheticised, sanitised and commodified for touristic consumption. In this light, heritage conservation is also utilised as an effective tool for tourism development. Di Giovine (2009: 267) criticises this process as 'museumification of local culture', commenting that:

> By virtue of its designation, the citizens of Hoi An have to live under stricter statutes and regulations that extend from their public lives into their private lives. These laws are intended to maintain the ostensible authenticity of both the physical site, as well as the way of life... Museumified culture, then, is neither a preserved or ossified state of a people's pre-existing culture, nor a recovery

or a restoration of their 'correct' or 'traditional' way of life; it is something entirely new and original that organically emerges from the ongoing iterative process. Cultivated by a heightened exhibitionary sensitivity wherein one's 'culture' is specifically pinpointed, mapped and enacted for the benefit of an outside audience... It is at once entirely authentic and artificial – a completely organic phenomenon that stems from very contrived dynamics.

Many WHSs, particularly in developing countries, lack effective management strategies aimed at tackling rapidly increased tourism development. In this regard, the original aim of inscription to enhance conservation and protection becomes rather challenging and difficult to achieve, regardless of increased access to technical or expert services that WH designation brings in. The over-hyped belief in the potential of inclusion on the WH List as an effective tool for tourism development is generally implicated in the planning policy and the marketing and promotional strategies of destinations. But the effectiveness of WH designation in promoting tourism needs more rigorous empirical investigation. The degree to which WH designation generates the economic benefits of tourism needs to be more systematically analysed and examined. Interestingly, a few studies have challenged popular assumption that WHS status results in increased tourist arrivals, thereby bringing in economic benefits (see Cellini, 2011; Huang *et al.*, 2012). Huang *et al.* (2012) observe that WH listing in Macau has rather failed to enhance its tourism appeal on a longer term. It is further argued that the tourism-enhancing effect of WH listing varies among countries and regions. There should be more investigations on what determinants or variables in each country or region lead to significant differences in the effect of WH listing in attracting international tourists. It is important to maximise their privileged status to bring certain economic benefits to the local economy. But obviously, excessive tourism development could pose a threat to maintaining long-term sustainability of WHSs, while simultaneously acting as an invaluable opportunity to enhance the local or national economy. It is therefore important to emphasise that WHSs should not overtly exploit their status as a main tool for tourism development, particularly with regard to destination branding and marketing. Furthermore, too much attention on WHSs can lead to prominent targets in conflicts and wars. Frey and Steiner (2011) attribute WH status to a target for attack or destruction. Sacred places and monuments are regarded as effective targets because they are believed to embody a whole set of beliefs, ideals and identities (Golden, 2004). It is symbolic associations of heritage rather than its physical manifestations that become the primary target of attack and violence. Some notable examples are the destruction of the ancient bridge in Mostar, Bosnia and Herzegovina, the destruction of the great Buddhas at Bamiyan, Afghanistan, the recent destruction of the old city of Damascus and Aleppo, Syria and the mosques and ancient manuscripts in Timbuktu, Mali.

Contrary to UNESCO's claim that WH status counteracts the globalising process of the world, particularly in relation to commodifying and homogenising cultural heritage, it is argued that UNESCO and its universal protocols and practices in heritage management are a clear example of globalising heritage (Askew, 2010). As discussed before, heritage discourses and practices in the West have become predominant under conditions of globalisation. It should also be noted that WH, from its inception, has been inherently related to global politics. It is argued that the operational mechanisms inherent in the convention often result in a reinforcement of the politics of protection that were unequally developed and incoherently practised from one region to the next (Musitelli, 2002: 325). UNESCO's universal principles employed in the designation and management of WHSs are criticised as being deeply Eurocentric and developed for Western contexts, without fully considering varying and intricate local dynamics with the past in non-Western contexts

(Munjeri, 2004; Scholze, 2008; Long and Labadi, 2010). Meskell (2002) even claims that the concept of WH is flawed in that it privileges the Western idea of heritage, with greater emphasis on material culture that is distinctly European in origin. As explicated in Chapter 1, Smith (2006: 11) brings attention to 'Authorised Heritage Discourse' (AHD) as a dominant Western discourse of heritage, which is based on the 'power/knowledge claims of technical and aesthetic experts, and institutionalized in state cultural agencies and amenity societies'. It can be argued that UNESCO's principles in the operation and management of heritage are in line with the key principles of the AHD. Perceiving World Heritage Convention as an authorising institution of heritage, Smith (2006: 99) cogently argues that:

> This imbalance is not simply caused by disproportionate nominations by European countries, but by the AHD that frames and legitimizes the assumptions made in the listing criteria. The World Heritage List itself is a process of meaning making – it is a list that not only identifies, but also defines, which heritage places are globally important. The listing process creates or recreates sites as universally important and meaningful. Once again, the process of listing is an act of heritage management that is itself an act of heritage in which, on this occasion, a sense of universal 'human identity' is created. That the human identity that is performed through the List tends to be European is expressive of the degree to which the listing process is informed by, and reinforced, the European AHD.

However, there emerges an irony here in the way non-European countries competitively bid for WH listing that continues to ensconce them in this privileged locus of AHD, which needs further exploration. Along with the listing process, the process of heritage conservation and development at WHSs is also largely conditioned by the AHD. Buildings and urban features regarded as priorities for preservation in a historic city follow the Eurocentric values which do not fully consider the importance of the social fabric of the built environment in conservation. In this regard, AHD has been criticised for its elitist dominance and social exclusion in heritage conservation and development. Drawing on the case of the Ancient City of Pingyao in China, Wang (2012) claims that despite the economic development of tourism its WH designation brings out, heritage development and urban conservation has led to community exclusion and displacement. As emphasised in Chapter 9, community involvement is essential in facilitating the sustainable development of heritage tourism.

Furthermore, UNESCO places greater emphasis on universal, consensual and immutable values and qualities inherent in heritage, thereby often leading to assessing heritage as simply concerned with uncovering fixed heritage values that already exist in an object, place and practice. But heritage needs to be recognised as an active social relation or process (Smith, 2006), open to constant contestations and negotiations. The notion of idealised and rigid temporality in WHSs needs thus to be challenged. Accordingly, it is stated that:

> The monument to which 'heritage' is attributed speaks of an idealized time that is not simply traced back to a particular point in the past, pinpointed to some neatly delimited present or projected into a specific date in the future. Rather, it is filtered through ongoing and iterative social relations, allowing the present imagination to conceptualize the past and the future, in all of the vagaries to which it refers.

(Di Giovine, 2009: 93)

There also emerges a criticism pertaining to UNESCO as a main force in facilitating homogenised cultural globalisation in the preservation and development practices of WHSs in non-Western contexts (see Logan, 2002). In their recent study on examining the relationship between tourism, heritage and community at the Luang Prabang WHS in Lao People's Democratic Republic, Staiff and Byshell (2013) criticise WH theory and practice that conceptualises Luang Prabang as static and unified. They further challenge the dichotomy between tourism and heritage evident in WH practices as over-simplified, without fully taking account of the perspectives of the local communities, particularly within non-Western contexts. The way this WHS is experienced and appreciated by both locals and tourists is by no means undifferentiated. Luang Prabang is thus reconceptualised as a 'place that is constantly remade in a non-directional and non-linear process of endlessly becoming' (Staiff and Byshell, 2013: 109). Popular and prevalent accusations of tourism as a force of destructing heritage in non-Western contexts need thus to be remediated and reassessed. Importantly, heritage and tourism need to be revalued and renegotiated within the cultural context in which heritage is situated. Non-Western and non-traditional heritage has not been, as emphasised, fully embraced within the confines of WH practice (Munjeri, 2004; Bertacchini *et al.*, 2011). Munjeri (2004) claims that Europe's cultural heritage is over-represented in relation to the rest of the world and the architecture of the 'elitist' including castles, palaces or cathedrals is mainly included in the WH Lists. In this regard, there emerges a critical concern as regards the focus on the 'universal' nature of WH. According to Salazar (2010: 135):

> the very concept of universal heritage is increasingly contested. After all, it privileges an idea originating in the West and requires an attitude towards culture that is also distinctly European in origin. Within the discourse of universal heritage, there is little room for specific cultural, political or religious positions that diverge from Western, secularist viewpoints.

As of 2013 the number of WHSs amounts to 86 in Africa including four transboundary properties and 73 in Arab States out of 962 sites worldwide. This is relatively small compared to 462 nominations in North America and Europe. UNESCO has endeavoured to move away from a Eurocentric focus by way of developing a new set of assessment criteria considering local sensitivity and diversity, particularly in relation to the recognition of intangible heritage in non-Western countries.

Despite UNESCO's concerted efforts on the ideal of establishing the globalised and institutionalised heritage system, its operation and management has not necessarily overcome nation-state-based power structures and nationalist agendas (Long and Labadi, 2010). Askew (2010) claims, however, that attributing AHD as merely being Eurocentric undermines a critical factor, normative values and purposes of nation-states in operating and managing UNESCO's global heritage system. It is observed that UNESCO's member states mainly use the processes of nominating and promoting WHSs for their own domestic agenda of cultural hegemony, state nationalism and tourism development rather than achieving internationalist and universal ideals as specified in the principles. This can be linked with using the global to achieve the local by way of the actions of nation states that legitimise UNESCO's work within the context of WH listings. In a similar vein, Frey and Steiner (2011) claim that national interests dominate, rather than global interests, in the selection and decision-making of the WH List. Furthermore, UNESCO tends to stress the importance of heritage as a national property, thus neglecting the often conflicting diversity within nation states, which problematises and overlooks the varying socio-cultural and geo-political implications of heritage for different ethnic or cultural groups within a nation.

As emphasised in Case study 7.1, selecting and promoting the elements of the past, either tangible or intangible, for WH designation is not free from political influences. The process is often conditioned by the complex and intricate dynamics between local, national and global politics. In addition, the universal efficacy and global applicability of WHSs should not be overtly emphasised in the management paradigms and practices of individual WHSs. Each unique locality and specific context in which individual sites are situated needs to be fully considered and incorporated. Finally, it is important to monitor and control unnecessary changes or modifications in and around WHSs but here also emerges one important question to be considered: can heritage ever stay the same? WHSs, particularly cities, are often perceived as places not allowed to implement any modern changes and modifications. Both Seville and Liverpool have been threatened with delisting due to their plans to build high skyscrapers adjacent to their designated area. Liverpool is currently enlisted on the WH List in Danger (38 sites in 2013).

Case study 7.1: The politics of WH inscription

The process of WH inscription generally follows a top-down approach. The initiative has to be taken by the government of the state party, which has to supply UNESCO with a tentative list of potential sites to be inscribed. The relevant ministry then compiles a dossier of nomination for each proposed site including a detailed concept for the management and preservation of the site after WH status has been accorded. The Republic of Niger signed the UNESCO Convention in 1974 and two natural WHSs have been designated. But no cultural sites have yet been successfully inscribed. The town of Agadez is situated in the north of Niger and has 77,000 inhabitants of various ethnic origins, including Tuareg, Hausa, Songhay and Arab. Over the centuries, inter-marriage between these ethnic groups has led to the constitution of a distinct group called the Agadassawa in Hausa language, who mainly reside in the old quarters today. Founded in the eleventh century, Agadez soon became an important trading post and a centre for the manufacture of handicrafts along principal routes for the caravans crossing the Sahara. Although the sultan still plays an important role in organising and leading religious feasts and local festivals, the power of the sultan has substantially diminished in recent years. There exist different actors in the organisa-tional, top-down framework of the formalised process of inscription, which operate at international (the French embassy and the French consulting firm CRA Terre spe-cialising in clay architecture), national (the minister of culture and the director of the Department of Patrimony and Museums) and local (the representatives of the regional and local administration, local intellectuals and the reigning sultan and his court) lev-els. In Niger, the state has failed to introduce a cultural policy promoting a national identity, encompassing all ethnic and regional differences within its territory. The government officials in Niger prefer to abstain from the nomination of Agadez as a WHS due to the pressure put on decision-makers by their peers to support and to give an advantage to their home regions, politically and economically. There are a range of reasons for the failure of the nomination of Agadez: the prevailing regionalism and collective memories, the struggle for economic and political resources, the hierarchi-cal organisation of the process and a weak cultural policy. The global recognition of Agadez as a WHS remains momentarily arrested in local and national politics.

Source: an excerpt from Scholze (2008).

Neoliberalism, heritage tourism and privatisation

Neoliberalism is grounded in the premise that 'human well-being can best be advanced by the maximization of entrepreneurial freedoms within an institutional framework characterized by private property rights, individual liberty, unencumbered markets, and free trade' (Harvey, 2007: 22). Neoliberalism as a political economic practice has further accelerated the spread of global capitalism, thereby opening up the advent of neoliberal globalisation. A systematic examination of underlying forces and agents that have propelled neoliberal globalisation is therefore essential in clearly understanding this contemporary phenomenon. The main tenet of neoliberalism is, according to Negussie (2006), deregulation with a reduced role of the state through the selling of public sector assets. In order to maximise entrepreneurial freedom, state interventions in markets should ideally be kept to a minimum. Under neoliberalism, markets become a major force in political as well as economic and social–cultural domains. This shift in power is clearly implicated in the development of heritage tourism. Neoliberalism creates a framework for commodification of heritage. Heritage is actively employed to enhance the market appeal of the places and destinations concerned. Expansion of heritage, in terms of both scope and use, is an inevitable choice in increasingly competitive markets (both with other forms of tourism and within heritage tourism). Neoliberal forces have facilitated the process of commodification in heritage, thus leading to an unprecedented growth of the heritage industry in which markets become a major drive in privatising heritage – see Chapter 4 for detailed discussions on the commodification of heritage.

The commercial values of heritage have gained momentum as neoliberal forces become implicated in managing heritage. In this regard, heritage conservation is often treated in purely economic terms, mainly as a source of profit and development. Subsequently, private sector involvement in conserving and managing heritage has become normative on a global scale. Significant cuts in public funding and increasing pressure of global market forces have led to the privatisation of heritage conservation and management (Starr, 2010). Various processes of privatisation have been evident in heritage sectors all across the globe. Heritage properties previously owned and managed by state and local authorities have been increasingly sold to private developers in the international market. Even Italy, the home of classical antiquities and European heritage, has come to the fore on the issue of privatising its rich heritage such as old towns, medieval palazzos, archaeological sites, museums and beaches (Benedikter, 2004). In examining the implications of neoliberal conventions and practices for managing built heritage, Negussie (2006) employs a cross-cultural study of urban conservation in Ireland and Sweden during the post-1950 period. The pervasive process of privatisation has led to new ownership structures in the management of built heritage. Neguissie (2006) brings an important question to the fore as regards the issues of public access to privatised heritage buildings and sites that were formerly publicly owned, categorised as a part of 'national heritage'. Increasing privatisation of heritage has led to reducing its public access, thereby counteracting the process of democratising heritage. The consideration of leases rather than sales is suggested as a possible solution for maintaining the public sector's engagement in safeguarding national heritage. It is also revealed that neoliberalist changes on policies have redefined the role of and relationship between public and voluntary sectors. There is clear evidence of increased reliance on the voluntary sector to deliver services in Sweden. This study substantiates the ways in which practices related to neoliberal policies are locally and contextually specific, further emphasising that differing cultural–political contexts have implications in different capacities and structures for conserving and managing built heritage.

On the positive side, the process of privatisation can contribute to both increasing efficiency in protecting and managing heritage and improving the quality of visitor experiences. Many heritage sites are now eager to increase their economic viability by way of organising a variety of commercial events, including advertisements, wedding celebrations and exhibitions. Below are some examples of WHSs that have been used for various commercial purposes (see Case study 7.2).

Case study 7.2: The use of WHSs for commercial events and films

Machu Picchu, Peru	In 2000, a commercial for Peruvian beer Cusquena used the Intihuatana, a fifteenth-century granite sundial, as a makeshift bar. During the filming a crane collapsed and broke a corner of the sundial, resulting in criminal charges being filed against the production company, US publicity firm J. Walter Thompson.
The Great Wall of China	Italian fashion brand Fendi used the Juyongguan section of the Great Wall as a stage set for an exclusive fashion show in 2007. The event cost around US$ 10 million, involving a payment to the government-run China Great Wall Society.
The Colosseum, Rome	The Colosseum has been used as the location for concerts by Paul McCartney (2003), Elton John (2005) and the MTV Europe Music Awards (2004).
Petra, Jordan	A special tribute concert, which included Placido Domingo and José Carreras, was held in 2008, commemorating the life of the late tenor Luciano Pavarotti. *Indiana Jones and the Last Crusade* (1989)
Ait Ben-Haddou, Morocco	*Lawrence of Arabia* (1962) *Gladiator* (2000) *Alexander* (2004)
Angkor, Cambodia	*Tomb Raider* (2001)
Tongariro National Park, New Zealand	*The Lord of the Rings* (2001, 2003)
Blenheim Palace, UK	*Gulliver's Travels* (2010) *The Young Victoria* (2008) *Harry Potter and the Order of the Phoenix* (2007)
Huang Shan, China	*Crouching Tiger Hidden Dragon* (2000)

Source: Starr (2010).
See also http://www.blenheimpalace.com and http://www.visitjordan.com.

The use of heritage for commercial purposes is, however, unmistakably exposed to a barrage of concern and criticism regarding the challenges faced in the ethics and value of heritage. The public outcry regarding the decision to privatise certain heritage sites in Italy has been insurmountable. Particularly in the case of Venice selling advertising on its historic buildings and sites (e.g. Piazza San Marco and the Rialto Bridge) has drawn critical public concerns. Commercial activities in heritage have been justified as a means to pay for their expensive restorations and conservations. If kept to an optimum level, the use of heritage monuments for advertising could be a viable option for heritage conservation at a time of insufficient public funding. However, there still emerges a grave concern that this influx of consumer capitalism and privatisation will fatally damage the aesthetics of heritage, finally leading to turning Venice into a Disneyfied contemporary touristscape (Hatherley, 2012). The use of heritage for commercial activities including advertising and publicity has lately become more popular and widely practised across the globe. Uncontrolled and mismanaged commercialism could, even if utilised as a temporary measure for imminent financial gains, lead to damaging the cultural integrity of the history and culture concerned, which needs to be understood as the main implication of neoliberalism for heritage management. Furthermore, little information is publicly available regarding how actual payments of using heritage sites are made and used for their conservation and management (Starr, 2010). It is obvious that a certain level of business activity is mutually beneficial, thereby enhancing the relationship between the private sector and heritage. However, the private sector needs to pay substantial attention to the ethical and sustainable operation of heritage.

More responsible and ethical approaches taken by companies and business organisations would be essential in successfully managing heritage, particularly through corporate social responsibility (CSR). CSR is a specific application of the notion of environmental and social auditing to business practice. However, it is claimed that the tourism industry is well behind other industries in terms of CSR, not to mention of the absence of ethical leadership in the tourism industry (Mowforth and Munt, 2003). The concept of CSR is becoming gradually incorporated as both a philanthropic paradigm and a regulatory mechanism in heritage sectors. This concerted support from business has, along with such NGOs as the WHF and the GHF, been instrumental in supporting heritage conservation in both developed and developing countries. The private sector's involvement in conserving and managing heritage is regarded as one effective area in an attempt to achieve ethical responsibility, community participation and sustainable development as key practices of CSR. The restoration of the Hall of Mirrors at the Chateau de Versailles was successfully completed with the financial support (€12 million) of BTP Vinci, the construction group in France in 2007. In 2011, Diego Della Valle, head of the internationally renowned shoe firm Tod's in Italy, agreed to sponsor a €25 million restoration of the Colosseum in Rome (see Figure 7.2). There has since emerged a speculation that the company was given a right to place its logo on visitors' tickets sold to tourists every year for the next 15 years (Leitch, 2012). Early in 2013, another Italian fashion luxury brand, Fendi, decided to fund €2.18 million in restoring the Trevi fountain in Rome. Fendi's logo will be displayed on building site signs during the repairs in return for funding and a plaque commissioned by the city of Rome will be hung for up to four years near the restored fountains once the work is complete (Davies, 2013). In addition, heritage sites in developing countries often benefit greatly from the assistance of foreign companies and international partnerships. The GHF plays a crucial role in protecting

Figure 7.2 The Colosseum in Rome, Italy, under restoration (taken by Zuzana Lescisinova)

and sustaining endangered heritage sites in developing countries (see Global Heritage Fund, 2012). The GHF has worked very closely and collaboratively with private sectors, including Singapore Airlines, DigitalGlobe and Google Earth. The commercial sector's active engagement in conserving heritage has provided a welcoming and indispensable financial source at a time of limited government sponsorship and responsibility for heritage. Private sponsorship in heritage conservation should not, however, be tainted with attempts to use it for the publicity and marketing of a brand or a company. Appropriately, Starr (2010) warns that certain commercial activities could contradict the principles and values of heritage, as clearly illustrated in the case of Venice above. Furthermore, careful approaches need to be made regarding compromising priorities that both local communities and partners have in mind as well as overcoming cultural differences and communication barriers.

As another solution to control an excessive drive in privatising heritage, a globalist and neoliberal government needs to resort to nationalist politics where appropriate and necessary. In both developed and developing countries, the process of privatisation in managing heritage is often severely criticised by the general public. However, it is not uncommon that states often opt for close collaboration with the private sector, without fully recognising or considering the collective concern raised by the public. Here, market forces take precedence over national politics. Moreover, it is not unsurprising to realise that national politics even turn to supporting market forces. Therefore, below is a very rare recent example of preventing market forces from taking over woodlands and forests in the UK, amidst its increased neoliberal governance and reduced market regulation (see Case study 7.3).

However, national parks in the UK have not been free from dangers of privatisation. The forces of privatisation such as the mining and tourism industry have threatened protected lands, thereby bringing to the fore the tensions between environmental protection and economic development. Neoliberal governments often succumb to the market, as emphasised, which is the most powerful force in play. A recent decision made in liberalising the planning restrictions in the UK will undoubtedly lead to furthering commercial-oriented modification and development in the national parks.

The increasing prevalence of privatisation in heritage is not often easy to be controlled or interfered by public involvement, particularly in developing countries where the power of the decision-making is limited to small elitist groups in central governments. The proliferation of neoliberal economic policies in developing countries has seen a surge of capitalist enterprises with a particular emphasis on local goods and services, including

Case study 7.3: Woodlands U-turn

Environment Secretary Caroline Spelman in the UK had backed plans to sell off 250,000 hectares of woodland in 2011. However, a fierce public outcry and opposition forced the government to make a u-turn. On 4 July 2012, the Independent Panel on Forestry published its Final Report. According to the report, England's woodland had been hugely undervalued and should be kept in public hands. The experts calculated woodland costs around £20 million a year to the taxpayer – or 90p per household – but benefits people, nature and the economy to the tune of £400 million. The Panel's chair, the Right Reverend Bishop James Jones emphasised:

> There is untapped potential within England's woodlands to create jobs, to sustain skills and livelihoods, to improve the health and wellbeing of people and to provide better and more connected places for nature. Government investment is now needed to kick start these changes which will repay itself many times over in terms of public benefit.

More importantly, woodlands and forests are fundamental parts of English heritage and collective identity. They have symbolic as well as cultural significance in the maintenance of national solidarity. Therefore, a decision to privatise English woodlands was regarded as 'environmental vandalism'. The plans of privatisation were intended to give the private sector, community and charitable groups greater involvement in woodlands by encouraging a 'mixed model' of ownership. The government further insisted the terms would have ensured public access to protected 'heritage forests' such as the Forest of Dean and the New Forest by giving them to community groups. However, the concern was immediately raised that this could threaten public access, biodiversity and result in forests being used for unsuitable purposes. Half a million people including Dame Judi Dench and the Archbishop of Canterbury signed a petition against it. Here, a neoliberal government has finally yielded to conservative politics, which requires the state to be the guardian of woodlands from commercial exploitations.

Sources: Cohen (2012); http://www.woodlandtrust.org.uk.

culture- and heritage-related products (see Scher, 2011). In order to enhance market appeal in competitive international contexts, local culture and heritage are perceived as effective economic tools on which to capitalise. Within the context of the Caribbean, Scher (2011) contends that heritage tourism development in the region is an inevitable outcome of neoliberalist economic pressures and challenges. He further elaborates that:

> Neoliberalist economic strategies have often promoted local, non-traditional, export products that create intense competition within the region, but limit market conflict with other, usually larger, external economies... the structuring force of neoliberalism produces an emphasis on culture (a non-competitive market niche), yet also provides the hegemonic module of what counts as culture; that which is remembered and recalled by consumers as appropriate and legitimate to a region, is shaped by both global factors and local history or tradition. Cultural products then need to be recognisable to the target consumer: the

foreign visitor. The result is a greater investment in managing cultural products and practices in order to preserve their economic potential and serve the expectations of consumers.

(Scher, 2011: 8–9).

Despite the concern over excessive commodification or Disneyfication of heritage, it seems to be inevitable for heritage and the private sector to become increasingly interdependent and mutually beneficial. Excessive involvement of the private sector in conserving and developing heritage could actually decrease its value. However, it should not be overlooked that heritage continues to be an important and meaningful part of history and society when it continues to influence and interact with human life. Ethically and sustainably managed heritage through meaningful public, private and third sector partnership would contribute to enhancing the overall subjective well-being of society. Therefore, more careful approaches and legislation need to be made in order to achieving the balance between profit-making activities and the ethical and moral values of heritage sites.

Heritage tourism, localities and 'glocalisation'

As emphasised, the process of globalisation, both economic and cultural, has crucially contributed to the homogenisation of places and cultures. Local cultures are increasingly replaced by appealing transnational symbolic forms originating elsewhere (Van Maanen, 1992) through global homogenisation. A huge rise in global tourism is regarded as one of the main culprits for accelerating the worldwide distribution of homogeneous culture. Standardised tourism products and services across the globe have diluted the distinctive characteristics of local culture and heritage. Regardless of the dispersal of a homogenised and unified culture under the pervasive influence of globalisation processes, however, it is crucial to note that globalisation may not necessarily override the distinctive characteristics of the local. Rather ironically, globalisation has also facilitated the era of increasing heterogeneity (see Appadurai, 1996). Subsequently, globalisation has generated an appreciation and awareness of local cultures and uniqueness, thereby facilitating 'to think local and act global' (Wahab and Cooper, 2001: 147). The term 'glocalisation' has been adopted from the marketing field, where it refers to large-scale micro-targeting towards increasingly differentiated consumers with localised contexts (Robertson, 1995). Glocalisation is denoted as the 'intertwined processes whereby new boundaries are created between local-to-global orders' (Salazar, 2010: 133). Within socio-cultural contexts, the process of 'glocalisation' entails reappropriating and reinterpreting distinctive local (national) culture and identity within global settings, especially as a resistance to the increasing dominance of homogenised global cultures. There emerges a constant struggle to search for differences in sameness and sameness in differences. Nation states are defined and redefined through creating and maintaining certain cultural distinctions and uniqueness in which tradition and heritage are key components (Meethan, 2001). The multiplicity and diversity of local cultures and identities should not be either overlooked or underestimated. As Meethan (2001: 35) maintains: 'One of the notable aspects of globalisation has been the reassertion of the region or locality as the basis for social interaction and focus of both political and social identity.'

Furthermore, globalisation has ironically led to the advent of 'the age of nostalgia and traditionalism, which could be defined as a modern ideology promoting tradition'

(Eriksen, 2007: 103). The age of transnational movement has seen a sharp upsurge of interest in memory and nostalgia inherent in heritage tourism development. Jones and Desforges (2003) strongly support Harvey's (1989) notable claim that a deep-felt sense of belonging to specific cultures and places can be fortified as a reaction to globalisation. A recent surge of interest in local culture, heritage and tradition within tourism contexts is inextricably bound up with reaffirming and re-emphasising 'place-based identities' in increasingly homogenised tourism environments, influenced by the processes of globalisation. Nation states are defined and redefined through the creation and maintenance of cultural distinction and uniqueness in which tradition and heritage are crucial components (Meethan, 2001). Here, local cultural distinction and uniqueness play a central role in the survival and success of the tourism businesses in increasingly global tourism markets (Swarbrooke, 2001). In this regard, heritage tourism development can contribute to maintaining and fortifying the cultural distinction and uniqueness of each nation or region. It can be argued that the global and the local should be understood as interrelated and overlapping forces in suggesting a broader understanding of social and cultural transformations in contemporary societies. Appropriately, Giddens (1991: 22) maintains that the process of globalisation needs to be understood as an ongoing and persistent 'dialectic of the local and the global'. Concomitantly, Hall (1992: 304) claims:

> There is a new interest in 'the local' together with the impact of 'the global'. Globalisation… actually exploits local differentiation. Thus, instead of thinking of the global replacing the local, it would be more accurate to think of a new articulation between 'the global' and 'the local'.

Even in economic terms, juxtaposing the global and the local proves to be positive in enhancing the appeal of both global and local products. Using an example of Knorr soups and sauces, de Mooji (2000) claims that the logo and packages of this global brand remain similar worldwide but the contents are varied reflecting local tastes. In analysing the process of the McDonaldisation of Israeli culture, Ram (2004) observes that the opening of McDonald's in Israel has led eventually to reviving and refining falafel, its national food. Through the McDonaldisation of Israel's culinary habits, the old authentic falafel has been replaced by a new commodified version of falafel. It is further explicated that

> the interrelations of McDonald's and the falafel are not simply a contrast between local decline and global rise. Rather, they are a complex mix, though certainly under the banner of the global. Indeed, the global (McDonald's) contributed somewhat to the revival of the local (the falafel). In the process, however, the global also transformed the nature and meaning of the local… The 'new falafel' is a component of both a mass-standardized consumer market, on the one hand, and a post-modern consumer market niche, on the other.
>
> (Ram, 2004: 15)

Accordingly, a new theoretical resolution is suggested in enhancing the understanding of the global–local encounters – a global–local, structural–symbolic model that highlights the interspersing between a structural homogenisation process and a symbolic heterogenisation process (Ram, 2004: 23–7). Cittaslow can be understood as another interesting example of manifesting local symbolic heterogenisation in the process of structural global homogenisation (see Case study 7.4).

Case study 7.4: Cittaslow: Slow City movement

The movement of Cittaslow was initiated in 1999 by Paolo Saturnini, past Mayor of Greve in Chianti, a little town of Tuscany in Italy. The main premise of the movement was to encourage a different way of development in towns, with an emphasis on improving life quality. The Cittaslow movement rapidly spread to the different towns of Italy such as Bra, Orvieto and Positano and was finally endorsed by the founder of the Slow Food movement, Carlo Petrini. Slow Food was founded as an international non-profit organisation in 1989 in order to counteract fast food and fast life. It began as a response to the disappearance of local food traditions and reduced interest in local food and cooking methods at an increasing influx of globalisation. The main goal of Cittaslow, was and still is today, to permeate the philosophy of Slow Food, which is ecological and gastronomic movement, to both local communities and government of towns. There are currently 147 Cittaslow towns in 24 countries across the world making Cittaslow an internationally recognised standard. Cittaslow is an international accreditation that acknowledges the dedication and commitment of community members to sustain and enhance local tradition and heritage. To achieve the status of 'Slow City', a city must agree to accept the guidelines of Slow Food and work to improve conviviality and conserve the local environment. Slow Cities seek to promote dialogue and communication between local producers and consumers. The main aims of the movement are to enhance environmental conservation, sustainable development and the quality of urban life. Slow Cities provide incentives to produce food using natural and environmentally friendly techniques. Furthermore, substantial focus is placed on maintaining the authenticity of local products, craft and food traditions and unspoiled landscapes, thereby enhancing the sustainability of local communities. Yaxi in Jiangsu province in eastern China, a village of 20,000 people, was designated China's first 'Slow City' by Cittaslow International in 2010. Given growing concerns over the fast-changing economic and socio-cultural fabric of China, it cannot be denied that the designation of Yaxi as a 'Slow City' is a positive and welcoming effort to protect local traditions and heritage. Yaxi is not only a pioneer for China, but also one of the first Slow Cities in the developing world.

Sources: Bergman (2011); www.cittaslow.org.

However, it is often the case that the entitlement of Slow City is invariably associated with increasing global media attention, which often leads to increasing tourism appeal. In examining the influences of Cittaslow on destination development in three Cittaslow towns in Northern Italy (Bra, Abbiategrasso and Levanto), Nilsson *et al.* (2011) observe that Cittaslow is not primarily used for destination development or marketing in order to avoid mass tourism development. Of central importance is to improve place-specific resources, local identity and heritage preservation by way of organising and promoting 'slow' events using local gastronomy. But it is also emphasised that Cittaslow is increasingly vulnerable to overexploitation as an effective means of destination and tourism marketing. It cannot be denied that both movements are undoubtedly appealing as an effective marketing tool of the destinations concerned. Destination marketing and subsequent global tourism development could lead haphazardly to facilitating the process of standardisation and homegenisation of local heritage and tradition, which will eventually taint the non-commercial ethos of this locally focused practice. Despite its critical focus placed on valuing local tradition and heritage in these movements, there emerges a risk that operational and management paradigms and practices can be homogenised during the global expansion. Nonetheless, these localised practices still need to be understood, as discussed above, as an effective means of facilitating local heterogenisation processes despite increasing structural homogenisation. More careful approaches in implementing policies and practices need to be ensured to achieve small-scale and community-led sustainable forms of development. A more flexible and less rigid understanding of the intricate dynamics between global and local will contribute to appreciating and reappreciating these movements, particularly with regard to their symbolic ramifications. Finally, it is also criticised that both Slow Food and City movements mainly serve middle-class people by way of promoting middle-class lifestyles (see Knox, 2005; Nilsson et al., 2011). In particular, Slow City movement could be irreducibly associated with the process of gentrification in old historic towns, thereby exacerbating class stratification and struggle. Following the practices of the Slow Food and Slow City movements, there has even emerged a new tourism model – Slow Tourism. Slow Tourism development is perceived as an alternative approach to mass tourism development on a global scale. In conceptualising Slow Tourism, Conway and Timms (2012) link the slow traveller's qualitative experiences with the benefits they provide for destinations, including local stakeholders. Here, greater emphasis is placed on local stakeholders, while valuing community participation as a crucial agent for development. The main tenets of Slow Tourism can thus be effectively implicated in the sustainable development of such tourism as ecotourism, nature tourism and heritage tourism. More rigorous empirical investigation will be needed regarding how Slow Tourism development can protect and promote local heritage.

A strong sense of local, regional or national identity, either self or collectively imbued, is needed to secure people's grounded existence. In this regard, heritage can make a constructive contribution to strengthening 'place-based identities' and enhancing clear socio-cultural linkages with local or national pasts. Consequently, heritage tourism experiences could encourage people to contemplate connections with unique local or national pasts, reaffirming an awareness of their own cultural authenticity and national solidarity within a wider globalised environment. It is also critical to note that globalisation and glocalisation are closely intertwined in the appropriation and development of heritage. Both global and local discourses, dynamics and divergences play a profound role in facilitating the flexible and multifaceted approaches to representing and interpreting heritage within tourism contexts. Globalisation poses a threat to heritage, however, it can also provide an impetus for reviving and reinventing local heritage, for both local and global communities. Heritage could therefore play a discursive role in enhancing the nuanced and intricate dynamics between the global and the local, the homogeneous and the heterogeneous and the universal and the particular.

Conclusion

There has emerged a growing economic and cultural interdependence between the countries under conditions of globalisation. Globalisation is undeniably bound up with the information technology revolution and international tourism development that have rendered traditional cultural forms and societal structures less meaningful and distinctive. It cannot be denied that heritage has become a commercial entity presumably commensurate with market viability and profitability. Heritage is increasingly utilised for commercial purposes and profit-making activities. Critical focus is increasingly placed on perceiving the values of heritage as being customer-oriented and economically driven within the practices of neoliberalism. Concerted efforts need to be made not to overtly exploit the commercial orientations and values in managing heritage. WHSs are global heritage products, selected, designated and managed by UNESCO regulations and procedures, which are often criticised as following European and Western frameworks. There emerges a need to develop local legislation and regulations that carefully consider specific local circumstances and situations. Despite its original purpose of protecting and conserving heritage, WH designation can pose a threat to the long-term sustainability of heritage by way of excessive tourism development and commercial activities. Therefore, a tendency to advocate for WHSs in certain countries with the rich allure of reaping economic benefits through tourism needs to be carefully monitored. Apart from realising these economic benefits are not necessarily made through WH listing, the wider implications for sustainable management of such WHSs can be more critical if the anticipated economic values are not realised. Heritage tourism has been actively employed as a means to recreate and promote a unique sense of place in homogenous global tourism settings. Heritage tourism can thus contribute to facilitating symbolic heterogeneity in global tourism development, thereby fortifying and enhancing 'place-based' identities in increasingly placeless and interconnected tourism settings. Importantly, globalising forces may not necessarily overpower the essential dynamics of national cultures and identities. Instead, there emerges a strong tendency in re-evaluating and reinforcing distinctive local heritage and identities in newly established global contexts. A heightened significance on the local, hetereogenous and particular practices of heritage is another clear manifestation of heritage tourism development under the process of globalisation.

Research questions

1 Explain and analyse the ways in which globalisation has impacted on heritage and its tourism development.
2 'WHSs can be seen as a manifestation of cultural imperialism'. Discuss this statement and develop your own critique.
3 Why are the principles of WHSs criticised as being Eurocentric and developed for Western contexts?
4 Using relevant examples, discuss how neoliberalism has facilitated the process of privatisation of heritage sectors.
5 What are the positive consequences of private sectors' involvement in managing heritage?
6 What is 'glocalisation'? Explain how the process of glocalisation has been incorporated in the practices of heritage tourism.
7 Critically reflect on 'Slow Food' and 'Slow City' movements as local resistance to globalising heritage and assess the extent to which such movements may be relevant in your chosen town or region?
8 Suggest the ways in which heritage can contribute to enhancing the intricate and dialectic dynamics between the global and the local, the homogeneous and the heterogeneous and the universal and the particular.

Learning material

Frey, B.S. and Steiner, L. (2011) World Heritage List: does it make sense? *International Journal of Cultural Policy*, 17(5): 555–73.

Harvey, D. (2007) Neoliberalism as creative destruction, *The ANNALS of the American Academy of Political and Social Science*, 610(March): 22–44.

Held, D. and McGrew, A. (2003) *The Global Transformations Reader*, 2nd edn, Cambridge: Polity.

Hopper, P. (2007) *Understanding Cultural Globalization*, Cambridge: Polity (Chapters 4 and 5).

Kirshenblatt-Gimblett, B. (2006) World heritage and cultural economics, in I. Karp, C.A. Kratz, L. Szwaja and T. Ybarra-Frausto (eds) *Museum Frictions: Public Cultures/Global Transformations*, Durham, NC: Duke University Press, pp. 161–202.

Logan, W.S. (2002) *The Disappearing 'Asian' City: Protecting Asia's Urban Heritage in a Globalizing World*, Oxford: Oxford University Press.

McGrew, A. (1992) A global society? in S. Hall, D. Held and T. McGrew (eds) *Modernity and its Futures*, London: Polity, pp. 61–116.

Meethan, K. (2001) *Tourism in Global Society: Place, Culture, Consumption*, Hampshire: Palgrave (Chapters 2 and 3).

Nilsson, J.H., Svard, A.-C., Widarsson, A. and Wirell, T. (2011) 'Cittaslow' eco-gastronomic heritage as a tool for destination development, *Current Issues in Tourism*, 14(4): 373–86.

Ram, U. (2004) Glocommodification: how the global consumes the local – McDonald's in Israel, *Current Sociology*, 52(1): 11–31.

Robertson, R. and White, K.E. (2007) What is globalization? in G. Ritzer (ed.) *The Blackwell Companion to Globalization*, London: Blackwell, pp. 54–66.

Salazar, N.B. (2010) The globalisation of heritage through tourism: balancing standardisation and differentiation, in S. Labadi and C. Long (eds) *Heritage and Globalisation*, London: Routledge, pp. 130–46.

Scher, P.W. (2011) Heritage tourism in the Caribbean: the politics of culture after neoliberalism, *Bulletin of Latin American Research*, 30(1): 7–20.

Scholze, M. (2008) Arrested heritage: the politics of inscription into the UNSECO World Heritage List: the case of Agadez in Niger, *Journal of Material Culture*, 13(2): 215–32.

Smith, L. (2006) *Uses of Heritage*, London and New York: Routledge (Chapter 3).

Staiff, R. and Bushell, R. (2013) Mobility and modernity in Luang Prabang, Laos: re-thinking heritage and tourism, *International Journal of Heritage Studies*, 19(1): 98–113.

Starr, F. (2010) The business of heritage and the private sector, in S. Labadi and C. Long (eds) *Heritage and Globalisation*, London: Routledge, pp. 147–69.

Wang, S. (2012) From a living city to a World Heritage City: authorised heritage conservation and development and its impact on the local community, *International Development Planning Review*, 34(1): 1–17.

Weblinks

Operational Guidelines for the Implementation of the World Heritage Convention: the criteria for World Heritage selections
http://whc.unesco.org/archive/opguide12-en.pdf

World Heritage Alliance
http://www.youtube.com/watch?v=1h9n7QmCiAk&list=PLFFDE70AE9CCBA434

Friends of World Heritage
http://www.youtube.com/watch?v=TdFP30WJrCc

Granada's Alhambra Palace, Spain
http://www.guardian.co.uk/travel/video/2010/aug/26/alhambra-palace-granada-spain

World heritage conversations: Edinburgh
http://www.ewht.org.uk/world-heritage-conversations

Hoi An ancient town, Vietnam
http://whc.unesco.org/en/list/948/video

The Ancient City of Pingyao, China
http://globalheritagefund.org/video/pingyao

WHSs and tourism: Curonian Spit, Lithuania and Russia
http://www.youtube.com/watch?v=xOCB8K0FgAw

China in transition
http://vimeo.com/29992277

Slow Food movement
http://video.nationalgeographic.com/video/places/culture-places/food/italy_slowfood

8 Heritage marketing

Marketing, tourism and destination branding

Marketing is the management function that is involved in identifying, anticipating and satisfying customer requirements profitably according to The Chartered Institute of Marketing (2009: 2). Marketing as a concept is closely associated with, but not limited to, business firms and, at its simplest, it normally entails the task of identifying and stimulating demand for the products or services of a given organisation (Kotler and Levy, 1969). Kotler (1984: 92) defines marketing as 'the process of planning and executing the conception, pricing, promotion, and distribution of ideas, goods, and services to create exchanges that satisfy individual (customer) and organizational objectives'. Marketing is grounded in the principle of anticipation in that the success of a product or service cannot be assured until it has been consumed (Misiura, 2006). In this sense, marketing planning needs to devise detailed strategies in order to meet the anticipated outcome of an involved company or institution. In principle, marketing is mainly concerned with enhancing both business profits and consumer satisfactions. Therefore, marketing involves identifying suitable target markets or audiences and promoting a product or service by way of developing effective strategies. The marketing function of a business or other entity therefore encompasses product development, pricing, place (distribution) and promotion, the so-called 4Ps originally introduced by McCarthy (1981). The marketing mix is defined as 'the mixture of controllable marketing variables that the firm uses to pursue the sought level of sales in the target market' (Kotler, 1984: 92). However, particularly within the context of services marketing including tourism, four additional Ps have recently been contemplated, including process, personnel, physical assets (environment) and personalisation (customisation) (Goldsmith, 1999). Hudson (2008) claims that additional variables have been added to better communicate with and satisfy customers in service production process. Due to the intangible nature of services, any tangible aspects of services are useful for customers to understand the nature of the service experiences. Therefore, the services marketing mix includes people, physical assets, process and personalisation along with the traditional four Ps (see Table 8.1).

Crucially, contemporary marketing is thought to make a perceived shift from its product-centric view to a customer-centric orientation. In other words, focus is increasingly placed on identifying customer needs, and developing, modifying and innovating existing products and services in order to best meet those needs with the aim of achieving the overall long-term goal of the organisation (Kotler and Levy, 1969; Goldsmith, 1999; Vargo and Lusch, 2004). This shift in marketing is somewhat reflected by the transition from Fordist to post-Fordist consumption practices, which is explained in greater detail in Chapter 1. Within the context of tourism destinations, marketing is perceived as a strategic approach to developing a given place or destination with a long-term goal that transcends the need for increasing visitor numbers and expenditure (Buhalis, 2000; Ritchie and Crouch, 2003). The destination that is perceived as an amalgamation of a

Table 8.1 *Marketing mix for heritage tourism services*

	Product	*Place*	*Promotion*	*Price*
Traditional 4Ps of marketing	Heritage artefacts, sites, monuments and events (tangible/ intangible)	Location Accessibility	Advertising PR Sales promotion	Admission fees Discounts Allowances Memberships
	People	*Physical assets*	*Process*	*Personalisation*
Additional 4Ps of services marketing	Visitors (education/ entertainment) Employees (recruiting/ training/ volunteering)	Facilities Presentational and representational methods (Signage/ interactive media) Retail outlets	Face-to-face contact Online service Virtual consumption Interaction with visitors	Customised/ personalised visitor experiences

wide range of products of natural, socio-cultural, historical, environmental, infrastructural and super-structural nature offers a unique set of experiences sought after by tourists (see Murphy *et al.*, 2000). Tourism destination marketing is thus closely bound up with the idea of place-making for and by tourists and other interested parties through employing a plethora of media such as films, TV, magazines and travel books in order to (re) produce objects and subjects for tourist gaze and consumption (see Urry, 2002). Tourism marketing may be seen as the professionalisation of the tourist quest for sublime experiences through a stimulation of desires, awareness of places and new ways of seeing and consuming such places (Urry, 2002). Marketing in a destination context then facilitates and enhances the construction of an imaginary bridge between the various images and imagery of the promoted destination and prospective tourists' perceptions of how their expectations and experiences may be satisfied through the consumption of such places. Ritchie and Crouch (2003: 6) mull over the possibility of the socio-cultural attributes of a destination constituting a 'dominant determinant of competitiveness'. Heritage, as a unique socio-cultural attribute of a destination, could thus serve as an active agent to recreate, rejuvenate and enhance the destination images.

The focus on strategic destination marketing is thus rationalised on two interrelated grounds, namely the changing and dynamic consumer tastes and preferences and the increasing global competition that challenges the conventional conceptions of tourist demand and supply patterns. It is becoming increasingly evident that contemporary trends in tourism demand posit inherently sophisticated tourist profiles and consumption patterns against what are perceived as the static and standardised conceptions of tourist experiences (see Shaw and Williams, 2004; Claver-Cortes *et al.*, 2007; Kolar and Zabkar, 2010). The spectre of a perceived loss of appeal to prospective tourists, of previously well-established destinations and subsequent decline in the absence of rejuvenation or repositioning strategies serve to underscore the significance of strategic destination marketing (Poon, 1993; Agarwal, 2002; Zhang and Jensen, 2007). Subsequently, those with responsibility for managing a tourist destination must aim at providing and enhancing unique, authentic and inimitable experiences, so as to positively influence tourist demand. Sustained efforts should thus be made in establishing relevant strategies through which such an influence can be achieved.

In marketing, branding is primarily a process by which messages are conveyed to the consumers, including potential consumers. These messages need to be simple and consistent and possibly reinforced by experience. One of the great advantages of branded products is that they are an infinitely renewable resource, as long as their value can be maintained and reinforced through careful marketing. Clearly established destination brand is considered to be indispensable for successful destination marketing. Morrison and Anderson (2002) define destination branding as a way of promoting a destination's exclusive identity by differentiating it from its competitors. It is agreed that destination branding is essential for the destinations to establish a unique identity and differentiation point to which tourists can be attracted and which also provides sustainable advantage in the competitive market (Morgan et al., 2002; Baker and Cameron, 2007; Ekinci et al., 2013). Destinations seek to create a worldwide recognisable identity through promoting their unique attributes, either physical, cultural or a combination of both. The challenge for them is to decide upon a differentiation point that would make consumers identify the destination from a range of other choices that offer the same products. Place promotion and marketing is unquestionably bound up with 'the systematic production and presentation of tourism placed within the media in general, and the travel industry in particular' (Williams, 2009: 193). The promoted images of places and destinations play a crucial role in the process of strategic planning and marketing.

Despite the contentious nature of what constitutes heritage tourism (Yale, 1991; Poria et al., 2003), an increasing interest in the consumption of the (authentic) heritage of the (exotic) other continues to be a key attraction in tourism destinations (Silberberg, 1995; Laws, 1998; Kolar and Zabkar, 2010). Here, one important question is raised: what role does heritage marketing play in the wider remit of destination marketing? Heritage is expected to play a significant role in shaping, maintaining and promoting the images and identities of destinations. Heritage acts as one of the essential factors, as illustrated in Table 8.2, in determining the brand images of the countries.

Table 8.2 *Heritage and culture top 15 in Country Brand Index 2012–13*

Heritage and culture ranking	+/– 2011	Overall rank
Italy	0	15
France	0	13
Japan	+3	3
Switzerland	+7	1
United Kingdom	+7	11
Peru	–2	40
Germany	+11	7
Israel	–5	27
Egypt	–1	58
Canada	+15	2
Spain	–4	19
Sweden	+1	4
Austria	–4	17
New Zealand	+1	5
Norway	+1	10

Source: adapted from FutureBrand (2013).

While European countries typically dominate in the heritage and culture dimension in the Country Brand Index, countries such as Japan, Peru, Egypt and New Zealand, which are renowned for historical sites, cultural traditions and iconic natural wonders, are listed among the top 15. But it is important to note that there is no one country in the world without its unique history and heritage. It is often the case that some countries fail to construct and promote their own unique brand images and identities construed from heritage, culture and tradition. It appears that it is the perceptions and images of heritage that are counted in branding rather than actual qualities and merits of heritage in countries. Therefore, emerging heritage destinations need to realise the significance of developing effective marketing strategies including branding which can enhance the perceptions and images of heritage. But they should also be critical of possible negative consequences that heritage marketing may bring out. It cannot be denied that heritage in each country offers a very unique and different tourism product and experience in its own right. There can be some cases, therefore, in which aggressive branding can damage or debase the integrity and authenticity of heritage. Although it is useful to realise the efficacy of branding and its relevance for both established and emerging heritage tourism destinations, excessive emphasis on using heritage for branding can risk the long-term sustainability of heritage by way of attracting unprecedented attention from global media and tourism.

Importantly, the process of branding has been described as a highly complex and politicised activity in its own right (Pride, 2001; Morgan et al., 2002; Ryan and Silvanto, 2010). Ryan and Silvanto (2010) perceive stakeholder management and politics as key components of destination branding. Various studies have been carried out to investigate the forms of power in destination branding and the impact that various stakeholders' interests have on its development (Marzano and Scott, 2009). Every stakeholder group including local residents or businesses must understand and be informed of the outcomes of the destination brand (Baker and Cameron, 2007). The process of branding should thus be a cooperative process, which is closely associated with involving and managing various stakeholders. Prideaux and Cooper (2002) emphasise that positive outcomes from marketing initiatives including branding can only be achieved through stakeholder collaboration and unity. Emotional branding is conceptualised as a 'relational, communal, participatory, sensory, and emotive view of consumer–brand relationships' (Thompson et al., 2006: 50). Given both psychological and social meanings and values of brands, branding needs thus to be viewed as a holistic process combining physical attributes with emotional dimensions. Destination branding is related to developing and promoting the identity and images of destinations, thereby helping to establish emotional connections with tourists. Although branding is generally associated with creating slogans and designing logos promoting the image of a destination, there has been increasing focus on emotional approaches to destination branding (Hosany et al., 2006; Kolb, 2006; Gobe, 2008). It comprises an active interaction between destinations' assets and the way in which they are perceived by tourists. Scarce attention has been paid, however, to analysing the emotional connections between destination brands and tourists and to investigating the implications of emotional branding in effectively promoting destinations. Hosany et al. (2006) conclude that destination marketers should focus on delivering promotions that highlight the unique personality of tourism destinations, based on the emotional aspects of destination image. Kolb (2006) suggests that emotional branding is a specific model of branding that builds the links with the visitors around a particular lifestyle. It is clear that the essence of branding is mainly concerned with creating an emotional relationship with consumers by way of developing effective communication campaigns (Morgan et al., 2002) and unique personalities or images (Baker and Cameron, 2007).

Heritage marketing

As has been explicated, heritage in a contemporary context is regarded as an industry, consciously controlled and planned in order to maximise its market appeal. In the past, heritage sites were mainly for education and cultivation. However, heritage is now a marketable product and heritage tourism is a consumerist-oriented phenomenon whose marketing tends to be driven by capitalist tendencies (Rowan and Baram, 2004). Heritage tourism products have become varied and wide-ranging, including artefacts, heritage sites and events, institutions and lifestyle. In general, heritage attractions offer both material attributes (buildings, monuments and events) and immaterial services (interpretations, education and entertainment), which are holistically integrated as an experience. The resources derived from the past are staged, packaged and promoted for touristic consumption, by ways of varying representation and interpretation processes. Given the increasing competition among heritage sites and attractions and their customer (visitor)-oriented approaches, a need to employ effective marketing strategies has come to prominence in contemporary heritage scenes. Along with the increased use of new information and communication technologies, heritage marketing has substantially contributed to attracting a much wider section of society. Successful and effective marketing within the context of heritage tourism has wide-ranging implications as a means of preserving and conserving a historic environment and regenerating a locality, as well as generating a commercial profit. Given that one of the main purposes of heritage tourism management is to protect and conserve the past, heritage marketing does not necessarily entail attempts to increase visitor numbers through advertising. Instead, it helps to target certain consumers and control their visits while improving heritage conservation. The employment of membership, friends or loyalty schemes in heritage sites and museums are good examples of strategic marketing. A careful balance needs to be made, however, between heritage conservation and commercial values in any marketing plans of heritage attractions and events.

Heritage is, as emphasised before, both a tangible and an intangible remnant of the past. It should be noted that heritage marketing needs to carefully consider the intrinsic nature of the heritage being promoted, either tangible or intangible. When intangible heritage is promoted, its marketing strategies and focuses need to be differentiated from those of tangible heritage sites and attractions. The unique intangible heritage of local indigenous communities is often utilised to create a brand that can be appealing and saleable to tourists. Of particular concern here is that the overuse of certain cultural symbols, historical values and sacred icons in marketing intangible heritage for tourism can demoralise and debase the local communities. This negative consequence is particularly noticeable when the communities, as a key stakeholder, are not properly involved in the marketing process (see George, 2010). Ashworth *et al.* (2007) identify dissonance as an intrinsic nature of heritage. It is argued that dissonance is implicit in the market segmentation that perceives heritage as an economic commodity. The inherent conflicts between the economic uses and social uses of heritage become evident in the process of secularising and popularising heritage in the process of destination branding and marketing. Branding heritage for tourists' consumption, particularly sacred or sensitive heritage, can lead to explicitly endorsing and possibly aggravating the issues of heritage contestation and dissonance. Heritage is unmistakably associated with politics, as extensively illustrated and discussed in Chapter 5. Heritage often represents and signifies the inherent and subtle conflicts and tensions among different groups and people. This dissonant and contested nature of heritage poses a challenge in branding and marketing heritage. One dominant discourse or narrative of heritage can often be represented and emphasised in heritage branding.

Therefore, it is not uncommon that multiple and varying interpretations of heritage are not clearly manifest in and through branding heritage. Moreover, the ways in which certain heritage is promoted for national branding are not necessarily a real portrayal of how it is recognised or valued. In discussing Australia's recent tourism destination marketing, Pomering and White (2011) observe that indigenous Australian culture and heritage are presented and promoted as essential elements of Australian national identity. The appeal of indigenous and aboriginal communities is fully embraced in national branding and marketing. However, it is criticised that the images used for promotion are incongruous with the factual identity of indigenous communities in Australia. Heritage branding and marketing requires closer cooperation and careful negotiation between the different stakeholders concerned, including the local communities. In examining the impact of political influences on the promotion and use of the WHS as a destination brand, Ryan and Silvanto (2010) argue that democracy and political instability have a significant impact on the decisions of national tourism offices to promote their WHSs as tourist destinations. Democracy is identified as a key element in facilitating and achieving a common consensus among stakeholders on the nature and special meaning of WHSs as destination brands.

Chhabra (2009: 307) views the main aim of heritage marketing as 'designing promotional strategies and message content appropriate for selected and suggested target markets'. In order to identify target markets, market segmentation is an essential and important marketing component, particularly at an early stage of marketing planning and development. The main purpose of market segmentation is to develop appropriate marketing strategies specific to each target group. Given that heritage tourists are of a heterogeneous nature, market segmentation is an essential marketing tool in identifying and accommodating the different interests and needs of heritage tourists. For Misiura (2006: 79), market segmentation is:

> the process of dividing a total market (or sub-market) using the principles...
> in order to create one or more homogeneous groups or segments that can then
> be targeted effectively, based on the accessibility of these customers and the
> resources of the organization.

Likewise, heritage attractions and organisations can use different variables in order to identify different target markets, thus developing specific marketing strategies:

- demographic characteristics (gender, age, position in family lifecycle);
- socio-economic and cultural characteristics (social class/status, education, income, race, religion, ethnicity, sub-cultures);
- psychographic characteristics (lifestyle and personality).

In the existing literature, various attempts have been made to divide heritage tourists into sub-groups by way of demographics (Chen and Hsu, 2000), socio-economic positions (Richards, 2001) and attitudes in interpretation (Poria *et al.*, 2001, 2009). Despite its effectiveness as a marketing tool, however, market segmentation approaches are criticised as being only revenue-oriented without considering the long-term sustainability of management (Tsiotsou and Vasaoti, 2006). As an area for future research on market segmentation in heritage marketing, it will be interesting to examine how changing demographics or lifestyles and the subsequent changes in tourists' decision-making processes and preferences will affect the ways in which heritage will be marketed and promoted.

Heritage marketing needs to adopt a 'visitor-focused management tool that can be used to help heritage sites achieve not only their financial but also their non-financial objectives' (Hausmann, 2007: 176). Here, non-financial objectives can include life-long learning, social inclusion and community participation. Poria *et al.* (2009) claim that the motivations of heritage tourists are different and these differences are related to the preferences for interpretation. It is thus suggested that heritage settings should be marketed differently according to interpretation preferences and products and activities provided. Marketing activities need to be varied depending on tourists' interests, needs and demands (see Case study 8.1).

The focus of heritage marketing needs to be placed on establishing and enhancing emotional connections between heritage and tourists. As is the case with destination branding explained in the previous section, emotional branding could contribute to developing and maintaining long-term and perennial relationships between heritage and tourists. Therefore, it is significant to develop 'images' and 'stories' of heritage provoking emotional associations that tourists could relate to. It is important to note that emotional aspects of heritage experiences are not just limited to the domestic tourism contexts in which heritage often acts as a symbolic agent through which national identity and memory can be sustained and communicated. In general, heritage establishes an emotional relationship with tourists who come to interact with different cultures and values outside of their own. Emotional associations within heritage contexts could be expanded to a broader context of culture, religion and politics, as well as personal circumstances. It is also important to note that intangible heritage including intangible elements of tangible heritage is closely associated with emotional

Case study 8.1: Long-term marketing strategies at Edinburgh Castle, Scotland

- VisitScotland Partnership: major route to market for international audience – Annual partnership contract covers VisitScotland visitor print, online presence, advertising and sponsorship in VisitScotland Information Centres, local marketing and new 'Days Out' smart phone App.
- Landmark Bedroom Folders (on display in 95 per cent of bedrooms in all Scotland holiday accommodation).
- Listings and features in publications such as Hudsons and This is Edinburgh.
- Historic Scotland Print Collateral: Edinburgh Castle Leaflet (350,000 annually), Edinburgh Castle What's On Leaflet (10,000 monthly).
- Online advertising: Trip Advisor, Facebook, PPC, The List website.
- Promotions: use of past-trialled promotions to change visitor engagement behaviour. For example, a campaign was launched in 2010 to get 18 per cent off the Edinburgh Castle ticket when buying online, which brought the admission price to under £10 per adult. This successful campaign engendered a move away from visitors buying tickets on the day, thus increasing traffic to the website and reducing the queue time at the admissions desk on site.
- Events: Mother's Day promotional activity, major annual Easter event.
- PR and media visits.

Sources: http://www.visitscotland.org/research_and_statistics.aspx; http://www.scotland.org; http://www.edinburghcastle.gov.uk.

and emotive dimensions of heritage, which can be effectively promoted by emotional branding. Substantial focus is even increasingly placed on the intangible nature of tangible heritage, often manifest as values, symbols and meanings of tangible heritage. This tendency is clearly reflected in contemporary heritage marketing in which the intangible nature of tangible heritage is essentially utilised in order to impart powerful and effective images and stories of heritage. Notwithstanding its significance and relevance to heritage contexts, however, it should be noted that emotional branding overly used in promoting certain elements of heritage can also create tensions and conflicts among the audiences who might not feel emotionally connected with the way in which heritage is promoted. Inauthentic emotional branding messages and promises can also have a negative impact on tourists' self-conceptions of heritage (see Thompson *et al.*, 2006). As a consequence, the brand image can be sensationalised and contested, thereby challenging its long-term sustainability.

Substantial effort has been made in recent years to promote visitations at heritage sites and to increase public awareness of them, despite the fact that historic sites often have small and fairly limited marketing, advertising and promotional budgets. Along with satisfying the existing market groups, the purpose of heritage marketing lies in market creation, thereby generating new target market groups. Below are some useful self-checklist points for heritage marketers to consider prior to drafting new marketing plans:

- What specific new target markets could we aim to attract?
- How can we reach these new competitors?
- How do we design and structure our marketing material and relate to the new market groups?
- What would we promote in the stories, contents and experiences that we offer in order to attract the attention of new target markets?
- What is both the physical and psychological carrying capacity of the attraction?
- What have other attractions done to attract these same market groups? Any successful marketing strategies we could learn from?
- How will we evaluate the success of new marketing strategies?

Furthermore, given the perceived significance of heritage tourism within a given destination, its marketing can be recontextualised to address those constantly emerging and changing consumption practices and patterns in tourism so as to ensure overall destination competitiveness. Some questions and issues that may be addressed through heritage marketing within a destination context include but are not limited to the following:

1   What constitutes the heritage product (generic product definition), who consumes such products (target market), how and why (analysis of demand and consumption behavioural patterns)?
2   What special value or differential advantage arises from the heritage products on offer, and what tools are being used to sell the heritage products and innovate and readapt them for various consumers with distinct tastes and preferences?
3   To what extent is heritage marketing underpinned by research to ensure the viability, suitability and sustainability of heritage products and services?
4   What provisions are being made to accommodate new opportunities or challenges arising from the current heritage products being marketed (e.g., commodification vs authenticity, sustainability, conflicts arising from the politics of representation, etc.)?
5   How can/should heritage products be employed in diversifying tourism experiences at a destination or destination rejuvenation/repositioning efforts, with particular

regard to relieving the adverse effects of either mass tourism or tackling certain challenges arising from climate change, including potential impacts on both cultural and natural heritage attractions?

Finally, there often arises a need to employ de-marketing strategies in some cases where heritage sites become too popular and overly congested by tourist visits, which can have a negative impact on the conservation of heritage (Bennett, 1997; Leask and Fyall, 2006; Smith, 2009). Beeton and Benfield (2003) perceive de-marketing as an intrinsic element of marketing management. Medway and Warnaby (2008) assert that demarketing is particularly effective in situations where the products offered are based on finite and non-renewable sources, of which heritage and tourism could be an essential part. Some notable examples would be popular WHSs of universal significance, including the Taj Mahal in India, the Lhasa palace in Tibet and the Pyramids in Egypt. De-marketing is defined as the 'aspect of marketing that deals with discouraging customers in general or a certain class of customers in particular on either a temporary or permanent basis' (Kotler and Levy, 1971: 76). It is critical to note that there emerges a need to de-market natural heritage sites as well as cultural heritage sites. Natural heritage sites, particularly designated as WH, contain rare and fragile landscapes and indigenous flora and fauna. Without any particular marketing activities, these sites receive a great horde of tourists all year round, which poses a critical threat to the sites carrying capacity and long-term sustainable management. In this context, some marketing strategies that discourage tourists from visiting the sites and attractions could be employed in order to maintain carrying capacity and focus on the preservation of the site (Smith, 2009) (see Case study 8.2).

Case study 8.2: De-marketing strategies employed in Kakadu National Park, Australia

Kakadu National Park is the biggest national park in Australia which is renowned for the world's highest concentration of aboriginal rock art. It is located within the Alligator Rivers Region of the Northern Territory of Australia, which covers an area of 1,980,400 ha (4,894,000 acres), extending nearly 200 kilometres from north to south and over 100 kilometres from east to west. The first remains of human occupation in Australia, dating from nearly 40,000 years ago, have been identified here. Kakadu National Park was designated as a WHS in 1981 and is now one of the most popular tourist attractions in Australia. As regards visitor management, the current management plan (2007–14) highlights the following points:

- The Board of Management has agreed on ten principles to guide tourism in the park. These principles include a statement that Kakadu is first and foremost home to Bininj, and that the pace and level of tourism development will be determined by the traditional owners.
- More ways will be looked at for Bininj to benefit from tourism – for example, from employment, Bininj-run businesses or joint ventures.
- Promotion of the park will make sure that the right things are said about Kakadu and the right pictures are shown.
- Bininj will guide decisions about any new activities that could be developed, such as camping areas or bushwalking.
- Tour operators will be required to do a course before being allowed to work as guides in Kakadu.

Figure 8.1 Kakadu National Park, Australia (taken by Alex Chapman)

In order to conduct commercial tours in Kakadu National Park, a permit or a licence needs to be acquired. The one-year fee for a standard land-based tour permit is 100 Australian dollars (for up to four trips each year) and $500 (for more than four trips each year). The three-year fee is $500 (for up to four trips each year) and $1,500 (for more than four trips each year). The relevant fee needs to be paid at the time of application. A licence will need to be applied for special activities including safari camps, which will take effect from 1 April 2014. Kakadu National Park passes contribute directly to the running costs of the park and help to maintain its natural environment and tourism services. All international and interstate visitors aged 16 years and over need to buy a park pass before they arrive at Kakadu National Park. All Northern Territory residents and children under 16 are free. A park pass costs $25 for 14 consecutive days, which can be purchased online prior to the visit. Legislation in Australia also requires National Parks to promote both visitation and preservation. Enhancing public awareness and educating potential visitors regarding how to conserve parks without overuse is also regarded as a key factor in assuring the long-term sustainability of the park. A new management plan is being developed and will be put into practice from 2014.

Sources: http://www.environment.gov.au/parks/kakadu;
http://www.environment.gov.au/parks/publications/kakadu/pubs/fs-summary.pdf.

New technologies and new marketing strategies for heritage tourism

As highlighted in Chapter 2, critical focus is increasingly placed on experiences in the mode of experience economy. Williams (2006) circumscribes experiential marketing as marketing initiatives that offer consumers in-depth and tangible experiences, in order to provide them with sufficient information to make a purchase decision. Contemporary consumers seek unique and differentiated experiences through their consumption activities. There even emerges a new term – storysumer (story + consumer) – which refers to consumers who are looking for, and attracted by, stories. Therefore, companies and organisations are keen on promoting their brands and products through stories, which can be included in experiential marketing. Hudson (2008: 433) identifies clear differences between traditional and experiential marketing. In experiential marketing:

- The main focus is placed on customer experiences and lifestyles, which provide sensory, emotional, cognitive and relational values to the consumer.
- There is a focus on creating synergies between meaning, perception, consumption and brand loyalty.
- It is argued that customers are not rational decision-makers, but rather driven by a combination of rationality and emotion.
- It is argued that experiential marketing requires a more diverse set of research methods in order to understand consumers.

An overall shift in emphasis from selling the products to selling the experiences has been clearly reflected in heritage marketing. Heritage marketing is increasingly becoming familiar with concepts such as 'value for money' and 'edutainment'. With an increasing number of heritage sites charging an entrance fee, tourists expect heritage managers to provide an appropriate value proposition in return for their payment. The potential for adopting an experiential and consumption-based approach to marketing has been recognised in heritage attractions, including both traditional heritage sites and new and purpose-built heritage attractions with commercial orientations. Accordingly, there has been a move away from the predominant focus on tangible and material elements of heritage such as monuments, buildings and artefacts to intangible and experiential elements of heritage attached to tangible heritage. Heritage attractions are positioned at the forefront of this fascination with creating and delivering memorable and powerful experiences. Contemporary heritage tourists are constantly and voraciously looking for new cultural experiences and discoveries and they are keen on consuming the stories and images heritage creates through marketing. It is obvious that heritage managers need to employ more innovative and diverse marketing strategies focusing on experiences in order to enhance the appeal of heritage sites in increasingly competitive tourism markets.

Compared to a traditional and product-focused approach to marketing, experiential heritage marketing emphasises the roles and expectations of the visitors as distinctive components in the consumption process (Leighton, 2007). Therefore, experiential marketing could contribute to furthering the potential of heritage consumption with visitor-oriented and imaginative activities. However, it should be noted that the application of experiential marketing to heritage needs to consider the distinctive nature of heritage. It is explicated:

> The adoption of an experiential, consumption-based approach to heritage is problematic for a sector whose very appeal lies in the priceless museum collection, the magnificent monument or the imposing building. There are significant barriers to adopting an experiential approach in the shape of stakeholders, such as funding bodies, conservation groups, civic trusts and local, national and international government. There are also innate tensions between commercial objectives and curatorial goals, between visitor access and preservation and between scholarship and entertainment.
>
> (Leighton, 2007: 118)

Despite its growing popularity, a focus on experiences embraced in heritage marketing is not an exception to criticism. There emerges a concern that too much focus on experiences could lead to facilitating sanitised, commodified and popularised representations of the past, which lies at the core of the debates on commodification of heritage. Leighton (2007) warns about the risk of destroying the intrinsic appeal of heritage, its exclusivity, by way of mainly facilitating consumption-oriented experiences in marketing. The popularist and interpretive approach embraced in experiential marketing could result in undermining the importance of product features and benefits (e.g. sites and collections). It can thus be a challenging task to make an optimum and sustained balance between a more conventional and object-based approach and an experience-focused approach in heritage marketing. Experiential marketing needs to be incorporated as a supplementary strategy in order to meet the demands, needs and expectations of an increasingly diverse range of heritage tourists, without losing sight of the potentially negative implications for over-marketed heritage.

In tandem with high-speed internet connections and mobile internet connectivity, new technologies and online services have radically changed the web over the last several years. These changes have had a substantial impact on the ways in which people are connected and communicated. Compared to other sectors, the heritage sector has rather slowly responded to these changes. But reduced budgets in the heritage sector and an increasing focus on performance measures in customer-focused management have propelled heritage attractions and organisations to diversify their marketing strategies to attract wider audiences. Employing new technologies can help heritage marketers reach new audiences and engage them in different ways. For example, school children and young adults find visual and interactive media in heritage attractions both appealing and informative (see Case study 8.3). In general, e-marketing refers to new marketing methods using digital technologies such as websites, mobile devices and social media. e-marketing has been employed as supplementary to traditional marketing methods, including PR, direct mail, advertising and word-of-mouth. The biggest benefit of e-marketing lies in its flexibility and cost-effectiveness. For small-scale heritage attractions that have a limited budget for publicity and marketing activities, e-marketing could serve as an effective tool to find new markets and enhance global reach, thereby developing and consolidating their brand identity. The use of Facebook and Twitter serves not only as effective marketing tools but also engaging platforms for the discussions and debates by online audiences. New online audiences are not passive recipients of heritage products and services. They have become more critical of what they consume and experience and eager to share their experiences with peers, thereby acting as 'prosumers (producers and consumers) of travel experiences' (Tsiotsou and Ratten, 2010: 537). Importantly, it should be noted that heritage marketing utilising online networks and social media could bring out some drawbacks as well as benefits. Tourists' comments and reviews become readily available online and can be widely spread with the real-time use of social media. Any negative peer review uploaded and distributed by social media could instantly have a negative impact on the images and reputations of heritage sites.

Customer relationship management (CRM) is mainly concerned with efficiently and effectively increasing and retaining profitable customers by way of selectively initiating, building and maintaining relevant customer relationships (Payne and Frow, 2006). CRM is grounded in the principles of relationship marketing, with an emphasis on individualised or 'one-to-one' marketing, which emerged in the 1980s (see Bendapudi and Leone, 2003). Since the 1990s, the interest in attracting, maintaining and enhancing customer relationships has been significantly on the increase. The two terms – relationship marketing and CRM – have been used interchangeably in both theory and practice. But Zablah *et al.* (2004) emphasise a clear distinction between relationship marketing and

Case study 8.3: Tate Online

Tate Online is widely recognised as one of the best museum websites across the globe. Tate Online was launched in 1998 with the aim of increasing public awareness and understanding of art. Following the development of the Tate Online strategy from 2010–12, the website was relaunched in early 2012 with a complete restructure of the site's content, innovative design and new technical architecture. Tate Online has made extensive use of social media in a number of recent audience participation projects, particularly in partnerships with Flickr, Blurb, Threadless and MySpace. Tate Online has also developed key strategic developments, including Tate Kids, Tate Papers, Tate Channel and TateShots. In order to promote lifelong learning, Tate Kids focuses on facilitating children's creativity through an online community where children can upload their own art works, display them next to Tate collection works and comment on each other's works. The site also offers a range of interactive programmes including games to encourage children to explore works in the Tate's collections and create their own online responses. The hope is that children who join Tate Kids will want to explore their interest in art further by joining Tate Collectives when they get older. Tate Collectives support teenagers and young people to develop their creativity. For adult learners, Tate Online has developed Creative Spaces in collaboration with eight other national museums and has developed a range of online courses where students are able to try techniques at home, upload images of their own work and discuss them with other participants on the course. Tate Online offers a virtual space for visitor-led discussions and debates. The Great British Art Debate website has been established to encourage young people to explore questions of identity, to engage with Tate's and the partners' collections online and to share their ideas and experiences through interactive websites and social media. Tate Online is also keen on developing and enhancing international collaboration and exchange. Turbinegeneration is a project that aims to link schools, galleries, artists and cultural institutions worldwide through contemporary art and ideas. With the advent of social media and online publishing platforms, online users' contribution to developing content as authors and editors has sharply increased. Tate Online is also eager to distribute its content to third-party websites, including YouTube, iTunes, iTunes U, Flickr, Wikipedia and Google Earth. A range of audio and video podcasts are available online, including audio tours, interviews and recordings of talks and discussions.

Source: http://www.tate.org.uk/learn/online-resources.

CRM. Relationship marketing differs from customer relationship management in that it is concerned with managing relationships with multiple stakeholders rather than only customers (Ryals and Payne, 2001). Furthermore, CRM utilises technological tools as a essential part of the strategic management of customer relationships. However, it is important to note that CRM is not just limited to the application of technology. It is also argued that CRM does need to consider close collaboration with other key stakeholders (Payne and Frow, 2006). CRM has recently been embraced in the heritage sectors as a means to improve and enhance customer relationships and management. In general, various heritage support groups including friends and membership schemes comprise the substantial portion of repeat visitors. They play an important role in maintaining the economic sustainability of the heritage sites or organisations by making donations and subscriptions. Moreover, developing and maintaining effective customer relationships through these schemes could also contribute to achieving the goals of conservation and social sustainability of heritage. Despite increasing recognition of its significant role in strategic management and marketing as a business philosophy, CRM is not exempt from criticism. It is suggested that a poor understanding of the strategic focus of CRM could lead to an inappropriate exploitation of customers, with particular reference to a service provider's misuse of intrusive technology (Frow *et al.*, 2011). It is thus important to emphasise the significance of carefully managing and protecting visitor information and profiles through close monitoring in heritage marketing. Moreover, the specific circumstances of different heritage attractions and organisations need to be considered in planning the key components of an effective CRM strategy.

There has been little attention given to the significance of a sustainable marketing approach in heritage tourism marketing literature, except some notable studies attempting to relate the concept of sustainable marketing to heritage places (Fuller, 1999; Gilmore *et al.*, 2007; Chhabra, 2009). Overall, there is limited guidance available in which sustainable marketing can contribute to balancing preservation and tourism development at heritage sites (Donohoe, 2012). There thus emerges a need to plan and develop an all-embracing and holistic marketing framework that enhances a long-term sustainability of heritage tourism management. In an attempt to design an effective sustainable marketing protocol for the museums selected, Chhabra (2009) proposes a hypothetical sustainable heritage tourism marketing model (SHTM) which is crafted along strategic marketing criteria, including measures such as environment analysis, level of local community involvement, partnership and maintenance of traditional, preservation-based objectives of the museums. It is revealed that there is a gap between the philosophical underpinnings of the proposed model and the existing marketing strategies. Therefore, it would be correct to state that destination branding has to comply with the principles and guidelines implied by sustainable development. Timur and Getz (2009) assert that even though each stakeholder group has different interests and aims regarding sustainable tourism development, there are some goals of sustainability that they share and should be working together towards the same desired outcomes. Heritage tourism marketing needs to incorporate more fundamental changes in stakeholder's collaboration. It should adopt a collaborative approach at the local community level, with residents and local government and businesses cooperating and working together. Joint marketing activities in collaboration with transportation, accommodation, attractions and other facilities could be both effective and economical (see Case study 8.4).

Heritage marketing needs to be planned, developed and managed as part of the integrated and holistic marketing of destinations. VisitEngland, the national tourist board in the UK, announced a partnership with *The Guardian* in launching the 'Think of England' campaign in January 2013. The campaign ran for three months, with the purpose of boosting domestic tourism by encouraging more Britons to take a holiday in England in 2013. The campaign, partly funded by the government's Regional Growth Fund, promoted a range of themes that highlight some of the best holiday experiences on offer in England, including romantic heritage sites and cultural cities. It is evident that heritage marketing is essential in creating, maintaining and enhancing the appeal of heritage to both existing and prospective tourists. However, it should be borne in mind that too much competitive pressure construed from aggressive marketing within the sector could lead to damaging and demoralising the intrinsic values of heritage. For heritage marketers, there raises a critical need to understand the intricate dynamics between heritage marketing and conservation. In order to achieve sustainable marketing practices in heritage, greater emphasis

Case study 8.4: London Shh...

London Shh... (Small historic houses) is a marketing alliance of small historic houses in central London which retain the stories of famous former residents. It currently includes Benjamin Franklin House, Dr. Johnson's House, Handel House Museum, Keats House Museum, John Wesley House and Freud Museum. It continues to recruit new small historic houses across London. The London Shh... houses can be rented out for various functions and parties, including weddings and conferences. It actively uses social media including Facebook and Twitter as an effective marketing tool.

Figure 8.2 Tweets from London Shh...

Figure 8.3 Dr Johnson's House and Benjamin Franklin's House, London, UK

Source: http://www.londonshh.org/home.html.

needs to be placed on holistic and strategic aspects of marketing such as market fit and orientation rather than mere promotional and revenue-generating activities. Heritage sites and attractions mainly employ quantitative data collected from surveys and question-naires in order to acquire visitor-related information. However, given the heterogeneous and complicated nature of both heritage and heritage tourists, there emerges a call for more qualitative data that help to unravel individualised perceptions and meanings of heritage and heritage visits. The regular implementation of existing marketing strategies is essential in enhancing their effectiveness in competitive heritage markets. A more rig-ourous use of e-marketing strategies will be facilitated in the future, therefore it is critical to examine and evaluate how heritage tourists respond to and interact with new technolo-gies. Finally, sustainable marketing should be planned, developed and implemented in collaboration with other sustainable management strategies and heritage practices.

Conclusion

The primary goal of marketing is, in a strict business sense, to make and maximise profits. Heritage has become increasingly recognised as a major economic resource in many cities and towns, and industry-based and business-oriented approaches including management and marketing strategies are crucial to maximise an attraction's appeal as a lucrative business. As previously highlighted, heritage in a traditional sense was hardly related to profit-making qualities and provisions. But the significance of marketing, as part of strategic management plans and procedures, is clearly recognised and incorporated in the practices of contemporary heritage management, in particular relation to tourism devel-opment. As an essential part of destination marketing and branding, heritage marketing could contribute to enhancing both heritage conservation and commercial activities and values. However, it should also be noted that both heritage and destination marketing are inherently political activities. In this regard, marketing, particularly in relation to strategic branding, could often lead to facilitating and intensifying the conflicts and discrepancies between stakeholders. Therefore, heritage branding and marketing should take the con-tested nature of heritage and heritage construction into careful consideration, thus fully integrating stakeholder management and collaboration as an essential element of strategic branding and marketing activities. The shift in emphasis from products to experiences has been clearly integrated in contemporary heritage marketing. Creating and promoting memorable and powerful experiences becomes essential in increasing the appeal of heritage sites in competitive tourism markets. Focus is also increasingly placed on establishing and promoting emotional connections between heritage and tourists in heritage branding, as is the case with destination branding. Heritage marketing strategies need to be diversified to attract wider audiences. The development of new technologies, particularly the use of social media and mobile network connections, has made some fundamental changes in the ways in which heritage is marketed and promoted to contemporary tourists, in particular relation to younger generations. Furthermore, new marketing strategies including CRM and sustainable marketing practices are increasingly integrated in promoting and managing heritage.

Research questions

1. Discuss the ways in which heritage marketing is related to managing heritage.
2. What are both the positive and negative implications of using heritage in destination marketing and branding?
3. Why are emotional connections between heritage and tourists important? Discuss how emotional aspects of heritage can be incorporated in marketing strategies.
4. Critically evaluate both the advantages and disadvantages of experiential and emotional heritage marketing.
5. How does a destination determine if it is achieving its goals with regard to heritage marketing? What indicators should or could be used in evaluating the marketing and branding performance of one heritage site or attraction compared to that of other competitors?
6. Explain the possible drawbacks of the increasing prevalence of e-marketing in heritage.
7. Try to devise some de-marketing strategies in your chosen popular heritage site.
8. Critically evaluate the ways social media has been employed in contemporary heritage marketing.
9. Try to develop a framework for sustainable heritage marketing in developing countries.

Learning material

Baker, M.J. and Cameron, E. (2007) Critical success factors in destination marketing, *Tourism and Hospitality Research*, 8(2): 79–97.
Beeton, S. and Benfield, R. (2003) Demand control: the case for demarketing as a visitor and environmental management tool, *Journal of Sustainable Tourism*, 10(6): 497–513.
Chhabra, D. (2009) Proposing a sustainable marketing framework for heritage tourism, *Journal of Sustainable Tourism*, 17(3): 303–20.
Kolar, T. and Zabkar, V. (2010) A consumer-based model of authenticity: an oxymoron or the foundation of cultural heritage marketing? *Tourism Management*, 31(5): 652–64.
Kolb, B.M. (2006) *Tourism Marketing for Cities and Towns*, Oxford: Butterworth-Heinemann.
Leask, A. and Fyall, A. (2006) *Managing World Heritage Sites*, Oxford: Butterworth-Heinemann.
Leighton, D. (2007) 'Step back in time and live the legend': experiential marketing and the heritage sector, *International Journal of Nonprofit and Voluntary Sector Marketing*, 12(2): 117–25.

Medway, D. and Warnaby, G. (2008) Alternative perspectives on marketing and the place brand, *European Journal of Marketing*, 42(5/6): 641–53.

Morgan, N.J., Pritchard, A. and Pride, R. (2002) *Destination Branding: Creating the Unique Destination Proposition* (revised 2nd edn), Oxford: Butterworth-Heinemann.

Pomering, A. and White, L. (2011) The portrayal of indigenous identity of Australian tourism brand advertising: engendering an image of extraordinary reality or staged authenticity? *Place Branding and Public Diplomacy*, 7(3): 165–74.

Prideaux, B. and Cooper, C. (2002) Marketing and destination growth: a symbiotic relationship or simple coincidence? *Journal of Vacation Marketing*, 9(1): 35–48.

Rowan, Y. and Baram, U. (eds) (2004) *Marketing Heritage: Archaeology and the Consumption of the Past*, Oxford: Altamira Press (Chapter 1).

Ryan, J. and Silvanto, S. (2010) World heritage sites: the purposes and politics of destination branding, *Journal of Travel & Tourism Marketing*, 27(5): 533–45.

Tsiotsou, R. and Ratten, V. (2010) Future research directions in tourism marketing, *Marketing Intelligence & Planning*, 28(4): 533–44.

Weblinks

Fota House and the 'marketing mix' (The Irish Heritage Trust)
http://m.youtube.com/watch?v=s1lknHDogJ4

Destination branding
http://www.macvb.org/intranet/presentation/DestinationBrandingLOzarks6-10-02.ppt

Nova Scotia Tourism Brand, Canada
https://vimeo.com/11491728

Tate Online Strategy 2010–12
http://www.tate.org.uk/research/publications/tate-papers/tate-online-strategy-2010-12

Joust in the royal tournament (online game developed for Hampton Court, UK)
http://henryviiiheadsandhearts.viral-game.co.uk/?c=stf

Kakadu Culture Camp
http://www.environment.gov.au/parks/publications/kakadu/culturecamp.html

ABC's podtour of Kakadu National Park
http://www.abc.net.au/local/stories/2010/03/16/2847217.htm

VisitScotland hopes 'Brave' film will boost tourism
http://www.bbc.co.uk/news/uk-scotland-18490069

The Jane Austen tour of Bath (app)
https://itunes.apple.com/gb/app/austen-tour/id469404965?mt=8

9 Heritage tourism and sustainable development

Sustainability, sustainable development and tourism

There is no one comprehensive definition of sustainability in the context of tourism that embraces the multiple and complex ramifications of the phenomenon. Mowforth and Munt (2009) claim that the principles of sustainability are neither absolute nor immutable. While there is no universal consensus on the definition, its innate equivocality allows the concept to remain flexible and adaptable depending on each circumstance and context. The interpretations of sustainability are thus varied, multidimensional and contextual. Concurrently, sustainability needs to be conceptualised, contextualised and interpreted differently between individuals, organisations and countries (Mowforth and Munt, 2009). Within the remit of tourism development, it is important to acknowledge that various definitions of sustainability can be more used as a general guideline than a prescriptive norm in order to avoid the whole concept of sustainability becoming abstract and somewhat elusive. As Cater (2006: 23) suggests, a 'one size fits all' approach to sustainable tourism will only serve to 'reinforce rather than reduce the very inequalities that it may attempt to reduce'. A variety of criteria needs to be developed and applied to assess the sustainability of tourism products and practices. The concept of sustainability has been linked to managing both current and future development by way of attempting to maintain the balance between environment, economy and an equitable society (Nasser, 2003). It is also essential to realise that sustainability has been increasingly incorporated in economic and socio-cultural areas and issues beyond the remit of environmental concerns. The criteria are generally concerned with the enhancement of the community in terms of environmental, economic and socio-cultural well-being (Mowforth and Munt, 2009). Sustainability can also be understood as strategic management that strives to minimise the direct and indirect costs of a given activity while maximising the attendant benefits, both locally and globally (Weaver, 2006). Ideally, sustainable tourism development needs to be ecologically sensitive, economically viable and socially equitable (Nicholas et al., 2009).

The term 'sustainable development' has increasingly become a buzzword and its practical application is attempted in wider environmental and socio-cultural contexts. But it is important to recognise that sustainable development is not necessarily a new idea (Hall, 1988; Butler, 1999). Hall (1988) argues that an idea of sustainable development has been prevalent since the advent of industrial society since the 1870s. But taking environment into consideration in the principles and processes of development is a fairly recent phenomenon. It was 1987 when the World Commission on Environment and Development published a report named *Our Common Future* (WCED, 1987), which introduced environmental issues to the political development arena. This report is also known as 'the Brundtland Report' in recognition of former Norwegian Prime Minister Gro Harlem Brundtland's leading role as Chair of the World Commission on Environment and

Development. It defines the concept of sustainable development as 'development that meets the need of the present without compromising the ability of future generations to meet their own needs' (WCED, 1987: 43). Two concepts underpinned within the definition are elaborated:

• the concept of 'needs', in particular the essential needs of the world's poor, to which overriding priority should be given; and
• the idea of limitations imposed by the state of technology and social organization on the environment's ability to meet present and future needs.

(WCED, 1987: 43)

It is widely acknowledged that this remains the most popular and well-circulated definition so far (Landorf, 2009). Four sustainable principles are further outlined in the report:

1   holistic planning and strategic decision-making;
2   preservation of essential ecological processes;
3   protections of human heritage and biodiversity;
4   growth that can be sustained over the long term.

However, there emerges a criticism that the Brundtland Report did not, despite recognising a need for economic growth in developing countries, engage with the necessity to balance this against the unsustainable lifestyles adopted in wealthier, developed nations (Landorf, 2009: 54). The publication of the Brundtland Report paved the way for the Rio summit and the adoption of Agenda 21 in 1992 and the World Summit for Sustainable Development, referred to as Rio+10 held in Johannesburg, South Africa, in 2002. Agenda 21 was ratified at the United Nations Conference on Environment and Development (UNCED), entitled 'Earth Summit', held in Rio de Janeiro, Brazil, in 1992. Agenda 21 proposed a number of practical strategies for achieving and implementing a conceptual framework of sustainable development outlined in the Brundtland Report. Importantly, both the Brundtland Report and Agenda 21 placed great emphasis on developing and enhancing the sustainable development of natural resources and environmental issues. There yet existed a substantial lack of focus on implementing the strategies for managing cultural heritage resources. Sustainable development is perceived as a process that ensures that 'we pass onto the next generation a stock of [natural and built] capital assets no less than the stock we have now' (Garrod and Fyall, 2000: 683). Sustainable development is mainly related to environmental issues and concerns, while maintaining economic development. The core of sustainable development lies in the idea of allocating and conserving natural and cultural resources in a sustainable manner in every process of development (Wager, 1995: 520). However, it should be noted that sustainable development as a concept is location-specific and context-specific, as is the case with the concept of sustainability. Clear theoretical analysis of sustainable development is of paramount significance in applying the concept of sustainable development to the context of tourism development. Hunter (1997) brings attention to the significance of conceptually reconnecting the concerns of sustainable tourism with those of sustainable development. Sustainable tourism research should not be isolated from the continuing debates on the meaning and implications of sustainable development. More importantly, it is argued that sustainable tourism should be regarded as an 'adaptive paradigm which legitimizes a variety of approaches according to specific circumstances' (Hunter, 1997: 851).

Furthermore, there is a critical need for more rigorous intellectual engagement with such broad concepts as 'sustainability' and 'sustainable development' when applied to other contexts such as tourism development. It is fallible to assume that these concepts provide a rigid theoretical framework that can be universally applicable to different contexts and locations. Undifferentiated application of these concepts could maintain and reinforce existing hegemonic perspectives inherent in power relations between developed and developing countries. Sustainability can be used as a means of supporting and enhancing the bases of power by elitist social groups in developing countries (Mowforth and Munt, 2009). Here, sustainability could serve as a 'discourse that is contested and through which power circulates' (Mowforth and Munt, 2009: 374). From an idealist perspective, regulations are generally perceived to be critical in maintaining and enhancing sustainability in the context of tourism. However, it should be noted that regulations do not necessarily improve the empowerment of local communities and people. Particularly in developing countries where regulations are often related to securing and reinforcing the power of a minority of elitist people, more careful approaches are critical in achieving the long-term sustainability of tourism development through collaboration and cooperation among different stakeholders.

Heritage tourism and sustainable development

In the heritage arena, sustainable development has undeniably become a key principle, a fundamental way of thinking in heritage management in recent decades. Achieving sustainable development in heritage management has become a major concern for both academics and practitioners alike. It has been generally acknowledged that there exists a close association between the fundamental elements of the heritage mission and the principles of sustainable development (Phillips, 1995; Garrod and Fyall, 2000; Pollock-Ellwand, 2011). Even within the discipline of archaeology and heritage studies, there emerges critical recognition of the social value of heritage as an effective medium for facilitating the long-term sustainability of communities and destinations. The traditionally held 'curatorial approach' in heritage management is not entirely synonymous with the more generally accepted notion of sustainable development (Garrod and Fyall, 2000). As explicated in Chapter 3, the heritage conservation movement in a collective sense is largely rooted in nineteenth-century Europe and America, which saw the establishment of agencies and the legislation of laws to protect valuable natural and cultural resources. Compared to this, sustainable development is a fairly recent phenomenon. Garrod and Fyall's (2000) study suggests that heritage sites tend to emphasise conservation and education rather than their contemporary use and local community. Likewise, there is a widely held belief that sustaining heritage is mainly concerned with addressing technical issues, such as minimising physical damage to built heritage (Tweed and Sutherland, 2007).

It is significant to recognise that conservation-focused approaches in heritage management are often devoid of social context. This point is concurrent with Keitumetse (2011) who claims that the field of heritage management is guided by the discipline of archaeology which focuses on tangible elements of heritage at the expense of intangible heritage. In this regard, it is essential to recognise that conservation-driven heritage management is not always in alignment with sustainability imperatives, not to mention the possible risks business-oriented approaches may run. McKercher and du Cros (2002: 45) recognise sustainability as one of fundamental principles in discussions of cultural heritage management. Sustainability of heritage is interpreted as follows (see also Table 9.1).

Table 9.1 *Sustainable development strategic imperatives in WCED (1987) and their potential relevance to heritage management*

Sustainable development strategic imperatives	Relevance/lessons for heritage management
Changing the quality of growth by meeting human needs by increasing productive potential and ensuring equitable opportunities for all.	Sustainable heritage tourism incorporating aspects of intangible (community-based) and tangible (physical) heritage.
Ensuring a sustainable level of population.	Monitoring access to monuments; establishing and abiding by carrying capacity levels as well as limits of acceptable change for heritage resource utilisation, particularly in relation to tourism development.
Reorienting technology and managing risk.	Virtual heritage interpretation and high-tech presentation and representation.
Merging environment and economics in decision-making.	Merging other uses of the historic environment with sustainable practices of heritage tourism.
Participation of all concerned citizens at the national level.	Active and meaningful local community involvement in natural resource management through implementation of cultural heritage perspectives.
The emergence of partnerships.	Sustainable development in broader heritage management perspectives that include human–environment interactions.

Source: adapted from Keitumetse (2011).

- Cultural heritage assets should be used only in culturally appropriate and sustainable ways.
- Each cultural heritage asset will have its own meaning and assessable cultural significance or values.
- Some cultures differ in their view about how much intervention or change can occur before an asset ceases to be authentic.
- Some heritage assets are too fragile or sacred to be fully accessible to the public, including tourists.
- The identification, documentation and conservation of heritage assets are essential parts of the development of sustainability.
- Consultation of stakeholders is an important part of developing an asset sustainably.

It is widely acknowledged that heritage interpretation as an essential constituent of heritage management plays a significant role in facilitating and supporting the sustainable development of heritage tourism (Moscardo, 1996; Tubb, 2003; Landorf, 2009). Heritage interpretation is regarded, as discussed in Chapter 3, as a key factor in creating mindful visitors, thereby ensuring both effective management and conservation of built heritage for sustainable tourism development (Moscardo, 1996). According to Moscardo (1996: 393):

Mindful visitors will understand the consequences of their actions and be able to behave in ways that lessen their impacts on a site. Mindful visitors will also have a greater appreciation and understanding of a site, and such understanding can provide both support for changing their behaviors on site and for the conservation of the site.

There has also been increasing awareness that respecting local community and encouraging its involvement is of paramount significance in achieving and enhancing sustainable development and management of heritage. Involving a wider range of stakeholders from the decision-making process plays a key role in facilitating the sustainable development of heritage tourism. Pollock-Ellwand (2011) emphasises the significance of an integrated approach to heritage conservation and sustainable development in place of divided approaches to natural and cultural conservation, environmental and economic processes and tangible and intangible resources. It is further argued that searching for a shared perspective that unites the consideration of natural and cultural systems remains the biggest challenge for both heritage conservation and sustainable development. Accordingly, heritage conservation needs to be holistic, considering its repositioning within a wider social and environmental context. New management philosophies and innovative practices need to be actively incorporated in enhancing sustainable development in heritage management and conservation.

McKercher and du Cros (2002: 43) define cultural heritage management as 'the systematic care taken to maintain the cultural values of cultural heritage assets for the enjoyment of present and future generations'. Therefore, sustainable cultural heritage management is the management that ensures the present use of cultural assets without compromising the ability of future generations to use and benefit from those assets (Garrod and Fyall, 2000: 691). This is not as easy as it may appear, especially for developing countries, whose economic growth is prioritised over the need for preserving heritage resources. However, increasing focus has been placed on the significance of respecting natural environment and cultural assets, which is essential in facilitating economic development in a sustainable manner. An 'economy first' approach has thus been criticised as not fully considering the possible socio-cultural and environmental consequences of economic development. Even in developed countries, there has been a heightened realisation of the social dimension of sustainable development as a qualitative indicator in considering and evaluating the contribution of heritage to individuals and communities (see Case study 9.1).

Case study 9.1: Sustainable framework for heritage and tourism

Council of Europe Framework Convention on the value of cultural heritage for society

This treaty, adopted in 2005, underscores the significance of cultural heritage in enhancing the sustainable development of contemporary societies. It reflects a shift from the question 'How and by what procedure can we preserve the heritage?' to the question 'Why should we enhance its value, and for whom?'. It is based on the idea that knowledge and use of heritage form part of the citizen's right to participate in cultural life as defined in the Universal Declaration of Human Rights. Heritage is conceptualised both as a resource for human development, the enhancement of cultural diversity and the promotion of intercultural dialogue, and as a tool for an economic development model based on the principles of sustainable resource use.

Section II – Contribution of cultural heritage to society and human development
Article 9 – Sustainable use of the cultural heritage
To sustain the cultural heritage, the Parties undertake to:

a   promote respect for the integrity of the cultural heritage by ensuring that decisions about change include an understanding of the cultural values involved;
b   define and promote principles for sustainable management, and to encourage maintenance;
c   ensure that all general technical regulations take account of the specific conservation requirements of cultural heritage;
d   promote the use of materials, techniques and skills based on tradition, and explore their potential for contemporary applications;
e   promote high-quality work through systems of professional qualifications and accreditation for individuals, businesses and institutions.

Sources: Council of Europe, 2006;http://conventions.coe.int/Treaty/Commun/QueVoulezVous.asp?NT=199&CM=8&CL=ENG.

The Global Code of Ethics for Tourism

In 1999, the United Nations World Tourism Organization (UNWTO) General Assembly adopted the Global Code of Ethics for Tourism as a framework to tackle these issues. The code, adopted in 2001 by the UN General Assembly, is a comprehensive set of principles designed to guide stakeholders, such as governments, local communities, the tourism sector and professionals, as well as visitors, in the responsible and sustainable development of tourism.

Article 3: Tourism, a user of the cultural heritage of mankind and a contributor to its enhancement

1   Tourism resources belong to the common heritage of mankind; the communities in whose territories they are situated have particular rights and obligations to them;
2   Tourism policies and activities should be conducted with respect for the artistic, archaeological and cultural heritage, which they should protect and pass on to future generations; particular care should be devoted to preserving and upgrading monuments, shrines and museums as well as archaeological and historic sites which must be widely open to tourist visits; encouragement should be given to public access to privately-owned cultural property and monuments, with respect for the rights of their owners, as well as to religious buildings, without prejudice to normal needs of worship;
3   Financial resources derived from visits to cultural sites and monuments should, at least in part, be used for the upkeep, safeguard, development and embellishment of this heritage;
4   Tourism activity should be planned in such a way as to allow traditional cultural products, crafts and folklore to survive and flourish, rather than causing them to degenerate and become standardized.

Source: http://www.unwto.org/ethics/full_text/en/pdf/CODIGO_PASAPORTE_ING.pdf.

In order to enhance sustainable development of heritage tourism, it is critical to develop and facilitate integrated and informed approaches that incorporate both tangible and intangible heritage, connect communities with heritage environment and strengthen social and economic heritage values. Economic benefits may be paramount to the success of heritage tourism development, however, non-economic benefits such as community empowerment and participation and social cohesion also need to be counted as integral factors in influencing heritage conservation and sustainable development. Sustainability should be incorporated in heritage planning and management as a 'potential for bringing heritage conservation, tourism and economic development into a balanced and constructive relationship' (Loulanski and Loulanski, 2011: 843). Importantly, sustainable development should not be exploited, in all its guises and facets, as an effective marketing tool to develop and promote heritage tourism, as evident in certain practices of eco tourism development such as 'greenwashing'. Finally, there is a critical need, as Pollock-Ellwand (2011) emphasises, to develop an integrated and collaborative approach between heritage conservation and sustainable development that seeks innovations in partnerships, policies and perspectives. Hence, it is important to examine how different stakeholders define sustainable development in a way that reflects their particular interest and how their different interest can be contested, negotiated and integrated in achieving sustainability in heritage tourism development.

Stakeholder collaboration and heritage management

As explicated in Chapter 3, the relationship between heritage and tourism is often characterised by the conflicts and tensions inherent in conservation and development. There is a critical need to call for the systematic examination and analysis of an interdependent and interrelated relationship between heritage and tourism. In order to achieve sustainable development in heritage tourism in the long term, therefore, it is crucial to employ a collaborative approach between heritage management and tourism development (see Aas *et al.*, 2005; Nyaupane, 2009; Pollock-Ellwand, 2011). This goal is more of a complicated task than it would appear. There are two schools of thought on sustainable tourism. The functional approach evaluates tourism and its impact on the tourist destination as a cultural resource. On the contrary, the political economy approach focuses on the 'structural inequalities in world trade, characterised by severe distortions and imbalances in the share of income and profits from tourism that remain inside a peripheral economy' (Nasser, 2003: 476). In this approach, critical emphasis is placed on the roles the government play in intervening in the market and encouraging active local involvement. Nasser (2003: 476) further emphasises:

> it is vital to integrate planning for sustainable tourism with national development plans in general and sector targets in particular. It is also necessary to recognise the mutually dependent interests of the public and private sectors in tourism. It is in the government's interests to create the conditions and business environment within which private local business can make a reasonable profit.

The active and continued engagement of a range of stakeholders is of pivotal significance in achieving a long-term, holistic and sustainable development of heritage tourism. Stakeholder theory was originally developed in the field of business management with the purpose of identifying the roles of stakeholders in a corporation that are key to its management (Nicholas *et al.*, 2009). In tourism literature, the application of stake-holder theory has been fairly limited in areas such as tourism planning and development processes. In most of the literature, substantial focus is placed on identifying key stake-holders and emphasising the significance of their collaboration in tourism planning and development (Jamal and Getz, 1995; Ritchie and Crouch, 2003; Nyaupane, 2009). It is contended that stakeholder involvement needs to be incorporated in any sustainable tour-ism plan in order to reduce conflict (Byrd, 2007). Recognising the potential of tourism as a driver for sustainable development, the UNWTO, in line with the Global Code of Ethics for Tourism, has created TOURPACT: a framework for Tourism Partnerships for Development. TOURPACT is a network of stakeholders committed to achieving the Millennium Development Goals (MDGs), advancing CSR through tourism and building a tourism sector that generates social and economic benefits for host communities while contributing to tourism growth.

There is no universal definition of 'stakeholder' in tourism literature. Derived from the field of strategic management studies, a stakeholder is defined as any individual or group who can affect or is affected by the achievement of an organisation's objectives (Freeman, 1984). According to Friedman and Miles (2006), the main groups of stakeholders include:

- customers;
- employees;
- local communities;
- suppliers and distributors;
- shareholders.

Similarly, stakeholder theory recognises that there are multiple parties involved in the management process such as governmental bodies, political groups, local communities and associated business enterprises (Friedman and Miles, 2002). In the context of tour-ism, the relevance of stakeholder theory is comparatively new and limited. Timothy and Boyd (2003) define stakeholders as interest groups involved in the conservation of herit-age and heritage tourism activities such as heritage conservation advocacy groups, public agencies, business associations, NGOs and other groups who directly and indirectly ben-efit from heritage tourism development. Heritage brings a range of benefits to different stakeholders. Nyaupane (2009: 158) explains:

> for individuals and households, it [heritage] provides a variety of artistic, aes-thetic, spiritual, cognitive and recreation needs. For private companies, it is a source of profits through tourism. For cities, towns and local authorities, her-itage is a means of improving the community image. Heritage has a strong community connection. From a community perspective, the aim of heritage conservation is to enhance the environment... connecting individuals to the place and the culture.

It is significant to identify a common ground and interest between different stakehold-ers, even from the stage of planning tourism development. Collaboration is defined as a 'process through which parties who see different aspects of a problem can con-structively explore their differences and search for solutions that go beyond their own limited vision of what is possible' (Gray, 1989: 5). Collaboration is thus viewed as a 'fundamental ingredient in sustainable development' (Sautter and Leisen, 1999: 312). In this light, it is critical to identify and legitimise all potential stakeholders in the planning process, including those who can represent the local community, and facilitate their mutual understanding for shared ownership and consensus (Mowforth and Munt, 2009). Key to a collaborative approach is to engage all interested stakeholders in the decision-making process. In particular, those who could be most impacted by tourism development need to be directly involved in developing decision-making (Jamal and Tanase, 2005) (see Table 9.2).

Table 9.2 *Challenges in stakeholder cooperation and public participation*

Formulating a clear idea of different stakeholder groups can be difficult.	Unravelling the identity and structure of different stakeholder groups can be time consuming and the results are not obvious. For example, different agencies can be involved in the management of a site and have different goals and objectives.
Open discussion may be seen as a threat to one's power and control.	Some stakeholders are unwilling to support wider participation, especially when it is seen as a threat to their authority. This situation eventually creates a climate of distrust, limiting the site manager's ability to deal with the public.
The most vocal critics can dominate the participation process.	Public hearings can become forums in which the most vocal critics of a plan can dominate discussions and exclude others from the process. This can happen if an organised lobby group is heavily represented.
Large numbers of people may be overlooked because they are not as vocal as other groups.	While most people will have an opinion, many will not feel strongly about the issue. This large majority risks being ignored. Consideration of these groups is essential to ensuring long-term public support.
Hierarchical structures may inhibit stakeholder participation in decision-making.	In many societies the formal structure of institutions and organisations as well as cultural norms may make it difficult to elicit the opinions of certain groups making stakeholder participation in formal meetings impossible. A few powerful agencies may dominate, overwhelming other stakeholders and blocking cooperation.
Public participation may be more a form of appeasement than a way to solicit stakeholders' input.	Offering local communities the opportunity to participate raises expectations about acceptance of their suggestions.
Overemphasis on involving stakeholder groups can lead to a failure to recognise certain effects on resources.	Managers must understand how stakeholders perceive impacts and define acceptability. However, many stakeholder groups can have limited knowledge about natural and cultural resources and may be unaware of potential negative impacts. While public participation is necessary, over-reliance on public input can lead to inaction and a deterioration of conditions over time.

Source: Pedersen (2002: 39).

Differences in values, interests, expectations and priorities among various stakeholders may create conflicts in managing and preserving heritage, thereby posing operational challenges and difficulties (Nyaupane, 2009). In examining heritage complexity and tourism in Lumbini, one of the most important Buddhist sites in Nepal, Nyaupane (2009) claims that the locals, mainly Hindus and Muslims, view their heritage as a source of economic development rather than a spiritual aspiration. Compared to this, the Nepalese government uses the site for maintaining and enhancing national pride, promoting tourism and resorting to international support. Here, each stakeholder differently perceives the meaning and significance of this heritage site. Western-oriented approaches and practices may not necessarily consider operational, structural and cultural limits to community participation in developing countries (Tosun, 2000). It would thus be desirable to establish local organisations that could play a crucial role in enhancing public awareness concerning the significance of community participation and engagement, as illustrated in Case study 9.2.

Furthermore, there is a risk of overemphasising the need for ecological protection to achieve sustainable development in developed countries, leading to underestimating the benefits of such natural resources for local people and neglecting the livelihood needs of local communities (Scheyvens, 2002). An overemphasis on conserving natural resources to enhance the tourist experience may undermine the local and cultural imperatives of utilising these resources. This point is concurrent in the context of heritage tourism development. Too much focus on Western-oriented heritage development and conservation in developing countries could lead to undervaluing the role of the community in the protection and management of heritage, thereby deteriorating the cultural identity and integrity of the local people and their connections with heritage. Therefore, sustainable heritage tourism development in developing countries needs to recognise the main concerns and needs of their local community as a focal point of address.

Community involvement and participation

There has been an increasing focus on involvement and participation of local communities as a central focus of sustainable development (Prentice, 1993; Tosun, 2000; Stronza and Gordillo, 2008; Darcy and Wearing, 2009; Hung *et al.*, 2011). Participation has been regarded as inherently positive for change and development (Mowforth and Munt, 2009). Particularly, community participation has become integral in the ideal of people-centred approaches to development. Tosun (2000: 615) defines that:

> Community participation refers to a form of voluntary action in which individuals confront opportunities and responsibilities of citizenship... community participation is a tool to readjust the balance of power and reassert local community views against those of the developers or the local authority, or to redefine professionalism, which may determine the conditions of successful participation and prevent manipulation of a community in the participation process.

According to Murphy (1985), participation suggests empowerment on the part of the community affected by development. Focus on participation has been dominant in sustainable development perspectives within the realms of ecotourism (see Scheyvens, 2002; Stronza and Gordillo, 2008). Importantly, local residents' support and participation also play an integral role in facilitating sustainable development in heritage tourism. In recent literature on heritage tourism, focus has been placed on understanding

Case study 9.2: Heritage Watch in Cambodia

Heritage Watch, a non-profit organisation, was founded in 2003 in order to preserve Southeast Asia's cultural heritage. Heritage Watch launched an innovative project of heritage protection and poverty reduction at one of Southeast Asia's largest temple complexes, the ancient Khmer capital of Koh Ker in 2007. This project was supported by various organisations and private donors, including Friends of Khmer Culture, Pepy Ride, the Fonds Famille vanBeek and Lonely Planet. This tenth-century site, home to dozens of magnificent temples, was isolated for much of the last century by war, landmines and poor roads. But due to recent demining efforts and improved roads, Koh Ker is now poised to become a major tourist destination. Through the project, Heritage Watch promoted the protection of the temple complex while providing a sustainable development strategy. The area is among the poorest in Cambodia where the majority of local people are disabled landmine victims who mainly rely on farming and forest scavenging for subsistence. This poverty has naturally exacerbated looting at Koh Ker, which was heavily plundered in the 1990s. However, much of this remarkable site is still intact, and its future protection hinges on the local community being able to benefit from the coming economic boom. Heritage Watch provided training in heritage protection and conservation for the local community, organising and equipping community patrols to protect the temples from looting. It also established a baseline survey of past looting at the temples and, using this, recent thefts can easily be detected. These patrols were provided with training in basic environmental management, including picking up litter and emptying rubbish bins. Training in tourism at a basic level was also provided, so that the villagers could establish sustainable businesses near the temples – such as refreshment stands, ox-cart tours of the site and traditional craft sales. Village women and the disabled, some of the most disadvantaged groups in the community, will be trained in the production of these crafts. Income was generated by the villagers through the sale of craft goods, ox-cart rides and other products. Perhaps most importantly, this project illustrated to the entirety of Cambodia that protecting heritage is more financially advantageous than destroying it.

Source: www.heritagewatchinternational.org.

residents' attitudes and perceptions towards tourism impacts on heritage and its sustainable development in their communities (Uriely *et al.*, 2002; Nicholas *et al.*, 2009; Chen and Chen, 2010; Lenik, 2013). Resident involvement in planning provides communities with the opportunity to raise their concern in relation to promoting as well as conserving and protecting their own heritage (Timothy and Boyd, 2003). Nasser (2003) argues that encouraging local involvement in achieving sustainability surpasses moral obligation. The local population's longer-term perspective is invaluable in that it ensures respect and reappreciation of old lifestyles and traditions. Therefore, local participation can serve as a main actor in achieving sustainable heritage tourism development on a longer-term basis.

In examining the participation of local residents in managing New Lanark WHS in the Greater Glasgow and Clyde Valley area of Scotland, Garrod *et al.* (2012) assert that local residents play active roles in decision-making at New Lanark. They also point out that New Lanark aims to practise a 'consultative' approach to engaging local residents, thereby attempting to maintain a sustainable community in the longer term. However, three main limitations on its consultative approach are identified as follows:

- Local residents have formal representation on only one of the three subsidiaries of the trust (the New Lanark Trust), which serves to limit their ability to influence decision-making to issues related directly to housing.
- Local residents living on site are engaged with more intensively than those living in the surrounding area, suggesting that the interests of the latter group have less salience in the trust's decision-making.
- Consultation tends to take place in an ad hoc manner and the agenda seems to be determined mainly by the trust, which may limit the degree to which consultation may actually have a tangible impact on decision-making.

(Garrod *et al.*, 2012: 1169)

The increased sense of local cohesion has been categorised as a neo-populist perspective that idealises bottom-up strategies that are, in general, small scale and local driven as a resistance to top-down approaches. Scheyvens (2002) proposes that it is essential to empower disenfranchised groups with opportunities to have greater control over their own lives. Central to this idea is utilising local resources and skill bases, while retaining cultural integrity. The principles of the neo-populist approach thus offer a platform for understanding sustainable development, stressing the need for local communities to be central to the planning and management of tourism development. This shift in focus needs to be clearly reflected in planning the sustainable development of heritage tourism. Given social and intangible values of heritage in sustaining the cultural and historical integrity of a community, local participation in planning, managing and promoting heritage tourism should be prioritised before taking any other stakeholders' perspectives into consideration (see Case study 9.3). Furthermore, encouraging community participation in heritage management and conservation can play a crucial role in facilitating the subaltern and alternative discourses of heritage (see Figure 9.1).

Participation is not, however, free from criticism (Koch, 1997; Cooke and Kothari, 2001; Darcy and Wearing, 2009). Koch (1997) identifies a range of potential constraints to high levels of community participation. A sense of ownership on the part of the local community is crucial in encouraging active community participation. In the context of heritage tourism, a sense of cultural ownership over heritage can be enhanced by community participation. But interestingly, Cooke and Kothari (2001: 172) warn that participation could act as an 'unjustified exercise of power'. This point is closely related to unequal political structures and relations inherent in participatory approaches and exercises. Unclear proprietorship over land and resources and control by external organisations, for example, could lead to discouraging local participation (Koch, 1997). In certain cases, participation could lead to reinforcing the traditional top-down and bureaucratic approach to development practices, thereby discouraging close cooperation among stakeholders. Darcy and Wearing (2009: 196) regard public participation in planning as inherently flawed, claiming that:

> it [public participation] can fail to address the needs of those members of the community who are not involved in a pressure group and who may be less educated, articulate or may not be politically connected, yet are also affected by the development.

Participatory forms of democracy can only be realised on a formal institutional level without a clear understanding of the local needs and effective mechanisms to motivate active

Case study 9.3: The benefits of community participation, Heritage Lottery Fund, UK

The Heritage Lottery Fund (HLF) was set up in 1994 to distribute money raised by the National Lottery to heritage projects throughout the UK. The HLF gives grants to support a wide range of projects involving the local, regional and national heritage of the United Kingdom. Below are the benefits of community participation identified by the HLF as a guideline for heritage projects.

For your project
- Increasing the range of skills, knowledge and experience in your project.
- Bringing richness, new perspectives and new ideas or ways of working.
- Ensuring the project reflects local needs, represents communities in a sensitive way and avoids negative impacts.

For your organisation
- Creating links with the community and providing powerful ambassadors for your organisation.
- Building new skills and experiences that your organisation can use for other work and in the future.
- Showing public accountability.
- Inspiring and demonstrating organisational change and innovative practice.

For individuals involved
- An opportunity to use existing skills and experience while gaining new ones.
- Gaining confidence.
- Meeting people and/or feeling part of their community.
- Seeing their ideas and work recognised and knowing that they have made a difference.

For your local community
- Transferring skills and experience that individuals gain to other community projects and activities.
- Strengthening local pride, sense of community and quality of life.
- Linking people together so they feel less isolated and have more support within their community.
- Learning about and enjoying their local heritage.
- Organisations working more closely together and identifying opportunities for joint projects.

For heritage
- More people feeling committed to their local heritage and valuing it.
- People taking action to look after heritage.
- Better use of heritage assets.

Sources: Heritage Lottery Fund; http://www.hlf.org.uk/HowToApply/goodpractice/Documents/Thinking_about_community_participation.pdf.

Figure 9.1 Community participation in Giong festival, Hanoi, Vietnam

community involvement (Hailey, 2001). This tendency has been extensively observed in heritage tourism development, particularly in relation to the relative lack of power assigned to the locals in developing their locality for tourism in developing countries. There is often a wide consensus that it is the sole responsibility of the government to protect and develop heritage. The increasing popularity of heritage tourism has led, however, to a realisation that the involvement of local communities is essential in sustainable heritage management. Local communities involve different individuals and groups encompassing different political goals, socio-economic positions and cultural aspirations. In developing a strategy promoting sustainable development of both natural and cultural resources in Angkor, Cambodia, Wager (1995) contends that the involvement of local community residents in managing the WHSs can foster respect of sustainable heritage (see Figure 9.2). In examining the factors that influence local community residents' support for the Pitons Management Area (PMA) as a WHS in St. Lucia and their support for sustainable tourism development, Nicholas *et al.* (2009) establish independent variables such as community attachment, environmental attitudes and involvement in the PMA. The findings construed from 319 resident samples suggest that community attachment positively influences their support behaviours and environmental attitudes indirectly influence the support behaviours through perceptions about the PMA. In comparison, the level of involvement in the PMA has no significant bearing on support for sustainable tourism development. However, this does not negate the need for increased involvement of local residents in the activities of the PMA. Community involvement is a critical element of sustainable tourism development at WHSs in developing countries, as is the case with other heritage sites and settings. In the case of the ancient city of Pingyao in China, community involvement and local residents' needs are not included in the local plans for both conservation and development, although specified at the level of central government (Wang, 2012). The critical lack of community involvement in preserving and developing heritage, along with decentralised decision-making at the central and local levels, has transformed Pingyao from a traditional-living city into a historic tourist city, devoid of the local population and activities in its historic centre (Wang, 2012: 2). The historic town of Vigan in Philippines was appointed as a model of best practices in WHS management in 2012. Among various factors, collaborative stakeholder involvement including active local participation proved essential in successfully managing the town (see Case study 9.4).

Figure 9.2 Angkor Wat, Cambodia (taken by Kapsu Lee)

Case study 9.4: The historic town of Vigan, Philippines

In October 2012, the historic town of Vigan (Philippines), inscribed on the WH List in 1999, was recognised as a model of best practices in WHS management. Vigan's successful and sustainable management has been achieved with relatively limited resources, which should make it adaptable to sites in all countries; the integration of local community and a multifaceted approach to the protection of the site. Below are some exemplary practices used to enable the active participation of local stakeholders:

- Even before the site was inscribed as a WHS, public fora and multistakeholder workshops were organised to formulate a vision statement for the city and formulate cultural tourism strategies to uplift the city's economy and well-being. Likewise, a series of public hearings were held to provide all stakeholders with the opportunity to voice their opinions regarding the enactment of each of the legislative measures to safeguard the built heritage of the city. This is quite an achievement, considering that the legislative measures have curtailed to a great extent the right of homeowners to develop their private properties according to their wishes.
- Composed of owners of historic properties within the protected zones, the Save Vigan Ancestral Homeowners Association, Incorporated (SVAHAI) was

organised to empower homeowners and enable their active participation in the conservation programme of the city government. All matters pertaining to safeguarding and conservation of the protected zones are brought to the attention of the SVAHAI members. Published jointly by the city government and UNESCO, a Heritage Homeowner's Manual, a practical and user-friendly management tool, has been distributed to guide the custodians in the maintenance, repair and adaptive re-use of their historic properties, thereby promoting responsible stewardship of their heritage.

- The Vigan Tourism Council composed of various stakeholders from academia (universities and colleges), craft industries, the infrastructure sector (transportation and communication), the business sector (association of souvenir shops, furniture makers, hotel and restaurant owners) and religious and government sectors was established to help in the development of an appropriate tourism industry in the city.
- The Vigan Conservation Council, which reviews and approves applications for construction, renovation, restoration and other works in the core and buffer zones of the heritage district, is provided for by Ordinance No. 7 S 2006. It is composed of representatives from the local government, the academe, the SVAHAI, NGOs and the church.

Sources: http://whc.unesco.org/uploads/news/documents/news-948-1.docx; http://whc.unesco.org/en/news/948.

Despite its potential to solve major issues of tourism development, incorporating community participation leaves a challenging task in the context of developing countries (Cater, 1991; Brohman, 1996; Tosun, 2000). Apart from the obvious barriers represented by asymmetries of power and legislative systems that potentially undermine public voice, Tosun (2000) further identifies more immediate restrictions on local decision-making such as a lack of expertise, minimal financial resources, cultural traditions and ways of life, and lack of trained human resources. Li (2006) supports this view in recognising efficiency to be more important than fairness. It is argued that involving the local community in the decision-making process can be very costly and inefficient. In order to increase equity within the communities, sound practices regarding social structures need to be implemented; even though community members may still not be in control, they should at least have an avenue available for direct consultation (Wearing, 2001) (see Table 9.3).

In managing heritage tourism in developing countries, each specific local circumstance needs to be considered in developing policies and formulating institutional framework. Furthermore, local governments need to be more proactive in encouraging community participation as a main vehicle for heritage conservation and tourism management. Well-planned and well-informed community participation can play a crucial role in enhancing sustainable development in heritage tourism. Reflecting the concerns and interests of local people, even some hidden stakeholders such as the poor and women, in the tourism development of heritage resources needs to be prioritised, thereby pursuing democratic decision-making and developing procedures. Closer cooperation with a variety of international agencies, NGOs and businesses would also contribute to facilitating the sustainable development of heritage tourism. Heritage is closely related to constructing, reconstructing and maintaining the cultural identities of local people. Learning lessons from Western

Table 9.3 *Limitations to community participation in the tourism development process in developing countries*

Operational limitations	Centralisation of public administration of tourism
	Lack of coordination
	Lack of information
Structural limitations	Attitudes of professionals
	Lack of expertise
	Elite domination
	Lack of appropriate legal system
	Lack of trained human resources
	Relatively high cost of community participation
	Lack of financial resources
Cultural limitations	Limited capacity of poor people
	Apathy and low level of awareness in the local community

Source: Tosun (2000).

paradigms could be helpful, however it should be borne in mind that context-specific approaches considering the distinctive local cultural characteristics of developing countries are essential in achieving the sustainable development of heritage tourism.

Conclusion

In the existing tourism literature, there is a plethora of definitions of sustainability and sustainable development on a general level. The overabundance of these definitions often leads to complicating their applications and operations in specific contexts of tourism development such as heritage tourism. There thus emerges a critical need for different and varied interpretations of sustainability which are location- and context-specific. The concept of sustainable development is malleable, as Hunter (1997) claims, and each specific location and context needs to be carefully considered in its application. In this regard, it would be useful to have a clear and universal definition and operational guidelines that could be generally applicable to managing heritage sites and settings. However, it is of crucial significance to fully consider the individual characteristics and contexts of each heritage attraction and the implications in further enhancing the quality of sustainable development. Furthermore, it is essential to understand interconnection and interdependence between cultural heritage management and sustainability. Defining and effectively managing stakeholders is a prerequisite in ensuring their collective responsibility for achieving longer-term goals in sustainable heritage tourism development. Community involvement and participation is integral to sustainable heritage tourism development. A sense of cultural ownership of heritage sites and settings on the part of local communities can be enhanced by way of encouraging active community participation. Conflicts and contingences among various stakeholders can be a major source of dissonance in heritage management. Identifying a common interest and ground between different stakeholders is essential in achieving the long-term sustainability in heritage conservation and management. Finally, Western paradigms and practices of heritage management need to be reviewed, modified and reappropriated for the sustainable planning and management of heritage tourism in developing countries.

Research questions

1 Try to develop the definitions of sustainability and sustainable development within the context of heritage tourism.
2 Why is sustainability important in heritage tourism development?
3 Discuss ways in which heritage tourism can contribute to enhancing social sustainability in the destinations concerned.
4 Using relevant examples, identify and explain different interests and roles of major stakeholders in popular WHSs for tourism.
5 Try to devise a sustainability indicator that can be applied to heritage tourism management.
6 Why is it important to recognise and incorporate different stakeholder viewpoints and interests in enhancing the sustainable development of heritage tourism?
7 Critically discuss the main issues that impede active community involvement in developing countries.
8 Suggest some ways in which local participation and involvement could be enhanced in heritage management.

Learning material

Aas, C., Ladkin, A. and Fletcher, J. (2005) Stakeholder collaboration and heritage management, *Annals of Tourism Research*, 32(1): 28–48.
Cater, E. (2006) Ecotourism as a Western control, *Journal of Ecotourism*, 5(1&2): 23–39.
du Cros, H. (2007) Too much of a good thing? Visitor congestion management issues for popular world heritage tourist attractions, *Journal of Heritage Tourism*, 2(3): 225–38.
Garrod, B. and Fyall, A. (2000) Managing heritage tourism, *Annals of Tourism Research*, 27(3): 682–708.
Garrod, B., Fyall, A., Leask, A. and Reid, E. (2012) Engaging residents as stakeholders of the visitor attraction, *Tourism Management*, 33(5): 1159–73.
Hunter, C. (1997) Sustainable tourism as an adaptive paradigm, *Annals of Tourism Research*, 24(4): 850–67.
Li, W. (2006) Community decision-making: participation in development, *Annals of Tourism Research*, 33(1):132–43.
Mowforth, M. and Munt, I. (2009) *Tourism and Sustainability: Development, Globalisation and New Tourism in the Third World* (3rd edn), London: Routledge.
Nyaupane, G.P. (2009) Heritage complexity and tourism: the case of Lumbini, Nepal, *Journal of Heritage Tourism*, 4(2): 157–72.
Scheyvens, R. (2002) *Tourism for Development: Empowering Communities*, Edinburgh: Pearson Education.
Tosun, C. (2000) Limits to community participation in the tourism development process in developing countries, *Tourism Management*, 21(6): 613–33.
Uriely, N., Israeli, A.A. and Riechel, A. (2002) Heritage proximity and resident attitudes toward tourism development, *Annals of Tourism Research*, 29(3): 859–62.

Weblinks

Go Green! Edinburgh WH Map
http://www.ewht.org.uk/uploads/downloads/Go%20Green%20EWH%20Map.pdf

Community tours Sian Ka'an, Mexico (Green Livings Project)
http://vimeo.com/29992277

Voices of the Galapagos
http://vimeo.com/38369962

The role of local communities in WH and sustainable development
http://www.youtube.com/watch?v=r-KJVOX3agM

Albania: fighting poverty through cultural heritage
http://www.youtube.com/watch?v=GzBHryWLzDU

Old Palestinian village in Lifta, Israel
http://video.pbs.org/video/1893628343

UNESCO Eco Learning Programme in Göreme National Park and Rock Site of Cappadocia, Turkey
http://www.youtube.com/watch?v=JS39vDdfi4k

The Raleigh Project in Nottingham, UK
http://www.bbc.co.uk/news/uk-21508679

The historic town of Vigan, Philippines
http://whc.unesco.org/en/list/502/video

Heritage tourism and cities

Culture, heritage and tourism development in cities

There is a general lack of clear definitions on urban tourism in the existing tourism literature. Urban tourism development is inherently complex and diverse. The research on urban tourism was not regarded as a distinctive academic field prior to the 1980s (Edwards *et al.*, 2008). Despite increasing focus on cities and their tourism development, there has been a paucity of systematic analysis and evaluation concerning the roles of tourism in the context of urban development and regeneration. Urban tourism development is undeniably bound up with post-Fordist, post-industrial and postmodern transitions and ramifications. In a post-Fordist economy, cities are repositioned as the centre of consumption, not production. The post-industrial and postmodern transition of cities since the 1980s has led to the remaking and transformation of cities and their identities. Here, tourism plays a significant role in creating, recreating and reinforcing new place identities within a wider framework of economic restructuring and redevelopment (Coles, 2003; Shaw and Williams, 2004; Williams, 2009). The emergence of the symbolic economy in cities in the 1970s and 1980s was, according to Zukin (1995), founded upon the increasing prominence of culture industries. Cities increasingly used culture as a main economic base and the visual display and consumption of culture serve as cities' main driver for production. In the process of changing the roles of cities as a place of consumption, culture was regarded as the most significant factor in revitalising and restructuring the urban economy. It is claimed that the use of the arts was the main drive in transforming New York City from a place of production to a place of consumption. According to Zukin (1995: 7–8):

> Building a city depends on how people combine the traditional economic factors of land, labor, and capital. But it also depends on how they manipulate symbolic languages of exclusion and entitlement. The look and feel of cities reflect decisions about what – and who – should be visible and what should not, on concepts of order and disorder, and on uses of aesthetic power. In this primal sense, the city has always had a symbolic economy... What is new about the symbolic economy since the 1970s is its symbiosis of image and product, the scope and scale of selling images on a national and even a global level, and the role of the symbolic economy in speaking for, or representing, the city.

Heritage, arts and culture in this context serve as the main agent in facilitating the symbolic economy of cities. In a similar vein, Hall (2000) advocates that the urban economy is becoming increasingly dependent on the production and consumption of culture, thereby leading to the burgeoning of creative cities. Culture is also regarded as a balanced tool for both the conservation of heritage and the development of new entertainment complexes in cities (Smith, 2007). This emphasis on culture and heritage in cities has facilitated the development of cultural clusters as a main hub of urban regeneration and tourism development. In general, the main purpose of developing cultural clusters is to revitalise a particular area of the city, mainly city centres, by way of providing cultural facilities and activities for both residents and tourists. In addressing the idea of clusters and the new economy of competition, Porter (1998: 78) defines a cluster as 'a geographically proximate group of interconnected companies and associated institutions in a particular field'. This type of collaboration can provide an efficient and flexible economic synergy for the community, while creating a new economy of competition. Cultural clusters in cities mainly comprise of various cultural heritage attractions including museums, galleries and arts and heritage centres as unique local resources and assets. Notable examples of good practice exist in the Museumsinsel (Museum Island) in Berlin, the movie industry in Hollywood, the clothes industry in Hong Kong and the theatre district in Covent Garden, London. Culture-led redevelopment could contribute substantially to fostering new images for cities and towns (Evans, 2001; Norris, 2003; Miles and Paddison, 2005).

The city of Baltimore began to rapidly deteriorate during the process of de-industrialisation. According to Norris (2003: 145), the population declined from 950,000 in 1950 to about 651,000 in 2000 and the employment rate in the metropolitan area by 2000 dropped to only 33 per cent. These numbers clearly indicate Baltimore's deterioration in an economic and industrial sense. Therefore, culture-led and tourism-driven city redevelopment projects were vehemently supported by the city's civic and business leaders, thereby redeveloping the city's existing landmarks such as the water-front area, the aquarium and the museums (see Figure 10.1). Heritage and cultural tourism attractions now serve as a main appeal of the city to both international and domestic tourists. The tourism industry in Baltimore has steadily grown, yielding $79,681,155 as tourism-related sales tax revenue in 2010 (http://www.sagepolicy.com/wp-content/uploads/2009/03/visitbaltimore1110.pdf).

Figure 10.1 Old Wharf, Fells Point, Baltimore, USA (taken by Shinhee Park)

However, economic revitalisation utilising the appeal of urban cultural and heritage resources cannot be disassociated from its negative consequences. Importantly, it should be noted that culture-led regeneration is not a panacea for long-standing economic and social issues and problems immanent in an urban context. Moreover, there remain significant uncertainties over the long-term benefits of culture-led regeneration (Tucker, 2008). The main goals of culture-led regeneration projects are indelibly bound up with facilitating economic development as well as enhancing urban image. Culture-led regeneration becomes overtly propelled by excessive commercial development including property and corporate development and urban entre-preneurialism, rather than focusing on the protection of local communities and their cultural identities. As clearly emphasised in the two examples below, excessive commercial develop-ment could counteract the original goals of urban regeneration projects (see Case study 10.1).

Case study 10.1: Urban redevelopment: commercial exploitation of heritage?

The Southbank Centre, London

The Southbank Centre is located on the south bank of the river Thames and is one of Britain's premier art centres. It comprises three main buildings – the Royal Festival Hall, the Queen Elizabeth Hall and the Hayward Gallery. The Royal Festival Hall underwent a substantial renovation between 2005 and 2007, improving the general quality of the venue, including the auditorium, the entrance areas, café and the lay-out of the foyers. A familiar blend of chain restaurants including Yo! Sushi, Eat, Giraffe, Strada and Wagamama and other retail shops were added as new visitor facilities. There ensued a barrage of criticism from the public regarding the com-mercial uses of the public spaces, raising significant concern about turning the area into an identikit retail outlet or shopping mall. A new plan for redeveloping the Hayward Gallery and the neighbouring Queen Elizabeth Hall is being currently pushed forward. There is a consensus that the excessive commercial redevelopment of the Southbank Centre has already reached a saturation point. Moore (2012) warns that this new plan will further the commercial transformation of the Southbank in which any place unconsumed by branding and marketing is regarded as a missed opportunity for commercial exploitation. It is further explicated that the new plan ignores a need to retain non-commercial public space and sustain the architectural and historical values of the buildings. A lack of funding for redevelopment can facilitate possibilities of attracting money-making businesses. It is important to put unused spaces into use through renovation and redevelopment. Also, commercial use of some spaces would definitely enhance the appeal of the buildings and outdoor areas. However, practicality and convenience should not always take precedence over the maintenance of aesthetics and heritage. The encroachments of commerce and consumerism need to be carefully controlled and monitored.

Sources: Moore (2012); www.southbankcentre.co.uk.

'Shanghai-style' redevelopment in Liverpool

Liverpool has recently been transformed into one of the UK's leading urban tour-ism and business destinations. At its heart of transformation lie various urban regeneration projects. As part of the regeneration, Liverpool's historic waterfront has gone through a major facelift. However, plans to create a 'Shanghai-style' high-rise waterfront in Liverpool posed a threat to its WH status. Liverpool's waterfront was granted WH status in 2004 on the grounds that 'Liverpool is an outstanding example of a world mercantile port city, which represents the early development of global trading and cultural connections throughout the British Empire'. Peel Holdings planned to develop the northern docklands, with skyscrapers including the tallest UK building outside London, apartment blocks and a ferry terminal, thereby regenerating former and disused dockland and replicating the drama of Shanghai on Merseyside. However, it was warned that, in the report commissioned by English Heritage, new buildings would have a significant negative impact on the WHS and its outstanding universal value, particularly affecting such heritage assets as the Victoria Clock Tower and the Stanley Dock tobacco warehouse. In a statement, English Heritage said:

> If the scheme in its current form goes ahead, in our view the setting of some of Liverpool's most significant historic buildings will be severely compromised, the archaeological remains of parts of the historic docks are at risk of destruction and the city's historic urban landscape will be permanently unbalanced.

Despite controversies, a £5.5 billion waterfront development, which could put Liverpool's WHS status at risk, was approved in a city councillors' planning meeting in March 2012. The application will now be referred to the secretary of state for communities and local government who will decide if it requires a public inquiry. Careful consideration needs to be taken in making such an optimum development, while retaining its WH status. Dresden in Germany lost its WH status in 2009 after the construction of a new four-lane bridge.

Sources: Carter (2011); http://www.bbc.co.uk/news/uk-england-merseyside-17270508.

As illustrated above, it is often not a choice between development and conservation in heritage but between appropriate and inappropriate development. The actual benefits to the local people and economies of cities need to be taken into full consideration. The human dimension of urban development with an emphasis on socio-cultural provisions should not be overlooked. The support of local communities is essential to the success of culture-led regeneration. It is rather unreasonable to expect that cities should remain static as time progresses. In many cases, redevelopment and regeneration cannot be achieved without commercial development led by private sectors. Capitalising on heritage and cultural sources for urban regeneration becomes inevitable and often necessary. However, it should be noted that commercial development could have negative as well as positive impacts on local heritage and people. Both private developers and public sectors need to prioritise the long-term sustainability of local communities and their historical and cultural authenticity over anticipated economic gains.

Heritage tourism: a panacea for regenerating cities?

The term heritage has long been associated with ancient sites and monuments. It has also been closely related to rural resources and contexts rather than urban assets. However, the potential of heritage becomes recognised as an important asset and resource for maintaining and promoting the appeal of cities and towns. Concurrently, tourism is increasingly viewed as a panacea for the economic recovery and regeneration of cities. Accordingly, Law (1993:1) identifies four factors propelling tourism development in cities:

- The decline of long-established manufacturing activities.
- The need to create new economic activities or face high unemployment.
- The perception of tourism as a growth industry.
- The hope that tourism development will result in the regeneration and revitalisation of urban cores.

Heritage emerged as a last resort after de-industrialisation in many industrial towns and regions. Industrial heritage including old mines, quarries and breweries have been reopened as industrial heritage attractions employing previous workers. In many localities, heritage became the only growth area with substantial support from local authorities. The advent of urban tourism development utilising local heritage in the UK, for example, was closely associated with the industrial crisis in the 1980s. Many local and city councils were initially reluctant to invest in tourism development. However, their various attempts to develop different industries came to no fruition and tourism seemed to be seen as the last resort to bring vitality back to a sluggish economy. This phenomenon was not just confined to the UK but widely practised in many post-industrial cities and towns all across the globe. Heritage tourism development as new economic activities is expected to contribute to restructuring and regenerating the urban economy. Heritage in this context becomes identified as both a profitable resource and an innovative niche. Therefore, the historic core of cities has incorporated new tourism development over recent years, with particular reference to the juxtaposition of heritage and commercial development, an outcome of global economic transition. Orbaşli (2000) claims that history has become a product that can be marketed, sold and recreated for tourists. It should also be noted that an increasing predominance of global culture within the historic core of cities has effaced the clear boundaries between the local and the global. Mordue (2005: 181) emphasises:

> The result is a de-differentiation of the local and global in which local particularity becomes disembedded... Thus, when tourists seek place distinction, they are complicit in a paradoxical effacement of local difference by the industry... This 'glocalization' both ensures the 'quality' of the 'product' in universal terms and compels the staging of place particularities and local cultures as attractions.

Both heritage sites (e.g., attractions and towns) and events (e.g., festivals and special events) play a crucial role in enhancing the images of cities as unique and distinctive tourism destinations. The popularity of urban heritage tourism can, however, lead to standardising both heritage products and experiences in cities and towns. Rojek (1995: 146) points out that the majority of increased 'universal cultural space' shares the same aesthetic and spatial references as their foundation. There is clear evidence worldwide that many cultural and heritage projects lack their own uniqueness and creativity, thereby reproducing and duplicating the same facilities and features. Standardised and homogenous processes and products of urban development are ubiquitous across national and cultural boundaries. This can be attributed to the wide dispersal of global approaches to urban development. In criticising global and 'top-down' approaches in urban development, Chang *et al.* (1996: 286–7) claim:

> Cities differ in their inheritance of urban forms and undertake heritage conservation for varied reasons. Local political and economic aspirations also differ, ensuring that the heritage theme adopted by planning authorities varies from place to place. Thus, although heritage tourism may be the chosen strategy, different destinations tend to accentuate peculiar to their culture and location as a way to differentiate themselves from competitors.

Heritage tourism claims to be low volume and high value, exerting its appeal as a profitable niche in tourism markets. Too much emphasis has been, however, placed on publishing the successful stories of utilising heritage and culture in city regeneration projects. There also exist the limitations of heritage-focused and culture-driven projects. Under the disguise of small, differentiated and individualised products, urban heritage tourism can often provide mass-produced and standardised packages, thereby creating 'tourist bubbles' (see Fainstein and Judd, 1999). Similar heritage attractions reproduced in various regions lead to fierce competition. Despite increasing recognition of heritage as profitable products, it is of paramount significance to realise the inherent risk of excessive commodification that will eventually lead to seriously damaging and distorting local heritage. Academic research on the host residents' perception of tourism development on their community has substantially increased over recent years (Ko and Stewart, 2002; Lee *et al.*, 2007; Jackson, 2008). However, Lee *et al.* (2007) raise a concern that there is a paucity of empirical research concerning the relationship between resident attitudes and support for tourism development. Studies of tourism impacts have been mainly concerned with focusing on rural areas in developing countries. This is also not uncommon within the context of heritage tourism. Therefore, Lee *et al.*'s (2007) study on social and environmental impacts of tourism in a large urban area of York in the UK provides an interesting perspective as it deals with issues of urban tourism and historic resources in a developed country. Such negative impacts of tourism as traffic congestion, lack of parking spaces, litter and the lack of community participation in managing urban tourism are observed and discussed.

In examining the impacts of globalisation on historic districts and centres in Latin America, Scarpaci (2005) reveals that residents in historic centres are largely pessimistic about the benefits of heritage tourism development and remain politically inactive in resolving their situation. It is further revealed within the context of Latin America that local authorities do little to enhance residential buildings whereas too much emphasis is being placed on promoting tourism and commercial enterprises. In examining the impacts of heritage tourism development on the residents of Shi Cha Hai hutong in Beijing, Gu and Ryan (2008) observe that there is a growing concern about the levels of intrusion caused by tourism development into the everyday life of the residents in the hutong (see Figure 10.2).

There also ensues a certain level of skepticism regarding the positive capacities of tourism development in terms of creating employment and preserving the nature of the hutong. Many residents do not regard the preservation of buildings and built heritage as a means to maintain a way of life. Instead, they believe that it is the architectural heritage that attracts tourism and it is tourism that confers commercial values to that architectural heritage. The understanding of the hutong as a special architectural heritage and social entity proves to be more significant than the economic benefits tourism may bring. This study demonstrates the social values of heritage in maintaining and enhancing place attachment and community sustainability.

Figure 10.2 The hutong of Shi Cha Hai in Beijing, China (taken by Sohyun Park)

Heritage, urban regeneration and gentrification

The conflicts between heritage and commerce are often evident in urban development and regeneration. It is important to note that maintaining the historical fabric of cities and enhancing their market appeal is, in principle, rather contradictory. Preserving and conserving heritage is fundamentally regarded as antithetical to its commercial uses, including tourism development. However, it is interesting to observe that urban heritage conservation has often been initiated, developed and promoted as a primary and invaluable component of urban redevelopment and regeneration. In the late 1960s, a critical need was identified to protect historical districts in urban contexts. The Civic Amenities Act legislated in 1967 in the UK, for instance, required all local planning authorities to designate and protect conservation areas. Following this, the practice of designating conservation areas in cities has become prevalent in various parts of the world. It seems to be quite ironic to recognise the interlinked and interdependent relationship between heritage conservation and urban regeneration. In this sense, urban heritage conservation can be regarded as rather a permanent process of 'newing' in the construction and promotion of modern urban landscape (Relph, 1987). Through restoration and conservation, urban heritage, such as historical districts, becomes endowed with its new uses and commercial purposes, particularly within the context of urban tourism development. According to Relph (1987: 223):

> Historic districts are popular tourist venues, so some of the buildings are usually taken over by tourist-oriented restaurants and boutiques; others become museums and information centres, while some are turned into the offices of designers, architect, lawyers and similar professionals who seem to find heritage districts attractive and good for business. The overall result is a spanking new townscape paradoxically made of partially old structures.

Here, heritage becomes a value-added entity that enhances the touristic appeals and images of cities and towns. In this way, heritage conservation is a fairly capital- and economic-driven activity rather than merely focusing on protecting the historic environment. Urban heritage in this light serves as an effective economic tool in post-industrial contexts, which is often regarded as a 'cure for all' remedies. Commercial values of heritage have further gained great prominence within the increasing influx of neoliberalist approaches to urban restructuring and development, as discussed in Chapter 7. However, the conservation and reproduction of heritage for commercial reproductions, such as touristic consumption, could divorce products from its milieu, through which heritage becomes excessively developed as commercial and profitable products. The utilisation of heritage for urban regeneration is prevalent in developing countries as well as developed countries. It is widely acknowledged that old historic cores of cities in many developing countries are damaged and destructed by an excessive obsession with modernisation, ranging from Istanbul, Beijing and Mumbai (Henderson, 2002; Gugler, 2004; Daher, 2005). This point is well encapsulated in Steinberg's (1996: 464) sharp observations, highlighting that:

> The desire for 'modernization' by governments and top decision-makers in most developing countries often led them to believe that only new and 'modern' housing was worthwhile. Anything old or in a traditional style was considered of little value and was torn down or, at best, ignored. Older housing normally concentrated in the inner parts of the city, was often in a state of physical deterioration, overcrowded and lacking in services. It was easy to label such areas as 'slums', to be removed at the earliest convenient opportunity.

Historical districts and old historic cores of cities in developing countries are now faced with different challenges: to preserve the authentic character of the areas while striving to achieve economic viability and sustainability under the influence of globalisation. The Historic Old Salt Development Project in Jordan was developed as part of the overall strategy to upgrade the tourism sector, which incorporates urban regeneration and heritage management. Daher (2005) argues that the practice of heritage management in Jordan is tied up with sporadic agents of power that generate shock treatments and modest outcomes rather than an institutionalised practice. There also exist two tiers of decision-making processes – local and central – that lessen the efficiency of operating and managing the project. Moreover, Mowforth and Munt (2009) identify the key threats historic tourism resources face in urban contexts in developing countries. There emerges a pressure of urban expansion and change. Tourism development and promotion of historic resources have widely been regarded as a main tool for economic growth and regeneration. But this has not always been the case. The use of tourism for urban redevelopment can also lead to issues such as commercial exploitation and gentrification.

Historically, the inner city was associated with being the underside of society, which often poses threats and challenges for city development. Short (1991: 50) explicates:

> As myth, the inner city is the dark underside of the city, a place of crime and disorder, a tariff-free zone for traditional moral values. In the nineteenth century it was the place of the working classes, the source of disease and crime, the home of the crowd. In the twentieth it has become the locale of the underclass, a black hole of contemporary civilization.

The process of gentrification, as part of urban regeneration, is thus regarded as the cure for inner city ills (Caufield, 1994; Lees, 2000; Slater *et al.*, 2004). As an effective and powerful political solution, gentrification is strategically employed to develop and promote new images of the places in the context of globalisation and neoliberalism. In the literature on gentrification there exists a dichotomy between demand and supply-side explanations and justifications – the emancipatory city versus the revanchist (revengeful) city. The emancipatory city thesis focuses on the gentrifiers themselves and their forms of agency (Lees, 2000). It rests on the ideal vision of reproducing and resettling old inner-city neighbourhoods, leading to creating a new kind of emancipatory space in which tolerance and equality could be sustained. Here, gentrification is conceptualised as an emancipatory social practice, a positive and ideal construct through which opportunities for social interaction and tolerance could be created (Caufield, 1994). In sharp contrast to the emancipator city thesis, the revanchist city thesis draws clear attention to the privilege of the middle class and the underlying complexity of gentrification, particularly in relation to issues of inequalities imposed on the working class such as displacement and injustice. Smith (1996) develops interesting and thought-provoking perspectives to understanding the complex interfaces between race/ethnicity and gentrification in the 1990s. Despite the fact that both approaches endeavour to analyse the causes and consequences of gentrification, they fail to recognise the specific and individual nature of each spatial and temporal context. It is essential to emphasise that the analysis and assessment of gentrification should consider spatial and temporal differences. There is a critical need to develop more rigorous empirical research with theoretical specificity in various regional and local contexts.

Furthermore, it should be critical to recognise that the process of gentrification encompasses such sensitive issues as class and race. Class politics is clearly encapsulated in the process of gentrification (N. Smith, 2002). It is also argued that gentrification has become a powerful political solution to urban problems with political connotations (Eisenschitz, 2010). However, it should be noted that gentrification often displaces or aggravates rather than resolving the political issues and problems. In the disguise of 'cultural shift' and 'economic regeneration', gentrification has facilitated the influx of the professional middle class in inner cities. As witnessed in Harlem, New York, and Brixton and Hackney, London, gentrification has been successful in renovating dilapidated buildings and encouraging commercial and corporate developments in these areas with strong ethnic and racial diversity. However, these unique inner-city areas of metropolitan cities, which were once noted for the diversity of communities and cultures, have been increasingly homogenised by intense commercial and corporate developments under the banner of 'rejuvenation', 'regeneration' and 'redevelopment' over recent decades. Regeneration policies have been utilised as a driving mechanism for the spread of gentrification across national boundaries, thereby facilitating global urban competition (N. Smith, 2002). This concurs with Eisenschitz's (2010) claim that gentrification is unmistakably dependent on neoliberal politics. Harvey (1989) succinctly asserts that the neoliberal turn has restored class power to rich elites in contemporary society. Urban development at increasing geographical scales has led to 'burgeoning processes of creative destruction that entail the dispossession of the urban masses of any right to the city whatsoever' (Harvey, 1989: 12). Harvey (1989: 8–9) emphasises:

> Quality of urban life has become a commodity for those with money, as has the city itself in a world where consumerism, tourism, cultural and knowledge-based industries have become major aspects of urban political economy… This is a world in which the neoliberal ethic of intense possessive individualism and its cognate of political withdrawal of support for collective forms of action can become the template for human personality socialization.

There emerges a barrage of criticism regarding the ways in which these traditional working-class urban areas largely renowned for ethnic diversity have turned into a new hub for the middle class during the process of gentrification.

There is a very close line between the use of heritage resources for economic development and its exploitation for gentrification. Throughout the process of gentrification, urban heritage and aesthetics have become commodified, thereby repositioning their appeal as a solution of choices in the market. A new, market-driven economy immediately recognises the potential of heritage in cities and invests in enhancing the infrastructure and service of heritage. Drawing on a case study of the socio-spatial transformation of New Orlean's Vieux Carré (French Quarter) over the past half-century, Gotham (2005) pinpoints that the growth of tourism has encouraged gentrification by way of facilitating consumption-oriented activities in residential space. Tourism gentrification is referred to as the 'transformation of a middle-class neighbourhood into a relatively affluent and exclusive enclave marked by a proliferation of corporate entertainment and tourism venues' (Gotham, 2005: 1099). It is argued that research on tourism gentrification is warranted by the distinctiveness of the patterns inscribed by the process. First, tourism gentrification highlights the twin processes of globalisation and localisation that define modern urbanisation and redevelopment processes. Second, the concept of tourism gentrification presents a challenge to traditional explanations of gentrification that assume demand-side or production-side factors drive the process. According to Gotham (2005: 1103):

> The example of tourism gentrification provides the conceptual link between production-side and demand-side explanations of gentrification while avoiding one-sided and reductive conceptions. On the production side, for example, tourism is about shifting patterns of capital investment in the sphere of production, new forms of financing real estate development and the creation of spaces of consumption. On the demand side, the socio-physical spaces associated with gentrification are also the 'highly visual expression of changing patterns of consumption in cities' (Carpenter and Lees, 1995: 288).

Gentrification is neither a cure-all remedy nor a panache for economic regeneration. As Gotham (2005: 1114) claims, gentrification needs to be understood as a 'multidimensional process that is fraught with conflict and tension'. Gentrification is also an evolutionary process, which is time- and place-specific (N. Smith, 2002). Both benefits and drawbacks of gentrification in inner-city areas need to be clearly understood and considered by all stakeholders, including public and private sectors and local people. The increasing influx of global and corporate businesses replacing traditional and independent businesses could lead eventually to creating homogeneous, undifferentiated and lifeless urban communities. Here, community involvement and participation are of paramount significance in minimising and preventing any possible disadvantages to local communities and people. Ideally, governments need to play a crucial role in monitoring and controlling commercial forces rapidly redefining contemporary cities. However, it is often the case that governments, both central and local, facilitate a conscious and deliberate utilisation of commercial forces in urban renewal and redevelopment. In this regard, gentrification is strategically harnessed and dominated by an amalgam of governments and private sectors. The proliferation of gentrification is now not just limited to the US and Europe but has spread worldwide. The rapid expansion of gentrification in old historic quarters in developing countries has often intensified the forced displacement of poorer local communities, as evidenced in Case study 10.2.

Case study 10.2: The Sulukule Urban Regeneration Project, Istanbul

Sulukule, officially named Hatice and Neslişah Sultan, is one of the oldest permanent Roma settlements in the Fatih district of Istanbul, Turkey. The first Romani community settlement in Sulukule is believed to date back to the eleventh century. Throughout history, the Romani people have been renowned for their music, dancing and entertainment. However, they have been isolated and discriminated for generations, including the Byzantine rule and the Ottoman reign. Since the early 1990s, local governments have been keen on rejuvenating the areas of Sulukule. In January 2006, the Sulukule Urban Regeneration Project was approved by the Istanbul Metropolitan Municipality Council. The municipality website justifies the project as a necessity to combat urban decay and slumming of the areas, which create a range of negative socio-economic problems and cultural issues. It further emphasises the significance of this urban renewal project for safety reasons, claiming that the poor condition of the houses in Sulukule is vulnerable to threats of earthquakes (Uysal, 2012). Despite worldwide protests, social movements in Istanbul including The Sulukule Platform (SP) and UNSECO interferences, the planned evictions and demolitions started in 2008. The 3,400 Roma living in Sulukule were forced to resettle in Taşoluk, approximately 40km away from Sulukule after selling their homes for 500 Turkish Lira (£175) per square metre to private investors and the Fatih municipality (Letsch, 2011). The areas have been replaced by 'Ottoman style' new townhouses and new commercial developments. The new life for the Romans in Taşoluk has not been as promising as it first sounded. Displaced families find it difficult to adapt to the modern mass houses, lack of community feel and high rent prices in their forced resettlement. The majority of families have returned to Sulukule despite higher rental prices compared to their previous rents.

The Sulukule Urban Regeneration Project has been widely criticised as undervaluing and ignoring the Romani identity, only focusing on the improvement of physical decay of the areas. The project aims to secure the sustainability of the neighbourhood, thereby maintaining economic development and promoting urban integration. However, too much focus is placed on enhancing the physical and environmental quality of the urban areas, without taking into consideration the socio-cultural aspects of sustainability, in relation to maintaining the cultural identity of the Romani community. The enforcement of the Sulukule Urban Regeneration Project led to activating social movements. The SP, a grassroots organisation, comprises of a range of actors such as NGOs, locals in Sulukule and independent activists, including professionals, academics and artists. It criticises the illusionary nature of the project, further accusing it as a gentrifying tool to displace the Romani community at the heart of Istanbul rather than a genuine development plan to conserve Sulukule or to improve the quality of the neighbourhood. Despite the eventual failure to stop the project, various attempts to resist the process of gentrification made by the SP are really commendable. Uysal (2012: 16–17) elaborates on several of the distinctive features used as unique local resistance in Istanbul, claiming that:

> First, SP emerged as an opposition against gentrification... It was not founded only by middle class gentrifiers but also by locals who have

been living in Sulukule for generations, though professional supports played important roles in raising the profile of SP. Second, SP has an ethnic and cultural identity. The emphasis on ethnicity and culture made SP a spokesman for all the Roma in Istanbul… Unlike other social movements in Istanbul, SP gained not only wide domestic support but also international assistance… SP played a part in refreshing political debate on the so-called participative character of local governance… Finally, this experience of urban resistance encouraged locals to openly express their Romani identities.

As one conspicuous example of an urban regeneration project burgeoning in developing countries, many promises by the Sulukule Regeneration Project focusing on conservation and redevelopment became tainted with issues such as displacement, exclusion and ensuing poverty of the local people. Here, the darker and less promising side of urban regeneration and redevelopment, propelled by both public sectors and corporate commercial developments, has come to prominence. But it is rather positive that the SP continues to challenge local authorities and protest the forced loss of local identity and community.

Sources: Letsch (2011); Uysal (2012).

As highlighted in the Sulukule Regeneration Project in Istanbul, the complex processes of urban regeneration encompass political as well as economic and cultural ramifications. Recently, cities in developing countries have increasingly been at the forefront of urban regeneration and gentrification debates. It is often believed that the process of gentrification is a necessary agent for enhancing the sustainability of inner-city areas. There is a tendency that gentrification in developing countries is regarded more as physical renewal with less emphasis on its social functions (see Song and Zhu, 2010). The excessive redevelopment of historic neighbourhoods in Istanbul is still underway despite fierce protest and contestation from residents, campaigners and professionals, including academics and architects. As part of Istanbul's public development projects in 2012, about 50 neighbourhoods including Tarlabasi are earmarked for urban renewal projects, which will cost up to 7.5 billion Turkish liras (£2.69 billion) (Letsch, 2012).

Festivals, events and urban tourism development

As essential intangible heritage, festivals have played a significant role in sustaining the cultural identity and integrity of cities. Traditional festivals contribute to building, maintaining and enhancing community cohesion and identity (Derrett, 2003). Festivals encompass both communal and participative dimensions. The word festival derives its meaning from the Latin word, *festum*, meaning feast. In tandem with repositioning cities as landscapes of consumption (Zukin, 1995), many cities have been eager to develop various new festivals as well as reinvigorating traditional festivals. The process of globalisation has further influenced the burgeoning of festivals in cities. Festivals and events are increasingly viewed as 'entrepreneurial displays, as image creators capable of attracting significant flows of increasingly mobile capital, people and services' (Quinn, 2005: 931). Festivals and events are, in this regard, often viewed as effective solutions to enhance the image of cities while maximising economic benefits. Cultural forms of consumption, of which festivals are part, can actively maintain and enhance the images of local communities (Bailey *et al.*, 2004). Scotland has actively used festivals as its main appeal to attract both domestic and international tourists. A variety of festivals running all year round in different cities and towns of Scotland has unmistakably contributed to recreating and promoting the images of Scotland as a tourism destination with a strong focus on culture and heritage. Glasgow, in particular, is a good example of actively incorporating festivals in reviving the city's image and status (see Table 10.1).

Special events are also regarded as an effective means of facilitating and promoting tourism development in cities. The European Capital of Culture is one notable example of annual events that are mainly culture- and heritage-oriented. Initiated as a means of bringing EU citizens closer together in 1985, the European Capital of Culture has become one of the most prestigious and high-profile cultural events in Europe. It serves as a platform to showcase the cultural profile and development of a designated city for one year. Its designation has greatly contributed to enhancing the profile of cities internationally, particularly in relation to tourism development. Liverpool was designated as the European Capital of Culture in 2008, which played a major role in transforming the city's image as culture- and heritage-oriented (see Kokosalakis *et al.*, 2006; Shukla *et al.*, 2006). The event attracted 9.7 million visitors to the city (a 34 per cent increase on annual figures) and generated £753.8 million for the economy (Carter, 2011). Before 2008, the main images of Liverpool were often associated with social deprivation that emerged from the 1980s. The city has been repositioned, however, as a modern and multifaceted place with a vibrant and diverse cultural life since the successful hosting of the event. Despite its undisputed success as an effective tool for place branding and cultural regeneration, it is unrealistic to expect

Table 10.1 *2013 calendar of festivals and events in Glasgow, Scotland*

Month	Festival/Event
January	Celtic Connections
February	Glasgow Film Festival
March	Glasgow International Comedy Festival
April	Glasgow International Festival of Visual Art Aye Write! Glasgow's Book Festival
May	Southside Festival
June	West End Festival Glasgow International Jazz Festival Glasgow Mela
July	Merchant City Festival SURGE
August	Piping Live? Glasgow International Piping Festival
September	Doors Open Day
October	Glasgay! Scottish Mental Health Arts And Film Festival

Source: http://www.glasgowlife.org.uk/arts/cultural-festivals/Pages/home.aspx.

that a one-off cultural event could eradicate deep-rooted social and economic issues inherent in cities. Quinn (2005: 939) explicates:

> The crux of the problem appears to lie in the failure of cities to acknowledge the critical importance of understanding and responding to the needs of local places, and of closely linking city marketing and urban regeneration strategies with the specificities of particular city contexts… City authorities seem to misunderstand the social value of festivals and construe them simply as vehicles of economic generation or as 'quick fix' solutions to city image problems.

Furthermore, the expected positive change might be confined to the city centres and tourist areas without making any substantial impact on the neighbourhoods of local communities. The long-term sustainability of such events needs to be carefully considered from an early stage of planning and development.

Quinn (2005) warns that festivals can engender local continuity by way of constituting realms where local knowledge and culture can be rejected and revised. It clearly draws attention to the danger of exploiting festivals and events as a tourism resource without carefully considering their possible negative impacts. Moreover, tourism development could play a positive role in reawakening the significance of traditional festivals in cities as a main agent for claiming place-based local identities. In packaging and promoting the tradition of festivals, locals could act as 'active strategists' and 'ingenious cultural politicians' (Adams, 1995). As emphasised in Chapter 9, active local participation in the decision-making process is therefore key to successful heritage management, which needs to be clearly implicated in the management and promotion of festivals and events. In this light, de Chavez's (1999: 37) insightful suggestion is of particular relevance in emphasising the significance of local participation in the planning and management of festivals. 'Unless indigenous peoples have a direct participation in the planning, implementation, and regulation of tourism activities that affect them, and unless benefit-sharing mechanisms are put in place, tourism can never rebound to their interest.'

On the contrary, local communities can also exploit tourist expectations for their own benefits, selectively portraying and promoting certain elements of their cultural heritage. Heritage tourism is generally regarded as a positive contribution to strengthening community identity and social cohesion (Palmer, 1999). In order to maximise the potential of festivals and events as opportunities for community interaction and cohesion as well as tourism development in the urban context, a final decision also needs to be made by local people over the extent to which traditional elements of festivals need to be transformed, commodified and promoted as special events for touristic consumption.

Conclusion

As a main base of symbolic economy, culture and heritage have become the centre of repositioning cities as places of consumption. The emphasis on culture and heritage in cities has facilitated the development of urban tourism over recent decades. Urban tourism development is closely associated with rejuvenating, recreating and promoting urban heritage. Urban heritage has actively been conserved and utilised for urban development and regeneration, however, its excessive development often leads to the criticism of commodification. Capitalising heritage sources for urban regeneration and development can make both positive and negative impacts on local heritage and people. Furthermore, the popularity of heritage regeneration and development projects including urban tourism development can lead to standardising heritage products and experiences, leading to ubiquitous and homogeneous urban development across national and cultural boundaries. It is also important to note that the process of gentrification is not any longer a by-product of global cities such as London and New York. It is now widely incorporated as an effective urban development strategy in developing countries all over the globe. Despite its economic benefits, gentrification is not a cure-all remedy for economic regeneration in cities. It should be perceived as an evolutionary process that encompasses political as well as economic and cultural ramifications. The issues of race, class and ethnicity deserve careful scrutiny in order to enhance an in-depth understanding of gentrification. Festivals and events utilising heritage play a significant role in sustaining the cultural identity of cities, while enhancing the images of cities and maximising economic benefits. As is the case with other urban regeneration and development projects, active local consultation and participation need to be prioritised in the planning and management of festivals and events.

Research questions

1   Explain the ways in which cities have transformed from a place of production to a place of consumption.
2   Discuss both benefits and drawbacks of culture-led and heritage-focused regeneration projects.
3   Explain and critically assess the roles heritage play in urban regeneration and redevelopment.
4   Using some relevant examples, discuss the ways in which gentrification has further contributed to class division in inner cities.
5   What are the main characteristics of tourism gentrification?
6   Discuss and critically evaluate the ways in which the gentrification process influences the social sustainability of local communities in developing countries.
7   Discuss both positive and negative impacts of special events and festivals such as the European Capital of Culture as an urban development strategy and how their long-term sustainability can be ensured.

Learning material

Ashworth, G.J. and Tunbridge, J.E. (2000) *The Tourist–Historic City: Retrospect and Prospect of Managing the Heritage City*, Oxford: Pergamon/Elsevier (Chapters 3 and 5).
Bailey, C., Miles, S. and Stark, P. (2004) Culture-led urban regeneration and the revitalization of identities in Newcastle, Gateshead and the North East of England, *International Journal of Cultural Policy*, 10(1): 47–65.
Gibson, L. and Stevenson, D. (2004) Urban spaces and the uses of culture, *International Journal of Cultural Policy*, 10(1): 1–4.
Gomez, M.V. (1998) Reflective images: the case of urban regeneration in Glasgow and Bilbao, *International Journal of Urban and Regional Research*, 22(1): 1–16.
Gotham, K.F. (2005) Tourism gentrification: the case of New Orleans' Vieux Carré (French Quarter), *Urban Studies*, 42(7): 1099–1121.
Gu, H. and Ryan, C. (2008) Place attachment, identity and community impacts of tourism: the case of a Beijing hutong, *Tourism Management*, 29(4): 637–47.
Gugler, J. (ed.) (2004) *World Cities Beyond the West: Globalization, Development and Inequality*, Cambridge: Cambridge University Press.
Lees, L. (2000) A reappraisal of gentrification: towards a 'geography' of gentrification, *Progress in Human Geography*, 24(3): 389–408.

Miles, S. and Paddison, R. (2005) Introduction: the rise and rise of culture-led urban regeneration, *Urban Studies*, 42(5/6): 833–9.

Quinn, B. (2005) Arts festivals and the city, *Urban Studies*, 42(5/6): 927–43.

Scarpaci, J.C. (2005) Plazas and barrios: heritage tourism and globalization in the Latin American *Centro Histórico*, Tucson, AZ: University of Arizona Press (Chapters 2, 6, and 7).

Shukla, P., Brown, J. and Harper, D. (2006) Image association and European capital of culture: empirical insights through the case study of Liverpool, *Tourism Review*, 61(4): 6–12.

Slater, T., Curran, W. and Lees, L. (2004) Gentrification research: new directions and critical scholarship, *Environment and Planning A*, 36(7): 1141–50.

Smith, N. (2002) New globalism, new urbanism: gentrification as global urban strategy, *Antipode*, 34(3): 427–50.

Tucker, M. (2008) The cultural production of cities: rhetoric or reality? Lessons from Glasgow, *Journal of Retail and Leisure Property*, 17(1), 21–33.

Uysal, U.E. (2012) An urban social movement challenging urban regeneration: the case of Sulukule, Istanbul, *Cities*, 29(1): 12–22.

Williams, S. (2009) *Tourism Geography: A New Synthesis* (2nd edn), London: Routledge (Chapter 9).

Zukin, S. (1995) *The Cultures of Cities*, Malden: Blackwell (Chapter 1).

Weblinks

Regenerating neighbourhoods with cultural heritage
http://www.youtube.com/watch?v=xkjEzYg1PwU

Baltimore Tourism Barometer (2010)
http://www.sagepolicy.com/wp-content/uploads/2009/03/visitbaltimore1110.pdf

Southwark notes: whose regeneration? Regeneration and gentrification in Southwark, South London
www.southwarknotes.wordpress.com

Urban regeneration in Liverpool
http://www.youtube.com/watch?v=zWLkP2A5sK0

Urban regeneration and social sustainability
http://www.youtube.com/watch?v=JFssF-nvVaE

Save our heritage: a short film regarding rapid gentrification of Dalston in Hackney, London
http://vimeo.com/32541973

Open Dalston: a not-for-profit membership company to support the sustainable community development of Dalston
www.opendalston.blogspot.com

The Sulukule Affair: Roma against expropriation
http://www.errc.org/cms/upload/media/02/F6/m000002F6.pdf

The fight for historical buildings in Moscow
http://www.youtube.com/watch?v=ERWNpkX93Pk

Scotland interactive festivals map
http://www.creativescotland.com/explore/showcase/festivals/interactive-festivals-map

Edinburgh festivals impact study final report (2011)
http://www.eventscotland.org/funding-and-resources/downloads/get/56

11 Museums and heritage tourism development

The evolution of museums

Museums have played a crucial role in providing an understanding of identity, an invaluable sense of connection with the past and present, and a springboard for the future (Ambrose and Paine, 1993). The word 'museum' stems from Temple of the Muses, which refers to the Greek goddesses inspiring poetry, music and art related to human inspiration and creativity. In Europe, Middle Age collections of objects were mainly for courts and churches, mostly in a non-systematic manner. But with the rise of Humanism in the fourteenth century, collections became systematic. The concept of *Wunderkammer* (wonder room) and *Kabinette* (cabinet) emerged as an antecedent type of museum throughout the Renaissance period. With the advent of geographical discoveries in the late fifteenth and sixteenth centuries, increasing attention was paid to appreciating the culture of curiosity, in which the tradition of collection grew substantially. This fascination with curiosities was continued in the following centuries as is evident from the case of the Grand Tour. As explicated in Chapter 1, the trip involved visiting sites connected with classical culture, particularly the cities of Italy, including Rome, Florence and Venice. The tradition of collecting objects of artistic and historical significance, as a memoir of the travelling experience during the trip, became very popular and prevalent. Along with the works of art and antiquities brought back, grand tourists cultivated their aesthetic tastes throughout their travels, which led to the enhancement of their private collections in both quantity and quality. One impressive example is Sir John Soane's museum in London. Sir John Soane was a prominent architect and academic in his time (1753–1837) and his trip to Rome during his grand tour inspired him to begin the collections of paintings, drawings and antiquities. His impressive private collection has now been turned into a museum open to the public.

The shift in the value of museums as a national heritage for educating the public was evident in the opening of the Louvre Museum in 1793. The French Revolution in 1789 emphasised the importance of national sovereignty as the key element of the newly established 'nation-state' (see Bennett, 1995; Tocqueville, 1998; Hunt, 2004). The birth of the public museum in France was thus underpinned by a new and radical political movement after the French Revolution. The French government established the Louvre with the intention of instilling the morality of a free nation to its people and ensuring the propagation of worthy virtues through the collections confiscated from the royal family and the church during the revolution. In support of legitimising a nation state, the public museum emerged as one systematic apparatus of the disciplinary society (Hooper-Greenhill, 1989). The establishment of the Louvre meant that the king's private collection was 'nationalised' and placed on display freely open to the public (Prösler, 1996). It is apparent that the museum represented the movement of republicanism or anti-clerical-ism, the concept spread by Napoleon's successful conquest. Hooper-Greenhill (1989: 68) further argues that the 'museum' was created as an instrument that exposed 'both the decadence and tyranny of the old forms of control, the *ancien régime*, and the democracy and public utility of the new, the Republic'. Therefore, the Louvre was employed as an ideological instrument to provide an authoritative narrative of state power (see Amato, 2006). According to Duncan (1999: 306):

> As a new kind of public ceremonial space, the Louvre not only redefined the political identity of its visitors, it also assigned new meanings to the objects it displayed, and qualified, obscured, or distorted old ones. Now presented as public property, they became the means through which a new relationship between the individual as citizen and the state as benefactor could be symboli-cally enacted.

The education of the public through museums contributes to the collective good of the state, thereby supporting the republic by offering an opportunity to all citizens to share in what would have become the private possessions of the privileged classes (Hooper-Greenhill, 1989). The Louvre as a public institution, representing national heritage and pride of the newly established republic, was a powerful agent through which a close relationship between the citizen and the state could be symbolically established (Duncan, 1999). This transformation of the Louvre as the prototype of the public art museum was influential in the establishment of national and regional museums across Europe in the nineteenth century, such as the Prado Museum in Spain and the Hermitage Museum in Russia. But interestingly, the development of national museums and galleries in Britain remained out of touch with the influence of the Louvre in comparison with other European countries. The establishment of the National Gallery clearly lacked revolutionary orienta-tions and the evolution of culture as an apparatus to foreground and support the state was slower in Britain compared to France (Duncan, 1999). It is further explicated:

> The founding of the National Gallery did not change the distribution of real political power – it did not give more people the vote – but it did remove a por-tion of prestigious symbolism from the exclusive control of the elite class and gave it to the nation as a whole. An impressive art gallery, a type of ceremonial space deeply associated with social privilege and exclusivity, became national property and was opened to all. The transference of the property as well as the shift in its symbolic meaning came about through the mediation of bourgeois wealth and enterprise and was legitimated by a state that had begun to recognize the advantages of such symbolic space.
>
> (Duncan, 1999: 322)

Concurrently, the role of museums evolved from a symbol of wealth and power into an ethical and educational forum for the public. The main purpose of museums became no longer confined to preserving a material culture of the past. Importantly, museums were not value-free cultural institutions. They were highly political and hegemonic, positioned and manipulated by power relations inherent in society. In this light, the museum func-tioned, as Hopper-Greenhill (1989) contends, as an instrument of discipline. Museums served as a symbolic signifier in instilling the general public with a strong sense of national belonging and solidarity. According to Bennett (1995: 102):

The museum, viewed as a technology of behavior management, served to organize new types of social cohesion precisely through the new forms of both differentiating and aligning populations it brought into being. Its functioning in this respect, however, needs to be viewed in a comparative light in order to appreciate the distinctive economy of its effort... the museum provided its complement in instilling new codes of public behaviour which drove a wedge between the respectable and the rowdy.

Founded in 1946, the main aim of The International Council of Museums (ICOM) was to take responsibility for carrying out UNSECO's policies on museums. A priority was placed on preserving the objects of historical and artistic significance. Therefore, its definition of museums initially focused on the significance of their content: 'The word "museums" includes all collections open to the public, of artistic, technical, scientific, historical or archaeological material, including zoos and botanical gardens, but excluding libraries, except in so far as they maintain permanent exhibition rooms' (ICOM Constitution, 1946).

Benton and Watson (2010) claim that the main responsibility of museum curators in the above definition is more related to preserving museum collections than enhancing the museum's potential interest to the general public. Over the last decades, the role of museums as a means to educate, inform and cultivate the general public has been increasingly recognised and appreciated and its changes are clearly specified in defining museums:

A museum is a non-profit, permanent institution in the service of society and its development, open to the public, which acquires, conserves, researches, communicates, and exhibits, for the purposes of study, education, and enjoyment, material evidence of man and his environment.

(ICOM, 1974)

A museum is a non-profit, permanent institution in the service of society and its development, open to the public, which acquires, conserves, researches, communicates and exhibits the tangible and intangible heritage of humanity and its environment for the purposes of education, study and enjoyment.

(ICOM, 2007)

The latter definition was adopted during the 21st General Conference in Vienna, Austria, in 2007 and it is now widely acknowledged as an official definition of 'museum' across the globe. As indicated, the definitions of museums have constantly evolved in line with changes and developments in society. It is interesting to note that intangible as well as tangible heritage is recognised as being worthy of preservation in museums. Furthermore, enjoyment along with education and study is highlighted as the main purpose of museums' existence in the service of society. Education is one of the primary determinants of cultural participation. It is essential to note that museums, first and foremost, are educational institutions more than any other purpose. In the past, museums mainly served as a cultural and educational institution for a minority of privileged elite groups (Merriman, 1991; Weil, 1995; Grek, 2009). Although this stereotypical understanding of museums still remains in the perceptions of the public, the educational remit of museums now aims to reach entire societies, regardless of class, gender and ethnicity. Museums strive to make their resources available in order to meet the needs of all users, both existing and potential, which is regarded as the main concern of museum education (Anderson, 1997). Here, enjoyment can be regarded as one efficient way to deliver the resources of museums to all visitors, thereby enhancing the benefits of museum education. Education and enjoyment are not necessarily mutually exclusive, rather complementing each other. It is crucial to understand that museums are both cultural assets and social institutions, in fulfilling their responsibilities of preserving their collections and making them accessible to the public. As part of public culture, museums function as 'places for defining who people are and how they should act and places for challenging those definitions' (Karp, 1992: 4). Museums are in a constant state of change as the values of a society become contested, negotiated and renegotiated over time.

The relationship between museums and tourism

Museums are now posited as the most popular tourist attractions across the globe. The increasing popularity of museums as major tourist attractions has led to recognising and re-emphasising their economic potential, thereby strengthening the links between the economy and culture (Stylianou-Lambert, 2011). One main advantage of museums and galleries as a tourist attraction lies in the fact that their non-literal nature obviously presents fewer barriers to tourists from other socio-cultural backgrounds and language traditions (Evans, 1998). Anderson (1997) also claims that museums communicate across the boundaries of language, culture and time. Museums and galleries are, for example, ranked by other language speakers as the most important factor in deciding to visit Britain (VisitBritain, 2010). Museums, in origin, are cultural and educational institutions whereas tourism is more of an industry that aims to make profits by providing products and services to tourists. However, both of them are becoming indelibly associated with each other in contemporary society, particularly in relation to museums' increasing business-oriented approaches and strategies to maximise their appeal and competitiveness as tourist attractions. According to Phelps (1994), tourism should be seen as a means of supplementing the income of a museum to enhance its prime function. Museums can derive direct and indirect benefits in economic terms through entrance fees, the sale of museum catalogues and souvenirs, catering facilities and the organisation of special events or programmes. Close collaboration between museums and tourism is essential in encouraging and enhancing national and local economies (Heilbrun and Gray, 2001). Here, strategic planning and marketing strategies in museums are increasingly perceived as a crucial element in maximising their appeal as popular tourist attractions. In particular, museums are at the forefront of developing city tourism focusing on culture and heritage. The presence of popular museums in cities contributes to enhancing the appeal of cities as a tourist destination, attracting a wide range of tourists (Van Aalst and Boogaarts, 2002). Likewise, the 'clustering' of museums in cities is considered to be effective in attracting tourists to one particular area (see Case study 11.1). Below are some examples of popular museum clusters worldwide:

- New York: Museum Mile;
- Amsterdam: Museumplein;
- Melbourne: Federation Square;
- Berlin: Museumsinsel;
- Frankfurt: Museumsufer;
- Tokyo: Kitanomaru Park.

Case study 11.1: The Museumsinsel (Museum Island) in Berlin, Germany

The Museumsinsel comprises of five museums situated on the northern part of an island in the centre of Berlin in the River Spree and has an area of almost one square kilometre. King Friedrich Wilhelm III commissioned the construction of the Royal Museum – now the Altes Museum – in 1830 in order to allow the general public to get access to the royal treasures of Germany. In 1841, Friedrich August Stüler proposed the idea to create a cultural centre on the island. The New Museum was completed in 1859 and the Old National Gallery in 1876. Kaiser-Friedrich Museum – today the Bode Museum – was added in 1904 and the final museum, the Pergamon, was completed in 1930. Sadly, nearly 70 per cent of the buildings were destroyed during World War II and, after the war, the collections were split up between East and West Berlin. In 1999, UNESCO placed Museumsinsel under its protection as a World Cultural Heritage site. Its new master plan, entitled 2015: Future Projection, is currently underway to ensure the long-term sustainable development of the museum complex. Along with restoring the buildings and colonnades, new 'Museumshöfe' ('museum courtyards') are being constructed on the other side of the Kupfergraben where archives, student repositories and restoration shops will be housed as a new service space in the Museumsinsel.

Source: http://www.berlin.de/orte/sehenswuerdigkeiten/museumsinsel/index.en.php.

The changing socio-cultural roles of contemporary museums

The fast-changing dynamics of contemporary society have unmistakably impacted on the ways in which museums are managed and promoted. Compared to traditional museums, which focus on collecting and conserving essentially educational repositories, contemporary museums have been eager to diversify their social and cultural functions and remits of services as well as to broaden their collections. The remit of museums has changed from being relatively elitist into more inclusive and service-oriented (Grek, 2009). Even though education is still regarded as the most significant role of a museum, museum visitors now expect to achieve a quality experience not only in terms of the exhibition and displays but also the interpretation and other services, including catering and retailing in museums. Cultural institutions including museums have become a unique intermediary between heritage and the audience (Prentice, 2001). The focus of museums has shifted towards communication and interactivity between the collections and the visitors. Museums are expected to turn into spaces for intercultural dialogue, heritage expression and performance (Simpson, 2007). The new role of museums is focused on the one hand within the educational context, but on the other, placed in the context of a leisure and tourism industry, dedicated to pleasure and consumerism (Hooper-Greenhill, 1994a; Foley and McPherson, 2000; Stephen, 2001). Within the past two decades, museums have shown an increasing importance in the leisure and tourism industry. Eight of the top ten UK visitor attractions in 2012 were museums and galleries and three UK museums (British Museum, Tate Modern and National Gallery) were in the top five most visited international art museums in 2012 (Association of Leading Visitor Attractions, 2012). However, despite museums' increasing concern with their recreational roles in the context of the leisure and tourism industry, visits to museums are certainly understood as a worthwhile and valuable experience which is closely associated with learning. It is the educational potential of museums, according to Hooper-Greenhill (1994b), based on their unique collections, that gives them their particular market niche within the leisure and tourism industry.

Traditionally, museums have been viewed as elitist institutions where the distinctions between classes are clearly demarcated (McTavish, 2006). But there are less clear distinctions between 'high' and 'popular' culture in terms of both collections and experiences, which is one of the main characteristics of postmodern museums. The number of museums has increased dramatically since 1980 and the range and scope of museums have been substantially expanded (see Case study 11.2). There has been:

- a marked broadening in the range of objects that are now deemed worthy of preservation and presentation;
- a shift towards the concept of the living, working museum as an alternative to the reverential aura of the conventional museum, from aura to nostalgia;
- less auratic museum displays;
- an extension of the business of presenting objects of interest for the public gaze beyond the confines of museums themselves and into other types of space.

(Urry, 1990: 129–32)

Postmodern museums are increasingly concerned with image and consumer satisfaction than collections of objects (Foley and McPherson, 2000). Contemporary tourists use the power of their imagination to receive messages and create their own sense of heritage and identity during their heritage tourism experiences, including visits to museums. As a response to this, contemporary museums are being transformed from being collection-focused to being public-oriented cultural institutions. Museums have become a place of consumption, a provider of the 'heritage product' and this change in the tourism arena places a new emphasis on the changing status of visitors as customers (Lewis, 1994; Gilmore and Rentschler, 2002; Timothy, 2011). Critical focus is increasingly placed on visitors' direct participation and interactivity in contemporary museums. According to MacCannell (1976), there are two main types of display in museums: one is collection, the other is representation. He conceptualises representation as an 'arrangement of objects in a reconstruction of a total situation' (MacCannell, 1976: 78). It involves its original context, such as 'painted background, facades of native huts, department store mannequins for the period costumes' (MacCannell, 1976: 78). The main aim of representation is to provide visitors with an authentic atmosphere of the objects in display, thus enabling them to recollect the total situation of the past in the display. There has been a clear shift of focus from collection to representation as a main mode of display in contemporary museums. Increased focus on representation is closely linked with the increasing significance of visitor experiences. Instead of merely displaying the collections in traditional glass cases, museums strive to provide visitors with opportunities to contextualise the collections in their experiences through enhanced representational and interpretational methods, often engaging all the sensory experiences.

Incorporating new technologies such as the use of multimedia (e.g., video interactive and audio guides) in enhancing representational and interpretational strategies is now a very common and popular practice in museums across the world. For example, the Nobel museum in Stockholm employs 160 monitors to create an impression of travelling through networks of innovation. Such use of high-tech media allows museums not only to diversify their audience, but also to compete more closely with other leisure institutions

Case study 11.2: Postmodern museums as tourist attractions

Museum of Broken Relationships (Zagreb, Croatia)

Olinka Vištica and Dražen Grubišić, two artists, founded this museum in Croatia after their own relationship broke up in 2006. The Museum of Broken Relationships grew from a travelling exhibition revolving around the concept of failed relationships and their ruins. The museum offers a chance to overcome an emotional collapse through creation by way of contributing to the museum's collection. Along with its permanent collection in Zagreb, established in 2010, which has become a significant tourism attraction, the museum has since toured internationally, including to Berlin, Belgrade, Cape Town, London, Istanbul, Singapore, Bloomington, St. Louis and Houston. Around 800 objects, often coloured by personal experience, local culture and history, have been donated to the project so far by members of the public. As of 22 March 2013, TripAdvisor put the museum at the top spot on the list of Zagreb's must-see sights.

Source: http://brokenships.com.

The Toilet Culture Park (Suwon, South Korea)

Established in 2012, the Toilet Culture Park was previously the home of Sim Jaeduck, the former mayor of Suwon. The museum building in itself is toilet-shaped and visitors are invited to use his original toilet, complete with a full-length glass door that clouds up when it's occupied. Collections include WC signs from around the world and toilet-themed works of art. Visitors can even purchase faeces shaped souvenirs. Several exhibits are intended to raise awareness of public toilets and sanitation in the developing world. Admission is free.

Sources: McCurry (2012); http://www.guardian.co.uk/world/2012/nov/09/south-korea-toilet-theme-park.

The Mob Museum (Las Vegas, USA)

The Mob Museum, also entitled the National Museum of Organized Crime and Law Enforcement, aims to present an authentic view of organised crime's impact on Las Vegas history and its unique imprint on the world. The museum reveals real stories of the events and people through engaging exhibits and multisensory experiences. The museum opened to the public on 14 February 2012 – the 83rd anniversary of the St. Valentine's Day Massacre in which seven men from the Bugs Moran gang were murdered by Al Capone's South Side gang. The main exhibits of the museum develop an in-depth understanding of such topics as how the mob is perceived and portrayed in pop culture, how Las Vegas attracted mobsters and how organised crime persists today.

Source: http://themobmuseum.org.

such as theme parks and heritage centres. The development of the internet has transformed the ways in which museums interact with their audiences. For example, podcasts, blogs and wikis are increasingly employed as effective educational and promotional methods in museums' virtual spaces. The recent upsurge in utilising such social media as Facebook, Twitter, LinkedIn and YouTube has led to further broadening the appeal of museums to a wider audience, particularly young and new audiences. New technologies have also impacted ways in which permanent collections in museums are installed and displayed. The National Maritime Museum in Greenwich, London, installed a permanent sculpture called 'Voyagers' in 2011 in its newly built Sammy Ofer wing. It is 20 metres long and stretches the full length of the room. Its surface is made up of 26 triangular facets, and at one end there is a spherical projector that shows the Earth. More than 300 images and movies from the museum's archives are tagged and those tags move as waves down towards the globe (see Case study 11.3).

Digitalising archives is another realm where new technology has replaced traditional methods of preserving museum archives. Memories and ideas as well as objects become preserved in digital format and displayed online (see 'the past online' in the weblinks section at the end of this chapter). Furthermore, the success of virtual museums has ensued worldwide: 24 Hour Museum, first launched in 1999, was the first national museum in cyberspace. The online museum provided information about each of the UK's 2,000 museums and galleries, with links to more than 300 museums and galleries that already had their own websites. It was given National Collection status, which only 12 other institutions in the UK including the British Museum, the National Gallery and the Natural History Museum have been given. Another notable virtual museum is Museu da Pessoa (The Museum of the Person), which was first launched in São Paulo, Brazil, and now located in Brazil, Portugal, the US and Canada. It aims to collect, preserve and share the life stories and experiences of every person in favour of social change. Using the medium of text, images, audio and video it is also responsible for democratising social memory and disseminating local life stories and values on a global scale (www.museudapessoa. net). Along with increased access to the collections, virtual museums can be utilised as effective mediums in incorporating the diverse views and different perspectives of both artists and general users, thereby challenging elitist museum practices. But despite many positive aspects of virtual museums, it should be noted that the personal and intimate experience of artworks in real museums cannot be replicated by the imaging technologies employed in virtual museums. Appropriately, McTavish (2006: 227) raises some insightful questions to dwell upon in the face of an increasing fascination with virtual museums:

- Do virtual museums undermine or reinforce traditional conceptions of the authenticity of artworks and museum visits?
- How are these websites experienced?
- Is the visitor offered greater freedom to engage with museum spaces and their contents online, is the power dynamic of conventional institutions reaffirmed?
- What happens when everyday people begin to produce the content of virtual museums, appropriating the roles of curator and even museum director?

McTavish (2006) challenges the predominant rhetoric of interactivity and increased access, often regarded as the benefits of virtual museums. It is argued that virtual museums are, like traditional museums, confronted with conflicting and contradictory messages between real and virtual and original and copy, particularly when using virtual reality galleries. Moreover, digitised collections in museums should not be overtly exploited in order to expedite the increasing focus on culture and heritage as commercial

Case study 11.3: Use of new technologies in museums

Rijkswidget

The Rijksmuseum in Amsterdam, Holland, is the first museum in the world to offer a 'widget'. The Rijkswidget allows virtual visitors to view a different work from the collection on a daily basis. Interestingly, the 'reverse side' of every work provides information about the work and the painter. The Rijkswidget is now available as an iPhone App. Users can choose one of 1,000 masterpieces collected in the museum, which are displayed by pressing the icon on the screen. The application also offers links to the museum's website for more detailed information. The Rijkswidget can be installed on websites, blogs and profiles on social networking sites.

Show Me

Show Me (www.show.me.uk) is a website for children, organised by Culture 24. The site is non-commercial and is a collection of online games and interactive content produced by the UK's museums and galleries for children aged 4 to 11. Interactive resources are organised and listed by topic and users can choose a topic ranging from Dinosaurs, Vikings, Tudors, Victorians or twentieth-century Britain. The site includes a new web tool, called Storymaker, with which children living in different cities send in their own stories and pictures, thereby creating a pool of useful information regarding each city reflecting their own points of view. All the information available on the site is from UK-based museums and galleries. The site also includes some useful information for parents and teachers in order to maximise its educational benefits.

Gallery One, The Cleveland Museum of Art

As part of a recent expansion project, The Cleveland Museum of Art has opened Gallery One. Visitors can explore digital versions of the artworks, see the original context of the artworks themselves and create their own works of art. Through interactive games, visitors can put their own bodies into the experience, matching poses with figurative sculptures, or browse the museum's collection by making different facial gestures. An interactive wall allows multiple visitors to see all 3,000 artworks on display at the same time and to create their own experiences by exploring connections between the artworks. Custom tours can be connected to a new iPad application that allows visitors to both navigate the museum through a director's tour and take tours made by other visitors.

Source: http://localprojects.net/project/gallery-one/#1.

entities, as evident in the recent popularity of online museum shops which will be discussed in detail below. A more critical and discerned use of technologies is essential in enhancing the inclusive and interactive nature of museums. The Museum of Modern Art (MOMA) in New York creates, for example, online exhibitions specifically and exclusively for its website. Real museum experiences need to be differentiated from experiencing the digital reproductions of the collection. Furthermore, the use of advanced and enhanced presentational and interpretational methods including new digital technologies are mainly incorporated in museums in (Western) developed countries. There can be significant discrepancies between museums in developed and developing countries in utilising new technologies as a tool for research, representation and promotion. As a consequence, dominant historical narratives and Western discourses can be reinforced and re-emphasised in this process. Both historical and everyday narratives of developed countries can be excessively recorded, narrated and displayed, whereas those of indigenous communities in non-Western contexts are largely under-represented. Finally, it seems inevitable that the original context and function of each object or artwork cannot be fully recontextualised and integrated in the process of digitising the collection.

The role of museum staff has also dramatically changed, from being strictly curatorial (collection, conservation, taxonomy) to one that is now increasingly marketing/managerial and leisure/entertainment-oriented. Certainly, there is an increasing need to develop effective marketing strategies based on the expectations and requirements of identified target audiences. Hooper-Greenhill (1994a) argues that the development of museum marketing has been encouraged by central government as part of the ideology of 'plural funding'. It is thus vital for museums to find strategies to attract other possible sources of funds, either from industry or the public. Therefore, each museum strives to develop and promote its image through a variety of different marketing strategies. Digital technologies are now widely employed as a cost-effective and powerful marketing tool, giving access to various information and collections and generating both virtual and actual visitors. The use of digital technologies in heritage institutions will be further discussed and illuminated in Chapter 12. Unlike goods marketing techniques, the practice of marketing in museums has to take into account the whole context of museums ranging from the collection and the staff to the public as service and not-for-profit organisations (McLean, 1997). Competitions may exist between museums and other groups of heritage attractions, such as historic houses and castles and between museums geographically close to each other, and which supply similar services. Furthermore, new and innovative marketing strategies including viral marketing have become essential in reducing the marketing costs while broadening the accessibility of museums to the general public, particularly younger generations who are not traditionally regarded as the main group of museum visitors. Viral marketing refers to marketing techniques that use pre-existing social networks to create and enhance brand awareness. It includes word of mouth, the internet, video clips, interactive flash games and images. Particularly, the use of social networking sites such as Facebook and Twitter as one of the main marketing tools has become increasingly universal and popular among museums across the globe. Following McLean (1994, 1997), museum marketing needs to be seen as the process, not as the product, by which a close relationship between museums and the public can be facilitated. Marketing in museums needs thus to be understood not just as commercially driven business practice but a holistic approach for enhancing the long-term sustainability of museums. The shift in perceived roles of museums as economic entities rather than cultural service is clearly evident in their repositioning roles as a tool for tourism development and urban regeneration. Undoubtedly, the recent changing social role of museums is immensely underpinned by the process of commodification. Museums are in competition with other tourism or leisure attractions such as newer heritage centres, thereby striving to adjust to the different requirements of commercial operation. There exist inherent tensions between the traditional 'museum professional' and newer 'commercialist/managerial' ideologies (see Foley and McPherson, 2000; Gilmore and Rentschler, 2002; Lord and Lord, 2009). The role of museum staff has thus shifted to a more commercial orientation, with a greater focus being placed on increasing income. Despite the critique of the 'Disney approach' in museums, commercial interests and orientations of museums are expected to increasingly become a central focus of museums in the future. However, it should be noted that an excessive focus on commodifying museums, as discussed in relation to other heritage attractions in Chapter 4, can lead to presenting history and culture purely as a set of commodities for touristic consumption.

New museums and new challenges

In tandem with some significant changes in traditional museums, there have also emerged new museums in the past two decades. New museums are defined as 'physically new institutions that are dedicated to the exhibition of cultural objects, artefacts and experiences' (Message, 2006a: 603). New museums mainly refer to a new modern construction and a remodelling of museums in Western cities, conferred an iconic status by the tourism industry. This museum boom was initiated in Western cities and then has gradually spread worldwide. An image of 'newness' and 'innovation' has become a symbol of new museums. Impressive architectural designs and strong iconic status as tourism landmarks are characteristic of new museums, ranging from the Guggenheim Bilbao, the Tate Modern in London, the Getty Centre in Los Angeles, the Jewish Museum in Berlin, the State Museum of São Paulo and Suzhou Museum in China. New museums are keen on dissolving rigid distinctions between 'high' and 'popular' culture and blurring different disciplinary boundaries. Therefore, they try to differentiate themselves from traditional museums by actively incorporating postmodern changes and resorting to different representational methods. Here, issues such as standardisation or homogeneity in their managerial and representational modes and methods cannot be overlooked. Message (2006a: 604) explicates:

> A certain homogeneity exists amongst new museums; they appear visually similar and they share a common approach to representing material culture and storytelling. Although variations based on the particulars of exhibition, mission and geographical location do exist, for the most part, these museums all signify newness by reference to a global lexicon that tends, problematically, to transcend issues of local context or regional identity.

The Guggenheim Bilbao is regarded as one of the most relevant examples of new museums that embodies a struggle between the global and local nexus. There have been opposing viewpoints surrounding the establishment of the Guggenheim Bilbao both in the media and academia. Some argue that the museum has played a significant role in regenerating the local economy and restructuring the urban landscape in the Basque region (Plaza, 1999). The museum's existence has developed the cultural infrastructure of the city and enhanced the city's image to the outside world. However, there has been a barrage of criticism that views its opening as a stark example of American cultural imperialism (see Case study 11.4).

Case study 11.4: The museum as a site of open contest – the Guggenheim Bilbao

As a state museum, the establishment of the Guggenheim Bilbao, from the initial moments of its inception, provoked ongoing and intensive debates between the different stakeholders. In 1991, the Basque Government officially announced the signing of an agreement with the Guggenheim Foundation of New York to build a museum in Bilbao. The Partido Nacionalista Vasco (Basque Nationalist Party) was the main partner in the coalition which constitutes the Basque Government. It strived to achieve political autonomy for the Basque area from the central Spanish government, thereby consolidating and enhancing Basque identity. The Basque Government defended its actions on the grounds that this lavish project would be a great investment in the future of the Basque Country. The heavy industries including the mining of iron ore, shipbuilding and the manufacture of steel had significantly declined since the 1970s. The government saw the museum as a key component of their strategy to improve the image of the country. Furthermore, the museum would be an integral part of a transatlantic axis, linked to Venice and New York (the homes of the two other Guggenheim museums). The government also planned to revitalise Bilbao by commissioning the construction of a series of impressive buildings, including a business centre, performing arts centre and a new terminal for the city's airport. The overall strategy behind these projects was to establish Bilbao as a European centre for service industries, modern technologies and upmarket tourism. Basque reaction to the agreement was, in general, very negative. Particularly, representatives of political parties criticised the elevated number of visitors the government claimed the museum would attract and argued that the money would be far better spent tackling directly the problems of the Basque Country. Creative artists were also vehement in condemning the project. Forming a collective group 'Kultur Keska', local artists regarded the museum as the central part of a shift in strategy from supporting local activities to sponsoring prestige projects imported from the United States. Other critics have seen it as an exemplar of the economically motivated 'culture of spectacle', where culture is treated not as a source of creativity and dynamism but as a profitable commodity. The establishment of the museum was regarded as part of 'Coca-colonisation' of non-American culture by American forces.

Source: an excerpt from MacClancy (1997).

Figure 11.1 The Guggenheim Bilbao, Spain

It is evident that the museum is unmistakably associated with the impact of globalisation on the contexts of local and regional museums. Following the main tenets of 'McDonaldisation', the term 'McGuggenisation' refers to the process through which a chain of Guggenheim museums, in collaboration with regional governments, become established around the world (see McNeil, 2000). Despite this prevalent concern over the impact of a global commodification process on local cultural domains, McNeil's (2000) reasoning suggests a different approach to this controversial issue. He argues that the museum has become indigenised by the Basque political elite. As a powerful symbol of the Basque identity in the contemporary world, the museum repositions the traditional working-class town of Bilbao as a post-industrial centre for culture, finance and tourism. This symbolic transition is strongly implicated in reimagining regional identity and national solidarity. Here, the process of 'McGuggenisation' is not just understood as a simple flow from global core to local periphery. Instead it is perceived as:

> a more complex negotiation of identity which includes the possibility of local actors 'indigenising' dominant cultures; the strength of a 'bourgeois regionalism' which is challenging the established European nation-state and which revalorises cities peripheral to the metropolitan core of the nation state; and the particularist reaction from radical sections of the Basque political community which raised questions over Basque cultural identity.
>
> (McNeil, 2000: 474)

More critical focus needs to be placed on examining how urban and economic restructuring is implicated in the territorial strategies of political groups. It is thus essential to develop a detailed analysis of specific events such as the establishment of the Guggenheim Bilbao in terms of how they are planned, represented, contested and negotiated. But importantly, new museums can be perceived as a distinctive form of reinforcing cultural imperialism. The dominance and enforcement of Western-centric, standardised management strategies and methods can undermine and dilute unique local cultural characteristics. Furthermore, representation of cultural differences, historical conflicts and political sensitivities still largely remain intact despite pragmatic changes in new museums (see Message, 2006a, b). Therefore, museum professionals need to be sensitive about representing competing and contradictory voices in interpreting and representing the collections. In this way, museums' social roles as cultural expression and identity communication could be greatly improved in contemporary societies (see McCarthy and Ciolfi, 2008). These points are clearly incorporated in conceptualising and contextualising a new and radical notion of 'post-museum'. According to Marstine (2006: 19):

> The post-museum actively seeks to share power with the communities it serves, including source communities. It recognizes that visitors are not passive consumers and gets to know its constituencies. Instead of transmitting knowledge to an essentialized mass audience, the post-museum listens and responds sensitively as it encourages diverse groups to become active participants in museum discourse... The post-museum does not shy away from difficult issues but exposes conflict and contradiction. It asserts that the institution must show ambiguity and acknowledge multiple, ever-shifting identities. Most importantly, the post-museum is a site from which to redress social inequalities.

Ecomuseum (ecomusée) is one relevant example in which key characteristics of 'post-museum' can be put into practice. Ecomuseum was originated in France in 1971. As opposed to traditional museums focusing on collecting and displaying specific items and objects, ecomuseums place greater emphasis on achieving a more holistic approach to both their collection and audiences, thereby enhancing the sustainable development of communities' cultural heritage (see Walsh, 1992). Community agreement and management are crucial in successfully operating ecomuseums, thereby achieving the long-term sustainability of community heritage and identity. Contrary to this original emphasis on community-based sustainability, however, there exist many commercially driven ecomuseums, purely developed as a marketing device for tourism development (see Corsane *et al.*, 2007). Local heritage of communities can be commodified, sanitised and secularised for tourists, which contradicts the main tenets of ecomuseum philosophy. It is therefore important to note that such main characteristics of ecomuseums as in-situ interpretation and active involvement of the local communities need to be carefully prioritised in practice.

As discussed before, the prevalence of musuems' commercial orientations alters the distinction between 'high' and 'popular' culture upon which traditional positioning of museums as a sanctuary for 'high' culture is founded. The desire for museums to be more accessible and democratised to a broader public often conflicts with their original mission as an elitist cultural institution. By examining the conflicting positions of a commercial shopping mall (the Carrousel du Louvre; see Figure 11.2) within the renovated Richelieu wing of the Grand Louvre, McTavish (1998) reveals the conflicts between aesthetic and consumer interests. The Louvre has long been considered the culmination of the 'high' art museum. It is argued that new consumer areas of the museum potentially undermine traditional distinctions between 'high' and 'popular' culture upon which museums are founded. However, McTavish (1998) demonstrates

Figure 11.2 The Carrousel du Louvre in Paris, France

that the distinctions between the two realms are still fairly palpable in appropriating and reappropriating newly added consumer areas in museums. The use of the Mona Lisa in advertisements for the Carrousel du Louvre can, for example, be perceived as an attempt to convey the changing, unstable and shifting relationship of the museum and the shopping mall, with particular reference to the function and status of the museum. Furthermore, distinctions of 'high' and 'low' culture are rearticulated in relation to gender, class and nationality in specific presentations and representations of the shopping mall. According to McTavish (1998: 182–3):

> In the Carrousel du Louvre, the shops initially welcomed by developers tended to be expensive ones, like Lalique crystal and Hermès, which catered to wealthy consumers. Clearly, the less affluent museum patron could feel uncomfortable in the aura of elegant refinement associated with these particularly 'French' luxurious shops. Furthermore, the type of boutique noticeably changes according to its location within the mall… Another indication of the potentially exclusionary effect of the shopping mall is its decoration… the plan and aesthetics of the commercial area make it seem like part of the Grand Louvre. The spacious mall, for example, is sheathed in the same beige limestone that covers the walls of the Richelieu wing… The foundations of the early palace are on display in what is deemed to be a commercial zone.

Albeit contradictory, the Carrousel du Louvre is a good example of juxtaposing commercial changes with the original purpose of museums. Recently, the Louvre has again been subjected to heated public debates as regards its plan to establish branches both within and outside France. The agreement made between the French Government and the city of Abu Dhabi to complete the Louvre Abu Dhabi has been fiercely criticised by the conservative art world as an act of denigrating the cultural values of museums like the Louvre with commercial interests. Due to the recent economic crisis, the project was suspended for two years while completing a review of its viability. The construction of the museum has been resumed and is now due to be completed in 2015. The museum is part of a cultural district on Saadiyat Island that will also include a franchise of the Guggenheim and the Zayed National Museum.

Museums now exist in a mixed economy funded by public support and various commercial practices such as cafeterias, restaurants and shops, both on site and online. To cope with increasing financial constraints, more and more museums are beginning to contract out their services, including catering and retailing facilities. Museums are increasingly concerned with concepts such as 'customer experience', 'value for money' and 'return on investment'. It is emphasised:

> Museums have changed, taking into account different visitor expectations and catering for interpretation and participation by different methods. This includes the development of both retail and catering outlets which attempt to replicate other sightseeing experiences and which are wholly aimed at 'customers'.
>
> (Foley and McPherson, 2000: 168)

Museums strive to organise and promote temporary exhibitions, so called 'blockbuster' exhibitions, in order to generate their additional income. Close cooperation between the public sector and private sector, such as the private sector sponsorship of 'blockbuster' exhibitions in museums, is essential in tackling the funding deficit the public museums currently face. Repeated use of popular themes and collections in temporary exhibitions of museums worldwide, however, has been criticised along with excessive commercial orientations inherent in the sales of tickets and souvenirs (Marstine, 2006). Both on site and online museum shops have become a key feature of museums' commercial activities. Both permanent and temporary exhibitions in museums offer prolific and profitable merchandising opportunities. On the positive side, retailing, catering and online business in museums can contribute to enhancing a broader appeal of museums to the general public. Commercial orientations of museums can substantially contribute to attracting a heterogeneous and broader public, thereby repositioning them as a popular tourist attraction in the domain of heritage tourism. However, as discussed before, careful attention needs to be paid not to overtly exploit the commercial interests of museums, which might lead to denigrating the cultural and educational values of museums. Museums ought not to be perceived as purely commercial entities but, at the same time, museums are no longer an elitist authoritative space preoccupied with the connoisseurship and conservation of their collections. It is important to perceive museums as an organic and discursive social space in which collections are reshaped and reconfigured through interactions with visitors and vice versa. Furthermore, becoming more democratic and accessible does not necessarily lead to abandoning or distorting certain intrinsic and traditional values of museums, including scholarship and preservation.

Conclusion

Museums as educational and cultural institutions have made a positive contribution to enriching our understanding of history and culture. Along with fulfilling their traditional roles and responsibilities, museums have increasingly enhanced their appeal in tourism and leisure markets. In order to adapt to the changing economic and political environment where public funding becomes very limited, museums strive to increase financial independence by way of improving the 'customer experience' and providing better 'value for money'. In order to increase their competitiveness in a contemporary tourism environment, museums have been keen on modifying and enhancing their management and marketing strategies. Rather than traditional glass display cases, a range of diverse representational and interpretational methods, including use of new technologies, are employed to maximise the appeal of museums and enhance visitors' direct participation, interactivity and experiences in contemporary museums. The development of the internet has fundamentally transformed the ways in which museums interact with their audiences. Furthermore, commercial practices of museums including museums shops and catering businesses have contributed to furthering the appeal of museums as tourist attractions. Museum visitors are increasingly seen as a market opportunity and innovative marketing strategies are essential in attracting a heterogeneous and broader public, particularly younger generations. Museums should sustain their intrinsic cultural and educational values in society, while striving to maximise new and commercial interests and opportunities as popular contemporary tourism attractions. Despite the increasing popularity and significance of new museums, furthermore, it should be noted that there remain certain challenges that new museums need to deal with, such as representation of cultural differences, historical conflicts and political sensitivities in both developed and developing countries.

Research questions

1   Explain ways in which museums were regarded as a 'disciplinary tool' for the public.
2   Discuss the ways in which the development of the internet has influenced contemporary museum management and practice.
3   What are 'new museums'? Evaluate both the positive and negative aspects of the increasing popularity and significance of 'new museums'.
4   Museums are increasingly associated with the process of commodification. What is your viewpoint on commodifying museums?
5   What kind of lesson could be learnt from the success of Guggenheim Bilbao as a tourist attraction?
6   Museums' policy is increasingly concerned with concepts such as 'customer experience', 'value for money' and 'return on investment', which compromises the integrity of collections and their long-term sustainability. Discuss.
7   What are some of the opportunities and/or risks arising from constant and never-ending change in the museum?
8   Use relevant examples to discuss how the digitisation of collections in museums has impacted the way we perceive museums and how museums relate to their communities.
9   As regards digitalising archives, should original items such as books, letters and photos still be kept in physical form, even after digital copies are made?
10   How can sustainable approaches in ecomuseums be incorporated in the practice of other museums?

Learning material

Amato, S. (2006) Quai Branly museum: representing France after empire, *Race and Class*, 47(4): 46–65.

Bennett, T. (1995) *The Birth of the Museum: History, Theory, Politics*, London: Routledge (Chapters 3 and 4).

Duncan, C. (1999) From the princely gallery to the public art museum: the Louvre museum and the national gallery, London, in D. Boswell and J. Evans (eds) *Representing the Nation: A Reader*, London: Routledge, pp. 304–31.

Foley, M. and McPherson, G. (2000) Museums as leisure, *International Journal of Heritage Studies*, 6(2): 161–74.

Gilmore, A. and Rentschler, R. (2002) Changes in museum management: a custodial or marketing emphasis? *Journal of Management Development*, 21(10): 745–60.

Hooper-Greenhill, E. (1989) The museum in the disciplinary society, in S.M. Pearce (ed.) *Museum Studies in Material Culture*, Leicester: Leicester University Press, pp. 61–72.

MacClancy, J. (1997) The museum as a site of contest: the Bilbao Guggenheim, *Focal Journal of Anthropology*, 1(7): 271–8.

Marstine, J. (2006) Introduction, in J. Marstine (ed.) *New Museum Theory and Practice: An Introduction*, Oxford: Blackwell, pp. 1–36.

McCarthy, J. and Ciolfi, L. (2008) Place as dialogue: understanding and supporting the museum experience, *International Journal of Heritage Studies*, 14(3): 247–67.

McNeil, D. (2000) McGuggenisation? National identity and globalization in the Basque country, *Political Geography*, 19(4): 473–94.

McTavish, L. (1998) Shopping in the museum? Consumer spaces and the redefinition of the Louvre, *Cultural Studies*, 12(2): 168–92.

McTavish, L. (2006) Visiting the virtual museum: art and experience online, in J. Marstine (ed.) *New Museum Theory and Practice: An Introduction*, Oxford: Blackwell, pp. 226–46.

Message, K. (2006a) The new museum, *Theory, Culture & Society*, 23 (2–3): 603–6.

Simpson, M.G. (2007) Charting the boundaries: indigenous models and parallel practices in the development of the post-museum, in S.J. Knell, S. MacLeod and S. Watson (eds) *Museum Revolutions: How Museums Change and are Changed*, London: Routledge, pp. 235–49.

Stephen, A. (2001) The contemporary museum and leisure: recreation as a museum function, *Museum Management and Curatorship*, 19(3): 297–308.

Weblinks

The cabinet of animosities
http://www.bbc.co.uk/programmes/p00ywhh7

Culture24
www.culture24.org.uk

The Museumsinsel, Berlin
http://blip.tv/InABerlinMinute/museumsinsel-gnyb-week-23-4240835

Thomas P. Campbell: weaving narratives in museum galleries
http://www.ted.com/talks/thomas_p_campbell_weaving_narratives_in_museum_galleries.html

Museum of Broken Relationships, Zagreb
http://edition.cnn.com/video/?/video/international/2011/03/21/wv.museum.relationships.bk.g.cnn

South Korea Toilet Museum
http://www.youtube.com/watch?v=2HWg9mMFN50

The Mob Museum, Las Vegas
http://www.youtube.com/watch?feature=player_embedded&v=Z5yIU-XtqC0#!

Technology in museums
http://www.youtube.com/watch?feature=player_embedded&v=1XAgDwuTjUQ
http://www.wired.co.uk/news/archive/2012-10-26/jake-barton-local-projects

Digital dig: the scanning technology revolutionising archaeology
http://www.bbc.co.uk/news/technology-21235980

The past online: a digital archive at the Imperial War Museum, London
http://www.bbc.co.uk/learningzone/clips/the-past-online/9569.html

12 Contemporary issues in heritage tourism

Intangible heritage and tourism

Greater emphasis on physical and material heritage rather than intangible and immaterial heritage has long been sustained in the practice of heritage protection and conservation. This tendency is deeply embedded in the Western approach to the values of heritage. A focus on tangible and material heritage has been, as discussed in Chapter 7, clearly incorporated in the WH paradigms and practices. The exclusive monumental focus of cultural heritage has mainly been emphasised in the selection and designation of WHSs. Perceiving heritage mainly as a tangible and material construction of the past, however, could lead to undermining the significance of intangible heritage, which is also a crucial element of history and tradition. Concurrently, UNESCO has gradually attempted to change its focus from a Eurocentric perspective by way of developing a new set of assessment criteria considering local sensitivity and diversity. Intangible heritage is clearly differentiated from the practice of WH in that:

> ICH [Intangible Cultural Heritage] attempts thus to shift from the universalism underpinning WH and the overall UNESCO early modernist perspective. The more inclusive and relativist idea of 'representativeness' replaces that of 'outstanding universal value'. More concretely, ICH involves a reflexive approach to heritage, as the potential of an element to be turned into something called 'heritage' is assumed to be established by its 'bearers'.
>
> (Bortolotto, 2010: 98)

As a conspicuous example of recognising cultural diversity, 'The Nara Document on Authenticity' commissioned in 1994 focuses on incorporating the values placed on symbolism in East Asia. The values of heritage and the qualities of authenticity are recognised as fundamental and intrinsic elements of heritage. The diversity of cultures emphasised here pave the way for extending the scope of heritage, including intangible heritage:

> All judgments about values attributed to cultural properties as well as the credibility of related information sources may differ from culture to culture, and even within the same culture. It is thus not possible to base judgments of values and authenticity within fixed criteria. On the contrary, the respect due to all cultures requires that heritage properties must be considered and judged within the cultural contexts to which they belong.
>
> (World Heritage Committee, 1994)

The Proclamation of Masterpieces of the Oral and Intangible Heritage of Humanity was initiated in 2001 in an endeavour to raise and enhance the awareness of intangible heritage at international as well as local and national levels. UNESCO declared, for the first time, 19 of the world's most remarkable examples of the oral and intangible heritage, all of which were later included on the Representative List of the Intangible Cultural Heritage of Humanity in 2008. Some examples included on the list were the Oruro Carnival (Bolivia), Kunqu Opera (China), Georgian Polyphonic Singing (Georgia) and the cultural space of Djamaa el-Fna Square (Morocco) (see Case study 12.1).

Case study 12.1: The cultural space of Djamaa el-Fna Square, Morocco

Djamaa el-Fna Square is situated near the medina of Marrakesh, included on the UNESCO WH List. A cultural crossroads, local people as well as tourists use it as a central meeting place for entertainment and trading – even medical treatment. Some of the activities encountered here are storytelling, acrobatics, music performances, comic acts and stunts, dancing, animal shows, snake-charming, glass and fire-eating. The square also hosts fortune-telling, astrology, numerology, one-hole miniature golf and preaching. Even dental, traditional herb medicine and henna tattoo businesses are established in the square. Trading includes fruit, bread, water-carrying and the rental of lanterns during dark evenings. Djamaa el-Fna Square dates back to the foundation of Marrakesh in 1070–1, and since then has been the symbol of the city. Travellers have long extolled its cosmopolitanism and vibrancy. It has been protected by law since the 1920s. Djamaa el-Fna Square is of historical, anthropological and artistic significance to Morocco and its people.

Figure 12.1 Djamaa el-Fna Square in Marrakech, Morocco

Threats: The growth and modernization of Marrakesh increase the vulnerability of Djamaa el-Fna Square. Traffic, pollution, city development plans and tourism are also taking their toll.

Action plans: The square aims to be a model of town planning that gives priority to people, culture, encounter and exchange. The ten-year action plan will identify major problems and link together institutions involved in preserving the square. Practitioners' rights will be protected and scientific inventories established. A National Scientific Institute of Oral Heritage will be created to study the history of Djamaa el-Fna Square.

Source: http://www.unesco.org/bpi/intangible_heritage/morroco.htm.

Nas (2002) emphasises that UNESCO's recognition of intangible heritage has a dual rationale in the area of conservation and identity construction. Faced with the process of modernisation, urbanisation and globalisation, there exists a clear risk of losing unique local cultural expressions and traditions. The significance of intangible heritage does not just lie in its cultural manifestations but in its connections with people and communities as a form of knowledge and skill transmitted from one generation to the next. Therefore, the preservation of intangible heritage at an intergovernmental level can contribute to revitalising local identities and creating new identities in a rapidly changing world. There raises a concern though that international and national intervention in protecting intangible heritage can dominate the process of such protection, thereby losing the complexity and diversity of local intangible heritage that it seeks to protect (see Chapter 7 for the critique of WHSs in general). The Convention for the Safeguarding of Intangible Cultural Heritage was finally adopted in 2003 by the General Conference of UNESCO. In the 2007 Convention for the Safeguarding of Intangible Cultural Heritage, the definition of intangible cultural heritage was elaborated as follows:

> The 'intangible cultural heritage' means the practices, representations, expressions, knowledge, skills – as well as the instruments, objects, artefacts and cultural spaces associated therewith – that communities, groups and, in some cases, individuals recognize as part of their cultural heritage. This intangible cultural heritage, transmitted from generation to generation, is constantly recreated by communities and groups in response to their environment, their interaction with nature and their history, and provides them with a sense of identity and continuity, thus promoting respect for cultural diversity and human creativity.
>
> (UNESCO, 2003: 2)

In 2008, the committee incorporated 90 elements (formerly proclaimed Masterpieces) into the Representative List. During the period from 2009 to 2012, it has also inscribed 167 new elements on this list. The committee meets annually to evaluate nominations proposed by states parties to the 2003 convention and decides whether or not to inscribe those cultural practices and expressions of intangible heritage on the convention's lists (see Table 12.1).

The Viennese coffee house (German: *Wiener Kaffeehaus*) has played a significant role in shaping and promoting Viennese culture, thereby maintaining the cultural identity of Vienna and its people. The 'Viennese Coffee House Culture' was listed in 2011 in the domain of social practices as intangible cultural heritage in the Austrian inventory of the 'National Agency for Intangible Cultural Heritage', a part of UNESCO. Inspired by the listing of the Viennese coffee house, interestingly, a group of students from Kingston University's interior design, architecture and landscape architecture departments (UK) are currently in the process of applying to get WH status for the London pub as a 'type' (Wainwright, 2012).

In tandem with the heightened significance of intangible heritage in the arena of heritage practice, as evidenced above, substantial academic attention has been paid to develop a systematic analysis of intangible heritage and tourism development (see González, 2008; George, 2010; Park, 2011). Intangible heritage and tangible heritage are often viewed as two separate realms of heritage, representing 'pre-modern and vernacular' and 'modern and authoritative' respectively. However, it is critical to recognise the deep-rooted interdependence between intangible heritage and tangible heritage. Memory, cultural knowledge and performance are grounded and embedded in tangible heritage while the value of tangible heritage derives from its cultural and symbolic significance. Furthermore, it can be argued that all heritage is, to a greater or lesser extent, intangible. Ashworth *et al.* (2007) claim that the symbolic worth of tangible heritage is closely linked to its intangible

Table 12.1 *Some examples on the Representative List of the Intangible Cultural Heritage of Humanity*

2012	Al'azi, elegy, processional march and poetry (Oman)
	Craftmanship of Horezu ceramics (Romania)
	Fiesta of the patios in Cordova (Spain)
	Traditional violin craftsmanship in Cremona (Italy)
	Rites and craftsmanship associated with the wedding costume tradition of Tlemcen (Algeria)
2011	Secret society of the Kôrêdugaw, the rite of wisdom in Mali (Mali)
	Fado, urban popular song of Portugal (Portugal)
	Jultagi, tightrope walking (Republic of Korea)
	Chinese shadow puppetry (China)
	Leuven age set ritual repertoire (Belgium)
2010	Gastronomic meal of the French (France)
	Gióng festival of Phû Dông and Sóc temples (Vietnam)
	Human towers (Spain)
	Mediterranean diet (Spain, Greece, Italy, Morocco)
	Hopping procession of Echternach (Luxembourg)
2009	Farmers' dance of China's Korean ethnic group (China)
	Indonesian Batik (Indonesia)
	Ijele masquerade (Nigeria)
	Tango (Argentina, Uruguay)
	Traditional Ainu dance (Japan)
2008	Barkcloth making in Uganda (Uganda)
	Cultural space of the Bedu in Petra and Wadi Rum (Jordan)
	Mask dance of the drums from Drametse (Bhutan)
	Wood crafting knowledge of the Zafimaniry (Madagascar)
	Cocolo dance drama tradition (Dominican Republic)

heritage. Deacon (2004: 311) argues that no heritage value is therefore completely 'tangible', given that all interpretations of place are human constructions. Subsequently, increasing focus is placed on conceptualising and contextualising intangible heritage of (tangible) heritage as values, meanings and perceptions inherent in (tangible) heritage. Munjeri (2004) argues that tangible and intangible heritage has recently moved towards convergence. Intangible heritage in this context is related to evoking the spiritual and symbolic aspects of sites or places. Tangible aspects of heritage provide symbolic foundations where intangible qualities prevail. Furthermore, it is intangible heritage of (tangible) heritage that renders the application of heritage in a given society and culture as valuable and enduring (Park, 2010a). As previously emphasised, individuals are increasingly recognised as important agents in conceptualising and interpreting heritage. This can be linked with incorporating individual narratives and subjective perceptions of heritage as essential elements of intangible heritage. Here, the meanings and values of heritage to which individuals confer are essential in enriching the understanding of heritage. In this light, the concept of intangible heritage has much wider and more significant implications in sustaining certain cultural values of individuals and communities. Obviously, intangible heritage is increasingly recognised as a profitable tourism resource. The excessive development of intangible heritage for tourism, particularly small and indigenous communities, can often lead to concerns over its ownership and copyrights. George (2010) brings attention to the difficulties of protecting intangible heritage, with specific reference to the issues surrounding intellectual property rights and ownership in appropriating intangible heritage for tourism. It is argued that cultural values of intangible heritage are converted into commercial products for exchange in tourism. In order not to challenge communities' ownership over intangible cultural heritage, developing and implementing legislation and strategies and encouraging all stakeholders' involvement could contribute to achieving a more equitable and sustainable approach that can benefit the communities.

Currently, there is a paucity of academic research, both conceptual and empirical, as regards the relationship between personal identity and intangible heritage (González, 2008). In examining the ways in which Japanese tourists experience intangible and experiential tourism through Flamenco tours in Spain, González (2008) points out that existential intangible heritage tourists seek, compared to leisure tourists, a deep integration into the authenticity of Flamenco. It is suggested that this finding can be integrated in developing the managerial strategies and practices of intangible heritage. As a scope for future research, it will be insightful to critically evaluate the complex and nuanced interrelationships between personal identity, authenticity and intangible heritage in both tourists and local communities. It will also be interesting to look at how varied interactions between tourists and local people including performers can influence their personal experiences of intangible heritage, identity and authenticity (see Zhu, 2012). However, developing the intangible heritage of aboriginal or indigenous communities for tourism can challenge their ownership and cultural integrity over the market value of intangible heritage. Marginal as well as hegemonic cultural expressions need to be carefully selected, protected and promoted as integral markers of identity, both personal and collective. It is also important not to impose the principles of safeguarding tangible heritage on the way intangible heritage is embraced in various national, international and intergovernmental practices of preservation and development. A more anthropological approach to heritage would contribute to enhancing the inclusive understanding of intangible heritage.

Heritage, citizenship and tourism

Neoliberalism and territorial and geographical reconfiguration harnessed by the process of globalisation have indelibly led to changing the dynamic relationship between state and citizen (Karim, 1997). The questions of identity, heritage and citizenship have shifted the focus on increasingly diverse and hybrid societies. Both heritage and citizenship has previously been conceptualised and contextualised within a national framework. However, heritage values now delimit and transcend individual nation-states, thereby highlighting a critical need to discuss heritage uses and functions in a wider framework beyond a national scale. In an age of increased mobility, it is difficult for a nation to remain as a primordial entity sharing a common race, language, ethnicity and heritage. Maintaining mono-cultural and mono-ethnic nations seems to be out of the question at a time of global assimilation and interdependence. Importantly, the increased recognition of cultural diversity and the proliferation of multiculturalism in Western societies have brought a new and challenging dimension in discourses of heritage. In multicultural and multiracial nations, heritage can be one effective medium to inform and teach citizenship, thereby helping to forge and maintain a sense of belonging (see Copeland, 2006b). Pretes (2003) argues that heritage tourism can help to inform tourists of a common national identity among distinct ethnic populations. Heritage can serve as a conceptual and symbolic medium in preserving the integrity and authenticity of different and distinctive groups as well as enhancing their relationships on the whole. Here raises a dilemma though: how can heritage of different groups be recognised and protected while creating and supporting common heritage in contemporary societies? Different and diverse exemplars of multi-ethnic and multicultural heritage need to be recognised and incorporated as key constituents of heritage in increasingly multiracial and multicultural heritage. Many mainstream heritage organisations have started to embrace the history and heritage of non-indigenous communities in their main discourses as an attempt to enhance diversity and social inclusion (Littler, 2005). Therefore, claims of culture and identity advanced by various minority groups including immigrants and aboriginals have become researched and contextualised (see Carens, 2000). However, multicultural heritage can be employed to 'embed essentialised ideas of cultural difference, whether through exoticising 'other' cultures or homogenising and sentimentalizing "local" white English heritages' (Littler, 2005: 10). Cultural differences and heterogeneities of non-indigenous communities need to be clearly reflected in the process of heritage selection, interpretation and management in hybrid and diverse contemporary societies.

The issue of multicultural identity and heritage needs to be more holistically integrated in theoretical studies of the relationship between heritage and citizenship. Brubaker (1996) maintains that discussions of citizenship in an age of the nation-state are largely about constructions of nationhood and nation, as well as meanings of belonging. However, the process of globalisation has transcended pre-established territorial boundaries, thereby reconceptualising and recontextualising the meanings of belonging and identity, such as the construction of the European identity. Here, heritage is constantly made and remade in the new challenging dynamics of nation-states, citizenship and global movement including tourism. In examining the nexus of citizenship, heritage and technology, Karim (1997) argues that the digital dissemination of heritage can contribute to establishing a renewed social contract between citizen and state. As emphasised in the previous section, heritage is essential in teaching citizenship. The use of digital technology encourages universal access to heritage, playing a role of 'essential communicative resources for citizenship' (Karim, 1997: 83). Concurrently, a range of heritage-related projects have been developed in an endeavour to strengthen new cultural identities in the European community (see Case study 12.2).

Both heritage and citizenship are identified as effective agents of global unity and identity (Copeland, 2006b). There emerges a heightened realisation of the discursive and dialectic relationship between heritage and citizenship in reconfiguring the issues of identity, belonging and inclusion in contemporary societies. It is also critical to note that heritage has become a symbol of cultural citizenship, both rights and duties of the citizens in national and global contexts. This line of thought will be insightful in future studies to unravel ways in which heritage informs and contests contemporary citizenship in an age of global mobility. It would thus be fruitful to conceptually explore ways in which heritage tourism can reinforce and re-enact a sense of what it means to be a modern citizen, opening up further discussions concerning the ethnic and cultural elements of transnational as well as national citizenship embodied in various heritage settings. It will also be interesting to systematically examine and analyse the ways in which ethnic heritage of different non-indigenous communities is contested and negotiated in the complex and intricate dynamics between national and transnational citizenship. Finally, comparatively less emphasis has been placed on unravelling how non-indigenous communities perceive and respond to the heritage of a host country. Non-indigenous communities tend to relate the notion of heritage to the history and tradition of their ancestral homeland, as discussed in Chapter 6, thereby creating a perceived distinction between cultural and political citizenship.

From digital heritage to virtual heritage

As illustrated in Chapter 8, technological advancements including digital technology have had a substantial impact on the ways in which heritage is produced and consumed in contemporary contexts. In particular, the internet has dramatically changed the way heritage engages with audiences. The special properties of heritage content comprising heterogeneity, intangibility and perishability make them extremely information-intensive and thus specially suited for presenting them in an electronic way (Liu et al., 2006). According to

Case study 12.2: Heritage projects in the European community

EUSTORY – history network for young Europeans

EUSTORY is an international network of historical research competitions for young people, which currently connects 22 civic organisations from 22 European countries. The mandate of EUSTORY is to view European history from the grass roots and to recognise the vast diversity of experience. Opposing the abuse of history as an ideological weapon, EUSTORY emphasises the view of history as a platform for intercultural understanding in Europe, which is clearly specified in the EUSTORY charter. EUSTORY is therefore not only a meaningful initiative of historical grass roots work in Europe, but also makes an important and pioneering contribution to European efforts towards peace and tolerance. Since the EUSTORY network was founded in September 2001 on the initiative of the Hamburg-based Körber Foundation, some 122,000 youth have already participated in EUSTORY history competitions with about 55,000 contributions.

Source: http://www.eustory.eu/#.

LEM – the learning museum

LEM is a new European project that started in 2010 and aims to create a European network of museums and cultural heritage organisations active in the lifelong learning arena. In order to face the challenges of present and future decades and in order to react to changing societies, museums are expected not only to be learning places, but also learning organisations themselves. As learning organisations, museums have to learn from communities, from the public and also from other agencies with whom they have to build alliances in order to achieve the aims set out by politics at the national and European level. LEM wants to support museums in all of this.

Source: http://www.lemproject.eu.

Liew (2005), images and videos have an important role in attracting heritage tourists. The practices of using digital technology have largely been incorporated in contemporary heritage management, both in situ and online. In July 2012, Web Lab, a series of interactive Chrome Experiments made by Google, was launched at the Science Museum in London where physical installations can be interacted through a web browser. This web-based exhibition enables online visitors to create music together, watch their portrait being drawn by a robot or track down individual photos on the web, to see where in the world images are stored. Advanced digital technologies have even expanded their scope and capacity in heritage conservation. CyArk, a non-profit organisation in the US, was founded in 2002 and has since digitised more than 30 endangered heritage sites ranging from the cave dwellings of the Anasazi people in Colorado, the ruins of Pompeii, the Mayan temples in Guatemala to the Hindu temple of Angkor Wat in Cambodia.

Heritage tourists now engage with heritage displays in much more participatory and engaging ways (see Case study 12.3). With the help of digital technologies, heritage has become more accessible and open to broader social groups. But this raises some fundamental

Case study 12.3: Reflecting the Past

The project, Reflecting the Past, along with five other projects, is supported by Heritage Sandbox, part of REACT (Research & Enterprise in Arts & Creative Technology), exploring new experiences around heritage. Tim Cole, an academic and historian at the University of Bristol, leads the project in collaboration with Interactive Places, an agency specialising in developing installations and apps for heritage organizations, and a laboratory at Plymouth University. Using a wide range of media – augmented reality mirrors, directional speakers and material objects – this project aims to create an immersive visitor experience that re-populates heritage properties by using mirrors with 'ghostings' of figures from the past. Newark Park in south Gloucestershire, a National Trust property, has been selected as one of the project's destinations. It was built in the Tudor period and several interesting historical characters including James Power-Clutterbuck, the son of the last owner, have been created as images in the mirrors. Visitors are placed into the past very literally through the illusion of figures created by the mirrors and the voices of these previous occupants. Pioneering the use of a new type of augmented reality mirror in heritage attractions, this project seeks to transform the contemporary experience for visitors, as they see not only their own reflection, but also glimpse the characters who have left their traces and conversations behind.

Source: http://www.react-hub.org.uk/heritagesandbox/projects/2012/reflecting-the-past.

questions to reflect upon: has digital heritage really become more democratic in terms of access and social inclusion? Digitising heritage including museums and archival collections could lead to, despite its overall effect of enhancing accessibility, the exclusion of a certain segment of society that is either digitally illiterate or uninterested (Karim, 1997; Grek, 2009). Grek (2009) argues that the focus on the delivery methods of education in contemporary practices of heritage, with particular regard to museums, can lead to unfulfilled educational potential. Currently, too much focus seems to be placed on visitors' personal and experiential learning experiences in heritage contexts. However, learning in and through heritage ought not just be related to learning through participation in entertaining and technological ways. Certain technological and global changes in heritage are inevitable but the social dimension of learning in heritage should not be overlooked. The use of new digital technologies needs to be perceived and employed as an alternative and informal tool in enhancing flexible and independent learning in heritage, rather than being completely oppositional to traditional heritage education. Diverse learning choices and contexts offered in heritage through digital technology may only contribute to enhancing the access and participation of the established heritage visitor groups. More empirical investigations would be insightful in future research that critically evaluate the ways in which the use of digital technology in various heritage settings may or may not facilitate enhanced access and participation of traditional 'non-visitor' groups, including disadvantaged and ethnic minority groups.

Heritage tourism and social media

As previously emphasised, there has been an increasing focus on visitors' participation and engagement in heritage experiences. Social media has unmistakably contributed to facilitating and enhancing the culture of participation in the way heritage is perceived and experienced in contemporary contexts (Giaccardi, 2012). The increasing utilisation of social media in heritage has led to a sustained emphasis on the significance of user-generated content, which has reshaped the way heritage information is produced, distributed and consumed. Information becomes widely and instantly shared through various channels of social media. Apart from popular social media platforms such as Facebook, Twitter and Flickr, there exists a plethora of new online applications, including podcasts, blogs, media and content syndication, online videos and discussion boards. History and heritage becomes readily available in everyday life. Iversen and Smith (2012: 128–9) emphasise the role of social media in encouraging heritage experiences in everyday contexts, commenting that:

> Social media and networked forms of communication reflect social practices that already exist as part of people's everyday lives and experiences. People actively create everyday experiences within and through the communication paradigm of social media. This creates a model of communication based on engagement and dialogue that is rooted in particular and situated in everyday practices. Thus, social media can be actively used as both a means for and a model of communication and interaction emphasizing engagement and dialogue.

Social media can play a pivotal role in facilitating heritage tourism experiences in everyday contexts by creating and sharing dialogical connections between heritage and tourists. Social media can also contribute to blurring the formal distinction between heritage as product and heritage as process in tourism experiences. Authorised and fragmented realms of the past can be recreated and repositioned as ongoing, interactive and inclusive heritage experiences. In 2010, the Museum of London released an augmented reality app for the iPhone, entitled *Streetmuseum*, which enables users to browse historical photos in various parts of the city. Using either the map or GPS, the app recognises the location and overlays the historical photograph over the real images. The photos stored in the archive of the Museum of London have been brought to life, creating an impression of a lived past in present contexts. Through the use of social media, tourists are able to share and communicate their personal experiences of heritage. But more importantly, tourists are increasingly involved in creating, managing and curating the content of heritage available in virtual spaces. Here, heritage tourists become active creators of heritage rather than merely remaining passive recipients in the making of heritage. Dominant hegemony of heritage representation and interpretation becomes more easily challenged, deconstructed and reconstructed in virtual social spaces than traditional face-to-face settings. Social media thus plays a significant role in making heritage more democratic and accessible.

Social media practices have been integrated in tourism research, particularly in relation to supporting online marketing activities (Gretzel, 2006), examining the role of search engines in online travel information searches (Xiang and Gretzel, 2010) and assessing online social network websites for Generation Y travellers (Nusair *et al.*, 2013). There has also been a surge of academic enquiries in examining and evaluating the role of social media in heritage studies. But scant emphasis has been placed on exploring individual engagement with cultural heritage and connecting heritage experiences to people's lives and settings (Giaccardi, 2012). There is little understanding in the existing literature regarding the use of social media as individual expressions and social constructions of heritage within tourism contexts. There emerges a critical need to qualitatively research the implications of incorporating social media in heritage tourism experiences, which would help further understand the ways in which social media may or may not contribute to the individual and contextual understanding and experience of heritage. Heritage managers need to realise the technological changes and dynamics in co-creating and communicating heritage narratives, thereby reaching out and promoting their heritage sites and practices to a wider section of society. It is correct to assume that social media plays a critical role in attracting the younger generations who are not generally part of traditional visitor groups. However, the age range using social media continues to expand and the use of social media will not differ greatly between generations in the near future. Despite their unprecedented growth and popularity, as clearly emphasised in the previous section, new technological changes in heritage need to be complemented as an auxiliary means to encourage more participatory and interactive heritage experiences.

Heritage accommodation: from hotels to hostels

Utilising and renovating historic buildings for heritage accommodation has become increasingly popular all over the globe. Despite their popularity and significance, heritage experiences derived from tourism services such as accommodation have not fully been examined and evaluated in the existing literature (Timothy, 2011). According to Timothy and Teye (2009), renovated or remodelled historic buildings are one of the most in-demand types of tourist accommodation. The economic values of heritage are emphasised in the transformation of historic buildings into heritage accommodation. A wide range of historic buildings have been converted into heritage accommodation, ranging from stately homes in England, shophouses in Singapore and Thailand, monasteries in Italy and Spain, to prisons in Finland and Canada and lighthouses in Scotland. The development of heritage accommodation can contribute to 'preserving historical buildings and utilizing them for alternative purposes rather than tearing them down to make way for new developments' (Timothy and Teye, 2009: 247). This use of heritage can also contribute to maintaining the historical ambiences of built heritage, thereby enhancing its long-term sustainability. It is interesting to note that this vernacular use has rapidly grown in different types of heritage, even including unusual and unconventional heritage for accommodation, as illustrated in the case study below on the conversion of nuclear bunkers in Albania (see Case study 12.4).

Heritage lodging establishments have become unique cultural, historical and ethnic markers of authentic environments in various tourism destinations (Chang, 1997). In examining the use of shophouses for boutique hotels in Singapore, Chang and Teo (2009: 363) claim that these spaces in urban contexts help to serve as 'representational spaces in Singapore's quest to be a modern metropolis with a historic flair'. Given that heritage is constantly recreated and reused in multiple ways depending on contemporary interests and demands, the use of old and historic buildings for tourist accommodation can be welcoming and beneficial as both identity and tourism markers in contexts where tradition is explicitly surpassed by modernity. In this light, it is interesting to note that heritage hotels have increasingly become popular in Asian countries. The usual concerns over the issues of authenticity and commodification are bound to emerge from the proliferation of heritage hotels and historic accommodation. Currently, there exists a significant paucity of academic research in examining and evaluating the emerging trends, uses and values of heritage accommodation. More rigorous research should be conducted in order to develop an insightful understanding of the complex dynamics between authenticity and commodification in the tourist experiences of heritage accommodation.

Case study 12.4: Albania's nuclear bunkers converted into hostels

During the Cold War in Albania, around 750,000 bunkers were built in fear of nuclear war. Albania is just 28,700 square kilometres in size and there are more than 26 bunkers per square kilometre. This project was instigated and led by the country's former dictator, Enver Hoxha, in the 1970s and 1980s. Since the demise of the country's communist government in 1992, this unique military infrastructure has apparently become of no use. Despite the fact they are the material remnants of the country's brutal and paranoid history, the bunkers remain as significant heritage that should not be lost. Two Albanian graduate students, Gyler Mydyti and Elian Stefa, started a project in 2010, entitled 'Concrete Mushrooms', which aims to catalogue the country's network of bunkers and encourage their new uses. In the blog of the project, it is clearly emphasised that:

> The priority of the 'Concrete Mushrooms' project is facing the symbol of xenophobia (bunker) with deliberate awareness for the purpose of inverting its meaning, the preservation of the memoir of a significant period of the Albanian history, giving bunkers value instead of having them as a burden and as a result the promotion of an underdeveloped touristic sector such as Eco-Tourism which has an enormous potential at the same time growing the financial viability, social and environmental sustainability.

A new book featuring step-by-step guides for converting derelict bunkers into everything from hostels and toilets to cafes and gift shops was launched at the Venice Biennale in 2012. In Lezhë on the Adriatic coast, 30 miles north of Tirana, a joint German–Albanian tourism venture, 'Bed & Bunker', officially launched in 2012, is in the process of transforming a bunker into a no-frills hostel for backpackers.

Sources: Geoghegan (2012); http://blog.concrete-mushrooms.com/?page_id=112.

Heritage and climate change

The World Monuments Fund (WMF) aims to monitor damage to heritage buildings and sites. The WMF identifies three major threats facing heritage sites as political conflict, tourism and climate change. Political conflict and tourism development have widely been discussed as the main culprits of damaging and denigrating heritage sites and experiences. On the contrary, climate change issues in heritage have remained largely unexplored. The impacts of climate change on both cultural and natural heritage have become evident across the globe in the past decade. International organisations including UNESCO, the WMF, the GHF and ICOMOS have started to seriously engage with the particular issues of climate change. But it was not until 2005 that the issue of climate change was brought to the attention of the World Heritage Committee. In 2007, UNESCO published Case Studies on Climate Change and WH in order to enhance public awareness of WHSs exposed to various climate change threats, including flooding in London, sea-level rise in Venice and its lagoon, Italy, desertification in Timbuktu, Mali and coral bleaching in the Great Barrier Reef, Australia (see Case study 12.5).

Case study 12.5: Climate change issues and cultural heritage

Historic cities: the case of Cesky Krumlov, Czech Republic

In 1992, the World Heritage Committee decided to inscribe the historic centre of Cesky Krumlov, a Czech city located south of Prague. Situated on the banks of the Vltava River, the town was built around a thirteenth-century castle with Gothic, Renaissance and Baroque elements. It is an outstanding example of a small central European medieval town whose architectural heritage has remained intact thanks to its peaceful evolution over more than five centuries. But the sites remain exposed to natural hazards, such as the severe floods that affected Eastern Europe in the summer of 2002. The WHSs of the historic centres of Prague and Cesky Krumlov suffered significant damage from these events. In Cesky Krumlov, the historic centre was flooded up to 4m and about 150 buildings from the medieval Gothic and Renaissance periods suffered considerable damage. It was only due to the preference of medieval builders in the Czech region to use stone, bricks and lime, instead of the less durable wood or raw bricks, that prevented the damage from being much worse. The biggest challenge encountered in the recovery of these floods was how to dry the waterlogged walls and structures before the winter brought frost damage. Preserving the authenticity of the sites after the floods proved to be difficult because of several pressures to replace historic features by modern materials assumed to be more resistant to floods.

Figure 12.2 The historic centre of Cesky Krumlov, the Czech Republic

Archaeological remains: the case of Chan Chan Archeological Zone, Peru

Chan Chan, capital of the ancient Chimu Kingdom, is one of the largest and most important pre-hispanic earthen architecture cities in the Americas. The architectural ensembles and the complexity of the urban design reflect the high political, social, technological and economic levels attained by the Chimor society between the ninth and fifteenth centuries, just before falling into the hands of the Incas. The archaeological complex, therefore, synthesises the historical evolution of ethnic groups in northern Peru that contributed to the development of the Andean culture. The El Niño-Southern Oscillation (ENSO) phenomenon consistently affects regional variations of precipitation and temperature over much of the tropics and sub-tropics. Over the northern coast of Peru, warm episodes of this oscillation are associated to large positive anomalies in precipitation. In coastal arid zones of northern Peru, the historical average of annual precipitation is only 20–150mm, but this area received up to 3,000mm of rainfall during the El Niño event of 1997–8. Intense precipitation is damaging the base of the earthen architecture structures. It leads to greater humidity in the lower parts of the buildings and, consequently, to an increase in salt contamination of the structures and to the growth of vegetation such as reeds and water lilies in the low-lying *huachaques*. A monitoring survey of the 68 wells has been underway since 2000, as part of a ten-year action plan in management, and it has revealed a progressive rise of the water levels that had already reached alarming heights in January 2003. Chan Chan Archeological Zone has been placed in the list of World Heritage in Danger since 1986.

Source: Colette (2007).

As evident in the case studies above, climate change causes adverse effects on cultural heritage as well as natural heritage. Less significant focus has been, however, placed on identifying and investigating the impacts of climate change on cultural heritage. World Heritage Centre (2007) recognises a lack of data pertaining to climate change impacts on WH cultural properties. Subsequently, various possible impacts on cultural heritage are identified:

> Archaeological remains and related evidence will be affected when the hydrological, chemical and biological processes of the soil change. Since historic buildings materials are more porous than modern constructions, any increases in soil moisture might result in greater salt mobilizations; consequently drying will cause salt crystallisation to damage decorated surfaces. Timber and other organic building materials may be subject to increased biological infestation in altitudes and latitudes that may not have been previously affected. Flooding may damage building materials not designed to withstand prolonged immersion. Increases in storminess and wind gusts can lead to structural damage. Desertification, salt weathering and erosion is already threatening cultural heritage in desert areas.
>
> (World Heritage Centre, 2007: 3)

Interestingly, the WMF list focuses on the 'human factor', anthropogenic factors in climate change, which link the change to human energy consumption and tourism development (Barthel-Bouchier, 2013). The impact of efforts to meet the challenges of climate change is also regarded as a significant threat to heritage. Environmental sustainability and historic preservation need to be integrated in the management strategies of heritage. There is currently a lack of adequate capacity and financial resources for research and its application, particularly in developing countries. Ongoing generic research on the issues of climate change needs to be incorporated in heritage management. Long-term monitoring of the impacts of climate change on heritage is critical in detecting and investigating any signs of possible threats and changes before any irreparable damages are made. It is also critical to raise awareness among the public of the impact of climate change. The challenge is to understand what climate change means for heritage, and hence consider what practical steps can be taken to adapt its built environment without damaging its historic and architectural importance (see Barthel-Bouchier, 2013).

Conclusion

It is critical to recognise the significance of intangible heritage, drawing attention to the deep-rooted interdependence between intangible and tangible heritage. The importance of tangible heritage is often grounded in its intangible values manifesting diverse symbolic meanings and embodiments. Overall, the inclusive and holistic understanding of intangible heritage would contribute to enriching the discussions around the values and practices of heritage. Recognition of intangible heritage could also enhance the understanding of the peripheral and marginalised version of heritage, which is often under-represented in the authorised version of heritage. Excessive commercial interest in developing intangible heritage for tourism can be carefully balanced by more anthropological approaches to heritage. Both heritage and citizenship are identified as effective agents of global unity and identity. The issue of multicultural identity and heritage needs to be more holistically integrated in theorising and integrating heritage and citizenship. Careful approaches need to be made in assessing, appropriating and reappropriating multicultural heritage as part of the mainstream display of social history in contemporary societies. The role of digital technology and social media has had a fundamental impact on contemporary uses of heritage. New technological changes in heritage need to be complemented as an auxiliary means to encourage more participatory and interactive heritage experiences. The use of digital technology as a presentational and communicative tool should not circumvent unique first-hand heritage experiences. Currently, there exists a general lack of academic research in the field of heritage accommodation and climate change issues. More empirical-based research will provide an enhanced understanding of protecting heritage in the face of increasing signs of climate change.

Research questions

1 Explain the interdependent nature of tangible and intangible heritage.
2 Discuss ways in which heritage and citizenship interact in multicultural societies.
3 What are the implications of digital or virtual heritage in enhanced access and participation in heritage?
4 What opportunities do digital technologies offer for collaboration between heritage sites and communities?
5 Discuss and critically evaluate the ways in which social media has enhanced tourists' participation in heritage.
6 How can cultural values and economic values be balanced in the increasing use of historic buildings for accommodation?
7 Using relevant examples, discuss the impacts of climate change on cultural heritage sites.

Learning material

Barthel-Bouchier, D. (2013) *Cultural Heritage and the Challenge of Sustainability*, Walnut Creek, CA: Left Coast Press (Chapter 3).

Colette, A. (2007) *Case Studies on Climate Change and World Heritage*, Paris: World Heritage Centre.

Giaccardi, E. (2012) Introduction: reframing heritage in a participatory culture, in E. Giaccardi (ed.) *Heritage and Social Media*, London: Routledge, pp. 1–10.

Grek, S. (2009) 'In and against the museum': the contested spaces of museum education for adults, *Discourse: Studies in the Cultural Politics of Education*, 30(2): 195–211.

Karim, K.H. (1997) Relocating the nexus of citizenship, heritage and technology, *The Public*, 4(4): 75–86.

Landorf, C. (2009) Managing for sustainable tourism: a review of six cultural World Heritage Sites, *Journal of Sustainable Tourism*, 17(1): 53–70.

Nas, P.J.M. (2002) Masterpieces of oral and intangible culture: reflections on the UNESCO World Heritage List, *Current Anthropology*, 43(1): 139–48.

Smith, L. (2006) *Uses of Heritage*, London and New York: Routledge (Chapter 2).

Timothy, D. and Teye, V. (2009) *Tourism and the Lodging Sector*, Oxford: Butterworth-Heinemann.

Weblinks

Day of the Dead, Mexico City
http://www.youtube.com/watch?v=GmeBn95DoMM

Commemorating Day of the Dead, Guatemala
http://www.bbc.co.uk/news/world-latin-america-20176934

The Dragon Boat Festival, China
http://www.unesco.org/archives/multimedia/?s=films_details&id_page=33&id_film=335

Viennese coffee house culture
www.bbc.co.uk/news/magazine-16538189
www.guardian.co.uk/travel/video/2011/jan/13/vienna-austria-coffee-houses-cafe

London pub
http://news.bbc.co.uk/1/hi/programmes/fast_track/9770685.stm

The real Downton Abbey
http://news.bbc.co.uk/1/hi/programmes/fast_track/9684249.stm

Heritage at risk: hazard map
http://archive.cyark.org/hazard-map

Buddhas in 3D: technology and the battle to preserve Asia's heritage
http://edition.cnn.com/2013/01/15/world/asia/china-digital-caves

Ben Kacyra: ancient wonders captured in 3D (CyArk)
http://www.ted.com/talks/ben_kacyra_ancient_wonders_captured_in_3d.html

Reflecting the past
http://www.watershed.co.uk/dshed/reflecting-past

The future cemetery, Britstol, UK
http://www.react-hub.org.uk/heritagesandbox/projects/2012/the-future-cemetery

An introduction to digital death
http://vimeo.com/16205659

Google's World Wonders project maps historic sites
http://www.telegraph.co.uk/technology/google/9301090/Googles-World-Wonders-project-maps-historic-sites.html

Streetmuseum: Museum of London
http://www.youtube.com/watch?v=qSfATEZiUYo

Pop-up museum
http://vimeo.com/21135962

Concrete Mushrooms: Albania's 750,000 inherited bunkers
http://vimeo.com/6710102

Wish you were here? Albania's Cold War bunker hostels
http://www.bbc.co.uk/news/world-europe-19871122

2012 World Monuments Watch (WMF)
http://cdn.wmf.org/downloads/2012-Watch-Map.pdf

References

Aas, C., Ladkin, A. and Fletcher, J. (2005) Stakeholder collaboration and heritage management, *Annals of Tourism Research*, 32(1): 28–48.

Adams, K.M. (1995) Making-up the Toraja? The appropriation of tourism, anthropology, and museums for politics in upland Sulawesi, Indonesia, *Ethnology*, 34(2): 143–54.

Adams, K.M. (1997) Ethnic tourism and the renegotiation of tradition in Tana Toraja (Sulawesi, Indonesia), *Ethnology*, 36(4): 309–20.

Addley, E. (2010) The second fall of Pompeii, *The Guardian*, 12 November.

Adi, H., Shahadah, A. and Nehusi, K. (2005) *Transatlantic Slave Trade*. Online. Available at: http://www.africanholocaust.net/articles/TRANSATLANTIC%20SLAVE%20TRADE.htm (accessed 29 September 2012).

Agarwal, S. (2002) Restructuring seaside tourism: the resort lifecycle, *Annals of Tourism Research*, 29(1): 25–55.

Ahmad, Y. (2006) The scope and definitions of heritage: from tangible to intangible, *International Journal of Heritage Studies*, 12(3): 292–300.

Amato, S. (2006) Quai Branly museum: representing France after empire, *Race and Class*, 47(4): 46–65.

Ambrose, T. and Paine, C. (1993) *Museum Basics*, London: Routledge.

Anderson, B. (1983) *Imagined Communities*, London: Verso.

Anderson, D. (1997) *A Common Wealth: Museums and Learning in the United Kingdom*, a report to the Department of National Heritage, UK.

Apostolakis, A. (2003) The convergence process in heritage tourism, *Annals of Tourism Research*, 30(4): 795–812.

Appadurai, A. (ed.) (1986) *The Social Life of Things: Commodities in Cultural Perspective*, Cambridge: Cambridge University Press.

Appadurai, A. (1990) Disjuncture and difference in the global cultural economy, *Public Culture*, 2(2): 6–10.

Appadurai, A. (2001) The globalization of archaeology and heritage: a discussion with Arjun Appadurai, *Journal of Social Archaeology*, 1(1): 35–49.

Ashworth, G.J. (1992) Heritage and tourism: an argument, two problems and three solutions, in C.A.M. Fleischer-van Rooijen (ed.) *Spatial Implications of Tourism*, Groningen: Geo Pers, pp. 95–104.

Ashworth, G.J. (1994) From history to heritage – from heritage to identity: in search of concepts and models, in G.J. Ashworth and P.J. Larkham (eds) *Building a New Heritage: Tourism, Culture and Identity in the New Europe*, London: Routledge, pp. 13–30.

Ashworth, G.J. (2012) Do tourists destroy the heritage they have come to experience? in T.V. Singh (ed.) *Critical Debates in Tourism*, Bristol: Channel View Publications, pp. 278–86.

Ashworth, G.J., Graham, B. and Tunbridge, E. (2007) *Pluralising Pasts: Heritage, Identity and Place in Multicultural Societies*, London: Pluto Press.

Ashworth, G.J. and Larkham, P.J. (1994) *Building a New Heritage: Tourism, Culture and Identity in the New Europe*, London: Routledge.

Ashworth, G.J. and Tunbridge, J.E. (1996) *Dissonant Heritage: The Management of the Past as a Resource in Conflict*, Chichester: Wiley.

Ashworth, G.J. and Tunbridge, J.E. (2000) *The Tourist–Historic City: Retrospect and Prospect of Managing the Heritage City*, Oxford: Pergamon/Elsevier.

Askew, M. (2010) The magic list of global status: UNESCO, World Heritage and the agendas of states, in S. Labadi and C. Long (eds) *Heritage and Globalisation*, London: Routledge, pp. 19–44.

Association of Leading Visitor Attractions (2012) 2012 Visitor Figures. Online. Available at: http://alva.org.uk/details.cfm?p=598 (accessed 6 August 2013).

Austin, N.K. (2002) Managing heritage attractions: marketing challenges at sensitive historical sites, *International Journal of Tourism Research*, 4(6): 447–57.

Azara, I. and Crouch, D. (2006) La Cavalcata Sarda: performing identities in a contemporary Sardinian festival, in D. Picard and M. Robinson (eds) *Festivals, Tourism and Social Change: Remaking Worlds*, Clevedon: Channel View Publications, pp. 32–45.

Azarya, V. (2004) Globalization and international tourism in developing countries: marginality as a commercial commodity, *Current Sociology*, 52(6): 949–67.

Bailey, C., Miles, S. and Stark, P. (2004) Culture-led urban regeneration and the revitalization of identities in Newcastle, Gateshead and the North East of England, *International Journal of Cultural Policy*, 10(1): 47–65.

Baker, M.J. and Cameron, E. (2007) Critical success factors in destination marketing, *Tourism and Hospitality Research*, 8(2): 79–97.

Barth, F. (1969) Introduction, in F. Barth (ed.) *Ethnic Groups and Boundaries: The Social Oganisation of Culture Difference*, Oslo: Norwegian University Press, pp. 9–38.

Barthel-Bouchier, D. (2013) *Cultural Heritage and the Challenge of Sustainability*, Walnut Creek, CA: Left Coast Press.

Basu, P. (2008) Confronting the past? Negotiating a heritage of conflict in Sierra Leone, *Journal of Material Culture*, 13(2): 233–47.

Baudrillard, J. (1983) *Simulations*, New York: Semiotext (translated by P. Foss, P. Patton and P. Beitchman).

Bauer, A.A. (2007) New ways of thinking about cultural property: a critical approach of the antiquities trade debates, *Fordham International Law Journal*, 31(3): 690–724.

Beck, L. and Cable, T.T. (2002) *Interpretation for the 21st Century: Fifteen Guiding Principles for Interpreting Nature and Culture*, Urbana: Sagamore.

Beech, J.G. (2001) The marketing of slavery heritage in the United Kingdom, *International Journal of Hospitality & Tourism Administration*, 2(3): 85–107.

Beeton, S. and Benfield, R. (2003) Demand control: the case for demarketing as a visitor and environmental management tool, *Journal of Sustainable Tourism*, 10(6): 497–513.

Belhassen, Y. and Caton, K. (2006) Authenticity matters, *Annals of Tourism Research*, 33(3): 853–6.

Bell, D. (2003) Mythscapes: memory, mythology, and national identity, *British Journal of Sociology*, 54(1): 63–81.

Bendapudi, N. and Leone, R.P. (2003) Psychological implications of customer participation in co-production, *Journal of Marketing*, 67(1): 14–28.

Benedikter, R. (2004) Privatisation of Italian cultural heritage, *International Journal of Heritage Studies*, 10(4): 369–89.

Bennett, M.M. (1997) Heritage marketing: the role of information technology, *Journal of Vacation Marketing*, 3(3): 272–80.

Bennett, O. (2005) Are we loving our heritage to death? *The Guardian*, 30 April.

Bennett, T. (1995) *The Birth of the Museum: History, Theory, Politics*, London: Routledge.

Benton, T. and Watson, N.J. (2010) Museum practice and heritage, in S. West (ed.) *Understanding Heritage in Practice*, Milton Keynes: The Open University, pp. 127–65.

Bergman, J. (2011) Rejecting life in the fast lane: Yaxi, China, takes it slow, *Time World*, 4 August.

Bertacchini, E., Saccone, D. and Santagata, W. (2011) Embracing diversity, correcting inequalities: towards a new global governance for the UNESCO World Heritage, *International Journal of Cultural Policy*, 17(3): 278–88.

Bessière, J. (1998) Local development and heritage: traditional food and cuisine as tourist attractions in rural areas, *Sociologia Ruralis*, 38(1): 21–34.

Billig, M. (1995) *Banal Nationalism*, New York: Sage.

Black, J. (1992) *The British Abroad: The Grand Tour in the Eighteenth Century*, New York: St. Martin's Press.

Blom, T. (2000) Morbid tourism: a postmodern market niche with an example from Althorp, *Norwegian Journal of Geography*, 54(1): 29–36.

Boniface, P. and Fowler, P.J. (1993) *Heritage and tourism in 'the global village'*, London: Routledge.

Boorstin, D.J. (1964) *The Image: A Guide to Pseudo-Events in America*, New York: Harper.

Bortolotto, C. (2010) Globalising intangible cultural heritage? Between international arenas and local appropriations, in S. Labadi and C. Long (eds) *Heritage and Globalisation*, London: Routledge, pp. 97–114.

Bourdieu, P. (2010) [1984] *Distinction*, London: Routledge.

Boyd, S.W. (2008) Marketing challenges and opportunities for heritage tourism, in A. Fyall, B. Garrod, A. Leask and S. Wanhill (eds) *Managing Visitor Attraction: New Direction* (2nd edn), Oxford: Butterworth-Heinemann, pp. 283–94.

Branigan, T. (2009) Communist heritage is good business as China prepares for 60th anniversary, *The Guardian*, 27 September.

Bressey, C. and Wareham, T. (2011) *Reading the London Sugar & Slavery Museum Gallery, Docklands*, London: Museum of London.

Briassoulis, H. and der Stroaten, J.V. (eds) (2000) *Tourism and the Environment: Regional, Economic, Cultural, and Policy Issues* (2nd edn), Dordrecht: Kluwer Academic Publishers.

Brohman, J. (1996) New directions in tourism for third world development, *Annals of Tourism Research*, 23(1): 48–70.

Brown, L. (2013) Tourism: a catalyst for existential authenticity, *Annals of Tourism Research*, 40(1): 176–90.

Brubaker, R. (1996) *Nationalism Reframed: Nationhood and the National Question in the New Europe*, Cambridge: Cambridge University Press.

Bruner, E.M. (1991) Transformation of self in tourism, *Annals of Tourism Research*, 18(2): 238–50.

Bruner, E.M. (1994) Abraham Lincoln as authentic reproduction: a critique of postmodernism, *American Anthropologist*, 96(2): 397–415.

Bruner, E.M. (1996) Tourism in Ghana: the representation of slavery and the return of the black diaspora, *American Anthropologist*, 98(2): 290–304.

Buhalis, D. (2000) Marketing the competitive destination of the future, *Tourism Management*, 21(1): 97–116.

Bushell, R. and Staiff, R. (2012) Rethinking relationships: World Heritage, communities and tourism, in P. Daly and T. Winter (eds) *Routledge Handbook of Heritage in Asia*, London: Routledge, pp. 247–65.

Butler, D.L. (2001) White-washing plantations: the commodification of a slave-free antebellum South, in G.M.S. Dann and A.V. Seaton (eds) *Slavery, Contested Heritage, and Thanatourism*, New York: Haworth Hospitality Press, pp. 163–75.

Butler, R.W. (1999) Sustainable tourism: a state of the art review, *Tourism Geographies*, 1(1): 7–25.

Buzinde, C.N. and Santos, C.A. (2008) Representations of slavery, *Annals of Tourism Research*, 35(2): 469–88.

Byrd, E. (2007) Stakeholder in sustainable tourism development and their roles: applying stakeholder theory to sustainable tourism development, *Tourism Review*, 62(2): 6–13.

Carens, J.H. (2000) *Culture, Citizenship, and Community: Contextual Political Theory and Justice as Evenhandedness*, Oxford: Oxford University Press.

Carnegie, E. and McCabe, S. (2008) Re-enactment events and tourism: meaning, authenticity and identity, *Current Issues in Tourism*, 11(4): 349–68.

Carpenter, J. and Lees, L. (1995) Gentrification in New York, London and Paris: an international comparison, *International Journal of Urban and Regional Research*, 19(2): 286–303.

Carter, H. (2011) Liverpool's heritage status 'at risk' from Shanghai-style plan, *The Guardian*, 16 May.

Cassia, P. (1999) Tradition, tourism and memory in Malta, *Journal of the Royal Anthropological Institute* (N.S.), 5(2): 247–63.

Catalani, A. and Ackroyd, T. (2013, in press) Inheriting slavery: making sense of a difficult heritage, *Journal of Heritage Tourism*.

Cater, E. (1991) *Sustainable Tourism in the Third World: Problems and Prospects*, Reading: University of Reading.

Cater, E. (2006) Ecotourism as a Western control, *Journal of Ecotourism*, 5(1&2): 23–39.

Caton, K. and Santos, C.A. (2007) Heritage tourism on Route 66: deconstructing nostalgia, *Journal of Travel Research*, 45(4): 371–86.

Caufield, J. (1994) *City Form and Everyday Life: Toronto's Gentrification and Critical Social Practice*, Toronto: University of Toronto Press.

Cellini, R. (2011) Is UNESCO recognition effective in fostering tourism? A comment on Yang, Lin and Han, *Tourism Management*, 32(2): 452–4.

Chadha, A. (2006) Ambivalent heritage: between affect and ideology in a colonial cemetery, *Journal of Material Culture*, 11(3): 339–63.

Chang, T. (1997) Heritage as a tourism commodity: traversing the tourist–local divide, *Singapore Journal of Tropical Geography*, 18(1): 46–68.

Chang, T.C. and Teo, P. (2009) The Shophouse Hotel: vernacular heritage in a creative city, *Urban Studies*, 46(2): 341–67.

Chang, T.C., Milne, S., Fallon, D. and Pohlmann, C. (1996) Urban heritage tourism: the global–local nexus, *Annals of Tourism Research*, 23(2): 284–305.

Chen, C.F. and Chen, P.C. (2010) Resident attitudes toward heritage tourism development, *Tourism Geographies*, 12(4): 525–45.

Chen, J. and Hsu, C. (2000) Measurement of Korean tourists' perceived images of overseas destinations, *Journal of Travel Research*, 38(4): 411–16.

Chhabra, D. (2009) Proposing a sustainable marketing framework for heritage tourism, *Journal of Sustainable Tourism*, 17(3): 303–20.

Chhabra, D. (2010) Back to the last: a sub-segment of Generation Y's perceptions of authenticity, *Journal of Sustainable Tourism*, 18(6): 793–809.

Chhabra, D., Healy, R. and Sills, E. (2003) Staged authenticity and heritage tourism, *Annals of Tourism Research*, 30(3): 702–19.

Claver-Cortes, E., Jose F., Molina-Azorin, J.F. and Pereira-Moliner, J. (2007) Competitiveness in mass tourism, *Annals of Tourism Research*, 34(3): 727–45.

Cohen, E. (1979) Rethinking the sociology of tourism, *Annals of Tourism Research*, 6(1): 18–35.

Cohen, E. (1988) Authenticity and commoditization in tourism, *Annals of Tourism Research*, 15(3): 371–86.

Cohen, R. (1997) *Global Diasporas: An Introduction*, London: UCL Press.

Cohen, T. (2012) 'Hugely undervalued' English forests will not be sold off after U-turn by the government, *Daily Mail*, 4 July.

Coles, T. (2003) Urban tourism, place promotion and economic restructuring: the case of post-socialist Leipzig, *Tourism Geographies*, 5(2): 190–219.

Coles, T.E. and Timothy, D.J. (eds) (2004) *Tourism, Diasporas and Space*, London: Routledge.

Colette, A. (2007) *Case Studies on Climate Change and World Heritage*, Paris: World Heritage Centre.

Connor, W. (1993) Beyond reason: the nature of the ethnonational bond, *Ethnic and Racial Studies*, 16(3): 373–89.

Conway, D. and Timms, B.F. (2012) Are slow travel and slow tourism misfits, compadres or different genres? in T.V. Singh (ed.) *Critical Debates in Tourism*, Bristol: Channel View Publications, pp. 365–73.

Cooke, B. and Kothari, U. (2001) *Participation: The New Tyranny?* London: Zed Books.

Cooper, C., Flectcher, J., Fyall, A., Gilbert, D. and Wanhill, S. (2005) *Tourism: Principles and Practice* (3rd edn), Harlow: Pearson Education.

Copeland, T. (2006) Constructing pasts: interpreting the historic environment, in A. Hems and M. Blockley (eds) *Heritage Interpretation*, London: Routledge, pp. 83–95.

Copeland, T. (2006b) *European Democratic Citizenship, Heritage Education and Identity*, Strasbourg: Council of Europe.

Corsane, G., Davis, P., Elliott, S., Maggi, M., Murtas, D. and Rogers, S. (2007) Ecomuseum evaluation: Experiences in Piemonte and Ligutia, Italy, *International Journal of Heritage Studies*, 13(2): 101–16.

Council of Europe (2006) *Council of Europe Framework Convention on the Value of Cultural Heritage for Society*, Strasbourg: Council of Europe.

Crang, M. (1994) On the heritage trail: maps of and journeys to Olde Englande, *Environment and Planning D: Society and Space*, 12(3): 341–55.

Cross, G.S. and Walton, J.K. (2005) *The Playful Crowd: Pleasure Places in the Twentieth Century*, New York: Columbia University Press.

Crouch, D., Jackson, R. and Thompson, F. (2005) *The Media and the Tourist Imagination*, London: Routledge, pp. 1–11.

Daher, R.F. (2005) Urban regeneration/heritage tourism endeavours: the case of Salt, Jordan 'Local actors, international donors, and the State', *International Journal of Heritage Studies*, 11(4): 289–308.

Dann, G.M.S. and Seaton, A.V. (2001) *Slavery, Contested Heritage and Thanatourism*, New York: Haworth Hospitality Press.

Darcy, S. and Wearing, S. (2009) Public–private partnerships and contested cultural heritage tourism in national parks: a case study of the stakeholder views of the North Head Quarantine Station (Sydney, Australia), *Journal of Heritage Tourism*, 4(3): 181–99.

Davies, L. (2013) Fendi throws coins in Rome's crumbling Trevi fountain, *The Guardian*, 28 January.

Davis, F. (1979) *Yearning for Yesterday: A Sociology of Nostalgia*, New York: Free Press.

Davison, G. (2008) Heritage: from patrimony to pastiche, in G. Fairclough, R. Harrison, J.H. Jameson and J. Schofield (eds) *The Heritage Reader*, London: Routledge, pp. 31–41.

de Chavez, R. (1999) Globalization and tourism: deadly mix for indigenous people, *Third World Resurgence*, 103. Online. Available at: http://www.twnside.org.sg/title/chavez-cn.htm (accessed 27 September 2012).

de Mooji, M. (2000) Global brands and global branding, in J. Beynon and D. Dunkerley (eds) *Globalization: The Reader*, London: Athlone Press, pp. 141–3.

Deacon, H. (2004) Intangible heritage in conservation management planning: the case of Robben Island, *International Journal of Heritage Studies*, 10(3): 309–19.

Derrett, R. (2003) Festivals and regional destinations: how festivals demonstrate a sense of community and place, *Rural Society*, 13(1): 35–53.

Dewar, K. (1989) Interpretation as attraction, *Recreation Research Review*, 14(4): 45–9.

Di Giovine, M.A. (2009) The heritage-scape: UNESCO, World Heritage, and Tourism, Lanham: Lexington Books.

Donohoe, H.M. (2012) Sustainable heritage tourism marketing and Canada's Rideau Canal world heritage site, *Journal of Sustainable Tourism*, 20(1): 121–42.

Dr Johnson's House (2012) *Dr Johnson's House @drJohnsonshouse*. Online. Available at: https://twitter.com/drjohnsonshouse (accessed 24 April 2013).

du Cros, H. (2001) A new model to assist in planning for sustainable cultural heritage tourism, *International Journal of Tourism Research*, 3(2): 165–70.

du Cros, H. (2007) Too much of a good thing? Visitor congestion management issues for popular world heritage tourists attractions, *Journal of Heritage Tourism*, 2(3): 225–38.

Duncan, C. (1999) From the princely gallery to the public art museum: the Louvre museum and the national gallery, London, in D. Boswell and J. Evans (eds) *Representing the Nation: A Reader*, London: Routledge, pp. 304–31.

Duval, D.T. (2003) When hosts become guests: return visits and diasporic identities in a Commonwealth Eastern Caribbean, *Current Issues in Tourism*, 6(4): 267–308.

Eco, U. (1986) *Faith in Fakes*, London: Secker & Warburg.

Edensor, T. (1998) *Tourists at the Taj: Performance and Meaning at a Symbolic Site*, London: Routledge.

Edensor, T. (2002) *National Identity, Popular Culture and Everyday Life*, Oxford: Berg.

Edwards, D., Griffin, T. and Hayllar, B. (2008) Urban tourism research: developing an agenda, *Annals of Tourism Research*, 35(4): 1032–52.

Eisenschitz, A. (2010) Place marketing as politics, in F.M. Go and R. Govers (eds) *International Place Branding Yearbook: Place Branding in the New Age of Innovation*, Hampshire: Palgrave Macmillan, pp. 21–30.

Ekinci, Y., Sirakaya-Turk, E. and Preciado, S. (2013) Symbolic consumption of tourism destination brands, *Journal of Business Research*, 66(6): 711–18.

El-Aref, N. (2009) Hands off, and we mean it, *Al-Ahram Weekly*, 938 (March). Online. Available at: https//weekly.ahram.org.eg/2009/938/eg7.htm (accessed 12 November 2012).

English Heritage (2011) *English Heritage Annual Report and Accounts 2010/11*, London: The Stationery Office.

Eriksen, T.H. (1991) The cultural contexts of ethnic differences, *Man*, 26(1): 127–44.

Eriksen, T.H. (2007) *Globalization: The Key Concepts*, Oxford: Berg.

Evans, G.L. (1998) In search of the cultural tourist and the postmodern Grand Tour, International Sociological Association XIV Congress, Relocating Sociology, July, Montreal.

Evans, G.L. (2001) *Cultural Planning: An Urban Renaissance*, London: Routledge.

Fainstein, S.S. and Judd, D.R. (1999) Global forces, local strategies and urban tourism, in D.R. Judd and S.S. Fainstein (eds) *The Tourist City*, New Haven: Yale University Press, pp. 1–20.

Fairclough, G. (2008) New heritage, an introductory essay: people, landscape and change, in G. Fairclough, R. Harrison, J.H. Jameson and J. Schofield (eds) *The Heritage Reader*, London: Routledge, pp. 297–312.

Falzon, M. (2004) *Cosmopolitan Connections: The Sindhi Diaspora, 1860–2000*, Leiden: Brill.

Fawthrop, T. (2011) Who does the Preah Vihear temple belong to? *Aljazeera*, 4 June.

Featherstone, M. (1996) Travel, migration and images of social life, in E.B.W. Gungwu (ed.) *Global History and Migrations*, Oxford: Perseus Books Group, pp. 239–77.

Featherstone, M. (2007) *Consumer Culture and Postmodernism* (2nd edn), London: Sage.

Feifer, M. (1985) *Going Places*, London: Macmillan.

Fladmark, J. (1988) *In Search of Heritage: As Pilgrim or Tourist?* Shaftesbury: Donhead Publishing.

Foley, M. and Lennon, J. (1997) Dark tourism: an ethical dilemma, in M. Foley, J. Lennon and G. Maxwell (eds) *Strategic Issues for the Hospitality, Tourism and Leisure Industries*, London: Cassell, pp. 153–64.

Foley, M. and McPherson, G. (2000) Museums as leisure, *International Journal of Heritage Studies*, 6(2): 161–74.

Freeman, R.E. (1984) *Strategic Management: A Stakeholder Approach*, Boston: Pitman.

Frey, B.S. and Steiner, L. (2011) World Heritage List: does it make sense? *International Journal of Cultural Policy*, 17(5): 555–73.

Friedman, J. (1999) The hybridization of roots and the abhorrence of the bush, in M. Featherstone and S. Lash (eds) *Spaces of Culture, City, Nation, World*, London: Sage Publications, pp. 230–56.

Friedman, A.L. and Miles, S. (2002) Developing stakeholder theory, *Journal of Management Studies*, 39(1): 1–21.

Friedman, A.L. and Miles, S. (2006) *Stakeholders: Theory and Practice*, Oxford: Oxford University Press.

Friedman, J. (1999) The hybridization of roots and the abhorrence of the bush, in M. Featherstone and S. Lash (eds) *Spaces of Culture, City, Nation, World*, London: Sage, pp. 230–56.

Fuller, D.A. (1999) *Sustainable Marketing: Managerial–Ecological Issues*, London: Sage.

FutureBrand (2013) *Country Brand Index 2012–2013*. Online. Available at: http://www.futurebrand.com/images/uploads/studies/cbi/CBI_2012-Final.pdf (accessed 24 April 2013).

Garrod, B. and Fyall, A. (2000) Managing heritage tourism, *Annals of Tourism Research*, 27(3): 682–708.

Garrod, B., Fyall, A., Leask, A. and Reid, E. (2012) Engaging residents as stakeholders of the visitor attraction, *Tourism Management*, 33(5): 1159–73.

Geoghegan, P. (2012) Albania watches impassively as bunkers become bunk-beds, *The Guardian*, 26 September.

George, E.W. (2010) Intangible cultural heritage, ownership, copyrights, and tourism, *International Journal of Culture, Tourism and Hospitality Research*, 4(4): 376–88.

Giaccardi, E. (2012) Introduction: reframing heritage in a participatory culture, in E. Giaccardi (ed.) *Heritage and Social Media*, London: Routledge, pp. 1–10.

Giddens, A. (1991) *Modernity and Self-Identity*, London: Sage.

Gilmore, A. and Rentschler, R. (2002) Changes in museum management: a custodial or marketing emphasis? *Journal of Management Development*, 21(10): 745–60.

Gilmore, A., Carson, D. and Ascencao, M. (2007) Sustainable tourism marketing as a world heritage site, *Journal of Strategic Marketing*, 15(2): 253–64.

GlasgowLife (2010) *Calendar of Glasgow's Cultural Festivals*. Online. Available at: http://www.glasgowlife.org.uk/arts/cultural-festivals/Pages/home.aspx (accessed 24 April 2013).

Global Heritage Fund (2012) Saving our vanishing heritage: Asia's heritage in peril. Online. Available at: http://www.globalheritagefund.org/images/uploads/docs/GHFAsiaHeritageinPeril050112_lowres.pdf (accessed 12 August 2013).

Gobe, M. (2008) *Emotional Branding: The New Paradigm for Connecting Brands to People*, New York: Allworth Press.

Goffman, E. (1959) *The Presentation of Self in Everyday Life*, Harmondsworth: Penguin.

Golden, J. (2004) Targeting heritage: the abuse of symbolic sites in modern conflicts, in Y. Rowan and U. Baram (eds) *Marketing Heritage: Archaeology and the Consumption of the Past*, California: Altamira Press, pp. 183–202.

Goldsmith, R. (1999) The personalised marketplace: beyond the 4ps, *Marketing Intelligence and Planning*, 17(4): 178–85.

Golomb, J. (1995) *In Search of Authenticity*, London: Routledge.

González, M.V. (2008) Intangible heritage tourism and identity, *Tourism Management*, 29(4): 807–10.

Gotham, K.F. (2005) Tourism gentrification: the case of New Orleans' Vieux Carré (French Quarter), *Urban Studies*, 42(7): 1099–121.

Goulding, C. (2000) The commodification of the past, postmodern pastiche, and the search for authentic experiences at contemporary heritage attractions, *European Journal of Marketing*, 34(7): 835–53.

Graburn, N. (1967) The Eskimos and 'Airport Art', *Trans-action*, 4(10): 28–34.

Graburn, N. (2001) Secular ritual: a general theory of tourism, in V.L. Smith and M. Brent (eds) *Hosts and Guests Revisited: Tourism Issues of the 21st Century*, New York: Cognizant Communication Corporation, pp. 42–50.

Graham, B. (2002) Heritage as knowledge: capital or culture? *Urban Studies*, 39(5–6): 1003–17.

Graham, B., Ashworth, G.J. and Tunbridge, J.E. (2000) *A Geography of Heritage: Power, Culture and Economy*, London: Arnold.

Graham, C. (2001) 'Blame it on Maureen O'hara': Ireland and the trope of authenticity, *Cultural Studies*, 15(1): 58–75.

Gray, B. (1989) *Collaborating: Finding Common Grounds for Multiparty Problems*, San Francisco: Jossey-Bass.

Greenwood, D.J. (1989) Culture by the pound: an anthropological perspective on tourism as cultural commoditization, in V.L. Smith (ed.) *Hosts and Guests: The Anthropology of Tourism* (2nd edn), Philadelphia: University of Pennsylvania Press, pp. 171–85.

Grek, S. (2009) 'In and against the museum': the contested spaces of museum education for adults, *Discourse: Studies in the Cultural Politics of Education*, 30(2): 195–211.

Gretzel, U. (2006) Consumer generated content: trends and implications for branding, *e-Review of Tourism Research*, 4(3): 9–11.

Gu, H. and Ryan, C. (2008) Place attachment, identity and community impacts of tourism: the case of a Beijing hutong, *Tourism Management*, 29(4): 637–47.

Gugler, J. (ed.) (2004) *World Cities Beyond the West: Globalization, Development and Inequality*, Cambridge: Cambridge University Press.

Hailey, J. (2001) Beyond the formulaic: process and practice in South Asian NGOs, in B. Cooke and U. Kothari (eds) *Participation: The New Tyranny?* London: Zed Books, pp. 88–101.

Halewood, C. and Hannam, K. (2001) Viking heritage tourism: authenticity and commodification, *Annals of Tourism Research*, 28(3): 565–80.

Hall, A. (1988) Community participation and development policy: a sociological perspective, in A. Hall and J. Midgely (eds) *Development Policies: Sociological Perspectives*, Manchester: Manchester University Press, pp. 91–107.

Hall, C.M. (1994) *Tourism and Politics: Policy, Power and Place*, Chichester: Wiley.

Hall, M. and Bombardella, P. (2005) Las Vegas in Africa, *Journal of Social Archaeology*, 5(1): 5–24.

Hall, P. (2000) Creative cities and economic development, *Urban Studies*, 37(4): 639–49.

Hall, S. (1992) The question of cultural identity, in S. Hall, D. Held and T. McGrew (eds) *Modernity and its Futures*, London: Polity, pp. 273–326.

Hall, S. (1993) Culture, community, nation, *Cultural Studies*, 7(3): 349–63.

Hall, S. (1996) Cultural identity and cinematic representation, in H.A. Baker, M. Diawara and R.H. Lindeborg (eds) *Black British Cultural Studies: A Reader*, Chicago: University of Chicago Press, pp. 210–22.

Hall, S. (2005) Whose heritage? Un-settling 'the heritage', re-imagining the post-nation, in J. Littler and R. Naidoo (eds) *The Politics of Heritage: The Legacies of 'Race'*, London: Routledge, pp. 23–35.

Halsall, D.A. (2001) Railway heritage and the tourist gaze: Stoomtram Hoorn-Medemblik, *Journal of Transport Geography*, 9(2): 151–60.

Handler, R. (1986) Authenticity, *Anthropology Today*, 2(1): 2–4.

Handler, R. and Saxton, W. (1988) Dissimulation: reflexivity, narrative, and the quest for authenticity in 'living history', *Cultural Anthropology*, 3(3): 242–60.

Hannabuss, S. (1999) Postmodernism and the heritage experience, *Library Management*, 20(5): 295–302.

Hannam, K. (2002) Tourism and development I: globalization and power, *Progress in Development Studies*, 2(3): 227–34.

Hannam, K. (2004) The ambivalences of diaspora tourism in India, in T.E. Coles and D.J. Timothy (eds) *Tourism, Diasporas and Space*, London: Routledge, pp. 246–60.

Hannam, K. and Knox, D. (2010) *Understanding Tourism: A Critical Introduction*, London: Sage.

Harewood (2007) Harewood 1807. Online. Available at: http://www.harewood.org/_documentbank/Harewood_1807_leafletFULL_web_2.pdf (accessed 24 April 2013).

Harrison, D. (2005) Introduction: contested narratives in the domain of World Heritage, in D. Harrison and M. Hitchcock (eds) *The Politics of World Heritage: Negotiating Tourism and Conservation*, Clevedon: Channel View Publications, pp. 1–10.

Harrison, D. and Hitchcock, M. (eds) (2005) *The Politics of World Heritage: Negotiating Tourism and Conservation*, Clevedon: Channel View Publications.

Harrison, R. (2010) Heritage as social action, in S. West (ed.) *Understanding Heritage in Practice*, Manchester: Manchester University Press, pp. 240–76.

Harvey, D. (1989) *The Condition of Postmodernity: An Enquiry into the Origins of Cultural Change*, Oxford: Blackwell.

Harvey, D. (2007) Neoliberalism as creative destruction, *The ANNALS of the American Academy of Political and Social Science*, 610(March): 22–44.

Hatherley, O. (2012) Venice's Rialto bridge will be desecrated by advertising, *The Guardian*, 20 September.

Hausmann, A. (2007) Cultural tourism: marketing challenges and opportunities for German cultural heritage, *International Journal of Heritage Studies*, 13(2): 170–84.

Hayes, D. and MacLeod, N. (2007) Packaging places: designing heritage trails using an experience economy perspective to maximize visitor engagement, *Journal of Vacation Marketing*, 13(1): 45–58.

Heilbrun, J. and Gray, C.M. (2001) *The Economics of Art and Culture*, Cambridge: Cambridge University Press.

Held, D. and McGrew, A. (2003) *The Global Transformations Reader* (2nd edn), Cambridge: Polity.

Hems, A. and Blockley, M. (2006) *Heritage Interpretation*, London: Routledge.

Henderson, J.C. (2000) War as a tourist attraction: the case of Vietnam, *International Journal of Tourism Research*, 2(4): 269–80.

Henderson, J.C. (2001) Heritage, identity and tourism in Hong Kong, *International Journal of Heritage Studies*, 7(3): 219–35.

Henderson, J.C. (2007) Communism, heritage and tourism in East Asia, *International Journal of Heritage Studies*, 13(3): 240–54.

Henderson, V. (2002) Urbanization in developing countries, *World Bank Research Observer*, 17(1): 89–112.

Henry, I.P. (1993) *The Politics of Leisure Policy*, Hampshire: Macmillan.

Herbert, D. (2001) Literary places, tourism and the heritage experience, *Annals of Tourism Research*, 28(2): 312–33.

Heritage Lottery Fund (2010) *Investing in Success*. London: HLF.

Herzfeld, M. (2010) Engagement, gentrification, and the neoliberal hijacking of history, *Current Anthropology*, 51(S2): S259–S267.

Hewison, R. (1987) *The Heritage Industry*, London: Methuen.

Hewison, R. (1991) Commerce and culture, in J. Corner and S. Harvey (eds) *Enterprise and Heritage: Crosscurrents of National Culture*, London: Routledge, pp. 162–77.

Hitchcock, M. (1996) *Islam and Identity in Eastern Indonesia*, Hull: Hull University Press.

Hitchcock, M. (1999) Tourism and ethnicity: situational perspectives, *International Journal of Tourism Research*, 1(1): 17–32.

Hitchcock, M. (2000) Introduction, in M. Hitchcock and K. Teague (eds) *Souvenirs: The Material Culture of Tourism*, Aldershot: Ashgate, pp. 1–17.

Hobsbawm, E. (1983) Introduction: inventing traditions, in E. Hobsbawm and T. Ranger (eds) *The Invention of Tradition*, Cambridge: Cambridge University Press, pp. 1–14.

Hobsbawm, E. and Ranger, T. (eds) (1983) *The Invention of Tradition*, Cambridge: Cambridge University Press.

Hollinshead, K. (1998) Tourism and the restless peoples: a dialectical inspection of Bhabha's halfway populations, *Tourism, Culture and Communication*, 1(1): 49–77.

Holloway, J.C. and Taylor, N. (2006) *The Business of Tourism* (7th edn), Harlow: Pearson Education.

Hopper, P. (2007) *Understanding Cultural Globalization*, Cambridge: Polity.

Hooper-Greenhill, E. (1989) The museum in the disciplinary society, in S.M. Pearce (ed.) *Museum Studies in Material Culture*, Leicester: Leicester University Press, pp. 61–72.

Hooper-Greenhill, E. (1994a) *Museums and their Visitors*, London: Routledge.

Hooper-Greenhill, E. (1994b) *The Educational Role of the Museum*, London: Routledge.

Horne, D. (1984) *The Great Museum: The Re-presentation of History*, London: Pluto Press.

Hosany, S., Ekinci, Y. and Uysal, M. (2006) Destination image and destination personality: an application for branding theories to tourism places, *Journal of Business Research*, 59(5): 638–42.

Howard, P. (2003) *Heritage: Management, Interpretation, Identity*, London: Continuum.

Huang, C., Tsaur, J. and Yang, C. (2012) Does world heritage list really induce more tourists? Evidence from Macau, *Tourism Management*, 33(6): 1450–7.

Hudson, S. (2008) *Tourism and Hospitality Marketing: A Global Perspective*, London: Sage.

Hughes, G. (1995) Authenticity in tourism, *Annals of Tourism Research*, 22(4): 781–803.

Hume, D.L. (2009) The development of tourist art and souvenirs – the arc of the boomerang: from hunting, fighting and ceremony to tourist souvenir, *International Journal of Tourism Research*, 11(1): 55–70.

Hung, K., Sirakaya-Turk, E. and Ingram, L.J. (2011) Testing the efficacy of an integrative model for community participation, *Journal of Travel Research*, 50(3): 276–88.

Hunt, L. (2004) *Politics, Culture and Class in the French Revolution*, California: University of California Press.

Hunter, C. (1997) Sustainable tourism as an adaptive paradigm, *Annals of Tourism Research*, 24(4): 850–67.

Huyssen, A. (2000) Present pasts: media, politics, amnesia, in A. Appadurai (ed.) *Globalisation*, Durham: Duke University Press, pp. 57–77.

Jones, R. and Desforges, L. (2003) Localities and the reproduction of Welsh nationalism, *Political Geography*, 22(3): 271–92.

Judd, D. (1999) Constructing the tourist bubble, in D. Judd and S. Fainstein (eds) *The Tourist City*, New Haven: Yale University Press, pp. 35–53.

ICOM (1974) ICOM Statutes, adopted by the 11th General Assembly. Online. Available at: http:// archives.icom.museum/hist_def_eng.html (accessed 15 September 2011).

ICOM (2007) *ICOM Statutes*. Online. Available at: http://icom.museum (accessed 9 September 2011).

ICOM Constitution (1946) . Online. Available at: http://archives.icom.museum/hist_def_eng.html (accessed 11 August 2013).

ICOMOS (2008) *The ICOMOS Charter for the Interpretation and Presentation of Cultural Heritage Sites*, the 16th General Assembly of ICOMOS, Québec, Canada.

Ioannides, D. and Debbage, K. (1997) Post-Fordism and flexibility: the travel industry polyglot, *Tourism Management*, 18(4): 229–41.

Ioannides, D. and Debbage, K. (1998) Neo-Fordism and flexible specialization in the travel industry: dissecting the polyglot, in D. Ioannides and K.G. Debbage (eds) *The Economic Geography of the Tourist Industry: A Supply-Side Analysis*, London: Routledge, pp. 99–122.

Iorio, M. and Corsale, A. (2013) Diaspora and tourism: Transylvanian Saxons visiting the homeland, *Tourism Geographies*, 15(2): 198–232.

Iversen, O.S. and Smith, R.C. (2012) Connecting to everyday practices: experiences from the Digital Natives exhibition, in E. Giaccardi (ed.) *Heritage and Social Media*, London: Routledge, pp. 126–44.

Jackson, L.A. (2008) Residents' perceptions of the impacts of special event tourism, *Journal of Place Management and Development*, 1(3): 240–55.

Jamal, T.B. and Getz, D. (1995) Collaboration theory and community tourism planning, *Annals of Tourism Research*, 22(1): 186–204.

Jamal, T.B. and Hill, S. (2002) The home and the world: (post)touristic spaces of (in)authenticity, in G.M.S. Dann (ed.) *The Tourist as a Metaphor of the Social World*, Wallingford: CAB International, pp. 77–108.

Jamal, T.B. and Kim, H. (2005) Bridging the interdisciplinary divide: towards an integrated framework for heritage tourism research, *Tourist Studies*, 5(1): 55–83.

Jamal, T.B. and Tanase, A. (2005) Impacts and conflicts surrounding Dracula Park, Romania: the role of sustainable tourism principles, *Journal of Sustainable Tourism*, 13(5): 440–5.

Jameson, F. (1984) Postmodernism, or the cultural logic of late Capitalism, *New Left Review*, 146(July–August): 53–92.

Jameson, J.H. (2008) Cultural heritage management in the United States: past, present, and future, in G. Fairclough, R. Harrison, J.H. Jameson and J. Schofield (eds) *The Heritage Reader*, London: Routledge, pp. 42–61.

Jenkins, J.G. (1992) *Getting Yesterday Right: Interpreting the Heritage of Wales*, Cardiff: University of Wales Press.

Johnson, N.C. (1999) Framing the past: time, space and the politics of heritage tourism in Ireland, *Political Geography*, 18(2): 187–207.

Jones, R. and Desforges, L. (2003) Localities and the reproduction of Welsh nationalism, *Political Geography*, 22(3): 271–92.

Jones, R. and Merriman, P. (2009) Hot, banal and everyday nationalism: bilingual road signs in Wales, *Political Geography*, 28(3): 164–73.

Judd, D. (1999) Constructing the tourist bubble, in D. Judd and S. Fainstein (eds) *The Tourist City*, New Haven: Yale University Press, pp. 35–53.

Kao, Y., Huang, L. and Wu, C. (2008) Effects of theatrical elements on experiential quality and loyalty intentions for theme parks, *Asia Pacific Journal of Tourism Research*, 13(2): 163–74.

Karim, K.H. (1997) Relocating the nexus of citizenship, heritage and technology, *The Public*, 4(4): 75–86.

Karp, I. (1992) Introduction, in I. Karp, C.M. Kreamer and S. Lavine (eds) *Museums and Communities: The Politics of Public Culture*, Washington, DC: Smithsonian University Press, pp. 1–6.

Keitumetse, S.O. (2011) Sustainable development and cultural heritage management in Botswana: towards sustainable communities, *Sustainable Development*, 19(1): 49–59.

Keller, P.F. (2000) Globalization and tourism, in W.C. Gartner and D.W. Lime (eds) *Trends in Outdoor Recreation, Leisure and Tourism*, New York: CABI, pp. 287–97.

Kelner, S. (2010) *Tours that Bind: Diaspora, Pilgrimage, and Israeli Birthright Tourism*, New York: New York University Press.

Kennedy, M. (2007) Images of slavery, *The Guardian*, 17 October.

Kerstetter, D., Confer, J. and Bricker, K. (1998) Industrial heritage attractions: types and tourists, *Journal of Travel & Tourism Marketing*, 7(2): 91–104.

Kim, H. and Jamal, T. (2007) Touristic quest for existential authenticity, *Annals of Tourism Research*, 34(1): 181–201.

Kim, S.S. and Lee, C.K. (2002) Push and pull relationships, *Annals of Tourism Research*, 29(1): 257–60.

Kirshenblatt-Gimblett, B. (2006) World heritage and cultural economics, in I. Karp, C.A. Kratz, L. Szwaja and T. Ybarra-Frausto (eds) *Museum Frictions: Public Cultures/Global Transformations*, Durham: Duke University Press, pp. 161–202.

Knox, P.L. (2005) Creating ordinary places: slow cities in a fast world, *Journal of Urban Design*, 10(1): 1–11.

Knudsen, B.T. (2010) The past as staged-real environment: communism revisited in The Crazy Guides Communism Tours, Krakow, Poland, *Journal of Tourism and Cultural Change*, 8(3): 139–53.

Knudsen, B.T. and Waade, A.M. (2010) Performative authenticity in tourism and spatial experience: rethinking the relation between travel, place and emotion, in B.T. Knudsen and A.M. Waade (eds) *Re-investing Authenticity: Tourism, Place and Emotions*, Bristol: Channel View Publications, pp. 1–19.

Ko, D.W. and Stewart, W.P. (2002) A structural equation model of residents' attitudes for tourism development, *Tourism Management*, 23(5): 521–30.

Koch, E. (1997) Ecotourism and rural reconstruction in South Africa: reality or rhetoric? in K.B. Ghimire and M.P. Pimbert (eds) *Social Change and Conservation: Environmental Politics and Impacts of National Parks and Protected Areas*, London: Earthscan, pp. 214–38.

Kohl, P.L. (2004) Making the past profitable in an age of globalization and national ownership: contradictions and considerations, in Y. Rowan and U. Baram (eds) *Marketing Heritage: Archaeology and the Consumption of the Past*, Oxford: Altamira Press, pp. 295–301.

Kokosalakis, C., Bagnall, G., Selby, M. and Burns, S. (2006) Place image and urban regeneration in Liverpool, *International Journal of Consumer Studies*, 30(4): 389–97.

Kolar, T. and Zabkar, V. (2010) A consumer-based model of authenticity: an oxymoron or the foundation of cultural heritage marketing? *Tourism Management*, 31(5): 652–64.

Kolb, B.M. (2006) *Tourism Marketing for Cities and Towns*, Oxford: Butterworth-Heinemann.

Kotler, P. (1984) *Marketing Management: Analysis, Planning, Implementation and Control* (8th edn), Upper Saddle River: Prentice Hall.

Kotler, P. and Levy, S.J. (1969) Broadening the concept of marketing, *Journal of Marketing*, 33(1): 10–15.

Kotler, P. and Levy, S. (1971) Demarketing, Yes, Demarketing, *Harvard Business Review*, November–December, 74–80.

Kumar, K. (1995) *From Post-industrial to Post-modern Society: New Theories of the Contemporary World*, Oxford: Blackwell.

Labadi, S. and Long, C. (eds) (2010) *Heritage and Globalisation*, London: Routledge.

Landorf, C. (2009) Managing for sustainable tourism: a review of six cultural World Heritage Sites, *Journal of Sustainable Tourism*, 17(1): 53–70.

Lanfant, M.F. (1995) International tourism, internationalization and the challenge to identity, in M.F. Lanfant, J. Allcock and E. Bruner (eds) *International Tourism: Identity and Change*, London: Sage, pp. 24–43.

Lash, S. (1990) *Sociology of Postmodernism*, London: Routledge.

Lash, S. and Urry, J. (1987) *The End of Organised Capitalism*, Cambridge: Polity.

Lau, R.W.K. (2010) Revisiting authenticity: a social realist approach, *Annals of Tourism Research*, 37(2): 478–98.

Law, C.M. (1993) *Urban Tourism: Attracting Visitors to Large Cities*, London: Mansell Publishing.

Laws, E. (1998) Conceptualising visitor satisfaction in heritage settings: an exploratory blueprinting analysis of Leeds Castle, Kent, *Tourism Management*, 19(6): 545–54.

Leask, A. and Fyall, A. (2006) *Managing World Heritage Sites*, Oxford: Butterworth-Heinemann.

Leask, A. and Yeoman, I. (1999) *Heritage Visitor Attractions: An Operations Management Perspective*, London: Cengage Learning.

Lee, T.J., Li, J. and Kim, H. (2007) Community residents' perceptions and attitudes towards heritage tourism in a historic city, *Tourism and Hospitality Planning & Development*, 4(2): 91–109.

Lees, L. (2000) A reappraisal of gentrification: towards a 'geography' of gentrification, *Progress in Human Geography*, 24(3): 389–408.

Leighton, D. (2007) 'Step back in time and live the legend': experiential marketing and the heritage sector, *International Journal of Nonprofit and Voluntary Sector Marketing*, 12(2): 117–25.

Leitch, L. (2012) The cobbler and the Colosseum, *The Telegraph*, 22 August.

Lenik, S. (2013) Community engagement and heritage tourism at Geneva Estate, Dominica, *Journal of Heritage Tourism*, 8(1): 9–19.

Lennon, J.J. and Foley, M. (1999) Interpretation of the unimaginable: the U.S. Holocaust Memorial Museum, Washington, DC and dark tourism, *Journal of Travel Research*, 38(1): 46–50.

Lennon, J.J. and Foley, M. (2000) *Dark Tourism: The Attraction of Death and Disaster*, New York: Continuum.

Leong, W.T. (1997) Culture and the state: manufacturing traditions for tourism, in J.T. Ong, C.K. Tong and E.S. Tan (eds) *Understanding Singapore Society*, Singapore: Times Academic Press, pp. 513–34.

Letsch, C. (2011) Turkish Roma make way for property developers in historic Istanbul district, *The Guardian*, 9 November.

Letsch, C. (2012) Istanbul sees history razed in the name of regeneration, *The Guardian*, 1 March.

Lewis, P. (1994) Museums and marketing, in K. Moore (ed.) *Museum Management*, London: Routledge, pp. 216–31.

Li, W. (2006) Community decision-making: participation in development, *Annals of Tourism Research*, 33(1):132–43.

Li, Y. (2003) Heritage tourism: the contradictions between conservation and change, *Tourism and Hospitality Research*, 4(3): 247–61.

Liew, C.L. (2005) Online cultural heritage exhibitions: a survey of information retrieval features, *Program: Electronic Library and Information Systems*, 39(1): 4–24.

Light, D. (2000) An unwanted past: contemporary tourism and the heritage of communism in Romania, *International Journal of Heritage Studies*, 6(2): 145–60.

Light, D. (2001) 'Facing the future': tourism and identity-building in postsocialist Romania, *Political Geography*, 20(8): 1053–74.

Light, D. (2007) Dracula tourism in Romania: cultural identity and the state, *Annals of Tourism Research*, 34(3): 746–65.

Light, D. and Dumbraveanu-Andone, D. (1997) Heritage and national identity: exploring the relationship in Romania, *International Journal of Heritage Studies*, 3(1): 28–44.

Light, D. and Prentice, R. (1994) Market-based product development in heritage tourism, *Tourism Management*, 15(1): 27–36.

Lindsay, K., Craig, J. and Low, M. (2008) Tourism and conservation: the effects of track proximity on avian reproductive success and nest selection in an open sanctuary, *Tourism Management*, 29(4): 730–9.

Littler, J. (2005) Introduction: British heritage and the legacies of 'race', in J. Littler and R. Naidoo (eds) *The Politics of Heritage: The Legacies of 'Race'*, London: Routledge, pp. 1–19.

Littrell, M., Anderson, L. and Brown, P. (1993) What makes a craft souvenir authentic? *Annals of Tourism Research*, 20(1): 197–215.

Liu, Y., Xu, C., Pan, Z. and Pan, Y. (2006) Semantic modeling for ancient architecture of digital heritage, *Computers & Graphics*, 30(5): 800–14.

Logan, W.S. (2002) *The Disappearing 'Asian' City: Protecting Asia's Urban Heritage in a Globalizing World*, Oxford: Oxford University Press.

Lominé, L. and Edmunds, J. (2007) *Key Concepts in Tourism*, Hampshire: Palgrave Macmillan.

London Shh... (2012) London Shh... @LondonShh. Online. Available at: https://twitter.com/LondonShh (accessed 24 April 2013).

Long, C. and Labadi, S. (2010) Introduction, in S. Labadi and C. Long (eds) *Tourism and Globalisation*, London: Routledge, pp. 1–16.

Lord, G.D. and Lord, B. (2009) *The Manual of Museum Management* (2nd edn), Lanham, MD: Altamira Press.

Loulanski, T. and Loulanski, V. (2011) The sustainable integration of cultural heritage and tourism: a meta-study, *Journal of Sustainable Tourism*, 19(7): 837–62.

Lowe, L. (1991) Heterogeneity, hybridity, multiplicity: marking Asian American differences, *Diaspora: A Journal of Transnational Studies*, 1(1): 24–44.

Lowenthal, D. (1998) *The Heritage Crusade and the Spoils of History*, Cambridge: Cambridge University Press.

MacCannell, D. (1973) Staged authenticity: arrangements of social space in tourist settings, *American Journal of Sociology*, 79(3): 589–603.

MacCannell, D. (1976) *The Tourist: A New Theory of the Leisure Class*, London: Macmillan.

MacClancy, J. (1997) The museum as a site of contest: the Bilbao Guggenheim, *Focal Journal of Anthropology*, 1(7): 271–8.

MacDonald, S. (1997) A people's story: heritage, identity and authenticity, in C. Rojek and J. Urry (eds) *Touring Cultures*, London: Routledge, pp. 155–76.

Macdonald, S. (2006) Undesirable heritage: fascist material culture and historical consciousness in Nuremberg, *International Journal of Heritage Studies*, 12(1): 9–28.

Mak, A.H.N., Lumbers, M. and Eves, A. (2012) Globalisation and food consumption in tourism, *Annals of Tourism Research*, 39(1): 171–96.

Marstine, J. (2006) Introduction, in J. Marstine (ed.) *New Museum Theory and Practice: An Introduction*, Oxford: Blackwell, pp. 1–36.

Martin, K. (2010) Living pasts: contested tourism authenticities, *Annals of Tourism Research*, 37(2): 537–54.

Marzano, G. and Scott, N. (2009) Power in destination branding, *Annals of Tourism Research*, 36(2): 247–67.

Masberg, B.A. and Silverman, L.H. (1996) Visitor experiences at heritage sites: a phenomenological approach, *Journal of Travel Research*, 34(4): 20–5.

McCain, G. and Ray, N. (2003) Legacy tourism: the search for personal meaning in heritage travel, *Tourism Management*, 24(6): 713–17.

McCarthy, E.J. (1981) *Basic Marketing: A Managerial Approach* (7th edn), Georgetown, ON: Irwin.

McCarthy, J. and Ciolfi, L. (2008) Place as dialogue: understanding and supporting the museum experience, *International Journal of Heritage Studies*, 14(3): 247–67.

McCrone, D., Morris, A. and Kiely. R. (1995) *Scotland – the Brand: The Making of Scottish Heritage*, Edinburgh: Edinburgh University Press.

McDowell, S. (2008) Selling conflict heritage through tourism in peacetime Northern Ireland: transforming conflict or exacerbating difference? *International Journal of Heritage Studies*, 14(5): 405–21.

McGrew, A. (1992) A global society? in S. Hall, D. Held and T. McGrew (eds) *Modernity and its Futures*, London: Polity, pp. 61–116.

McIntosh, A.J. and Prentice, R.C. (1999) Affirming authenticity: consuming cultural heritage, *Annals of Tourism Research*, 26(3): 589–612.

McKean, P. (1976) Tourism, culture change and culture conservation in Bali, in. D.J. Banks (ed.) *Changing Identities in Modern Southeast Asia*, The Hague: Mouton & Co, pp. 237–48.

McKercher, B. and du Cros, H. (2002) *Cultural Tourism: The Partnership Between Tourism and Cultural Heritage Management*, New York: Haworth Press.

McLean, F.C. (1994) Marketing in museums: a contexture analysis, in K. Moore (ed.) *Museum Management*, London: Routledge, pp. 232–48.

McLean, F.C. (1997) *Marketing the Museum*, London: Routledge.

McLean, F.C. (1998) Museums and the construction of national identity: a review, *International Journal of Heritage Studies*, 3(4): 244–52.

McNeil, D. (2000) McGuggenisation? National identity and globalization in the Basque country, *Political Geography*, 19(4): 473–94.

McTavish, L. (1998) Shopping in the museum? Consumer spaces and the redefinition of the Louvre, *Cultural Studies*, 12(2): 168–92.

McTavish, L. (2006) Visiting the virtual museum: art and experience online, in J. Marstine (ed.) *New Museum Theory and Practice: An Introduction*, Oxford: Blackwell, pp. 226–46.

Medina, L.K. (2003) Commoditizing culture: tourism and Maya identity, *Annals of Tourism Research*, 30(2): 353–68.

Medway, D. and Warnaby, G. (2008) Alternative perspectives on marketing and the place brand, *European Journal of Marketing*, 42(5/6): 641–53.

Meethan, K. (2001) *Tourism in Global Society: Place, Culture, Consumption*, Hampshire: Palgrave.

Merriman, N. (1991) *Beyond the Glass Case: The Past, the Heritage and the Public in Britain*, Leicester: Leicester University Press.

Merriman, N. (2000) *Beyond the Glass Case: The Past, the Heritage and the Public* (2nd edn), London: UCL Institute of Archaeology.

Meskell, L. (2002) Negative heritage and past mastering in Archaeology, *Anthropological Quarterly*, 75(3): 557–74.

Message, K. (2006a) The new museum, *Theory, Culture & Society*, 23(2–3): 603–6.

Message, K. (2006b) *New Museums and the Making of Culture*, Oxford: Berg.

Miles, S. and Paddison, R. (2005) Introduction: the rise and rise of culture-led urban regeneration, *Urban Studies*, 42(5/6): 833–9.

Millar, S. (1989) Heritage management for heritage tourism, *Tourism Management*, 10(1): 9–14.

Misiura, S. (2006) *Heritage Marketing*, Oxford: Butterworth-Heinemann.

Mitrašinovic, M. (2006) *Total Landscape, Theme Parks, Public Space*, Aldershot: Ashgate.

Mkono, M. (2012) Authenticity does matter, *Annals of Tourism Research*, 39(1): 480–3.

Moore, R. (2012) Why the Southbank Centre redevelopment plan is sheer folly, *The Observer*, 5 August.

Mordue, T. (2005) Tourism, performance and social exclusion in 'Olde York', *Annals of Tourism Research*, 32(1): 179–98.

Morgan, N.J., Pritchard, A. and Pride, R. (2002) *Destination Branding: Creating the Unique Destination Proposition* (revised 2nd edn), Oxford: Butterworth-Heinemann.

Morrison, A. and Anderson, D. (2002) Destination branding. Online. Available at: http://www.macvb.org/intranet/presentation/DestinationBrandingLOzarks6-10-02.ppt (accessed 4 October 2012).

Moscardo, G. (1996) Mindful visitors: heritage and tourism, *Annals of Tourism Research*, 23(2): 376–97.

Moscardo, G. and Ballantyne, R. (2008) Interpretation and attractions, in A. Fyall, B. Garrod and A. Leask (eds) *Managing Visitor Attractions: New Directions*, Oxford: Elsevier, pp. 237–52.

Moutinho, L. (1987) Consumer behavior in tourism, *European Journal of Marketing*, 21(10): 3–44.

Mowforth, M. and Munt, (2003) *Tourism and Sustainability: New Tourism in the Third World*, (2nd edn), London: Routledge.

Mowforth, M. and Munt, I. (2009) *Tourism and Sustainability: Development, Globalisation and New Tourism in the Third World* (3rd edn), London: Routledge.

Munjeri, D. (2004) Tangible and intangible heritage: from difference to convergence, *Museum International*, 56(1–2): 12–20.

Murphy, P. (1985) *Tourism: A Community Approach*, London: Routledge.

Murphy, P., Pritchard, M.P. and Smith, B. (2000) The destination product and its impact on traveller perceptions, *Tourism Management*, 21(1): 43–52.

Museu da Pessoa. Online. Available at: http://www.museudapessoa.net (accessed 24 April 2013).

Museum of London Docklands (2012) *Teacher Visit & London Sugar and Slavery Feedback Surveys: Interim Report*, London: Hope-Stone Research.

Musitelli, J. (2002) Opinion: world heritage, between universalism and globalization, *International Journal of Cultural Property*, 11(2): 323–36.

Nas, P.J.M. (2002) Masterpieces of oral and intangible culture: reflections on the UNESCO World Heritage List, *Current Anthropology*, 43(1): 139–48.

Nasser, N. (2003) Planning for urban heritage places: reconciling conservation, tourism and sustainable development, *Journal of Planning Literature*, 17(4): 467–79.

Negussie, E. (2006) Implications of neo-liberalism for built heritage management: institutional and ownership structures in Ireland and Sweden, *Urban Studies*, 43(10): 1803–24.

Newland, K. and Taylor, C. (2010) *Heritage Tourism and Nostalgia Trade: A Diaspora Niche in the Development Landscape*, Washington, DC: Migration Policy Institute.

Nicholas, L.N., Thapa, B. and Ko, Y.J. (2009) Residents' perspectives of a World Heritage site: The Pitons Management Area, St. Lucia, *Annals of Tourism Research*, 36(3): 390–412.

Nilsson, J.H., Svard, A.-C., Widarsson, A. and Wirell, T. (2011) 'Cittaslow' eco-gastronomic heritage as a tool for destination development, *Current Issues in Tourism*, 14(4): 373–86.

Nora, P. (1989) Between memory and history: Les Lieux de Mémoire, *Representation*, 26(Spring): 7–24.

Norris, D.F. (2003) If we build it, they will come! Tourism-based economic development in Baltimore, in D.R. Judd (ed.) *The Infrastructure of Play: Building the Tourist City*, New York: M. E. Sharpe, pp. 125–67.

Nuryanti, W. (1996) Heritage and postmodern tourism, *Annals of Tourism Research*, 23(2): 249–60.

Nuryanti, W. (ed.) (1997) *Tourism and Heritage Management*, Yogyakarta: Gadjah Mada University.

Nusair, K.K., Bilgihan, A., Okumus, F. and Cobanoglu, C. (2013) Generation Y travelers' commitment to online social network websites, *Tourism Management*, 35(1): 13–22.

Nyaupane, G.P. (2009) Heritage complexity and tourism: the case of Lumbini, Nepal, *Journal of Heritage Tourism*, 4(2): 157–72.

Oh, H., Fiore, A.M. and Jeoung, M. (2007) Measuring experience economy concepts: tourism applications, *Journal of Travel Research*, 46(2): 119–32.

Ong, A. (1999) *Flexible Citizenship: The Cultural Logics of Transnationality*, Durham: Duke Univeristy Press.

Ooi, C.S. (2002) *Cultural Tourism and Tourism Cultures: The Business of Mediating Experiences in Copenhagen and Singapore*, Copenhagen: Copenhagen Business School Press.

Orbaşli, A. (2000) *Tourists in Historic Towns: Urban Conservation and Heritage Management*, London: Spon Press.

Orbaşli, A. (2007) Tourism and the 'Islamic' town: social change, conservation and tourism in traditional neighbourhoods, in R. Daher (ed.) *Tourism in the Middle East: Continuity, Change and Transformation*, Bristol: Channel View Publications, pp. 161–87.

Orbaşli, A. and Woodward, S. (2012) Tourism and heritage conservation, in T. Jamal and M. Robinson (eds) *The SAGE Handbook of Tourism Studies*, London: Sage, pp. 314–32.

Palmer, C.A. (1999) *Heritage Tourism and English National Identity*, unpublished thesis, London: University of North London.

Palmer, G. (1993) *Death: The Trip of a Lifetime*, New York: Harper Collins.

Park, H.Y. (2007) *Heritage Tourism and Symbolic Representations of National Identity: An Ethnographic Study of Changdeok Palace (Seoul, South Korea)*, unpublished thesis, London: London Metropolitan University.

Park, H.Y. (2010a) Heritage tourism: a journey into nationhood, *Annals of Tourism Research*, 37(1): 116–35.

Park, H.Y. (2010b) *An Ethnographic Study of Changdeok Palace: Heritage Tourism and Symbolic Representations of National Identity*, Seoul: Jimoondang.

Park, H.Y. (2011) Shared national memory as intangible heritage: re-imaging two Koreas as one nation, *Annals of Tourism Research*, 38(2): 520–39.

Payne, A. and Frow, P. (2006) Customer Relationship Management: from strategy to implementation, *Journal of Marketing Management*, 22(1/2): 135–68.

Pearce, P.L. (1993) Fundamentals of tourist motivation, in D.G. Pearce and R.W. Butler (eds) *Tourism Research: Critique and Challenges*, London: Routledge, pp. 113–34.

Pedersen, A. (2002) *Managing Tourism at World Heritage Sites: A Practical Manual for World Heritage Site Managers*, Paris: UNESCO World Heritage Centre.

Peter, C. (2009) Fame is not always a positive asset for heritage quality! Some clues from buying intentions of national tourists, *Journal of Travel & Tourism Marketing*, 26(1): 1–18.

Peters, H. (1999) *Making Tourism Work for Heritage Preservation: Lijiang, A Case Study*, UNESCO and The Nature Conservancy, Yunnan, International Conference on Anthropology, Chinese Society and Tourism, Kunming.

Phelps, A. (1994) Museums as tourist attractions, in A.V. Seaton (ed.) *Tourism: The State of the Art*, Chichester: John Wiley & Sons, pp. 169–77.

Phillips, A. (1995) Conservation, in H. Newby (ed.) *The National Trust: The Next Hundred Years*, London: The National Trust, pp. 32–52.

Pidd, H. (2012) The Titanic memorial cruise: 'not a re-enactment', *The Guardian*, 8 April.

Pine, B.J. and Gilmore, J.H. (1998) Welcome to the experience economy, *Harvard Business Review*, July–August, 97–105.

Pine, B.J. and Gilmore, J.H. (1999) *The Experience Economy*, Harvard, MA: Harvard Business School Press.

Pitchford, S.R. (1995) Ethnic tourism and nationalism in Wales, *Annals of Tourism Research*, 22(1): 35–52.

Plaza, B. (1999) The Guggenheim-Bilbao museum effect: a reply to Maria V. Gomez's 'reflective images: the case of urban regeneration in Glasgow and Bilbao', *International Journal of Urban and Regional Research*, 23(3): 589–92.

Plog, S.C. (1990) A carpenter's tools: an answer to Stephen L.J. Smith's review of psychocentrism/allocentrism, *Journal of Travel Research*, 28(4): 43–5.

Plog, S.C. (1991) *Leisure Travel: Making it a Growth Market Again*, New York: Wiley.

Pollock-Ellwand, N. (2011) Common ground and shared frontiers in heritage conservation and sustainable development: partnerships, policies and perspectives, *International Journal of Sustainable Development & World Ecology*, 18(3): 236–42.

Pomering, A. and White, L. (2011) The portrayal of indigenous identity of Australian tourism brand advertising: engendering an image of extraordinary reality or staged authenticity? *Place Branding and Public Diplomacy*, 7(3): 165–74.

Poon, A. (1993) *Tourism, Technology and Competitive Strategies*, Wallingford: CAB International.

Poria, Y. (2007) Establising cooperation between Israel and Poland to save Auschwitz Concentration Camp: globalising the responsibility for the massacre, *International Journal of Tourism Policy*, 1(1): 45–57.

Poria, Y. and Ashworth, G.J. (2009) Heritage tourism: current resource for conflict, *Annals of Tourism Research*, 36(3): 522–5.

Poria, Y., Biran, A. and Reichel, A. (2009) Visitors' preferences for interpretation at heritage sites, *Journal of Travel Research*, 48(1): 92–105.

Poria, Y., Butler, R. and Airey, D. (2001) Tourism sub-groups: do they exist? *Tourism Today*, 1(1): 14–22.

Poria, Y., Butler, R.W. and Airey, D. (2003) The core of heritage tourism, *Annals of Tourism Research*, 30(1): 238–54.

Poria, Y., Reichel, A. and Biran, A. (2006a) Heritage site management: motivations and expectations, *Annals of Tourism Research*, 33(1): 162–78.

Poria, Y., Reichel, A. and Biran, A. (2006b) Heritage site perceptions and motivations to visit, *Journal of Travel Research*, 44(3): 318–26.

Porter, M.E. (1998) Clusters and the new economics of competition, *Harvard Business Review*, November–December, 77–90.

Prentice, R. (2001) Experiential cultural tourism: museums and the marketing of the new romanticism of evoked authenticity, *Museum Management and Curatorship*, 16(1): 45–70.

Prentice, R.C. (1993) *Tourism and Heritage Attractions*, London and New York: Routledge.

Prentice, R.C., Witt, S.F. and Hamer, C. (1998) Tourism as experience: the case of heritage parks, *Annals of Tourism Research*, 25(1): 1–24.

Pretes, M. (2003) Tourism and nationalism, *Annals of Tourism Research*, 30(1): 125–42.

Pride, R. (2001) Brand Wales: 'natural revival', in N.J. Morgan, A. Pritchard and R. Pride (eds) *Destination Branding: Creating the Unique Destination Proposition*, Oxford: Butterworth-Heinemann, pp. 109–47.

Prideaux, B. and Cooper, C. (2002) Marketing and destination growth: a symbiotic relationship or simple coincidence? *Journal of Vacation Marketing*, 9(1): 35–48.

Prösler, M. (1996) Museums and globalization, in G. Fife and S. Macdonald (eds) *Theorizing Museums: Representing Identity and Diversity in a Changing World*, Oxford: Blackwell, pp. 21–44.

Quinn, B. (2005) Arts festivals and the city, *Urban Studies*, 42(5/6): 927–43.

Ram, U. (2004) Glocommodification: how the global consumes the local – McDonald's in Israel, *Current Sociology*, 52(1): 11–31.

Rátz, T. (2006) Interpretation in the house of terror, Budapest, in M.K. Smith and M. Robinson (eds) *Cultural Tourism in a Changing World: Politics, Participation and (Re)presentation*, Clevedon: Channel View Publications, pp. 244–56.

Read, B. (1999) *A Changing Heritage: Construction and Change in the Representation of Bristol's Maritime Heritage Industry*, unpublished thesis, Bristol: University of Bristol.

Reiser, D. (2003) Globalisation: an old phenomenon that needs to be rediscovered for tourism? *Tourism and Hospitality Research*, 4(4): 306–20.

Reisinger, Y. and Steiner, C. (2006) Reconceptualising interpretation: the role of tour guides in authentic tourism, *Current Issues in Tourism*, 9(6): 481–98.

Relph, E. (1987) *The Modern Urban Landscape*, Baltimore: The John Hopkins University Press.

Richards, G. (1996) *Cultural Tourism in Europe*, Wallingford: CAB International.

Richards, G. (2001) The market for cultural attractions, in G. Richards (ed.) *Cultural Attractions and European Tourism*, Wallingford: CAB International, pp. 31–53.

Ritchie, J.R.B. and Crouch, G.I. (2003) *The Competitive Destination: A Sustainable Tourism Perspective*, Oxon: CABI Publishing.

Ritzer, G. and Liska, A. (1997) 'McDisneyization' and 'post-tourism': complementary perspectives on contemporary tourism, in C. Rojek and J. Urry (eds) *Touring Culture*, London: Routlege, pp. 176–201.

Rivera, L.A. (2008) Managing 'spoiled' national identity: war, tourism, and memory in Croatia, *American Sociological Review*, 73(4): 613–34.

Robb, J.G. (1998) Tourism and legends: archaeology of heritage, *Annals of Tourism Research*, 25(3): 579–96.

Robertshaw, A. (1997) 'A dry shell of the past': living history and the interpretation of historic houses, *Interpretation*, 2: 1–7.

Robertson, R. (1992) *Globalization: Social Theory and Global Culture*, London: Routledge.

Robertson, R. (1995) Globalization: time-space and homogeneity-heterogeneity, in M. Featherstone, S. Lash and R. Robertson (eds) *Global Modernities*, London: Sage, pp. 25–44.

Roders, A.P. and van Oers, R. (2011) World Heritage cities management, *Facilities*, 29(7/8): 276–85.

Rojek, C. (1995) *Decentring Leisure: Rethinking Leisure Theory*, London: Sage.

Rojek, C. (1999) Fatal attractions, in D. Boswell and J. Evans (eds) *Representing the Nation: A Reader*, London: Routledge, pp. 185–207.

Rowan, Y. (2004) Repackaging the pilgrimage: visiting the Holy Land in Orlando, in Y. Rowan and U. Baram (eds) *Marketing Heritage: Archaeology and the Consumption of the Past*, Oxford: Altamira Press, pp. 249–66.

Rowan, Y. and Baram, U. (eds) (2004) *Marketing Heritage: Archaeology and the Consumption of the Past*, Oxford: Altamira Press.

Rubinstein, W.D. (1993) *Capitalism, Culture, and Decline in Britain 1750–1990*, London: Routledge.

Ryals, L. and Payne, A. (2001) Customer relationship management in financial services: towards information-enabled relationship marketing, *Journal of Strategic Marketing*, 9(1): 3–27.

Ryan, J. and Silvanto, S. (2010) World heritage sites: the purposes and politics of destination branding, *Journal of Travel & Tourism Marketing*, 27(5): 533–45.

Safran, W. (1991) Diaspora in modern societies: myths of homeland and return, *Diaspora: A Journal of Transnational Studies*, 1(1): 83–99.

Salazar, N.B. (2010) The globalisation of heritage through tourism: balancing standardisation and differentiation, in S. Labadi and C. Long (eds) *Heritage and Globalisation*, London: Routledge, pp. 130–46.

Sampath, N. (1997) *Mas'* identity: tourism and global and local aspects of Trinidad Carnival, in S. Abram, J. Waldren and D.V.L. Macleod (eds) *Tourists and Tourism: Identifying with People and Places*, Oxford: Berg, pp. 149–71.

Samuel, R. (1994) *Theatres of Memory Vol. 1: Past and Present in Contemporary Culture*, London: Verso.

Sarmento, J. (2010) Fort Jesus: guiding the past and contesting the present in Kenya, *Tourism Geographies*, 12(2): 246–63.

Sassen, S. (1996) *Losing Control? Sovereignty in the Age of Globalization*, New York: Columbia University Press.

Sautter, E.T. and Leisen, B. (1999) Managing stakeholders: a tourism planning model, *Annals of Tourism Research*, 26(2): 312–28.

Saxe, D.W. (2009) Living heritage: an experimental model mixing heritage and entertainment, *Journal of Interpretation Research*, 14(1): 33–46.

Scarpaci, J.C. (2005) Plazas and barrios: heritage tourism and globalization in the Latin American *Centro Histórico*, Tucson, AZ: University of Arizona Press.

Scher, P.W. (2011) Heritage tourism in the Caribbean: the politics of culture after neoliberalism, *Bulletin of Latin American Research*, 30(1): 7–20.

Scheyvens, R. (2002) *Tourism for Development: Empowering Communities*, Edinburgh: Pearson Education.

Scholze, M. (2008) Arrested heritage: the politics of inscription into the UNSECO World Heritage List: the case of Agadez in Niger, *Journal of Material Culture*, 13(2): 215–32.

Seaton, A. (1996) Guided by the dark: from thanatopsis to thanatourism, *International Journal of Heritage Studies*, 2(4): 234–44.

Seaton, A. (2002) Thanatourism's final frontiers? Visits to cemeteries, churchyards and funerary sites as sacred and secular pilgrimage, *Tourism Recreation Research*, 27(2): 73–82.

Seaton, A. and Lennon, J. (2004) Thanatourism in the early 21st century: moral panics, ulterior motives and alterior desires, in T.V. Singh (ed.) *New Horizons in Tourism: Strange Experiences and Stranger Practices*, Wallingford: CAB International, pp. 63–82.

Seaton, A.V. (2001) Sources of slavery: destinations of slavery, *International Journal of Hospitality & Tourism Administration*, 2(3–4): 107–29.

Selwyn, T. (ed.) (1996) *The Tourist Image: Myths and Myth Making in Tourism*, Chichester: Wiley.

Shackel, P.A. (2003) Archaeology, memory, and landscapes of conflict, *Historical Archaeology*, 37(3): 3–13.

Shackley, M. (ed.) (1998) *Visitor Management: Case Studies from World Heritage Sites*, Oxford: Butterworth-Heinemann.

Shackley, M. (2001) *Managing Sacred Sites: Service Provision and Visitor Experience*, London and New York: Continuum.

Shaw, G. and Williams, A.M. (2004) *Tourism and Tourism Spaces*, London: Sage.

Short, J.R. (1991) *Imagined Country: Society, Culture and Environment*, London: Routledge.

Shukla, P., Brown, J. and Harper, D. (2006) Image association and European capital of culture: empirical insights through the case study of Liverpool, *Tourism Review*, 61(4): 6–12.

Silberberg, T. (1995) Cultural tourism and business opportunities for museums and heritage sites, *Tourism Management*, 16(5): 361–5.

Simpson, M.G. (2007) Charting the boundaries: indigenous models and parallel practices in the development of the post-museum, in S.J. Knell, S. MacLeod and S. Watson (eds) *Museum Revolutions: How Museums Change and are Changed*, London: Routledge, pp. 235–49.

Sirisrisak, T. (2009) Conservation of Bangkok old town, *Habitat International*, 33(4): 405–11.

Slater, T., Curran, W. and Lees, L. (2004) Gentrification research: new directions and critical scholarship, *Environment and Planning A*, 36(7): 1141–50.

Smith, A.D. (1991a) *National Identity*, London: Penguin.

Smith, A.D. (1991b) The nation: invented, imagined, reconstructed? *Millennium: Journal of International Studies*, 20(3): 353–68.

Smith, L. (2006) *Uses of Heritage*, London and New York: Routledge.

Smith, L., Shackel, P.A. and Campbell, G. (2011) *Heritage, Labour and the Working Classes*, London: Routledge.

Smith, M.K. (2002) A critical evaluation of the global accolade: the significance of World Heritage Site status for Maritime Greenwich, *International Journal of Heritage Studies*, 8(2): 137–51.

Smith, M.K. (2007) Towards a cultural planning approach to regeneration, in M.K. Smith (ed.) *Tourism, Culture and Regeneration*, Wallingford: CAB International, pp. 1–11.

Smith, M.K. (2009) *Issues in Cultural Tourism Studies* (2nd edn), London: Routledge.

Smith, N. (1996) *The New Urban Frontier: Gentrification and the Revanchist City*, London and New York: Routledge.

Smith, N. (2002) New globalism, new urbanism: gentrification as global urban strategy, *Antipode*, 34(3): 427–50.

Song, W. and Zhu, X. (2010) Gentrification in urban China under market transformation, *International Journal of Urban Sciences*, 14(2): 152–63.

Staiff, R. and Bushell, R. (2013) Mobility and modernity in Luang Prabang, Laos: re-thinking heritage and tourism, *International Journal of Heritage Studies*, 19(1): 98–113.

Starr, F. (2010) The business of heritage and the private sector, in S. Labadi and C. Long (eds) *Heritage and Globalisation*, London: Routledge, pp. 147–69.

Steinberg, F. (1996) Conservation and rehabilitation of urban heritage in developing countries, *Habitat International*, 20(3): 463–75.

Steiner, C.J. and Reisinger, Y. (2006) Understanding existential authenticity, *Annals of Tourism Research*, 33(2): 299–318.

Stephen, A. (2001) The contemporary museum and leisure: recreation as a museum function, *Museum Management and Curatorship*, 19(3): 297–308.

Stephenson, M.L. (2002) Travelling to the ancestral homelands: the aspirations and experiences of a UK Caribbean community, *Current Issues in Tourism*, 5(5): 378–425.

Stone, P. (2012) *What the Titanic can teach us*. Online. Available at: http://halifaxmag.com/2012/04/cover/what-the-titanic-can-teach-us (accessed 5 October 2012).

Strange, C. and Kempa, M. (2003) Shades of dark tourism: Alcatraz and Robben Island, *Annals of Tourism Research*, 30(2): 386–405.

Stronza, A. and Gordillo, J. (2008) Community views of ecotourism, *Annals of Tourism Research*, 35(2): 448–68.

Stylianou-Lambert, T. (2011) Gazing from home: cultural tourism and art museums, *Annals of Tourism Research*, 38(2): 403–21.

Swarbrooke, J. (2001) Organisation of tourism at the destination, in S. Wahab and C. Cooper (eds) *Tourism in the Age of Globalisation*, New York: Routledge, pp. 159–82.

Tarlow, P. (2005) Dark tourism: the appealing 'dark' side of tourism and more, in M. Novelli (ed.) *Niche Tourism: Contemporary Issues, Trends and Cases*, Oxford: Elsevier, pp. 47–58.

Tarnas, R. (1991) *The Passion of the Western Mind: Understanding the Ideas that have Shaped Our World View*, New York: Harmony Books.

Taylor, K. (2004) Cultural heritage management: a possible role for Charters and Principles in Asia, *International Journal of Heritage Studies*, 10(5): 417–33.

Taylor, D., Fletcher, S. and Clabaugh, T. (1993) A comparison of characteristics, regional expenditures, and economic impact of visitors to historical sites with other recreational visitors, *Journal of Travel Research*, 31(1): 30–5.

The Chartered Institute of Marketing (2009) *Marketing and the 7Ps*, Maidenhead: CIM Insights.

The Open University (2009) *Whose Heritage? Stories of Britain's Changing Attitudes to Heritage*, Northampton: CKN Print.

Thompson, C.J., Rindfleisch, A. and Arsel, Z. (2006) Emotional branding and the strategic value of the Doppelgänger brand image, *Journal of Marketing*, 70(1): 50–64.

Tilden, F. (1977) *Interpreting Our Heritage*, Chapel Hill: University of North Carolina Press.

Timothy, D.J. (2011) *Cultural Heritage and Tourism: An Introduction*, Bristol: Channel View Publications.

Timothy, D.J. and Boyd, S.W. (2003) *Heritage Tourism*, Harlow: Pearson Education.

Timothy, D.J. and Teye, V. (2009) *Tourism and the Lodging Sector*, Oxford: Butterworth-Heinemann.

Timur, S. and Getz, D. (2009) Sustainable tourism development: how do destination stakeholders perceive sustainable urban tourism? *Sustainable Development*, 17(4): 220–32.

Tivers, J. (2002) Performing heritage: the use of live 'actors' in heritage presentations, *Leisure Studies*, 21(3–4): 187–200.

Tocqueville, A. (1998) *The Old Regime and the Revolution*, Chicago: Chicago University Press.

Tomlinson, J. (1991) *Cultural Imperialism: A Critical Introduction*, London: Pinter.

Tosun, C. (2000) Limits to community participation in the tourism development process in developing countries, *Tourism Management*, 21(6): 613–33.

Towner, J. (1985) The grand tour: a key phase in the history of tourism, *Annals of Tourism Research*, 12(3): 297–333.

Tsiotsou, R. and Ratten, V. (2010) Future research directions in tourism marketing, *Marketing Intelligence & Planning*, 28(4): 533–44.

Tsiotsou, R. and Vasaioti, E. (2006) Satisfaction: a segmentation criterion for 'short term' visitors of mountainous destinations, *Journal of Travel and Tourism Marketing*, 21(1): 61–73.

Tubb, K.N. (2003) An evaluation of the effectiveness of interpretation within Dartmoor National Park in reaching the goals of sustainable tourism development, *Journal of Sustainable Tourism*, 11(6): 476–98.

Tucker, M. (2008) The cultural production of cities: rhetoric or reality? Lessons from Glasgow, *Journal of Retail and Leisure Property*, 17(1): 21–33.

Tunbridge, J.E. and Ashworth, G.J. (1996) *Dissonant Heritage: The Management of the Past as a Resource in Conflict*, Chichester: Wiley.

Tweed, C. and Sutherland, M. (2007) Built cultural heritage and sustainable urban development, *Landscape and Urban Planning*, 83(1): 62–9.

UNESCO (1972) *Convention Concerning the Protection of the World Cultural and Natural Heritage*, Paris: UNESCO World Heritage Centre.

UNESCO (2003) *Convention for the Safeguarding of the Intangible Cultural Heritage*, Paris: UNESCO World Heritage Centre.

UNESCO Brief History. Online. Available at: http://whc.unesco.org/en/convention (accessed 23 April 2013).

UNESCO World Heritage List Nomination. Online. Available at: http://whc.unesco.org/en/nominations (accessed 7 August 2013).

Uriely, N. (2005) The tourist experience: conceptual developments, *Annals of Tourism Research*, 32(1): 199–216.

Uriely, N., Israeli, A.A. and Riechel, A. (2002) Heritage proximity and resident attitudes toward tourism development, *Annals of Tourism Research*, 29(3): 859–62.

Urry, J. (1990) *The Tourist Gaze: Leisure and Travel in Contemporary Societies*, London: Sage.

Urry, J. (1991) The sociology of tourism, in C.P. Cooper (ed.) *Progress in Tourism, Recreations, and Hospitality Management* (vol. 3), London: Belhaven, pp. 48–57.

Urry, J. (1994) Cultural change and contemporary tourism, *Leisure Studies*, 13(4): 233–8.

Urry, J. (2002) *The Tourist Gaze* (2nd edn), London: Sage.

USI (2011) *Understanding Slavery Initiative*. Online. Available at: http://www.understandingslavery.com/index.php?option=com_content&view=article&id=314&Itemid=226 (accessed 1 October 2012).

Uysal, M. and Jurowski, C. (1994) Testing the push and pull factors, *Annals of Tourism Research*, 21(4): 844–6.

Uysal, U.E. (2012) An urban social movement challenging urban regeneration: the case of Sulukule, Istanbul, *Cities*, 29(1): 12–22.

Van Aalst, I. and Boogaarts, I. (2002) From museum to mass entertainment: the evolution of the role of museums in cities, *European Urban and Regional Studies*, 9(3): 195–209.

Van Maanen, J. (1992) Displacing Disney: some notes on the flow of culture, *Qualitative Sociology*, 15(1): 5–35.

Vargo, S.L. and Lusch, R.F. (2004) Evolving to a new dominant logic for marketing, *Journal of Marketing*, 68(1): 1–17.

Vesey, C. and Dimanche, F. (2003) From storyville to Bourbon Street: vice, nostalgia and tourism, *Journal of Tourism and Cultural Change*, 1(1): 54–70.

VisitBritain (2010) Culture and heritage. Online. Available at: http://www.visitbritain.org/Images/Culture%20&%20Heritage%20Topic%20Profile%20Full_tcm29-14711.pdf (accessed 5 September 2013).

VisitScotland (2013) Homecoming Scotland 2014. Online. Available at: http://www.visitscotland.com/see-do/homecoming-scotland-2014 (accessed 23 April 2013).

Voase, R. (2002) Rediscovering the imagination: investigating active and passive visitor experience in the 21st century, *International Journal of Tourism Research*, 4(5): 391–9.

Wager, J. (1995) Developing a strategy for the Angkor World Heritage Site, *Tourism Management*, 16(7): 515–23.

Wahab, S. and Cooper, C. (eds) (2001) *Tourism in the Age of Globalisation*, London: Routledge.

Wainwright, O. (2012) Should the London Pub get UNESCO World Heritage status? *The Guardian*, 12 October.

Walsh, J. (2008) Benidorm: one of the cultural wonders of the world? *The Independent*, 29 October.

Walsh, K. (1992) *The Representation of the Past: Museums and Heritage in the Postmodern World*, London: Routledge.

Walsh, K. (2001) Collective amnesia and the mediation of painful pasts, *International Journal of Heritage Studies*, 7(1): 83–98.

Wang, N. (1999) Rethinking authenticity in tourism experience, *Annals of Tourism Research*, 26(2): 349–70.

Wang, N. (2000) *Tourism and Modernity: A Sociological Analysis*, Oxford: Pergamon Press.

Wang, S. (2012) From a living city to a World Heritage City: authorised heritage conservation and development and its impact on the local community, *International Development Planning Review*, 34(1): 1–17.

Waters, M. (2001) *Globalisation*, London: Routledge.

Waterton, E. (2009) Sights of sites: picturing heritage, power and exclusion, *Journal of Heritage Tourism*, 4(1): 37–56.

Wearing, S. (2001) *Volunteer Tourism: Experiences that Make a Difference*, Wallingford: CAB International.

Weaver, D. (2006) *Sustainable Tourism: Theory and Practice*, Oxford: Elsevier.

Weaver, D.B. (2011) Contemporary tourism heritage as heritage tourism: evidence from Las Vegas and Gold Coast, *Annals of Tourism Research*, 38(1): 249–67.

Weil, S.E. (1995) *A Cabinet of Curiosities: Inquiries into Museums and their Prospects*, Washington: Smithsonian Institution Press.

Weiss, L.M. (2007) Heritage-making and political identity, *Journal of Social Archaeology*, 7(3): 413–31.

West, S. (ed.) (2010) *Understanding Heritage in Practice*, Manchester: Manchester University Press.

West, S. and Ansell, J. (2010) A history of heritage, in S. West (ed.) *Understanding Heritage in Practice*, Manchester: Manchester University Press, pp. 7–46.

Wight, A.C. (2005) Philosophical and methodological praxes in dark tourism: controversy, contention and the evolving paradigm, *Journal of Vacation Marketing*, 12(2): 119–29.

Wight, A.C. and Lennon, J.J. (2007) Selective interpretation and eclectic human heritage in Lithuania, *Tourism Management*, 28(2): 519–29.

Williams, A. (2006) Tourism and hospitality marketing: fantasy, feeling and fun, *International Journal of Contemporary Hospitality Management*, 18(6): 482–95.

Williams, S. (2009) *Tourism Geography: A New Synthesis* (2nd edn), London: Routledge.

Wilson, D. (1993) Time and tides in the anthropology of tourism, in M. Hitchcock, V.T. King and M.J.G. Parnwell (eds) *Tourism in South-East Asia*, London: Routledge, pp. 32–47.

Winter, T. (2004) Landscape, memory and heritage: new year celebrations at Angkor, Cambodia, *Current Issues in Tourism*, 7(4&5): 330–45.

Woollacott, M. (2012) On holiday with the Chinese: in China, *The Guardian*, 16 November.

World Commission on Environment and Development (WCED) (1987) *Our Common Future*, Oxford: Oxford University Press.

World Heritage Centre (2007) *Policy Document on the Impacts of Climate Change on World Heritage Properties adopted by the 16th General Assembly of States Parties to the World Heritage Convention*, Paris: UNESCO.

World Heritage Committee (1994) Nara Document on Authenticity. Online. Available at: http://whc.unesco.org/archive/nara94.htm (accessed 24 April 2013).

Wright, P. (1985) *On Living in an Old Country: The National Past in Contemporary Britain*, London: Verso.

Xiang, Z. and Gretzel, U. (2010) Role of social media in online travel information research, *Tourism Management*, 31(2): 179–88.

Xie, P.F. (2010) Developing ethnic tourism in a diaspora community: the Indonesian village on Hainan Island, China, *Asia Pacific Journal of Tourism Research*, 15(3): 367–82.

Xie, P.F. and Wall, G. (2003) Visitors' perceptions of authenticity at cultural attractions in Hainan, China, *International Journal of Tourism Research*, 4(5): 353–66.

Yale, P. (1991) *From Tourist Attractions to Heritage Tourism*, Huntingdon: ELM Publications.

Zablah, A.R., Bellenger, D.N. and Johnston, W.J. (2004) An evaluation of divergent perspectives on customer relationship management: towards a common understanding of an emerging phenomenon, *Industrial Marketing Management*, 33(6): 475–89.

Zhang, J. and Jensen, C. (2007) Comparative advantage: explaining tourism flows, *Annals of Tourism Research*, 34(1): 223–43.

Zhu, Y. (2012) Performing heritage: rethinking authenticity in tourism, *Annals of Tourism Research*, 39(3): 1495–513.

Zukin, S. (1995) *The Cultures of Cities*, Malden: Blackwell.

Zukin, S. (2012) The social production of urban cultural heritage: identity and ecosystem on an Amsterdam shopping street, *City, Culture and Society*, 3(4): 281–91.

Index

Please note page numbers followed by 'f' refer to figures and followed by 't' refer to tables.